How Is a Man Supposed to Be a Man?

Fertility, Reproduction and Sexuality

GENERAL EDITORS:

Soraya Tremayne, Founding Director, Fertility and Reproduction Studies Group and Research Associate, Institute of Social and Cultural Anthropology, University of Oxford.

Marcia C. Inhorn, William K. Lanman, Jr. Professor of Anthropology and International Affairs, Yale University.

Philip Kreager, Director, Fertility and Reproduction Studies Group, and Research Associate, Institute of Social and Cultural Anthropology and Institute of Human Sciences, University of Oxford.

Understanding the complex and multifaceted issue of human reproduction has been, and remains, of great interest both to academics and practitioners. This series includes studies by specialists in the field of social, cultural, medical, and biological anthropology, medical demography, psychology, and development studies. Current debates and issues of global relevance on the changing dynamics of fertility, human reproduction and sexuality are addressed.

For a full volume listing, please see the series page on our website:
http://www.berghahnbooks.com/series/fertility-reproduction-and-sexuality

HOW IS A MAN SUPPOSED TO BE A MAN?
MALE CHILDLESSNESS – A LIFE COURSE DISRUPTED

Robin A. Hadley

berghahn
NEW YORK · OXFORD
www.berghahnbooks.com

First published in 2021 by

Berghahn Books

www.berghahnbooks.com

© 2021, 2024 Robin A. Hadley
First paperback edition published in 2024

Library of Congress Cataloging-in-Publication Data
Names: Hadley, Robin A., author.
Title: How is a man supposed to be a man? : male childlessness-a life
  course disrupted / Robin A. Hadley.
Description: New York : Berghahn Books, 2021. | Series: Fertility,
  reproduction and sexuality ; volume 48 | Includes bibliographical
  references and index.
Identifiers: LCCN 2021017467 (print) | LCCN 2021017468 (ebook) |
  ISBN 9781800731875 (hardback) | ISBN 9781800731882 (ebook)
Subjects: LCSH: Fatherhood. | Childlessness. | Infertility, Male--Social
  aspects. | Older men--Family relationships. | Men--Identity.
Classification: LCC HQ756 .H3254 2021 (print) | LCC HQ756 (ebook)
  | DDC 306.874/2--dc23
LC record available at https://lccn.loc.gov/2021017467
LC ebook record available at https://lccn.loc.gov/2021017468

British Library Cataloguing in Publication Data
A catalogue record for this book is available from the British Library

ISBN 978-1-80073-187-5 hardback
ISBN 978-1-80539-129-6 paperback
ISBN 978-1-80539-392-4 epub
ISBN 978-1-80073-188-2 web pdf

https://doi.org/10.3167/9781800731875

To my wife Maryan for all her love, encouragement, faith, patience, support and wisdom:

I would not be complete without her.

In memoriam

This book is also dedicated to the memory of family, friends, colleagues and pets.

Margaret Mary and Kenneth Hadley
'Tony' Anthony Arthur Hadley
Ann Isabella Hadley
Betty Lister

Richard and Elsie Holme, the gentlest of giants – John Whitehead, Peter Reader and Andrew Davies

Mentor, photographer, microscopist: Francis 'Frank' Knowles

Author, researcher, counsellor: Lois Tonkin

Professor David Morgan

My girl: Sweep
My boy: Dylan
My girl: Keeta

CONTENTS

ILLUSTRATIONS

Figures

Tables

FOREWORD

Graham Handley

When I was invited to read Dr Hadley's study of male childlessness, I had no idea of the span of his investigation until
scrutiny of the chapter headings indicated a dense and wide coverage. I was immediately engaged, however, by the autobiographical
details revealed by the author. They are disarming, modest, a reve-
lation of human vulnerability, a moving prelude to his sympathetic
saturation in a hitherto little-recorded area of human unhappiness –
one which ranges from anguish to a reflex endurance or silent acceptance of the situation in which some men find themselves.

Strangely, I became aware of my own involvement, almost
obliquely, in the subject: I am an old man with children, but without
grandchildren. My wife and I discussed this occasionally before her
death, but it was generally a silent deprivation, a might-have-been
while we still had each other. It lingers with me, and perhaps this
accounts for my warm appreciation of the sympathetic ambience
that Dr Hadley has created in his dedicated focus on a representative selection of men who do not become parents, and their
resultant degrees of deprivation. His thoroughness goes together
with a residual commitment and understanding. He lays bare the
varying circumstances which contribute to male childlessness, and
these are examined and defined with insight and compassion, the
personal qualities that Dr Hadley brings to his study. There is an
empathy between the lines that is evident throughout, a kind of
emotional heartbeat. This sits beside the disciplined, scholarly citing of sources, the recognition of other work in this chosen area
whether direct or adjacent, and an evaluation of it. For the reader,
this cements the comprehensiveness of the appraisal.

And all the while we are aware of the author, and of those earlier revelations about himself and where he has come from – the uncomplaining but nevertheless significant partial hearing loss he has suffered, for example – which make him at one with those he is studying, each with his own particularized worry. Dr Hadley's academic dedication is not in doubt; his work has authority and resonance, but he is not a writer intent on statistics or displaying intellectual know-how. He is in fact a man among men, finely aware of human problems and sensitive to needs, inviting, encouraging confidences and promoting discussion which can only lead to fuller understanding and a wider dissemination of the problems and concerns voiced here.

His records of the participants interviewed are characterized by his awareness, his own self-critical stance and his outreaching sensitivity. At the same time, he is aware of the limitations of the exercise – his own, those of the person interviewed, the small numbers involved. The mere fact of exposure, however, carries its own message, not definitive but progressive, seeding where before there was aridity or silence. These probings are a template for the future; further, more extensive investigations and research will assuredly follow, hopefully with Dr Hadley at their forefront. The groundwork has been laid.

As a common reader, without any of the expertise evident in this book, I found the narrative sequence clear and easy to absorb, and this was further enhanced by the summaries and discussion which accompanied every headed sequence. Each chapter is complete in itself but leads seamlessly to the next area of relevant interest. The methodology established, the major aspects of 'non-fatherhood and the continuity of disruption' are clearly and directly defined. Let me in my turn make it clear that the reader becomes part of the experiences of others, almost a participant, because of the intimacies being revealed, either through cited examples or through the direct interviews which rivet our attention, compel our sympathy. As I indicated earlier, but wish to emphasize again here, the range of reference is impressive, from relevant books, articles, talks, discussions, areas central or adjacent to Dr Hadley's investigations, all deftly handled or crisply noted.

I have deliberately stressed that this is no limited or abstract academic excursion. Dr Hadley encountered, and successfully negotiated, the many frustrations he found in his way before the writing and recording of the interviews could be assured. His caring spirit and determination saw him overcome difficulties about costs and recruitments of participants, and battle to actually be in a position to undertake the research. He even records a verbal brickbat he received at a conference from a doubting, cynical colleague. He was not deterred; he was not in any doubt about the validity, indeed the necessity, of bringing to light the varying concerns of childless man, whether he is in a marital situation, is heterosexual, gay or single, has family, social or economic concerns. His age is subjected to scrutiny, and areas like his idea of seeing children as a form of continuity, or of making provision of some kind, are revealed. In each case the individual context (I am inclined to say vacuum) is opened up by meaningful investigation or participants' interviews.

These latter are sometimes unbearably moving, sometimes even anticlimactic as the interviewee either strives to find the words which echo his feelings or finds too many to put them clearly. And always we are aware of the tact and enabling stance of Dr Hadley. One can sense this just by reading, and at times we know that his presence carries in it the sympathetic power of silence. The reader has to live through the poignancy of the interviews, some perhaps revealing for the first time the hidden feelings, the buried fears for some of being thought to be paedophiles if they are seen with children. I was also very struck by the sense of isolation, social isolation, in some childless older men. I return, unashamedly, to my belief that this book is an experience, that it contains a sense of some urgency and that it has revealed an area of human experience which has not hitherto been accorded comprehensive investigation. The sample of the few, if that word can actually cover the extent suggested, can I think be taken as a sure indication of the many. And the research means that the problem or problems are now brought into the arena of public debate. The book is essentially valuable on this count, and the way that it is written – with warmth, commitment and empathy – means that it is accessible to ordinary readers, hopefully among them those directly affected by some form of the malaise described. Any important aspect of the human condition that needs amelioration or care, with the aim of beneficent action or relief, merits investigation.

Dr Hadley's research establishes the situation, variously defined, in the lives of childless men. Interested, concerned, sympathetic or doubting, whichever you are, go to his Introduction, meet the man, engage with his scholarship, embrace his humanity, hear in your minds the men he interviews and perhaps think of the many uninterviewed with their silent, unvoiced frustrations. This book was written with them in mind.

Graham Handley has spent his adult life researching and teaching at all levels, from secondary school to university honours degree. He has lectured on many part-time courses for the University of London, the WEA and various local authorities. As author and editor, he has published widely on nineteenth-century fiction, particularly on George Eliot, Elizabeth Gaskell and Anthony Trollope.

Acknowledgements

This book was only made possible with the assistance, encouragement, help, support and guidance of many people to whom I offer my heartfelt gratitude. First and foremost, all I have achieved so far is down to my wife, Maryan: I would not be who or where I am without her.

I deeply appreciate all at Berghahn Books for the opportunity to write this book and for their enduring patience and support. I am incredibly grateful to Graham Handley for his efforts on the manuscript and for writing such a moving Foreword. I am indebted to the men who participated in my studies. My profound thanks go to them for making themselves available to meet me and for their interest in my research. I would like to thank Professor Mo Ray and Dr Emma Head for all their advice, expertise, patience and support over the years. A special thank you to Liz Ballinger, who continues to be an immense support. Both Liz and Professor Phillip Prangnell helped initiate my academic journey by showing faith in me that I did not have. To both I say, 'Look what you started!' I truly thank you.

There are many in the academic community who have supported and helped me. Professor Gayle Letherby has led the way and given much advice and support. Take a bow, please, Hannah Marston, John Miles, Paul Simpson, Joan Stewart, Anna Tarrant, Dana Rosenfeld and Michael Carroll. I am particularly gratified that Alan Hopgood, Sarah Rutherford and Daniel Foxsmith included my work in their respective plays. I have received tremendous backing from many individuals, groups and organizations that form the 'childless' community: Jody Day (Gateway Women), Kirsty Woodard, the inspirational Sue Lister MBE and Ann Murray (York AWOC), Jason Bergen and The Full Stop podcast crew.

Due to lack of space, I am unable to acknowledge the many other people who contributed to this work, but my appreciation is no less heartfelt.

ABBREVIATIONS

ART   Assisted Reproduction Technology
AWOC   Ageing Without Children
AWwOC   Ageing Well Without Children
BNIM   Bio-Narrative Interview Method
BSA   British Sociological Association
DNA   Deoxyribonucleic acid
EU   European Union
HFEA   Human Fertilisation and Embryology Authority
ICSI   Intracytoplasmic Sperm Injection
IUI   Intrauterine Insemination
IVF   In Vitro Fertilization
LAT   Living Apart Together
MND   Motor Neurone Disease
NHS   National Health Service
ONS   Office for National Statistics
UN   United Nations
WHO   World Health Organization

INTRODUCTION

'I want to have your baby; you'll be a great Dad.' I have heard these words on relatively few occasions in my life, but each time my heart has either lifted with joy or plummeted with fear. As I approach sixty-two years of age, the words I hear now are, 'You would have made a great Dad.' Although my heart sinks a little, I dodge my sadness and move the conversation on. I am a childless man who has, at times, been desperately 'broody' to be a father. There have been times when I have ached to be a Dad. My reactions to 'broodiness' over the years have ranged across anger, elation, denial, depression, hurt, guilt, isolation, jealousy, relief, sadness, yearning and withdrawal. Infertility research has found that both men and women report similar reactions (Throsby and Gill 2004: 366). Consequently, this book is automatically auto/biographical; this approach situates the biographies of 'the researcher and the participants as data and as an inextricable part of the research process' (Carroll 2013: 547). The reasons for drawing on this approach (among others) are rooted in the landmark work of Charles Wright Mills (1959). Wright Mills (1959: 204) argued that 'The social scientist is not some autonomous being standing outside society, the question is where he [sic] stands within it.' Award-winning anthropologist Professor Marcia Inhorn (2012: 18) reasons that researchers should share their 'methodological toolkit' with readers. She argues that not to do so lessens the credibility of the research. The details of the methodology I used – the 'why, how, who, what and when' – are detailed in Chapter 3.

I believe that research in the field of older men who are involuntarily childless is important, not only because of the scarcity of material relating to the effects of involuntary childlessness on men as they age (Dykstra and Keizer 2009) but also because of the impact of actual and projected demographic change. The global demographic trend of increasing longevity and declining fertility rates has been widely reported (Rozer, Mollenhorst and Poortman 2017). In 2017, The Pew Center website reported that in the United States of America, 'Nearly one-in-five American women ends her childbearing years without having borne a child, compared with one-in-ten in the 1970' (Livingston and Cohn 2010). Comparable trends have been found in Australia (Corsetti 2017; Parr 2009), Canada (Grenier 2017), China (Feng 2017), Europe (Kreyenfeld and Konietzka 2017), South Africa (Masebe and Ramosebudi 2016) and New Zealand (Boddington and Didham 2008, 2009; Didham 2016).

This book focuses on men's experience of involuntary childlessness and is based mainly on the research I conducted for my Social Gerontology doctorate (Hadley 2015). Throughout the book, I am concerned with increasing the understanding of the experiences of men who, for whatever reason, involuntarily do not father. In doing so, I hope that this will lead to greater comprehension of men and the male experience. In addition to revealing the real-life impact of unwanted male childlessness, this book shows how to conduct rigorous research with people who are disenfranchised socially in the real world and systemically in the academic and political spheres: their experiences are not cherished, counted, courted or comprehended. In this Introduction, I begin by describing my own motivations for studying male involuntary childlessness. I then move on to give a guide to the layout of the book, followed by a brief summary of the content of each chapter.

Why Study Childless Men?

The incentive for undertaking research into male involuntary childlessness is grounded in my personal, professional and academic experience. My interest in male involuntary childlessness started as the subject of my dissertation for my Master of Arts in Counselling (Hadley 2008a). A number of clients had brought the subject to counselling and this had raised my awareness of the issue. The criterion for the subject of the dissertation was personal experience. I discussed the various topics with my supervisor Dr Liz Ballinger. I grew increasingly desperate as Liz gently rejected my grand schemes. I tentatively offered 'I was really broody in my thirties', and improvising from my own experience, detailed my feelings of 'broodiness'. Liz responded immediately, 'I've never heard of that before. Do that.' As I had been particularly broody in my mid-thirties, I wondered if other men had similar feelings. I am defining 'broody' as the behaviours, feelings, thoughts and urges that constitute the emotional and physical desire to be a parent. My reactions to my 'broodiness' have included: anger, depression, elation, guilt, isolation, jealousy, relief, sadness, yearning and withdrawal (Hadley 2008a, 2013). I was raised with the expectation of being a father: 'You'll have to make these difficult decisions when you have children of your own', was a favourite refrain of my parents in times of dispute. On the two occasions partners have told me they wanted to have children with me, my reactions have ranged between relief, panic, joy, fear and pressure. In the first instance, these related to my age (mid-twenties), employment, normative role assumptions and self-doubt regarding my emotional, economic and skill capacity to be a 'good' father. After 'trying' for a baby, that relationship ended just before I turned 30 years old. The second occasion was in my mid-thirties, by which time my self-doubt had abated and my thoughts around fatherhood were along the lines of, 'Yes, I can do this'. However, that relationship ended soon after that conversation. From my twenties onwards, my peers were becoming parents, and I became jealous of those who became fathers. For example, I told one friend, who had recently become a father, 'You have the life I should have had.' In my late thirties, I met my partner and, after the relationship became serious, we discussed my wish to become a father. I was in the position of either staying in a relationship with a wonderful woman or trying to locate a partner who wanted children with me. It was my choice and I placed our relationship first. However, I was conscious of not quite 'fitting' in with peers and not being able to access the social dividend of parenthood. In my early forties, I was also diagnosed with a 30 per cent hearing loss, and this, along with my counselling knowledge, gave me great insight into who, and how, I was.

A combination of that awareness, my counselling of involuntarily childless men and finding that there was little research on men's desire for fatherhood inspired me to consider taking my interest in 'male broodiness' further. However, my attempts to find a funded doctorate failed and as an interim measure, I self-funded a Master of Science (MSc) degree in research methods (Hadley 2009). In my MSc research study, I attempted to find the levels of desire for parenthood between women and men, non-parents and parents. One of my assumptions had been that women would be considerably 'broodier' than men would. The findings, however, showed that childless men were nearly as 'broody' as childless women (see Chapter 1). Moreover, the few studies that did call attention to the male experience were from a feminist perspective. Having gained a distinction in my MSc I then spent several months looking for a funded doctorate. In 2010, I was fortunate enough to be offered a full studentship by Keele University in the Centre for Social Gerontology, on the understanding that the study would focus on older childless men.

In the process of completing the Masters I had grown increasingly aware of how biological parenthood is accorded adult status in many different sociocultural forms, with the vast majority of societies and faiths exemplifying the parenthood ideal (Monach 1993). Moreover, I understood how those women who do not achieve the 'motherhood mandate' (Russo 1976: 144) and men the ideal 'package deal' (Townsend 2002) of work, relationship and fatherhood were subject to stigmatization (Brescoll and Uhlman 2005; Smith 1998; Veevers 1980). Furthermore, I had found that many sociological studies have concentrated on measuring women's marital status, fertility intentions, age at first birth and family size. Because of the historical attitude that fertility and family formation are relevant only to women, there is little available data on men's fertility intentions and history (Dykstra and Keizer 2009; Murphy 2009). Nonetheless, recently there has been an increase in both the academic and general media material on fatherhood, fathering and grandparenting (Arber and Timonen 2012; Doucet 2006; Lupton and Barclay 1997; Van Wormer 2019).

In the past, fatherhood has only been viewed through the lens of the cultural, legal and societal rules that dictated 'rights, duties, responsibilities and statuses' (Hobson and Morgan 2002: 11). Nevertheless, contemporary studies have highlighted the complex relationship between sociocultural practices and men's experiences of being a father, fathering, fatherhood and grandfatherhood (Brannen and Nilsen 2006; Doucet and Lee 2014). In many Western societies, the concept of fatherhood has moved from the traditional 'provider/disciplinarian' to an ideal of 'involved fatherhood'. In this type of parenting men are expected to be both intimate and involved parents (Hadley 2019a; Lupton and Barclay 1997, 1999). Nonetheless, research highlights the strains and limits between the practice and cultural ideal of 'involved fathering' (Daniels and Chadwick 2018; Featherstone 2009; Lupton and Barclay 1997). Some fathers have found that involvement in childcare and home life was fundamental to their sense of identity (Daniels and Chadwick 2018; Shirani, Henwood and Coltart 2012). Likewise, some new fathers have found work relationships improved because they 'could share that experience' with colleagues (Goldberg 2014: 158). Nicole Daniels and Rachelle Chadwick's (2018: 725) study of South African men found 'selfless masculinity' to be a key masculine ideal 'in which giving and service during birth was constructed as integral to being a good father and man'. However, Daniels and Chadwick observed that post-birth, there was a tension between maintaining caring and nurturing roles and traditional provider and protector roles. Equally, Caroline Gatrell et al. (2015: 235) found that some contemporary fathers struggle to balance 'the need, or desire, to engage in childcare' and breadwinning. Similarly, some 'stay-at-home-dads' described feeling strong social pressure to return to the traditional provider role (Shirani, Henwood and Coltart 2012). However, the large volume of academic literature and general media on motherhood highlights the small amount on fatherhood. Significantly, there is even less work on male involuntary childlessness and childlessness-by-circumstance (Hadley 2019; Throsby and Gill 2004).

The lack of men's voices in the literature surrounding reproduction is matched by a similar absence in ageing research (gerontology). Gerontological research in the last twenty years has focused on the lives of older women, mainly because of the disadvantageous status of women in terms of economics, health and care (Arber, Davidson and Ginn 2003; Fennell and Davidson 2003). Although in the past, women lived longer than men, demographic forecasts predict that the age of men's mortality will almost equal that of women in the next few decades. Moreover, demography highlights that with an ageing population there is also a growing demand for care in later life, because more people are living for longer with increased health issues.

The demand for both social and healthcare services increases with age, and recognition of the impact of this has raised serious concerns for governments, institutions and individuals regarding the cost and provision of such services (Pickard 2015; Wittenberg et al. 2008). For example, by 2033 the population of the United Kingdom is predicted to rise to 71.6 million, with those aged 85 and over more than doubling to 3.3 million (Office for National Statistics 2009). Those needing care are projected to grow by around 90 per cent by 2041, with carer numbers predicted to only increase by approximately 27 per cent (Pickard et al. 2009). Moreover, adult children typically undertake informal care with an 'oldest old' relative (Hoff 2015).

'Childless' adults are often seen as 'available to care' (Beth Johnson Foundation/Ageing Without Children 2016) and are 20–40 per cent more likely to provide support than equivalent adults with families (Pesando 2018). In the UK, 58 per cent of carers are female and 42 per cent male (Carers UK 2015), and it is estimated that by 2030 there will be at least two million people aged 65 and over without an adult child to support them if needed (McNeil and Hunter 2014; Pickard et al. 2012). Older childless men have smaller social networks and poorer behaviours in terms of health, diet, self-care and well-being than those married with children (Dykstra and Keizer 2009). Therefore, it is important to move beyond statistics and find the lived reality of being an older involuntarily childless man. An in-depth understanding of the why, how, what, when and who would give insight into individuals who are little understood.

All my academic work has been influenced by the work of feminist scholars (this is discussed further in Chapters 3 and 8). As a male researcher I acknowledge the influence feminist research and feminisms have had on qualitative research in general, and my work in particular (see Pease 2000, 2013). Drawing on that background, and in common with the sociological concept of reflexivity, I will now locate myself within this research by supplying a brief autobiography (Birch 1998). I am a White British, heterosexual male, 61 years old, divorced and remarried, with a non-genetic lifelong hearing impairment. I am the seventh youngest of eight children and I was born, raised and educated in Old Trafford, a working-class area of Manchester. I worked for thirty-one years as a scientific and technical photographer before training, and qualifying, as a counsellor. My academic background follows my multimodal counselling style, in that it draws on the knowledge, experience, myths and legends of different tribes. As such, and much like many childless people, I define myself by what I am 'not' – I am not solely a counsellor, educationalist, gerontologist or sociologist. However, I drew on all those fields, and more, in the undertaking of this study. I am a childless man who has, at times, been desperately affected by the desire to be a biological father (Hadley 2008b, 2012b, 2013). My age and childlessness reinforce the auto/biographical methodological foundations of this book. Moreover, my background and lived experience permeate this study in many ways – both consciously and unconsciously.

Wright Mills (1959: 216) urged social scientists to 'learn to use your life experience in your intellectual work: continually to examine it and interpret it. In this sense craftsmanship [*sic*] is the centre of yourself and you are personally involved in every intellectual product upon which you ... work.' Liz Stanley (1992) highlighted the relationship and intersection between a researcher's and participants' biographies by her use of the term 'auto/biography'. Michael Brennan and Gayle Letherby (2017: 156) argue the case for an 'autobiographical continuum' ranging from *auto*/biography to auto/*biography*. The former refers to academics who write about themselves and identify the significance of others in their story. The latter write about others but in the process recognize the importance of their own experience. However, auto/biography has been criticized for self-indulgence and as a means of covering poor work (Letherby 2002c; Merrill and West 2009). Nevertheless, the same accusation has recently been levelled at 'objective' research methods, including 'gold standard' clinical randomized control trials (Goldacre 2008, 2012). In addition, Cotterill and Letherby (1993: 67) argue that 'all academic research and subsequent writing involves, whether acknowledged or not, the weaving of the biographies of all participants and significant others'. Stanley (1992, 1993) meanwhile concludes that the 'auto/biographical I' demonstrates 'the active inquiring presence of the sociologists in constructing, rather than discovering, knowledge' (Stanley 1993: 41). The auto/biographical approach emphasizes that researchers are not detached, neutral observers and that self, involvement, privilege and power are acknowledged in the research process (Hugill 2012; Letherby 2002c). Moreover, I want to represent the participants as accurately as possible and believe that the auto/biographical approach automatically adds the important dimension of critical reflexivity to this work. This was demonstrated earlier in this chapter and will be apparent throughout the text – for example, in Chapter 3, where I describe the methodology and methods used, and then in Chapter 8, in how I arrived at my conclusions. Chapter 8 also contains my final reflections at the end of the study, and I acknowledge how the research has changed my understanding and worldview. In the Epilogue, I take a more 'improvised' approach to describe male childlessness, examine common myths around men and reproduction, suggest ways of working with men and draw on contemporary research to illustrate how men are the second sex in other fields as well as reproduction. Pen portraits of the participants are presented in Appendix 1. Each pen portrait is based on my notes taken post-interview, and each ends with a brief description of my reflections on the interview interaction. I therefore strongly believe that the approach I have taken is academically and sociologically credible, plausible and valid. Finally, central to my research is the enabling of the previously unheard voices of involuntarily childless men to be heard. On that basis alone, it would be both unethical and ironic not to include my own voice.

The Aims of My Research Study

The vast bulk of this book is based on my doctoral research study. The aim of that study was to address the gap in evidence surrounding older men's lived experiences of involuntary childlessness. To achieve that objective, I had to acknowledge the contextual background of an increasing ageing population, a falling fertility rate and the decline in familial support in later life. Likewise, the impact of involuntary childlessness on the men's health, identity, well-being, relationships, social networks and social interactions had to be explored. To understand the influences on how older men became involuntarily childless, the study aimed to:

- explore the participants' attitudes and behaviours in relation to the experience of involuntary childlessness;
- examine the influences on the participants' quality of life;
- suggest policy recommendations relating to the needs of involuntarily childless men as they age.

One objective of the study was to add to the debates surrounding reproduction and ageing by bringing the experiences of older involuntarily childless men to the attention of the public, academics, policymakers, service providers and practitioners. To address these research aims the study posed the following research questions:

Research question 1: What are men's attitudes and behaviours in relation to their experiences of involuntary childlessness?

Research question 2: How do men describe the influence of involuntary childlessness on their quality of life and relationships with close, familial and wider social networks?

Research question 3: What are involuntarily childless men's expectations of the future?

Research question 4: What are the future policy and service implications of the findings in relation to the above?

Structure of the Book

Following the Introduction, the book consists of a further eight chapters and an Epilogue, which are briefly described here.

The two chapters that immediately follow examine and evaluate the literature surrounding childlessness and ageing. In Chapter 1, I explore the contested meanings and understanding surrounding childlessness, including the exclusion and marginalization of men from the sociocultural narratives that surround parenthood and non-parenthood. I look at the key literature on the dynamic and complex issues that surround childlessness over the life course. Chapter 2 examines three aspects of ageing. Firstly, I explore the relationship between ageing and gender, before focusing on masculinity and ageing. I then scrutinize the broader implications of ageing and childlessness in the wider context of family and social relationships. I move on to propose that a biographical interview method would be a suitable means of gaining an in-depth understanding of involuntarily childless men's experiences over the life course. Chapter 3 depicts the methodological and theoretical foundation of, and the methods utilized in, the study. I examine the rationale for my use of a qualitative approach to my fieldwork that draws on life course, critical gerontological and biographical perspectives. I describe the stages of my fieldwork, from the pilot interview through to an explanation of the thematic analysis used to examine the participants' narratives.

The subsequent four chapters present the findings of my research. In Chapters 4 to 7, I describe the main themes that I have drawn from my analysis of my participants' life stories. Chapter 4 illustrates the different factors and events that influenced the men's involuntary childlessness. Chapter 5 elucidates the affect that not becoming a father had on the participants' 'closest', 'inner' and 'wider' relationships and social networks. Chapter 6 reports on the men's views of their childlessness and the impact it has had on their lives. Chapter 7 provides an insight into my participants' views of their economical position, health and thoughts regarding the future. Chapter 8 concludes the research, and in it I discuss my findings, both in relation to the earlier review of the literature and the research questions. I then move on to consider the contribution that my study has made to this area of research and highlight a possible theoretical approach and areas for further research. This is followed by an examination of the study, including its limitations.

The chapter concludes with my reflexive account of the study and final reflections on undertaking this research. Finally, in the Epilogue I discuss my experiences since completing the study and offer suggestions on how the findings may be used by practitioners and stakeholders from nursing, counselling and psychotherapy, and social work.

My research project was in the field of social gerontology: a field covering the sociology of ageing that tends to focus on later life. However, the subject of male childlessness has seldom been explored, even though it covers many of the disciplines of the humanities and the social sciences: for example, anthropology, demography, education, health, human geography, law, media, philosophy, politics, psychology, sociology and religion. Interest in my work has come from all those disciplines. Consequently, I have written this book from my background in gerontology, and I touch on many of the above areas. Accordingly, the likelihood is that a specialist in a particular discipline may be disappointed that I have not covered a specific subject in detail. I hope you understand that it was not possible for me to do so. However, I do hope that all readers can engage with the participants' experiences and apply their personal or professional lens to the material. Consequently, the book has been written so that the reader can dip in and out of chapters. For example, some scholars may be particularly interested in the methodological approach taken (Chapter 3). Others may be more interested in reading about the life stories and experiences of the men who participated in my research (Chapters 4 to 7).

Chapter 1

CONTEXTS OF CHILDLESSNESS

Introduction

In the majority of societies, biological parenthood provides an assured way to a valued social identity across the life course. Research into people ageing without children is a relatively new field with a paucity of literature from previous decades. The recent rise in interest in this subject reflects the increase in the population of childless older adults across the globe. Consequently, questions have arisen about the factors which influence the significance of childlessness and grandchildlessness in mid- and later life (Dykstra and Hagestad 2007b; Powdthavee 2011; Van Wormer 2019).

In this chapter, I examine the literature surrounding childlessness, including the effects of childlessness on attitudes and behaviour in close, familial and social relations, and any impact on health and well-being. This chapter is organized into six sections and draws on literature from a range of societies. The following section examines the definitions surrounding 'childlessness', and the third section explores the demographic context. The fourth section considers the material on voluntary and involuntary childlessness. Both the third and fourth sections also examine material on infertility and childless men, respectively. The fifth section focuses on childlessness in later life, and the final section provides a discussion of the material presented in the chapter.

Definitions

Childlessness, at its simplest, is the 'absence of children' (Houseknecht 1987: 369). However, it is only relatively recently that childlessness has started to be recognized as a substantive research subject in the social sciences (Dykstra 2009). Previously, social scientists had focused on social networks, family formation and relationships, fertility rates, childbearing age and marital status. Consequently, never-married, childless and, specifically, involuntarily childless men are mostly absent from research (Dykstra and Keizer 2009; Murphy 2009).

The term 'parenthood' has often been normatively used to refer to the role of heterosexual genetic parents within the context of a given cultural and social environment. However, this does not account for those who are biologically childless but who have social parental roles, for example adoptive or step parents (Bures, Koropeckyj-Cox and Loree 2009). Therefore, it is apparent that parenthood, and by implication non-parenthood (childlessness), cannot be categorized into discrete biological divisions. Table 1.1 highlights the diversity in types of biological and social parental realities (Marchbank and Letherby 2007). In addition, Table 1.1 demonstrates the impact that both medical treatments and social policy have had on family formation – for example, respectively through gamete donation (Beeson, Jennings and Kramer 2013) and equality legislation for lesbian and gay adopters (Hicks 2005). Childless adults are 'not a homogeneous group' (Wenger et al. 2007: 1434): childlessness affects all levels of society. Despite this, many studies have not clearly delineated who constituted being 'childless'. Frequently, research has included a conflagration of the never-married, the expected-to-be-childless, the childless-by-choice, the childless-by-circumstance, those who have outlived children or those whose children have left home (Dykstra 2009; Murphy 2009). The diversity of family life and different interpretations of childlessness has implications for all studies. Lack of clarity by researchers may lead to sampling issues that could confound the results or misrepresent individuals or groups (Hadley 2018a).

The terms 'childlessness', 'chosen childless', 'infertility', 'involuntary' and 'voluntary childlessness' are not as self-explanatory as often portrayed and have been frequently conflated, in research and practice (Letherby 1997: 47). Maura Kelly (2009: 158) has argued that academic literature is littered with discrepancies and inconsistent use of these terms (see also Letherby 1997, 2010; Letherby and Williams 1999). Furthermore, Anne Matthews and Ralph Matthews (1986: 643) have demonstrated the complexity inherent in the terms 'infertility' and 'involuntary childlessness' with their observation of the 'biological condition of infertility' and 'the social condition of involuntary childlessness.' James Monach (1993: 5) suggests that childlessness should be viewed as variable across the life course: 'It is probably more helpful to consider childlessness in general as a continuum, on which there are those clearly at either end, but there is a group in the middle whose position is not so simple and which may change over time.' Therefore, how individuals self-define their status may change over time and circumstance (Jeffries and Konnert 2002; Letherby 1997). There is a similar complexity concerning terminology in gerontological research and wider practice. Terms such as 'old', 'older', 'elderly' and 'senior' carry both positive and negative connotations depending on context, location and intent (Bytheway 1995, 2011; Calasanti and Slevin 2001). I acknowledge the complexity in many of the terms associated with both areas.

Fertility Trends, Intentions and Behaviours

In the Western world, on average, childlessness affects one in five women over 45 (Archetti 2019; Organisation for Economic Co-operation and Development 2015) and one in four men (Präg et al. 2017). Joseph Chamie and Barry Mirkin (2012) refer to 'Italy and Switzerland, where one in four women in their late 40s is childless', before asserting that in 'less developed countries the percentage of childless women in their late 40s is typically under 10 percent. And in some populous nations, such as India, Indonesia, Pakistan, South Africa and Turkey, the proportion of women remaining childless by their late 40s is below 5 percent.' The Organisation for Economic

TABLE 1.1. Diversity and difference in forms of parenthood.

- Biological parent(s) who raise their children.
- Biological parent(s) who do not raise their children (e.g. gamete donors).
- Biological parents who have fractured relationships with their children (e.g. through divorce).
- People who believe they are biological parents but are not: e.g. a man whose partner was impregnated by another man.
- People who adopt or foster.
- Social or step-parents with no biological children of their own.
- Lesbian or gay people who may co-parent a partner's biological child.
- Parents of a surrogate child.

Source: Marchbank and Letherby (2007: 193–99).

Co-operation and Development (OECD 2015) analysis of trends in childlessness across thirty-five OECD countries found that between the mid-1990s and 2010 the rate of childlessness fell in four countries: Chile, Luxembourg, Slovenia and Turkey. Furthermore, Cristina Archetti (2019: 175) argues that despite the significant level of childlessness, the childless are 'nearly non-existent from the perspective of the general population. Particularly the *involuntary* childless are virtually invisible' (original italics). Drawing on Renske Keizer's (2010) study, Archetti concludes that up to 90 per cent of childless people are involuntarily childless. Keizer (2010) examined the causes and consequences of childlessness in the Netherlands. She found that 10 per cent were 'chosen childless' and 10 per cent were 'infertile'. The remaining 80 per cent were 'childless-by-circumstance'.

A wide number of factors influence fertility trends (Boivin et al. 2018; Eggebeen and Knoester 2001; Jamieson et al. 2010; Purewal and Akker 2007; Qu and Weston 2004; Simpson 2006):

- women having their first baby in their thirties
- delay in partnering
- higher rates of birth outside of marriage
- increased demand for assisted conception
- preference for smaller families
- dual-earner households
- increase of cohabitation as the main form of couple households
- high rates of divorce/dissolution of couple relationships
- growth in solo living

In a large cross-sectional online study with data from seventy-nine countries, Boivin et al. (2018) investigated whether gender and country were factors in the decision-making of people who were trying to conceive. The study illustrates the complex intersection of sociocultural expectations on peoples' reproductive decisions. Although women were perceived to display a stronger desire for children than men, this has to be taken in the context of the significant difference in the number of male participants: 1,690 men compared to 8,355 women (Boivin et al. 2018: 91). The results state that compared to women, men had less of a personal desire for a child and rated economic, personal and relational willingness as less important. Men rated the social status of parenthood and subjective norms as major influences. Comparisons between countries found significant 'differences in personal desire for a child, partner's desire for a child, need for parenthood, preconditions, motivational forces and subjective norms' (ibid.: 90).

Jane Fisher and Karin Hammarberg (2017: 1289) argue that there are few population studies on men's desires, expectations and hopes to become fathers. Hammarberg and other authors conducted a systematic review of international academic literature to summarize men's attitudes, behaviours and knowledge related to fertility (Hammarberg et al. 2017). The authors examined forty-seven papers from fourteen countries and found that the majority of men desired and expected to become fathers, wished for at least two children and comprehensively viewed parenthood as central for contentment and fulfilment across their lifetime. In addition, Hammarberg et al. found that although men have an equivalent desire for parenthood to women, they have limited knowledge on the impact of age and other factors regarding fertility. Moreover, they were unrealistic in their expectations of both the likelihood of spontaneous conception and the efficacy of ART. Likewise, men's preconditions for parenthood included the suitability and willingness of partners, stable career and finances, and being at the right age or stage. The most common reason for women remaining childless is not finding a partner, and Hammarberg et al. (ibid.: 478) found that this was also true of men. Importantly, Hammarberg et al. argue that there is an increasing gap between the ideal biological and social ages to become a parent.

In a representative survey of German women ($n = 785$) and men ($n = 795$), Stöbel-Richter et al. (2005: 2853) found that childless men and women aged 31–40 had an equal desire to become parents. Stöbel-Richter et al. identified financial concerns as the strongest factors against parenthood, and financial security was also a factor in Australian (Thompson and Lee 2011b) and Canadian (Roberts et al. 2011) studies of childless men. Thompson and Lee surveyed 382 Australian male undergraduate psychology students aged 18–25 on their attitudes to the timing of parenthood. The results outlined that most wanted fatherhood in their late twenties or early thirties. Precursors before parenthood included 'be personally mature' and 'be in a stable relationship (preferably married)' with a 'permanent yet flexible career' and 'secure income'. Follow-up interviews with a subgroup revealed that becoming a father was seen as central to lifelong contentment and fulfilment. In addition to financial security, the participants in Roberts et al.'s (2011) study of five hundred biologically childless Canadian men aged 20–45 indicated that their partners' 'wish for children' and their 'suitability' as a parent were important preconditions. Significantly, 85 per cent of the men wanted to be a father, with 88 per cent wanting to be a father in the future – although this reduced with age.

Within the discussion on men's attitudes and intentions towards parenthood is the awareness of the paucity of material reporting on gay men's attitudes and intentions towards reproductive ideations and outcomes (Smith et al. 2019). In a study of German gay ($n = 628$) and heterosexual ($n = 638$) men aged 18–40 years, Dirk Kranz, Holger Busch and Christoph Niepal (2018) found that contrary to popular stereotypes, gay men were interested in fatherhood. Kranz, Busch and Niepal identified that 89.7 per cent of heterosexual men and 76.4 per cent of gay men expressed a desire for fatherhood. Slightly more than half of the heterosexual men affirmed fatherhood intentions, compared to slightly less than half of the gay men. Moreover, compared to younger men, the older men in each group showed less desire and intent for fatherhood. Correspondingly, a study of 133 New York gay youths (83 men and 50 women, aged 16–22) found that 86 per cent of the men and 98 per cent of the women expected to have children in the future (D'Augelli et al. 2007).

Studies of men have identified how significant the status of fatherhood is to men's sense of themselves and their social identity (Dudgeon and Inhorn 2003; Inhorn and Wentzell 2011; Inhorn et al. 2009a; Jones et al. 2019; Robb and Ruxton 2018; van Balen and Inhorn 2002). In their scoping review of research into fathers' experiences of neonatal death, Kerry Jones et al. (2019) found that the loss of role and status were widely reported. Esther Dermott (2008: 9–10) suggests that one of the factors affecting men's fatherhood intentions is 'the decision making of women'. Other elements include the fact that fatherhood is no longer assumed to be an automatic life event and the increased choice in types of personal relationships. However, Ann-Magritt Jensen (2010: 12) has argued that men may delay parenthood until women take on the majority of the domestic work. More recently, Jensen (2016) has identified the difference class has on childless men's desire to have children. She identified that upper-middle-class men and their partners discussed the timing of the first birth for over a year. Working-class men had few stable relationships and consequently had less deliberation regarding parenthood. Nick Parr's (2007) study found that attitudes towards family, health, money, women, work and leisure all influenced male procreative decision-making. Roberts et al. (2011) concluded that the most influential factors in men's procreative decision-making were financial security, partner intentions and suitability, and men's own attitude. Moreover, men aged between 35 and 45 stated that their perception of their partner's biological clock had an increased influence on their reproductive intentions.

The influence of early-years relationships – attachment theory (Bowlby 1979; Bretherton 1992) – on individual behaviours and motivations has been well established. Anxious attachment is the fear of abandonment by one's primary caregiver that becomes an internalized template for all subsequent intimate and social interactions and extends into adulthood (Vrtička, Sander and Vuilleumier 2012). Vrtička, Sander and Vuilleumier (2012: 531) argue that people with anxious attachment demonstrate 'a strong need for closeness, worries about relationships, and fears of rejection'. Nonetheless, the effect of upbringing on a person's reproductive outcome has seldom been studied. An online cross-sectional survey of 394 men and women aged over 50 in the UK found that people who were childless-by-circumstance were significantly more likely to have developed an anxious attachment to their primary caregiver in childhood (Hadley, Newby and Barry 2019). Furthermore, economists Richard Layard et al. (2014) deployed a prototype model based on the 1970 British Cohort Study dataset to measure the effect of childhood on well-being in adulthood. The results indicated that children's emotional health followed by the child's conduct were the strongest predictors of well-being in adulthood.

Infertility is defined as a disease of the reproductive system (Carroll 2019: xvii): a diagnosis of actual or potential infertility has lifelong implications for mental and physical health, well-being, and intimate and wider social relationships (Greil, Slauson-Blevins and McQuillan 2010; Mahlstedt 1985; Webb and Daniluk 1999). In 2017 it was estimated that between one in seven couples in the UK – approximately 3.5 million people – were affected by problems in conceiving (National Health Service 2017). It is problematic to identify precisely those who are involuntarily childless (Monach 1993: 15). Himmel et al. (1997) have suggested that between 10 and 50 per cent of the involuntarily childless do not seek help. Furthermore, Boivin et al.'s (2007) international review of twenty-five population surveys of infertility found that approximately only half those people with infertility issues sought any form of medical intervention. Involuntary childlessness is a term mostly associated with people during, or post-, Assisted Reproductive Technology (ART) treatment. Subsequently, the term is often used as a clinical classification. Nevertheless, the figures for the number of childless people are difficult to gauge, as those who do not seek medical treatment are not recorded (Monach 1993: 15). Anjani Chandra and Elizabeth Stephen (1998) have suggested that only half of couples in the US with infertility issues seek treatment, with non-treatment seekers differing on race and socio-economic status. Likewise, they propose that the rise in numbers of those seeking treatment between 1982 and 1995 was related to two factors: first, the rapid development and acceptance of ART, and second, 'baby boomers' who delayed parenthood and reached their 'later reproductive and less fecund reproductive years' (Chandra and Stephen 1998: 40). Similarly, more recent studies have found that men and women aged from their late teens to over 50 believed that delayed parenthood would be resolved by ART (Daniluk and Koert 2012, 2013; Thompson and Lee 2011a). Judith Daniluk and Emily Koert (2012, 2013) contend that a contributing factor to delayed childbearing is that men and women greatly overestimate their knowledge of ART procedures and age-related fertility factors. Moreover, although advanced maternal age and adverse birth outcomes have been well established, the corresponding association between advanced paternal age and adverse birth outcomes is less well known (Roberts et al. 2011: 1202).

The British Household Panel Study (Taylor et al. 2010) is an exception to the majority of demographic literature because it includes questions on both fertility intentions and behaviour (Jamieson et al. 2010). Ann Berrington's (2004) study found that females and males have generally comparable fertility, family building and completed family size intentions. However, only the fertility intentions of females were reported, as Berrington (ibid.: 12) argued that co-residency was 'unlikely to be the case for a significant minority of children of male respondents'. Furthermore, men especially may under-report the number of children they have previously fathered, in particular with those they no longer reside or have contact with (Rendall et al. 1999). In addition, Trudie Knijn, Ilona Ostner and Christoph Schmitt (2006: 180) suggest that the cost of adapting data-collecting instruments to include fatherhood intentions or history outweighs the benefits. The lack of available data on men's fertility is therefore partly down to the historical attitude that fertility and family formation are relevant only to women (Greene and Biddlecom 2000), combined with the contestable view that men's data may be unreliable, difficult to access (Berrington 2004) and, in most of the world, not collected. Crucially, because a mother's fertility history is recorded at birth registration, it is relatively simple to work out the level of women's childlessness. On the other hand, the non-collection of the father's fertility history means it is not possible to supply an estimate of the level of male childlessness in most of the countries of the world, including the UK. Consequently, one must conclude that the figures provided by the vast majority of institutions under-estimate the level of the childless population.

The change in fertility trends have led to a number of mainly demographic studies that attempt to develop models that would identify, and predict, the influences that affect fertility intentions (Hoffman and Manis 1979; Schoen et al. 1999; Schoen et al. 1997). Initial studies focused on structural items, such as social and economic status and the social value (costs and benefits) of children to parents (Hoffman 1975). The cost-benefit analysis approach was criticized for reflecting parents' decisions to stop having children (Hoffman and Manis 1979), with van Balen and Trimbos-Kemper (1995) reporting that childless couples were not deterred by costs. Moreover, Bagozzi and Loo (1978: 318) noted that 'to accurately predict fertility one must ... examine the attitudes and social re-lationships of families'. Subsequently, studies that incorporated attitudes and intentions items into their design confirmed that fertility intentions were reliable predictors of fertility outcomes (Langdridge, Connolly and Sheeran 2000; Schoen et al. 1999). A study of infertile Dutch couples by van Balen and Trimbos-Kemper (1995) found that the women reported a stronger desire for par-enthood than men. Happiness, well-being and parenthood were the highest motivators, while family name and religion were not frequently referenced. Langdridge, Connolly and Sheeran (2000) found a trio of core motivators for parenthood in their study of expectant and ART-ready British couples: to 'give love,' 'receive love' and 'become a family'. However, many of the scales devel-oped have been criticized. For example, many measured different point scales against different motivational items, and therefore reduced the generalizability of the findings. Moreover, implicit so-ciocultural differences and commonalities were not acknowledged (Armitage and Conner 2001; Langdridge, Sheeran and Connolly 2005; Purewal and Akker 2007).

In an attempt to consolidate scales, Langdridge et al. (2005: 125) developed the 'Reasons for Parenthood Scale' based on a postal survey of British white, married, childless couples (responses: men n = 393, women n = 481) aged 18–40. This study uniquely accounted for the fertility ideations of both female and male 'intenders' and 'non-intenders' (ibid.). 'Intenders' cited centrality of the family, bond between parents, giving love, aspiration and bond with child as main reasons. Both female and male non-intenders reported that 'other things' were more important than parenthood. Male non-intenders rated 'career', 'freedom' and 'responsibility', and female non-intenders rated 'partners wishes' (ibid.: 128). Furthermore, as age and length of marriage increased, the intention to become parents decreased (ibid.: 131). The findings followed 'traditional cultural expectations about masculinity, femininity, and childrearing' and all respondents highlighted the significance of their partner's opinion in fertility decision-making (ibid.). Although the authors acknowledge the limits of the study, such as only surveying white married couples, they suggest that the scale is appropriate for predicting fertility intentions and behaviours (Hadley 2009). Moreover, research conducted in Europe has highlighted that age, ethnicity and gender differences affect intentions towards parenthood (Bos, van Balen and van den Boom 2003; Rooij, Balen and Hermanns 2006). Critics of the quantitative measures approach to fertility behaviour scales suggest that its deterministic underpinnings assign a permanent attitude towards parenthood that fails to capture an individual's subjective processes (Purewal and Akker 2007: 79; Hadley 2008a, 2009).

In an effort to examine the sociocultural meanings of parenthood, a UK-based study individually interviewed thirteen participants (seven female and six male) from South Asian and White ethnicities, aged between 21 and 44 (Purewal and Akker 2007). The interviews used Langdridge et al.'s (2005) 'Reasons for Parenthood Scale' as a guide and the transcripts were analysed using Interpretative Phenomenological Analysis (IPA). This approach was taken in order to understand how individuals interpret, and make sense of, their personal and social experience (Smith and Osborn 2008). The findings revealed five themes common to both ethnicities: parenting as selfless, parenting as a fulfilling role, the significance of genetic ties, the importance of joint decision-making, and being prepared for parenthood (Purewal and Akker 2007: 81). The British South Asian participants indicated that life without children is undesirable, as the latter are the most important thing in their lives. The British South Asian males were strongly committed to the link between the genetic line and the family name. The sentiments expressed by the British South Asian participants are supported by the findings of Lorraine Culley and Nicky Hudson's (2009) study of infertility in British South Asian communities. White participants acknowledged the sociocultural values surrounding parenthood but also offered that 'there *could* be other important things in life' other than childrearing (Purewal and Akker 2007: 84, original italics). Both younger people and women participants viewed parenthood positively. The former saw parenthood as a unique bond and the culmination of a strong and close relationship. Women expressed the opinion that they would feel more fulfilled with a child than without. Moreover, women saw the meaning of fulfilment more positively and more deeply than males.

Purewal and Akker's study highlighted the influence that age, culture and gender had on attitudes and beliefs towards parenthood. Furthermore, although Purewal and Akker's socially constructive view produced nuanced and rich findings, their results were similar to the quantitative study of Langdridge et al. (2005). Overall, both forms of study demonstrated that the motivations for parenthood involve a complex negotiation between individual desires, relational dynamics and sociocultural norms. However, the cross-sectional nature of many fertility motivation studies does not account for how intentions and behaviours may evolve over time. Furthermore, the age range of the cohorts means that those at the older end of the age range may have experienced events which influenced their fertility intentions that the younger people did not (Robinson, Schmidt and Teti 2005: 5–6).

Childlessness

Biologically, 'no organism is advantaged by never conceiving' (Boivin, Sanders and Schmidt 2006: 352), and in most societies biological parenthood is a highly valued adult status. The attainment of genetic continuity brings privileges, kudos and an acknowledged positive social identity across the life course (Dykstra and Hagestad 2007a; Lisle 1996; Veevers 1973). All the main world religions exemplify the childbearing ideal (Monach 1993: 52), and becoming a parent is considered central to the life script of the 'normal, expectable life-cycle' (Dykstra and Hagestad 2007a; Franklin 1990; Neugarten 1969: 125). In Western society the pronatalist heterosexual norm is closely linked to the Judaeo-Christian tradition, which views children as a blessing, with 'barrenness' seen as unnatural (Daly 1999; Miall 1986). Moreover, the construction of parenthood as an unconscious, spontaneous and natural act permits an unreflective acceptance of the heteronormative, pronatalist ideal (Morison 2013).

All societies involve age-related transitions over the life course, with concomitant attendant roles and meanings surrounding each specific phase (Becker 1999; Goldberg 2014). Bernice Neugarten, Joan Moore and John Lowe (1965: 716) developed the concept of a 'social clock' to account for individuals' awareness of sociocultural expectations that link appropriate age to events, roles and behaviours. They proposed that people had absorbed the concept of the 'socio clock' to form an 'internal indicator' that was used to measure if they were 'on time' or 'off time' – for example, when it is socially acceptable to become a parent (Daly and Bewley 2013). This proposal is supported by Billari et al.'s (2011) analysis of the European Social Survey's (round three) study of twenty-five countries. Billari et al. found that there is a widespread social belief in the appropriate age and timing for parenthood. Neugarten (1979: 888) observed that the 'social clock' is critical in self-assessment and is evidenced when 'men and women compare themselves with their friends, siblings, work colleagues or parents in deciding whether they have made good', and 'always with a time-line in mind'.

Historically, discussions regarding reproduction have centred on 'women's and maternal processes' (Hinton and Miller 2013: 248) with little consideration for men's experiences. However, Marcia Inhorn et al. (2009b: 1) have argued that men have been assumed to be disengaged from reproductive intentions and outcomes, and as a result have been marginalized as the 'second sex'. For example, in a systematic review of parenting in the British print media, only one article related to men (Brown and Ferree 2005). This normative dynamic reinforces women's role as childbearing and nurturing and men's as providers and protectors (Connell 1995; Lupton and Barclay 1997). The evolution of social norms formed gendered roles that positioned male involvement in procreative decision-making as a taken-for-granted 'non-choice' and 'non-topic' (Morison 2013: 1140). North American political scientist Cynthia Daniels (2006: 5–6) proposes that the differential reproductive roles of men and women have been 'highly exaggerated' and have created embedded assumptions of male reproductive privilege. Consequently, she argues that those unchallenged assumptions demonstrate that reproductive difference does 'not just privilege but burden men'.

Those not participating in the dominant pronatalist heteronormative ideology of either the 'motherhood mandate' (Russo 1976: 144) for women or the male 'package deal' of work, relationship and fatherhood (Townsend 2002) have often been the subject of stigmatization (Blackstone and Stewart 2012; Brescoll and Uhlman 2005; Matthews and Matthews 1986; Sappleton 2018a; Veevers 1980). Moreover, a large range of deleterious stereotypes (for example, the labels of crones, hags and witches) have been applied to many lesbian and heteronormative older women for not attaining motherhood or grandmotherhood (Westwood 2016a, 2016b). Natalie Sappleton (2018a: 381) generalizes that 'childless and childfree women (but not men) experience social stigmas as a consequence of being cast deviant.' Conversely, there are studies that clearly show that men who challenge prescriptive stereotypes, such as gay men, house husbands, stay-at-home-dads and male primary school teachers, are often subject to discrimination, exclusion, isolation and mistrust (Letherby 2016; Rosenfeld 2003a; Sargent 2000; Smith 1998). Regarding older men, many have been subject to sexualized stereotyping ('dirty old men'). Nevertheless, the stigmatization of those not conforming to the pronatalist norm is apparent: many infertile people have hidden their experience and status to avoid stigma or to protect themselves or others from pain (Exley and Letherby 2001; Letherby 2016; Moulet 2005).

Family configuration is traditionally correlated with motherhood, and the majority of studies do not report on the fertility history or fertility intentions of men (Greene and Biddlecom 2000; Jamieson et al. 2010; Letherby 2002b; Throsby and Gill 2004). Moreover, studies of parenthood have concentrated on childbearing, and have focused on comparisons between those who do and those who do not have dependent children (Dykstra and Keizer 2009; Forste 2002; Wenger, Scott and Patterson 2000). The childless and the never-married disappear in such research, either through not being counted or being assigned to a category such as 'empty nesters' (Dykstra 2009). Parents whose children have left home or have died have also categorized themselves as childless (Murphy 2009), with Monach (1993: 16) pointing out that up to 20 per cent of the UK Census who reported themselves as childless do have children. Therefore, the lifelong childless and those whose children no longer live at home confound results, because those in parenting roles and those who are parents are inseparable (Dykstra 2009: 671).

Voluntary Childlessness

Voluntary childlessness is frequently defined as describing people who have the biological capacity to become a parent, but who do not choose, want or expect to have a child (Poston 1976). Parenting and childlessness are predominately associated with women. Childlessness has been culturally constructed as 'abnormal', 'deviant' and contrary to the dominant pronatalist ideal of biological parenthood (Grinion 2005; Lalos, Jacobsson and von Schoultz 1985; Veevers 1972, 1979). Many studies have reported childless women being stigmatized as 'greedy' or 'selfish' and as having 'privileged freedom' (Chancey and Dumais 2009; Gillespie 2000; Park 2002; Veevers 1973). Moreover, Rose O'Driscoll and Jenny Mercer (2018) argue that a dominant narrative surrounding childless women is that they will experience regret and loneliness in later life. Their grounded-theory study of twenty-one women from England, Scotland and Wales aged between 45–75 years old and who had chosen not to have children used semi-structured interviews. According to O'Driscoll and Mercer, the findings in fact demonstrated that as they age, childless women do not experience significant loss and regret. The experience of childlessness by lesbians, gay men, and bisexual and transgender people (LGBT) highlights issues that intersect with generational and sociocultural inequalities (Hadley 2018a, 2018c, 2019b). For older people of this population, non-parenthood has often been a feature of their lives, with contemporary research highlighting issues concerning discrimination, exclusion, isolation and prejudice (King and Cronin 2016; Simpson 2011; Westwood 2016b).

Recent studies have found that 'voluntarily childless' women and men have used a range of strategies to avoid social sanction: 'passing, identity substitution, condemning the condemners, asserting a right to self-fulfilment, claiming biological deficiency, and redefining the situation' (Park 2002: 21, 2005; Basten 2009, Blackstone and Stewart 2012). Tanya Koropeckyj-Cox and Gretchen Pendell (2007b: 910) analysed two United States nationally representative surveys to examine the attitudes towards childlessness of men and women aged 25–39. They found that childlessness was more acceptable to women than men, and that fertility intentions declined with increased age. College-educated men were the most negative compared with equivalent women who cited the opportunities offered by increased employment against the traditional female roles (see also Ayers 2010; Koropeckyj-Cox and Pendell 2007b: 911–12).

Similarly, Jamieson et al.'s (2010: 481) Scottish study found that men showed a preference for traditional 'provider' gender roles. Nonetheless, the younger men reported concern about their ability to fulfil that 'provider' role.

Jean Veevers (1980) argued that there were two types of childless people: those who chose 'childlessness' at an early age and those who decided to remain childless after a series of postponements. Following Veevers (1980), Sharon Houseknecht (1977, 1980, 1987) developed a typology of 'early-articulators' and 'postponers'. More recently, Leslie Cannold (2000, 2004, 2005) has contended that previous studies conflated delayed parenthood with voluntary childlessness and had not fully explored women's reproductive intentions. Moreover, Veever's (1980) and Houseknecht's (1987) claim that voluntarily childless people make fertility intention decisions when very young has been challenged by recent research highlighting the influence that attitudinal, life course, social and economic factors have on procreative decision-making (Cannold 2000; Basten 2009). Cannold (2000: 4–6) has argued that childless women are 'Childless-by-Choice' or 'Childless-by-Circumstance'. In her study, the latter were women who had not become mothers for social rather than biological reasons. Cannold (ibid.: 415–17) argued that the 'social clock' had as much an influence on women's procreative outcomes as the 'biological clock'. Cannold's (ibid.: 423) 'social clock' included attitudes of family and friends, the 'right' partner, economic considerations, location, education, religion and awareness of age. Similarly, findings from my MSc attitudinal survey (Hadley 2009) showed that both 'age' and the 'biological clock' were only reported by the female respondents as influences on reproductive decision-making.

The majority of studies into voluntary childlessness examine the experiences of women and couples (Basten 2009; Blackstone and Stewart 2012; Gillespie 2000, 2003; Mullins 2018; Park 2002, 2005; Sappleton 2018b). Alyssa Mullins's (2018: 119–20) use of Bourdieu's[1] (1986) concepts of habitus, capital and fields highlighted the complexity of the intersection of structural and agentic factors in childlessness. Mullins's contemporary quantitative study surveyed 972 American childless adults aged between 25 and 40 on their future parenthood intentions. Mullins (2018: 108) argued that there were two broad groups: the Temporarily Childless (TC) – those who wanted or probably wanted children – and the Voluntarily Childless (VC) – those who did not or probably did not want children. VC people were more likely to be single (never married), divorced or in an unmarried long-term relationship or cohabitating, to be a high earner and to be less traditional concerning gender roles (ibid.: 112, 117). Compared to VC people, TC people (ibid.: 111):

- viewed children as important to 'feeling complete as a man/woman'
- always thought they would be a parent
- thought life would be more fulfilling with children
- thought it was key for them to become a parent

In addition, marriage, time spent with friends, belief in pronatalist ideology and increased support for 'hands-on-father' childcare decreased the likelihood of voluntary childlessness. Nonetheless, Mullins reasoned that her findings supported some existing views of childlessness and challenged others. For example, her bivariate findings indicated higher social support for TC people. However, her multivariate analysis found the opposite (Mullins 2018: 118). In particular, she argued for a more nuanced discussion of voluntary childlessness. She went on to discuss the limitations of her study, noting that the sample was not representative of the US population.

Patricia Lunneborg (1999) identified a gap in the information on the fertility intentions of men and conducted 'an exploratory, not scientific' study of thirty voluntarily childless men. She surveyed male members of 'childfree' organizations using a self-developed questionnaire, 'Reasons Why People Say No To Kids' (Lunneborg 1999: 137). Follow-up interviews based on the men's responses were held with sixteen American and fourteen British men aged 27–55. The majority (twenty-two) were partnered and the remainder were single. From her findings, Lunneborg (1999: 4) constructed a tripartite typology: 'early-articulators', 'postponers' and 'acquiescers'. The first two categories followed Houseknecht's typology (1987). The 'acquiescers' adopted a neutral attitude and followed their partners' reproductive choices (Lunneborg 1999: 4). Lunneborg (ibid.: 131) asserts that this reflected the prevalent male belief that it was the woman's choice to have children and that 'children are women's *raison d'*être' (original italics). The men's motives for choosing childlessness related to time, freedom and identity, and these recall the items in the questionnaire (ibid.: 138). Lunneborg's findings support studies that have associated childlessness with the timing of transitional events (Hagestad and Call 2007) and men's attitudes towards both women and parenthood (Jamieson et al. 2010; Parr 2007, 2009). Unfortunately, Lunneborg's book does not reveal how she performed her analysis of either the questionnaire or the interviews. Nor does she explain the rationale for drawing the study's sample solely from childfree organizations or describe any bias she may have had regarding the subject or the participants. Many female researchers have reported both negative and positive gender dynamics regarding interviewing men (for example, see Gatrell 2006; Lee 1997; Lohan 2000; McKee and O'Brien 1983; Miller 2011). However, Lunneborg chose not to disclose any such details, and this may be an example of a researcher who does not recognize the presence of gender issues in research (Hackett 2008). Furthermore, Lunneborg did not acknowledge any cultural commonalities or differences between the American and British participants (Bancroft 2001; Knodel 2001).

Imogene Smith et al.'s (2019) contemporary Australian qualitative study explored the attitudes of eleven childless men aged 28–34 who had indicated they did not want children. Three of the men identified as homosexual and the remainder as heterosexual. Semi-structured interviews were conducted by a woman of similar age to the participants. The participants were volunteers from an ongoing longitudinal study and the data was analysed using Interpretive Phenomenological Analysis (IPA). The age of the men selected was an important factor, because the median age for first-time fatherhood in Australia is 33. Consequently, the authors believed that the 'pronatalist pressures would be most salient' (ibid.: 4) at this stage, in addition to effects from economic, health and relationship influences. The findings indicated that the men's attitudes to childlessness were inchoate with structural factors, with disquiet surrounding economics and population growth. On the other hand, none of the men committed themselves to a childless future, and few had had any sort of in-depth discussion regarding childlessness with their partner. The men did not see childlessness as central to their identity or as a fixed decision. Moreover, the men identified themselves as 'unconventional', with fatherhood viewed as a challenge to a valued freedom and an unknown responsibility.

Involuntary Childlessness

There is an extensive and diverse range of literature on infertility that spans from medical texts to descriptive pieces based on people's personal experience. Of the latter, the vast majority describe women's experiences and explore the personal journey of the authors

(Day 2013; Pfeffer and Wollett 1983). Although many address male infertility, it is usually in medical and technical terms rather than as actual experience – even when a male co-authors the material (for example, Houghton and Houghton 1984).

Infertility affects men and women equally and is defined by the National Institute for Clinical Excellence (NICE 2004: 9) as a 'failure to conceive after two years of unprotected sexual intercourse in the absence of known reproductive pathology'. Very few couples are completely infertile, the majority being 'sub-fertile'. However, this sub-fertile majority will experience the reality of infertility on either a temporary or a permanent basis, depending on whether or not they succeed in having a child. Because of this, the term 'infertile' is usually used to describe people in this situation. Those who have never achieved a pregnancy, or cannot conceive, are described as having 'primary' infertility. More common are those categorized as having 'secondary infertility', that is, they have had one or more pregnancies, have a child, cannot conceive or may have suffered miscarriage or a stillbirth (Hudson 2008; Human Fertilisation and Embryology Authority 2007/8). The typical route for an infertile couple may see them initially attempting to conceive naturally before seeking medical advice. Thereafter follows a series of tests to find a diagnosis for the cause of the childlessness. The diagnosis may lead to the possible use of Assisted Reproductive Technology (ART) treatments, with IVF (In Vitro Fertilization) being the most common in the UK.

Recent figures from the Human Fertilisation and Embryology Authority (2019) show that in 2017, 54,760 patients underwent 75,425 fertility treatment cycles with 21 per cent birth rate per embryo transfer of all IVF treatments. Those for whom treatment is unsuccessful are classed as 'involuntarily childless', and this term, although it has no medical basis, is a label applied to both individuals and couples post-treatment. However, there has been growing criticism of limiting the definition of 'involuntary childlessness' to only those who have accessed medical advice. The failure to include non-treatment seekers means that much infertility research cannot be generalized to the wider population (Greil, Slauson-Blevins and McQuillan 2010: 142–43). Moreover, quantitative studies of infertility are limited because of their reliance on clinic-based samples (McQuillan, White and Jacob 2003: 1009). In clinic-based research, there are significant power issues. For example, the researcher may be viewed as key in accessing services (for example, see Oliffe 2009: 77).

The diagnosis of actual or potential infertility has considerable implications for mental and physical health, social stress, relationships and well-being (Boivin 2003; Greil, Slauson-Blevins and McQuillan 2010; Lee 1996; Mahlstedt 1985; Menning 1980). Letherby (2012: 10) argues that the losses and absences that are implied with the term's 'infertility' and 'involuntary childlessness' do not reflect the complexity of the experience. For example, infertility treatment affects some relationships positively and others negatively, with 'deep and lasting hurt felt by many of the couples, although not all, at the experience of childlessness' (Monach 1993: 121; Letherby 1997; Moulet 2005). Moreover, many infertile people have hidden their experience and status to avoid stigma or to protect themselves or others from the pain. Christine Moulet (2005) has argued that psychological research has often conflated infertility and childlessness and focused on the early stages of successful or unsuccessful treatment. The process of adjustment to involuntary childlessness has frequently been described in stages, based on Kûbler-Ross's (1970) 'grief model': denial, anger, bargaining, depression and acceptance (Houghton and Houghton 1984; Letherby 2002a; Moulet 2005; Tonkin 2010).

Much infertility literature concentrates on the 'acceptance' or the 'resolution' of an individual's childlessness, with Letherby (1997: 283) identifying how 'the resolution of an individual's childlessness does not necessarily equal "complete" resolution'. Lois Tonkin (2010) has studied the psychosocial experience of twenty-seven New Zealand women, aged from 30 to their forties. She described her participants as 'contingently childless' (ibid.: 178): 'women who have always seen themselves as having children but find themselves at the end of their natural fertility without having done so for social rather than (at least initially) biological reasons.' Moulet's (2005) qualitative study of a single female and eight self-defined involuntarily childless couples aged 37–54 found three types of transitional process. Firstly, 'prompt acceptors' were mostly men who easily acknowledged a childless future and saw some advantages to childlessness. Secondly, 'movers-on', although pragmatic, also expressed a sense of loss. Finally, 'battlers' were mostly women, and a few men, who experienced a long, difficult process of negotiating the loss of their parental ideal. Consequently, there was no complete resolution, but an eventual adaption to childlessness (ibid.: 135, 138).

All societies have codes and rules on appropriate behaviour surrounding loss and bereavement. In her study, Lois Tonkin (2010) drew on both Doka's (2002) and Corr's (2004) conceptualization of 'disenfranchised grief', where some losses are not considered socially valid. Therefore, grievers are stigmatized, rendered invisible or have their feelings minimized. In ART, miscarriage and gamete loss are common occurrences. Fiona Littleton and Susan Bewley (2019) highlight the losses involved for the 281 women who participated in Robert Edward, Patrick Steptoe and team's innovative and experimental IVF research. More recently, Julia Bueno's (2019) groundbreaking book examined pregnancy loss across autobiographical, cultural, historical, medical, social and relational contexts. She demonstrated how miscarriage has been unacknowledged, silenced and minimized in many societies. Uniquely, Bueno explored how miscarriage affects men, and how men are structurally distanced from the loss and struggle to grieve in 'recognizable [i.e. female] ways'. Consequently, men face difficulties in knowing how to behave and relate to their partners, and in wider social situations.

Recent research challenges the perception that infertile men do not suffer the levels of distress that comparable women experience (Adler 1991; Domar et al. 1992; Domar, Zuttermeister and Friedman 1993; Lechner, Bolman and van Dalen 2007). Fisher et al.'s (2010) cross-sectional cohort survey of Australian men five years after a diagnosis of infertility found that men who did not become fathers suffered poorer mental health than those who had become fathers. Fisher et al. (ibid.: 6) concluded that the stereotype that infertile men 'are less distressed than women about potential loss of parenthood, and adjust more readily to childlessness appear[s] inaccurate'. Findings from the 1946 British Birth Cohort Study (Guralnik et al. 2009) of functionality tests on men and women, all aged 53 years, found differences between the health of never-married men, childless married men and married men with children. The unmarried and childless men faced greater risks of poor midlife physical function, even after adjustment for confounders such as social class, education and employment status. The authors conclude that for men, marriage and parenthood may protect against functional decline in middle age. However, they also acknowledge that poorer health in earlier life may influence relationship formation and parenthood. There were no marked differences in functional outcomes among women.

Male Involuntary Childlessness

There has been little published research into the effects of male involuntary childlessness (Culley, Hudson and Lohan 2013): 'Men have been terribly under researched in the parenthood motivation literature' (pers. comm., Darren Langdridge, 2008). Indeed, Marcia Inhorn et al. (2009a) contend that anthropology and social science research has almost exclusively focused on women's reproductive lives, their use of ART and their maternal and child nurturing experiences. Consequently, they argue that men have been marginalized in all literature, and that this has led to a serious omission concerning men's reproductive experiences in many disciplines. This, Inhorn et al. explain, has led to the untested and unprovable assumption that men are disengaged from matters of human reproduction. Accordingly, that assumption has become embedded in policy, the general media, and academic literature ranging from anthropology, demography, feminist studies, masculinities, psychology and social sciences. The fourteen chapters in Inhorn et al.'s edited book challenge this assumption, drawing on international and cross-cultural studies from America, Asia, Latin America and the Far and Middle East (see Hadley 2016b for a review of Inhorn et al. 2009a). In order to 'break the silence' around men's experience, feelings and thoughts, men are viewed as 're-producers' – 'reproductive partners, progenitors, fathers, nurturers, and decision makers' (Inhorn et al. 2009a: 3). Issues explored range over men's experience of childbirth, discourses surrounding sperm, family planning, fatherhood and fathering, genital surgery, infertility, male contraceptives, reproductive health, masculinity and the sexuality of 'heterosexuals, homosexuals, married and unmarried men' (ibid.). By drawing on a wide range of subjects from across the globe, Inhorn et al. identify that men are 'often heavily involved and invested in most aspects of the reproductive process'.

Similarly, Cynthia Daniels (2006) examines the discourses surrounding men, reproductive health and masculinity. She argues that structurally embedded, ideal masculine norms have systematically reduced and hidden men's reproductive vulnerability. Drawing on scientific, public media, legal, policy and political literature, Daniels (2006: 29) reasons that culture distorts the role of men in reproduction and reinforces gender stereotypes. She (ibid.: 6–7) carefully argues that four widely held cultural assumptions inform societal norms for male reproduction, or 'reproductive masculinities'. The four assumptions are: (1) men are secondary to biological reproduction; (2) men are less susceptible to reproductive harm and hazards, (3) men are virile and can father children, (4) men are less related to health issues in their children. Daniels critically explores each assumption by examining:

1. The history of scientific concepts surrounding reproduction from antiquity to the 1990s.
2. The worldwide decline in sperm and the increase of male reproductive diseases and disorders reported at the beginning of this century.
3. The increase in the commodification of sperm and the minimization of male infertility issues.
4. The acceptance of men's exposure to reproductive harm and denial of male-mediated foetal harm. (Daniels 2006: 8)

Daniel highlights how each informs the denial of men's vulnerabilities and supports idealized gender roles. For example, she challenges assumption four by reviewing the enquiry into the effect of Agent Orange on the children of veterans of the Vietnam War (2006: 129–37). It is interesting that Daniels does not draw on hegemonic masculinities[2] in her analysis. Nonetheless, she strongly argues that the reproductive ideals of masculinity 'are double-edged, for while they perpetuate assumptions about the superior strength of the male body, they lead to a profound neglect of male reproductive health and a distorted view of men's relationship to human reproduction.' Importantly, Daniels exposes the complex relationship between individual agency, structural institutions, and gender and reproductive relations. In addition, she forcefully argues for a transformation of gender relations through the recognition of 'a more just politics of reproduction' that would acknowledge 'that men and women share an interest in the health and well-being of children' (ibid.: 168). Daniels makes an excellent case for challenging the denigration of men's vulnerabilities without apportioning blame to individual men. Moreover, she challenges medical practitioners, policymakers, politicians, political activists and other stakeholders to value men and women equally.

In the decade and a half since Daniels's book was published, the significance of environment and lifestyle on fertility and reproductive health has been increasingly recognized. Within the general discourse of reproduction is the assumption that men are fertile from puberty until their demise. However, contemporary studies identify a decline in sperm efficacy from the age of 35 onwards, and a correlation between older fathers and babies born with genetic issues (Bray, Gunnell and Smith 2006; Goldberg 2014; Povey et al. 2012; Sartorius and Nieschlag 2010; Yatsenko and Turek 2018). Ana-Maria Tomova and Michael Carroll (2019: 205) demonstrate that lifestyle habits like alcohol, caffeine and recreational drug and tobacco consumption are risk factors for infertility. In addition, environmental and occupational contaminants have a detrimental effect on sperm quality and egg development. For example, air pollution, natural toxins and synthetic toxicants (chemical compounds) are linked to abnormal foetal development, infertility, miscarriage and poor pregnancy outcomes (ibid.: 207). Kevin Smith (2015: 775) has suggested a need for 'state-supported universal sperm banking' for younger men (aged 18) to account for the impact of the increasing age of fathers on debility and genetic disease. Concluding their review of literature on advanced paternal age (APA), Phillips, Taylor and Bachmann (2019) recommend that midlife and older men considering paternity should contemplate sperm banking.

There is a vast canon of literature focusing on women and reproduction that ranges from academic papers to the autobiographical. The latter category includes women's experiences of successful and unsuccessful ART and books on how to deal with involuntary childlessness (for example, Day 2013, 2016). By comparison, there are few academic books examining men's experience of infertility treatment. Two that have received critical acclaim are North Americans Marcia Inhorn's (2012) and Liberty Barnes's (2014). Professor Marcia Inhorn is a renowned medical anthropologist who has completed many studies on the impact of infertility by engaging with people in their everyday environment (via ethnographic research). Much of her research has centred on the Middle East and American Arabs. In her book *The New Arab Man: Emergent Masculinities, Technologies and Islam in the Middle East*, Inhorn argues that the experiences of Middle Eastern men are absent from research on ART. Moreover, vilifying stereotypes of Middle Eastern Muslim men as misogynistic oppressors of women, religious zealots and terrorists abound and are frequently embedded in theory. Inhorn challenges those stereotypes through her examination of the lived experiences of Middle Eastern men as they access ART in order to overcome childlessness and infertility. Her book is primarily based on the three-year study that she started in 2003: 'Middle Eastern Masculinities in the New Age of New Reproductive Technologies.' The sample consisted of 220 Lebanese, Syrian and Palestinian men, of whom 100 were fertile with infertile wives and 120 were infertile themselves. The majority of the men were Muslim, Lebanese, resident in the Lebanon and from all social classes. However, the participants' stated residence spread across fifty countries. By drawing on epidemiological reproductive history and anthropological life history methods, Inhorn produces a fine-grained person-centred account of the intersections between the experiential, the familial, Islam and other religions and orthodoxies, the political-economic environment, globalization, regional complexities, war, IVF clinicians, nurses, service providers, and 'the morally contentious world of assisted reproduction' (Inhorn 2012: 19).

The book is divided into two sections: 'Emergent Masculinities' and 'Islamic Masculinities'. Each chapter presents detailed accounts and rich narratives that brightly illuminate the agentic and structural nuances involved with ART in religious Islam. The first section expertly explores Middle Eastern men's lives in the context of '"the four M's": masculinity, marriage, morality and medicine treatment seeking' (Inhorn 2012: 30). In this section Inhorn's critique of masculinities theory centres on Raewyn Connell's (1995) popular concept of hegemonic masculinities. Drawing on her decades of research, Inhorn contends that hegemonic masculinities do not reflect how Middle Eastern men enact their manhood, not through brutality but through caring, nurturing and protecting their wives in a way 'characterised by a loving connectivity' (Inhorn 2012: 15). Acknowledging her change in perspective regarding masculinity, Inhorn advances her concept of 'Emergent masculinities', rooted in Raymond Williams's (1978) notion of 'emerging masculinities'. 'Emergent masculinities' reflect how her male participants' enactment of manhood was dynamically adapted to the changes in and challenges to ongoing socio-economic, physical and mental health, technology and the relational subtleties of their everyday lives. She identifies the medicalization of infertility and the change in narrative to one of a 'God-given disease' and exposes the relationship between the marketization of IVF and Intracytoplasmic Sperm Injection (ICSI) and couples' commitment to sharing reproductive expectations and issues. Importantly, Inhorn discusses the impact of the tradition of 'consanguineous connectivity' (marriage to cousins or related family). Consanguineous marriages are common, and contribute to maintaining family ties, finding partners and upholding community traditions. However, Inhorn argues that they contribute to the high level of male infertility and genetic disorders in the Middle East and have implications for the use of ICSI.

In the book's second section, Inhorn skilfully examines 'Islamic Masculinities' by painstakingly exposing the complexities of the men's experience of ART in relation to faith (Muslim and Christian). She explores the concerns surrounding semen collection and masturbation and adroitly evaluates the fatwas regarding the differing Sunni and Shia Islamic attitudes and approaches to ART and gamete donation. She demonstrates how, in the context of cultural and religious customs, Middle Eastern men's use of ART is challenging authorities and disrupting traditional narratives with a concomitant impact on the Middle Eastern sociopolitical world. She goes on to argue that 'New Arab men are rejecting the assumptions of their Arab forefathers', which include 'the four notorious Ps – patriarchy, patrilineality, patrilocality, and polygyny' (2012: 302). Moreover, she concludes that her participants' stories show that 'emergent masculinities entail love, tenderness, and affection as well as untold sacrifice and suffering' (ibid.: 317).

Inhorn's book is a tour de force of academic writing, balancing the experiential, political and theoretical in equal measure. She is clear in describing the issues that interest her as researcher and the limits of the study. Very few reviewers of the book raised any criticism, with only Ghauri (2014) mildly objecting to the phrase 'new Arab man'. Ghauri (ibid.: 236) asserts that the term could be seen as limiting 'the experience of men in the Middle East to a singular entity.' I disagree and believe that the phrase captures Inhorn's participants' way of being a Middle Eastern man in a context of political and economic flux and rapid technological change. Furthermore, Inhorn successfully achieves her aim to humanize the discourse on Middle Eastern men and on men and masculinity.

Liberty Walther Barnes's (2014) book is based on her ethnographic study of North American couples undergoing infertility treatment. Barnes, a medical sociologist, outlines her interest in the subject following her and her husband's experience of ART. Barnes's aim was to understand the intersection of medicine, health, femininity, gender, masculinity and reproduction by examining the social processes at both institutional and individual levels. She provides an in-depth exploration of the history and structure of the medical, scientific and technological aspects of reproductive medicine. Finding that there is little on the male experience of infertility, Barnes (ibid.: 125) argues that 'men's bodies, men's gendered medical experiences, and the medicalization of masculinity has been ignored' by putting the 'world of male infertility under the microscope' (ibid.: 2). Barnes held twenty-four separate telephone interviews with men and their wives, sampled from five fertility clinics. All the men were married, upper-middle-class and heterosexual. She also observed doctor–patient interactions and held interviews with doctors and clinical staff.

Barnes uses the lens of hegemonic masculinity to view the structural and agentic notions of masculinity. She characterizes

masculinity as both 'slippy' and 'sticky', with the former indicating
that masculine ideals are fluid and vary across individuals, groups,
location and time (Turner 2016). Those ideals of masculinity are the
permanent enactment of control and power; therefore, 'because of
its sticky quality, masculinity serves as the glue that cements the
colossal multi-tiered gender system apparatus together' (Barnes
2014: 163). Contrary to other research, Barnes argues that her
participants did not see infertility treatment as a challenge to their
masculinity. Against expectations of devastation, they framed the
use of medical intervention as supporting their masculinity. Barnes
(ibid.) recites how clinicians drew on a range of metaphors and
penis jokes to explain the diagnosis and treatment. She asserts that
these are 'employed to stabilize masculine identity and build trust
between doctors and patients' (ibid.: 63), functioning as a 'social
lubricant' (ibid.: 78) to uphold the embedded agentic and structural
norms of masculinity.

The limitations of the study are clearly outlined. For example,
Barnes notes that the men interviewed were not representative of
the population and the nature of the healthcare system in the USA.
Consequently, there are issues in generalizing the findings to other
countries. Issues that are not covered in her book include the effect of gender in her interviews with all her participants and the
limitations of using telephone rather than face-to-face interviews.
Antje Kampf's (2015: 403) review raises a few frustrations from the
perspective of a historian over some of the claims made, for example, 'referring to "countless anecdotes" (p. 13)'. In a similar vein,
Kristin Anderson (2014: 601) is concerned about the sole focus on
gender as opposed to class and race. Barnes leaves her critique of
the concept of hegemonic masculinity until the end of the book.
Consequently, there is the sense that the 'slipperiness' of men's
performance of being in the world did not quite fit the 'sticky' concept of hegemonic masculinity. Nevertheless, Barnes highlights
how sociocultural, medical, gender and identity aspects intersect
to reinforce the links of reproduction to women. Therefore, the invisibility of men and their reproductive experiences are structurally
embedded. Similarly, Inhorn argues that men are absent from ethnographic volumes and 'are "the second sex" in the scholarship
of reproduction, including anthropology' (2012: 6–7). Barnes and
Inhorn differ in their interpretations of men's performance of masculinities. However, they both found their respective participants
adapted their views of the ways of being a man to ones that went
against traditional stereotypes and theoretical frameworks.

There are few male scholars examining male childlessness, and similarly there are few accounts of men's experiences of childlessness, infertility or infertility treatment in the mainstream media. However, there are several books written by men describing their experiences of infertility, including those by Elliot Jager (2015), Steve Petrou (2018) and Glen Barden (2014). In addition, there is a short film by Rod Silvers (Silvers and Burnside 2011). Three of those authors' texts are fully auto/biographical: those of Jager, Petrou and Silvers. Journalist Elliot Jager (2015) describes the personal, psychological, sociocultural and theological aspects of his experience as an involuntarily childless Jewish man. He draws on his experience as a single child in an impoverished neighbourhood, abandoned by his father, and his unsuccessful IVF and reconciliation with his old-old father. However, he deftly weaves in politics, demography, genealogy, spirituality and interviews with ten other childless Jewish men (including gay, straight, married and single individuals) to illustrate the complexities of being a childless man in the heavily pronatalist context of contemporary Judaism. Jager examines in detail the cultural, religious and traditional aspects of fatherhood and the diminishment of childless men. For example, he explores the concept of 'kaddish'l': the duty of a son to 'recite the Kaddish prayer for the dead – linking God, eternity and children' (Jager 2015: 92). Consequently, he asks, 'What happens if you die without a "kaddish'l"?' Alongside existential and theological dilemmas, he describes issues that are common to infertile men across cultures, including 'otherness' and 'outsiderness', disenfranchised grief, ways of being in the world and complications in intimate relationships and wider societal contexts. Whereas Jager briefly alludes to his and his wife's ART treatment, the experience of IVF treatment is central to the books of both Steve Petrou (2018) and Glen Barden (2014), and the short film of Rod Silvers and Ray Burnside (2011).

Steve Petrou was born in Cyprus, where family is a central tenet of culture and parenthood is highly prized. He moved to the UK in the 1990s (aged 28) and views himself as an 'ordinary guy' and a 'fish and chip fryer' (Petrou 2018: 10). The aim of his book is to help others understand how men experience IVF. Although he draws on some demographic data and signposts relevant organizations, Petrou's focus is on his personal experience. His book is written in the first person and he counterpoints the 'traditional' Cypriot masculine narratives and attitudes – provider and protector – by ironically using the phrase 'I am/was King'. Written from the heart, Petrou's book reveals the canon of emotions that he felt through all the stages of IVF: anger, anxiety, depression, despair, fear, grief, hatred, hope, isolation, jealousy, loneliness and rage. Moreover, he details examples of his thoughts, moods and behaviours towards family, in-laws, friends, colleagues, health professionals and business associates during the period of the treatment. Petrou is clear that initially he was not concerned about becoming a father, but followed his wife's wishes to have children. Neither was he religious. However, following their first round of IVF and subsequent unsuccessful pregnancy, his view changed, and he wanted to be a father. Unfortunately, the baby, Xristos, did not fully develop and died. Further cycles of IVF eventually led to another pregnancy and premature delivery of twins via caesarean section. The first baby, Andrea, was stillborn, and the second baby was not breathing when delivered:

> Petros was out next. No movement or sound came out of him either. Yes, this is Hell! The blood drained from my face. The doctor wanted to let Petros die as he had no heartbeat and no oxygen went to his brain for ten minutes. By him taking that course of action, he was condemning me and my miserable life. No babies! No wife! Nothing! ... Full of despair and with tears in my eyes I told him, 'If you stop, you are not just killing my son, but also my wife. She will not be able to survive this. She will not be able to go home without at least one baby. Please, continue trying. Please!' ... Those few seconds of utter scare, despair and helplessness were the springboard that changed the course of my life. (Petrou 2018: 17)

Petros survived after many days in the neo-natal unit. He is now a fit and healthy young man. Aside from becoming a father, the changes alluded to by Petrou include empathy, tolerance and religion. Distinctively, Petrou's book reveals his inner voice and the struggle to balance what he wants, the need of others and the limitations of ideal sociocultural narratives.

Both Barden (2014) and Silvers (Silvers and Burnside 2011) use fictional characters – 'Mike' and 'Billy' respectively – in their stories. However, both characters are based on the respective author's experience of IVF. Both authors are working class and raised in England – Barden is White British from Brighton, while Silvers is British Asian from London. In a personal communication, Glenn Barden noted that 'Mike' is a 'blended' character formed from his own experiences and those of other men. 'Mike' is a man who wants to be a father, and that needs grows as his peers become parents. Barden describes in detail the whole process of ART, from deciding to try for a baby, not getting pregnant, accessing treatment, apprehension surrounding providing a sperm sample, diagnosis of low sperm count, Intrauterine Insemination (IUI) treatment, IVF using ICSI treatment, miscarriage and when – and if – to end treatment. As with Jager (2015) and Petrou (2018), Barden also weaves an educational theme throughout this bittersweet text, interleaving biological, demographic, medical, social and relational storylines. For example, he details the different medications that are given to women during treatment and their effects. In addition, he describes the differences between National Health Service (NHS) and private treatment. For example, the private clinic's sample room had a higher quality of furnishing and literature. A significant aspect of the book is how Barden reveals the tensions in relationships between 'Mike' and others: his girlfriend, parents, maternal grandparents, brother, peers and colleagues. An important theme that Barden explores is the impact on 'Mike's' sense of self: the emasculating effect of being a small cog in the ART machine, with concomitant impact on his identity and values and perceptions of his masculinity.

Rod Silvers wrote the script for 'England Expects' (Silvers and Burnside 2011) and concentrates on the intimate and close relationships of 'Billy', the male lead character, as he and his wife go through unsuccessful ART treatment. The film counterpoints Billy's hope for successful treatment with his hope that England will beat Germany in the quarterfinals of the soccer World Cup. Again, the tensions between Billy, family, friends and peers are highlighted. For example, Billy reacts angrily to an unthinking relative who has emailed a copy of their baby's scan to his partner. Similarly, other forms of social difference, such as stigmatization, mocking and 'outsiderness', are illustrated but not dwelt on – it is up to the viewer to observe the nuances in everyday interactions. As with the previous authors, Silvers shows the social and relational challenges that ART has for men. Both Barden (2014) and Silvers and Burnside (2011) use light-hearted humour to show the painful and difficult aspects of ART treatment in their bittersweet narratives. Moreover, Barden and Silvers illustrate how their childless male characters do not fit socially, with both Mike and Billy encountering circumstances in which they are seen as a threat of being a paedophile. All the authors – Barden (2014), Jager (2015), Petrou (2018) and Silvers (2011) – demonstrate the problems they encountered in not achieving the ideal of fatherhood. Significantly, they also highlight the lack of social narratives available for them to draw on, a lack which creates their 'social impotence'.

Contemporary psychological research has demonstrated that men's reactions to infertility are similar to women's (Fisher and Hammarberg 2017). For example, Saleh et al.'s (2003) cohort observational study of 412 men receiving treatment for primary infertility found that the psychological effects of male infertility were similar to those of sufferers from heart complaints and cancer. Nonetheless, Jordan and Revenson (1999: 341) note that in infertility research, 'most studies have not included men/husbands'. Mike Lloyd (1996) reported that the participation rates of males in infertility research had been strikingly low. Lloyd (ibid.: 451) argued that men's absence from infertility research had been wrongly 'condemned to be meaningful' without any grounds to justify the denunciation. Rather, men's non-participation had been interpreted as men not being interested in reproduction. As there is no biological basis for a connection between fertility and virility (Lockwood 2008), the importance placed on the 'fertility-virility link' (Lloyd 1996: 434) is a social construct and fundamental to both patriarchy and hegemonic masculinities – the empowerment of men over women, and other men (Connell 1995).

Childlessness has often been reported to 'enhance some elements of quality of life in women', with either no or negative associations with quality of life for men (Read and Grundy 2010: 333). One of the few studies to explore the relationship between male fertility and mortality is Weitoft et al.'s (2004) analysis of Swedish Census, Health, Multi-Generation and Death registers. Weitoft et al. postulated that there is a gap in health research knowledge because men's health, unlike women's, is viewed in terms of employment, not family role. The researchers examined the mortality and cause of death of men aged 29–54 and compared lone fathers and childless men to fathers who resided with their partner and children. The results demonstrated that lone childless men, and lone non-custodial fathers, had an increased risk of death through suicide, addiction, injury, external violence, poisoning, and lung and ischemic heart disease. Weitoft et al. (ibid.: 1457) argued that the higher mortality rate was connected to emotional instability and willingness to take risks, while parenting moderated risk-taking behavior. Analysis of the Swiss National Cohort study of the entire Swiss population indicated that generally, men had over twice the rate of unassisted suicide and a similar level of assisted suicide compared to women. When adjusted to account for underlying health problems (for example, cancer) the rate for unassisted suicide for men was nearly five times the rate for women, with a similar level for assisted suicide (Steck, Egger and Zwahlen 2018). Emily Grundy and Oystein Kravdal's (2008) analysis of Norwegian registers found that childless men in late middle age had higher mortality than fathers. Furthermore, Grundy and Kravdal's (2010) analysis of Norwegian register data found that both childless men and women had a higher risk of mortality for the majority of causes of death. Overall, Grundy and Kravdal (2008, 2010) concluded that the similarity between the genders points towards complex biosocial mechanisms that affect the fertility–mortality relationship.

Owens's (1982: 76) fertility-clinic based study of thirty pre-diagnosed infertile, married, working-class couples found that the men's desire for children 'was assumed ... [to be] natural'. Many studies report similar themes surrounding the desire for fatherhood: culmination of a loving relationship, enhancing and confirming status, fulfilling a role, giving pride, providing genetic legacy, appropriate age and stage, matching siblings and peers, giving pleasure and bringing company in later life (Inhorn et al. 2009a; Mason 1993; Owens 1982). Throsby and Gill (2004: 333) highlighted the lack of information on men's experience of IVF and fatherhood in general, and the way in which 'not being a father has received so little attention'. To evaluate the male experience of IVF treatment, Throsby and Gill used a feminist framework that viewed gender and technology as socially constructed. In taking such an approach, the authors acknowledged the debate between radical and liberal feminists regarding ART. Throsby and Gill's study focused on the experience of the male partners of thirteen couples who had ended unsuccessful IVF treatment at least two years before being interviewed. The participants' reactions fell into traditional gendered scripts, where the men felt powerless but remained silent and were 'strong' for their partners. The women felt isolated and devastated as their grief and sorrow was not shared. Throsby and Gill (ibid.: 344) outlined how the majority of the men had feelings of 'humiliation and inadequacy' due to not fulfilling the ideal of fathering of a child. The authors related this as integral to hegemonic masculinity (Connell 1995), wherein virility is proved by fertility. Consequently, the men questioned the 'sense of themselves as men' (Throsby and Gill 2004: 336), and this led them to reflect on their emotional, psychological and relational behaviours in the context of a pronatalist society. Two key components of the feminist perspective, mutuality and context (Morrow 2006), underpinned these findings. The former helped reveal the complex forces operating in social and intimate relationships, including those between interviewer and interviewee. The latter exposed the intersection between the participants' interpretation and their experience of their sociocultural environment (Hadley 2009: 21).

Similarly, Webb and Daniluk (1999) observed that infertility challenged men's masculinity, and that the men had to find ways to reconstruct their relationships and their sense of self. Nonetheless, Mary-Claire Mason (1993) found that some infertile men were more ambivalent about parenthood. Factors that influenced their reaction included relationship quality, personal coping strategies and ageing. One man noted that as he aged, his concern about not being a father lessened (ibid.: 89). A similar finding was reported in my research study (Hadley 2008a) of ten self-defined involuntarily childless British men, aged 33 to over 60. The older men were wistful about an opportunity lost, while the younger men expressed both fear and excitement in their attitude towards potential fatherhood (Lupton and Barclay 1997, 1999; Miller 2011). That study also demonstrated how experience of poor familial relationships in formative years affected all subsequent relationships. Those in relationships viewed their relationship as being of great importance. Fatherhood was viewed as a re-connection, replacement, repayment or repeat of childhood experience. All ten participants reported having experienced depression, with eight of the men stating that childlessness, to a greater or lesser extent, was an element in their mental health. The findings included themes of bereavement, isolation, addiction, substance abuse and social stress, and reflect those found in other research studies (see Dykstra and Keizer 2009; Fisher, Baker and Hammarberg 2010; Malik and Coulson 2008; Weitoft, Burström and Rosén 2004).

The importance of men's influence on fertility intentions has only relatively recently been taken into account (Berrington 2004; Dykstra 2009b; Hammarberg et al. 2017; Poston et al. 1983). Studies show that there is a notable difference between men and women in the influence that education and career achievements have on childlessness (Jensen 2016; Keizer, Dykstra and Jansen 2007; Parr 2007, 2010; Waren 2008). The Eurobarometer 56.2 survey of eight north-western European countries found that men defer parenthood more than women and that there are relatively more childless men over 50 in the UK (Knijn, Ostner and Schmitt 2006). Single men are more likely not to plan for children compared to married men. Knijn, Ostner and Schmitt (ibid.: 188) found that unemployment negatively influenced men's procreative plans and identified a positive correlation between more highly educated men and plans for fatherhood. Reasons 'childless' men gave for delaying parenthood included the need for a child's bedroom, the fear of a disabled child and the loss of freedom associated with family life (ibid.: 194). However, the lack of retrospective biological data limited the authors to the 18–39 age group. Moreover, Knijn, Ostner and Schmitt (ibid.: 191) proposed that national 'family-friendly' policies promoted shared parenthood and suggested that the lack of such policies in the UK reinforced the single breadwinner tradition. Nonetheless, Jensen (2016: 205) highlighted how in Norway, male childlessness has increased in parallel with the 'Daddy quota' (paternity leave). Jensen (2010) has argued that there are two reasons that childless men are ambivalent about accessing 'family-friendly' systems. Firstly, as fathers spend more time at home, employers may prefer childless men as employees. Secondly, childless men may find the rewards of work more attractive than the domestic and care work associated with paternity leave (ibid.: 9). In contrast, a contemporary Swedish study (Bodin, Plantin and Elmerstig 2019) found that fatherhood was not viewed as a career barrier. Although both Norway and Sweden are well known for their family-friendly policies, in the latter it is illegal to discriminate against parents in the workforce (ibid.). Waren and Pals (2013) argue that men's experience of 'voluntary' childlessness has received little attention. In their analysis of the 2002 USA National Survey of Growth, the authors found that age, race and never-married status were all predictors of 'childlessness' that were stronger for women than men. Childless men and women were older, white and unmarried compared to the other groups of men and women. Waren and Pals (ibid.: 167) argue that men had different reasons for choosing childlessness compared to women. Women's 'voluntary' childlessness correlated with higher education, economic independence and career advancement. None of those factors related to men's motivations for 'voluntary' childlessness. Unfortunately, the authors do not offer any motivations for men's 'voluntary' childlessness, although such men were more likely to have been unemployed than equivalent women (ibid.: 160). Moreover, cultural differences may restrict the generalizabilly of findings to other nations. For example, American women tend to view cohabitation as a prelude to marriage, whereas European women view it as an alternative living arrangement (ibid.: 167; see also Seltzer 2004).

Childlessness and Masculinity

Masculinities research has predominately concentrated on younger men in relation to education, crime, unemployment, the body and sexuality (Arber, Davidson and Ginn 2003: 4). However, there has been an increase in the study of fathering, fatherhood, 'involved fatherhood' and the ideals of 'New Man' (Goldberg 2014; Hadley 2018b; Machin 2015; Miller and Dermott 2015; Wall and Arnold 2007). This relatively recent interest in male reproduction high-lights the paucity of scholarship on any form of male childlessness. This is in stark contrast to feminist researchers, who have raised the issue of the absence of men's voices in all areas of scholarship concerning reproduction. In a study of the factors in the treatment of male sexual dysfunction, Stacy Elliot (1998) suggested that male masculinity and societal values were interwoven through strength, virility and vitality. To be validated within society a man had to be seen as potent, virile and fertile 'by the production of children' (ibid.: 4). Furthermore, in a review of anthropological studies on male infertility, Matthew Dudgeon and Marcia Inhorn (2003: 45) found that infertility had been seen to have a great effect on men's sense of self and noted that 'Men who fail as virile patriarchs are deemed weak and ineffective.'

Such is the dominance of the link between women and repro-duction that both Inhorn et al. (2009b) and Culley, Hudson and Lohan (2013) suggest that there is a very limited masculine script for men to draw on. Monach (1993) found the men in his study less likely to admit to being upset by infertility treatment than their wives or partners, except for men whose wives or partners were consistently distraught. Male reproductive impairment may result in overt displays of bereavement, guilt and shame (Crawshaw 2013; Mason 1993; Owens 1982; Webb and Daniluk 1999). Moreover, David Rawlings and Karen Looi (2007: 26) described Australian infertile men as having 'disenfranchised grief that can't be seen by other people'. An analysis of male infertility support group bulletin boards (Malik and Coulson 2008) found the anonymity provided a conduit for a wide range of difficulties and emotions to be discussed. Furthermore, Mason (1993) has suggested that men downplay any sense of loss and focus on their partner's needs. As her participants 'talked like women about having feelings of pain, loss, and loneli-ness', she argued that men and women's experiences of infertility have more in common than previously reported (ibid.: 184). Ac-cording to Moulet (2005: 166), her male participants indicated not only that they had 'missed out' on fatherhood roles, as noted earlier, but also roles like 'provider' and 'sage'.

It has been argued that men are more concerned with biological lineage and legacy than their partners (Wirtberg 1999). According to Crawshaw and Balen (2010: 9), the majority of people become adoptive parents after finding out they cannot have their own biological children. A three-year Canadian longitudinal study reported that infertile couples who adopted had greater life satisfaction than those who did not (Daniluk 2001: 445). Although her focus was on the relinquishment of biological parenthood, Daniluk emphasized the deep level of social and identity processes the couples undertook post-treatment. However, the sample comprised a large percentage of couples that had adopted or were in the process of adopting (62 per cent in total) (Daniluk 2001: 441; Moulet 2005). Nonetheless, a number of infertility studies have reported men's ambivalence concerning the pursuit, and achievement, of social parenthood (Monach 1993; Letherby 1997; Throsby and Gill 2004; Webb and Daniluk 1999). For example, the male partners of post-infertility-treatment couples expressed uncertainty towards non-biological parenthood and discounted the importance of a genetic legacy (Moulet 2005: 165). Letherby (1997: 176–77) argued that men in particular were the arbitrators against adoption. Although aware that biological children can be disillusioning, both Letherby (1997; 2010) and Throsby and Gill (2004) noted that their participants were mindful of 'horror' stories regarding adoption (Letherby 2010: 27). Webb and Daniluk's (1999) Canadian study found that the diagnosis of male factor infertility had greatly challenged six men's perceptions of self and assumed inevitable biological fatherhood. The diagnosis led to feelings similar to those reported by infertile women: grief, loss, powerlessness, guilt, inadequacy, betrayal, isolation and threat (ibid.: 20). All the men reported that over time, they had had to redefine their masculinity and had accepted their infertility as a major part of their lives (ibid.: 10). The generalizability of the findings was limited by the small sample size, the retrospective view of the participants and their parental role. However, this is one of the few studies to look at how men negotiated male infertility and to highlight how the men's attitudes changed over time.

The stigmatization of those not conforming to the heterosexual pronatalist norm has been well established, and many infertile people have hidden their experiences and status to avoid stigma or to protect themselves or others from pain (Exley and Letherby 2001; Lee 1996, 2003; Letherby 2016; Moulet 2005; Veevers 1975, 1980).

Men who do not comply with normative masculine expectations may 'find themselves under suspicion from both hegemonic men and women' (Sargent 2001: 19). Ann Dalzell's (2007) study focused on the experiences of five British gay men, 38–47, who wanted to be fathers but had little expectation that gay men could achieve this. Furthermore, some of the men felt an 'outsiderness' in peer, social, close and familial relationships (ibid.: 62). The study revealed that childless gay men experience a complex interaction between their identity and issues including bereavement, relationships, health and politics. Dalzell's participants' attitudes countered the positive view of the opportunities for non-heterosexual parenting given by Weeks, Heaphy and Donovan (2001: 164). Nonetheless, both Dalzell and Weeks, Heaphy and Donovan acknowledged that although there are many studies on how lesbians navigate childlessness and motherhood, there is a small but increasing volume of work focusing on gay men and parenthood. Dalzell and Weeks, Heaphy and Donovan (2001: 163) also identified 'the dominant construction of gay men presenting a risk to children'. In addition, Dalzell noted that her participants reported being discriminated against in close, familial, peer, work and social settings. Dalzell's study confirmed other research (Dalzell 2005; Purewal and Akker 2007) that has highlighted the association between men's experiences of childlessness and their upbringing, social expectations, self-image, health, bereavement, relationships, politics, policy and attitude towards virility and masculinity.

Childlessness and Later Life

Many studies highlight the importance of children in providing support for their ageing parents (Burholt and Wenger 1998; Dykstra and Fokkema 2011; Pesando 2018). Tanya Koropeckyj-Cox (2003) performed secondary analysis on in-depth interviews with three married, childless American men, two in their late sixties and the other in his early eighties. The men's involuntary childlessness was determined by different factors: wives' medical issues; the depression of the 1930s and the Second World War; age at first marriage (mid-fifties); and one man's wife's non-interest in parenthood. The men's life stories supported the findings of both Gunhild Hagestad and Vaughan Call (2007) and Parr (2005) regarding the timing of transitional events and 'historical time' (Neugarten and Datan 1973). The social networks of the three men varied considerably, from one man who had few social connections outside of the marital relationship to another who, with his wife, had a wide range of social ties through involvement in local community projects. Koropeckyj-Cox concluded that the process and status of childlessness was not viewed as a reflection on the men's identities or social position. Moreover, the overriding themes of self-identity were centred on traditional masculinities: being good providers; independence; economic safety; and professional achievement.

Recent studies have observed differences between parents and 'childless' individuals. Data from the Netherlands found that childless couples had less community-related social interaction than parents, but there was no difference in psychological well-being (Keizer, Dykstra and Poortman 2009). Wenger (2009) suggests that older childless people's social situation in later life depends particularly on gender, socio-economic status and the maintenance of early relationships with kin and non-kin networks. A comparative study of several countries indicated that older childless people are more likely to live alone than parents (Koropeckyj-Cox and Call 2007). Divorced, widowed and never-married childless men report higher rates of loneliness compared with women in similar circumstances. Furthermore, divorced and widowed childless men demonstrated higher rates of depression than divorced and widowed women (Zhang and Hayward 2001). Divorced and separated men aged over 50 reported poorer health, with higher rates of smoking and alcohol consumption than married, cohabiting or single men (Dykstra 2006). A tri-country study found connections between poor health behaviour and elderly childless people, with formerly married childless men having poorer physical health, smoking, depression and sleeping difficulties than partnered men (Kendig et al. 2007). Pearl Dykstra and Gunhild Hagestad (2007b: 1288) postulate that the childless are seen as vulnerable and 'a group at risk of social isolation, loneliness, depression, ill health, and increased mortality' compared to the 'social support, health and well-being' provided by the parent–child family alliance. Furthermore, Pearl Dykstra and Renske Keizer (2009) found that single non-parent men aged 45–59 were poorer socio-economically and psychologically compared to men in relationships.

The older childless tend to have smaller social networks than those who are parents, and consequently have reduced capacity to access informal care. While absence of children is not a disadvantage when health is good, it may become a problem when a childless person becomes ill, frail or loses their independence. The childless, unmarried or widowed have been shown to access formal care at younger ages and at lower levels of dependency than parents (Albertini and Mencarini 2011; Scott and Wenger 1995). In concluding her review of the trends, antecedents and consequences of childlessness for older adults, Dykstra (2009: 685) suggests that future studies on ageing should 'include men in research on childlessness', as studies of later life show the benefits that parental status gives. Moreover, in the USA, fatherhood has been shown to significantly positively affect both social and community engagement – including for older men whose children have left home (Eggebeen and Knoester 2001: 387; van den Hoonaard 2010).

One of the few studies to gather older people's detailed accounts of childlessness was conducted in New Zealand with thirty-eight participants: nine men and twenty-nine women, aged from 63 to 93 (Allen and Wiles 2013). As the sample was drawn from people who self-defined as 'childless', it included those who had outlived, were estranged from or had 'adopted out' children (ibid.: 210). Furthermore, the participants included the divorced, married, non-heterosexual, separated, single and widowed. Using life course, narrative gerontology and positioning theory, Allen and Wiles' findings supported the contention that childlessness is complex, fluid and diverse. Moreover, they highlighted the inadequacy of the voluntary–involuntary binary in representing the participants' experiences over the life course. Allen and Wiles found a wide variation in the participants' attitudes regarding their childlessness, which included positive views, no relevance, prevention of repetition of childhood experience, fatalism, loss, family obligations, health issues, cohort affect (Second World War), partner selection ('no Mr Right') and family dynamics (ibid.: 212). Allen and Wiles identified a difference between men and women's attitude to parenthood. The former did not refer to any form of 'paternal instinct' while the latter reported a 'maternal instinct'. Similarly, while some women had waited for 'Mr Right', there was no suggestion of waiting for a 'Miss Right' (ibid.). Instead, the men suggested that they had been the initiators in their relationship and marital decisions. The men's attitudes towards children ranged from sadness for those estranged from their own children to enjoyment of interactions with children. The men's routes to childlessness included preventing harm, the lack of children as an option for gay men, focus on career and doubts regarding the responsibility of being a father and husband. These narratives reflect both traditional heteronormative social narratives and the findings of other studies. Allen and Wiles's (ibid.: 216) study purposively included childless men. However, only one paragraph focused on the male experience. This may reflect both the greater number of women in the sample and the complexities of reporting a highly diverse sample that included self-defined childless biological parents.

Grandparenthood and Childlessness

In Western societies in the twentieth century, the falling fertility rate, increased longevity and social factors such as smaller and re-constituted families and increased rates of cohabitation and divorce have led to a change of family structure (Bengtson 2001; Chambers et al. 2009; Dykstra and Fokkema 2011). Allan and Jones (2003: 2–3) highlight that 'family organisation is not historically constant, either in its structure or content', but is responsive and related to historical transformations in the patterns of 'consumption, produc-tion, and reproduction'. This is not only a reflection of changing demographics but also a recognition of the effect of the wider social and economic change in postmodernity in the dynamics of family life and practice (ibid.). One result of the demographic change is an increase in the number of grandparents and a decrease in the number of grandchildren. This has led to a greater number of older adults, on average, being grandparents, for longer, to fewer chil-dren (Timonen and Arber 2012: 3) As a consequence, it is possible in the UK for a child to 'have relationships with eight grandparents (Hoff 2015: 15). Furthermore, older adults typically become grand-parents in their early to mid-fifties (Helosfan and Hagestad 2012) and tend to be in full-time employment, not be geographically close and have active leisure, social and employment commitments (Chambers et al. 2009: 63). Nonetheless, grandparenthood is an especially valued identity for older people (Tarrant 2012b; Timonen and Arber 2012). Importantly, in mid- and later life, the status of grandparenthood may act as a critical buffer against ageist discrim-ination and prejudice (Hadley 2018a).

The importance of the role of grandparents in contemporary family forms has been much written about in the social sciences (Ando 2005; Arber and Timonen 2012; Beeson, Jennings and Kramer 2013; Stelle et al. 2010; Tarrant 2012a; Umberson, Pud-rovska and Reczek 2010). Katherine van Wormer (2019: 10) proposes that grandparenthood has become a similar mark of status as parenthood, with concomitant social and familial expectations.

Furthermore, she asserts that little attention has been paid to older adults who do not become grandparents. To support her argument, van Wormer analysed the Academic OneFile search engine. This search engine listed over one thousand articles on grandparent roles, including cross-cultural intergenerational ties, the importance of grandparents to children and the role of caregiver grandparents. Nevertheless, there was no material on the denial or deprivation of the role of grandparent. Consequently, van Wormer deduced that there is a paucity of data examining the impact of childlessness on the wider family and particularly the older generation. As she is a grandmother herself, van Wormer's paper is auto/biographical, and she does draw on her own experiences and feelings. Unfortunately, she does not provide any details of her methodology or method apart from stating that she explores 'narrative data'. Nor is there any reference to any ethical standard or approval. Van Wormer examined online forums, newspaper articles and informal conversations. Her findings indicate a range of reactions to ageing without grandchildren, including disenfranchised grief, building familial and other ties and a sense of relief from childcare duties and projected gift giving. However, she does highlight four papers that examine 'happiness and care' of older people ageing without children (van Wormer 2019: 2).

In the USA, Echo Chang, Kathleen Wilbur and Merril Silverstein (2010) found that in terms of care received and psychological well-being, there was little difference between older childless disabled people and equivalent adults (this study is described in detail in the following chapter). Building on social science literature that described 'insignificant and sometimes negative correlation between the happiness and life satisfaction of parents', Nattavudh Powdthavee (2011: 3) examined the relationship between life satisfaction and grandparenthood. Powdthavee performed a secondary analysis of Wave 1 of the UK-based Understanding Society survey of over five thousand grandparents and over six thousand non-grandparents (aged 40 and above). He concluded that being a grandparent to at least one grandchild is associated positively with life satisfaction even when parenthood may not be. However, Powdthavee (ibid.: 16) argued that 'an investment in children may have a long-term psychological payoff, providing that our children also go on to have children of their own.' Similarly, in her study of 215 older Chinese grandparents in Hong Kong, Vivian Lou (2011) found that intergenerational relationships and activities protect against depressive symptoms. Lou was careful to note the importance of the cultural context of traditional Chinese family customs on her results. The importance of context of parent status and race is evidenced in Nicky Newton and Izora Baltys's (2014) mixed-methods study drawing on the Foley Longitudinal Study of Adulthood (FLSA; $n = 150$). The FLSA follows adults aged 55–58 (midlife) in the greater Chicago area (USA) for ten years. Drawing on Erikson's (1980) psychosocial concept of 'generativity' (providing for the next generation) in midlife, Newton and Baltys examined the extent to which parenthood, non-parenthood or grandparenthood were related to generativity by measuring four subtypes of generativity. Their findings highlight a nuanced view of midlife generativity, with non-parents generally recording lower levels of generativity than parents and grandparents. However, African Americans demonstrated the highest score of productive generativity (concern with the creation of products or ideas for future generations) of all parent statuses by race. Nevertheless, Newton and Baltys (2014: 189–91) highlight that contexts such as socio-economic status also play an important role in how people perform in midlife. In addition, Newton and Baltys are careful to point out the limitations of their study, including issues regarding sample size and how to interpret and measure generativity. Erickson's life cycle concepts are examined in Chapter 2.

Discussion

In this chapter, I have reviewed the literature surrounding 'childlessness', and have shown the development of research from that on 'voluntarily' childless women, who were seen as 'deviant', to recent research that demonstrates that both women and men are psychologically and physiologically deeply affected by infertility. There has been extensive research on women's reproductive bodies and lives, health, access to reproductive technology and experience as mothers and nurturers of children. Much of the material I have examined is from infertility and reproduction studies that have focused on women's bodies and lives. Consequently, men's experience has been excluded from the majority of the discourse surrounding both parenting and infertility. Moreover, it is only recently that men's attitudes towards, and experiences of, procreative intentions and outcomes have become of interest to researchers. Furthermore, the 'social clock' has been seen to be as significant for women in procreative decision-making as the 'biological clock'. The male 'biological clock' (andropause) has only recently received increased attention, and there has been little recognition of the 'so-cial clock' regarding men's procreative intentions. Similarly, there is little acknowledgement of non-grandparents in the literature on mid- and later life compared to the material on grandparenthood. A key issue to emerge from the literature explored in this chapter has been the absence of men, especially older men, from reproduc-tion research. Furthermore, limiting the definition of involuntary childlessness to only those who have accessed medical advice lim-its the generalization potential of any findings. This has directly affected the criteria for participation in this study, which rests on respondents defining themselves as childless men who wanted to be fathers (see Chapter 3).

Significantly, feminist researchers have highlighted the pau-city of material on male 'childlessness'. Scholars of masculinities have not considered reproduction, fatherhood, non-fatherhood or age as significant to being a man in the way that feminist scholars have regarding reproduction, motherhood and non-motherhood in the lives of women. The fact that scholars examining masculinity have not considered men who are infertile or do not reproduce is significant in itself. Scholars of masculinities often cite the con-cept of 'subordinated masculinities' and yet fail to reflect on which male voices are missing. Consequently, they are an agent of su-per-subordination, because they intentionally or unintentionally fail to report how they exclude an essential existential, agentic and structural element of being a man. Many government institutions have not collected longitudinal data on male fertility intentions or history, and consequently men who do not reproduce are not included in statistics and policy (rendering them structurally in-visible). Furthermore, the heteronormative ideal of women as 'mother/nurturer' is supported by only collecting women's fertility data. Not only have demographers reflected dominant social norms in only collecting fertility data on women, they have ignored how men view their reproductive role and intentions, negatively fo-cused on how men differ from women and not acknowledged how changes in socio-economic conditions have challenged the 'pro-vider' element of masculinity. Therefore, it is no surprise that many researchers have reported difficulty in recruiting male participants (see Culley, Hudson and Lohan 2013; Lloyd 1996; Throsby and Gill 2004). There are further methodological issues: for example, how women participants in a longitudinal study changed their status from mother to childless between one data collection point and the next (Murphy 2009). Moreover, extracting data from large datasets does not reveal if 'childlessness' was 'chosen' or 'circumstantial'.

The complex intersection between dominant social norms, health, socio-economics and individual agency has been shown to influence people's reproductive decision-making. The politics, policies and morals that form cultural and social norms are as diverse as their geographic locations. Consequently, care has to be taken in generalizing data from one country or geopolitical area to another (see Knijn, Ostner and Schmitt 2006; Waren and Pals 2013; Williams and Heighe 1993). This chapter ended with an appreciation of the different factors that affect older childless people's fertility decisions, and an examination of ageing without grandparenthood. The next chapter examines ageing and the lives of older men.

Notes

1. Pierre Bourdieu (1 August 1930–23 January 2002) was a French anthropologist, sociologist and philosopher. His work has had a major influence on sociology through his theory of sociology and the sociology of education. Bourdieu's work highlighted the diverse ways in which power operates in society, especially the varied and subtle ways it is maintained and transferred across generations. His pioneering concepts of cultural, economic, social and symbolic forms of capital; habitus; field; and symbolic violence have become very influential across a wide range of disciplines.

2. Raewyn Connell's concept of hegemonic masculinity has heavily influenced the field of masculinities, and this approach has been widely used since its development in the 1980s. Connell's (1995: 77) concept describes gender practices that uphold 'the dominant position of men and the subordination of women' through collaboration between institutional power and cultural ideals. To form his theory, Connell drew on feminist theory, Marxist sociology and Gramsci's hegemonic concepts of power. To illustrate the practice of masculinities and hierarchical differences amongst men, Connell used the feminist development of the social construction of gender. Connell developed hegemonic masculinities as a lens to view how various masculinities were formed, the function of power in their production, the relationships between hierarchy and the dialectic between practiced masculinities and social structure (Inhorn 2012).

Chapter 2

AGEING AND MALE INVOLUNTARY CHILDLESSNESS

Introduction

This chapter reviews the literature surrounding ageing in the light of older men's experiences of involuntary childlessness. To do this, I draw on material from demography, family studies, gender studies, public media, gerontology, life course studies, lifespan studies, masculinity studies and sociology. This provides a conceptual framework for understanding the current knowledge surrounding ageing and involuntary childlessness, and men's involuntary childlessness in particular. In the following section, I explore the demographic context in relation to ageing and childlessness and briefly discuss the population trends of Britain and Europe. I then consider the literature concerning ageing and the intersection of life course and lifespan perspectives. The next section explores ageing and gender, leading to a focus on men and masculinity. I then examine the literature on familial and wider social relationships, and in the sixth section, I discuss the chapter as a whole. The final section of this chapter draws together the insights gained from both literature review chapters to demonstrate the justification, relevance and approach of this book. The chapter ends with a reprise of the research questions.

Ageing

The study of ageing and its causes and effects has been a subject of focus for thousands of years (Laslett 1989; Thane 2005). Over the past half-century, theories about ageing have developed from the study of economic, demographic and social aspects of older people's lives to approaches such as political-economic, feminist, life course, continuity and humanist perspectives. In addition to institutional, sociocultural and economic processes, ageing research now also draws on individual biographical experience, gender, culture and race. Taking this view shows that the timing of events, roles, expectations and age are central in understanding the lives of involuntarily childless older men in the context of their interaction at micro, meso and macro environmental levels (Portacolone 2011: 9).

Childlessness has often been portrayed as a recent phenomenon, with many social scientists and demographers taking the 1950s as the analytical point of family change (Dykstra 2009). Demographers propose two transitions over the past two hundred years. The first lasted from approximately the 1800s until the 1930s, and the second took place in the mid-1960s (Aries 1980; Bottero 2011; Kneale, Coast and Stillwell 2009; Sobotka 2004; van de Kaa 2002). The two transitions were separated by the 'baby boom' period between the 1940s and early 1960s. However, that title is a misnomer: the steady decline in birth rate halted and the birth rate moved above replacement level. In Britain, there were two separate waves, the first between the late 1940s through to the early 1950s and the second in the early 1960s (Phillipson 2013: 82). The people who formed those post-Second World War cohorts have experienced, compared to earlier generations, a vastly different life (Arber, Davidson and Ginn 2003). For example, they experienced a range of social and cultural, economic and technological changes. Socioculturally, the decline in marriage and increase in divorce, equality legislation, legalization of homosexuality, increase in the average age of first birth and the recognition of new forms of kith and kin relationships were markers of generational difference. Economically, the advance of global economics and the increase in women's access to higher education and economic autonomy were significant changes to everyday life. The progress in technologies has been substantial – ranging from new reproductive technologies, including the availability of reliable contraception and ART procedures, to the rapid development of computing (Arber, Davidson and Ginn 2003; Bottero 2011; Sobotka 2004) and Information Communication Technology (ICT). For example, Hannah Marston (2019) has identified ownership of smartphones in the USA as illustrating a generational divide: 30 per cent of the

Silent Generation (1900–45) own a smartphone, compared to 67 per cent for Baby Boomers (1946–64), 85 per cent for Generation X (1965–76) and 92 per cent of Millennials/Gen Y (1977–95).

Demographic projections indicate that in the UK, there will be approximately two million people aged 65 and over without children by 2030 (Beth Johnson Foundation/Ageing Without Children 2016; McNeil and Hunter 2014; Pickard et al. 2012). The proportion of men in that figure is hard to judge, as Pickard et al. (2012: 536) define 'childlessness' as an 'absence of surviving child'. McNeil and Hunter (2014) combine Pickard's et al.'s (2012) study and Office for National Statistics (ONS 2009) data, without noting that the ONS does not record men's fertility history. Nevertheless, given that men's age of mortality has increased, there is a case that there will be more men living longer lives without having children. This has implications for the provision of health and social care in later life, given that most informal care for older people is undertaken by their adult children (Ivanova and Dykstra 2015; Pickard et al. 2009).

Following the financial crash of 2008, the shifting trends of global economics, demographics, politics and international and domestic migration have seen an intensification surrounding the problematization of 'ageing' by institutions (Phillipson 2013: 2). Governments, policymakers and social planners have had to reflect on the planning and policy implications regarding the needs and wishes of an increasing population of older people. Policies have focused on 'active' and 'successful' ageing in an effort to sustain independence and quality of life and reduce older people's susceptibility to chronic comorbidities in later life (Pike 2011). Physical activity is seen as a key in 'active' ageing and many health campaigns encourage older people to engage in physical exercise (Chodzko-Zajko, Schwingel and Park 2009). Andreas Kruse (2012: 12) contends that 'active' ageing is related to 'productivity', but extends the definition beyond labour, voluntary or material activities to include 'intellectual, emotional and motivational expressions of productivity'. 'Successful' ageing is mostly associated with Rowe and Khan's (1997) tripartite model that defined 'successful' as 'low probability of disease and disease-related disability, high cognitive and physical functional capacity, and active engagement with life'. In doing so, Rowe and Khan portrayed ageing in a 'preventative framework' accessed through modifications to individual behaviours (Phillips, Ajrouch and Hillcoat-Nalletamby 2010: 209). 'Successful' ageing may be summarized as the combination of active social engagement, well-being, absence of ill health and maintenance of functionality (Bowling and Dieppe 2005; Ray 2013; Rowe and Khan 1997). Nonetheless, Bowling and Dieppe (2005: 1550) have argued that the biomedical model has dominated the paradigm to the detriment of sociological, psychological and lay perspectives. Via the latter, people have often reported themselves as happy and well even with comorbidities (ibid.).

Appreciating the complexity of ageing in this way allows analysis of how involuntarily childless men experience ageing in midlife and later life. Additionally, it allows that individual experience and navigation of age-related transitions might vary, in different ways, in relation to the normative trajectory. Few sources of literature specifically define or theorize ageing (Simpson 2011, Phillipson 2013). I follow Ginn and Arber's (1995: 5–8) view of ageing as the relationship between the structural and material and the symbolic and discursive dimensions of existence. Equally, I follow Ginn and Arber (ibid.: 7–12) and Simpson (2011: 38) in viewing ageing as the dynamic interaction between chronology, physiology and social relationships. Chronology denotes the major ideas regarding time passing, and is referenced by the structural positions associated with being, for example, 18, 21, 65 or 100 years old. Physiological ageing signifies the physical ageing of the body and its changing functional capacity. Social ageing relates to transitions in the life course, which are affected by the dynamics of age, class, gender, sexuality and race.

Peter Laslett (1989) contended that the life course is defined by concepts that relate demography, biomedicine, chronology and stages of life. The stages are 'first age' (childhood); 'second age' (adulthood); 'third age' (ageing); and 'fourth age' (decline). The 'third' age describes a new period in the life course that is synonymous with freedom, choice, opportunity, potential and 'successful' ageing. The 'fourth' age is associated with 'dependence, decrepitude and death' (ibid.: 4). When the third and fourth ages begin and end is subject to ongoing debate, with the portrayal of the fourth age as one of unavoidable frailty and dysfunction being particularly contentious (Gilleard and Higgs 2000, 2010; Grenier 2012). The interactions between the chronological, physiological and sociological dimensions allow that ageing is uniquely experienced and that individuals may not follow the temporal markers that are associated with sociocultural norms. This lends weight to the argument that ageing and later life are part of an entire life course, and not a distinct period of 'being old' constructed by chronological social mandates (Grenier 2012: 20).

A central tenet of the literature on the theories of reproduction is the reporting of the psychological impact of childlessness. However, as we can see from the material above, theories of ageing tend to focus on structural issues: economics, class, gender and political characteristics. Parenthood and grandparenthood are significant symbols of successful ageing. Compared to the literature that charts trajectories and transitions using parenthood and family life as markers (Umberson, Pudrovska and Reczek 2010), there is little consideration of the pathways that 'childless' people navigate during mid- and later life (Allen and Wiles 2013; Van Wormer 2019). Rachel Moore, Megan Allbright and Kelly Strick (2016) argue that in midlife there is increased social pressure on childless people to become parents. Theorists of adult psychosocial development and ageing, such as Erik Erikson (1964, 1980; see also Sharkey 1997), Daniel Levinson et al. (1978) and Bernice Neugarten (Neugarten 1970; Neugarten and Datan 1973), have viewed people as developing across the lifespan. Neugarten linked temporal social structures and cultural norms to how an individual negotiates various age-related transitions (Neugarten and Hagestad 1976; Neugarten, Moore, and Lowe 1965; Neugarten 1974). She drew on demographic and sociological concepts to distinguish the stages of later life: 'young-old' (55–75), and 'old-old' (over 75), through age, health and activity (Neugarten 1974; Phillips, Ajrouch and Hillcoat-Nalletamby 2010: 213). Neugarten's argument is that as an individual moves across age-based stages, they may or may not comply with sociocultural expectations, and as a result, may feel 'on' or 'off' time. For example, the timing of entry and exit of employment affects a person's sense of self (Grenier 2012: 55–56). Beata Bugajska (2016) has identified the links between Laslett's (1989) four-stage typology of ageing and the psychosocial theories of lifespan development (see Erikson and Erikson 1997; Levinson et al. 1978; Neugarten 1974). Erikson's 'Adulthood' stage links to the 'young-old' stage of Neugarten's (1974) and the 'third age' stage of Laslett's (1989) theories. Likewise, Erikson's eighth stage, 'Old Age', relates to the 'old-old' and 'fourth age', respectively.

The majority of lifespan models regard personality development as complete on entering adulthood. The exception is Erik Erikson's eight major stages of psychosocial development, which cover the complete lifespan from infancy to old age (Erikson and Erikson 1997; Grenier 2012; Laceulle 2013). Erikson's stages of development are characterized by specific psychosocial crises.

Each crisis consists of two contrary dispositions (emotional forces): syntonic and dystonic. For example, in the first stage, Infancy, the conflict is between Basic Trust (syntonic) and Basic Mistrust (dystonic), and in the last stage, Old Age, the conflict is Integrity versus Despair (Erikson and Erikson 1997: 56–57). For optimal development to occur, each stage relies on the previous stage being successfully negotiated by achieving a healthy, balanced outcome between the two relevant forces (Rothrauff and Cooney 2008). Every healthy outcome leads to a 'Basic Virtue' or fundamental strength. For Infancy, this is 'Will', and for the last stage of Old Age it is 'Wisdom'. Erikson's (1964; Erikson and Erikson 1997) seventh stage theorized the significance of 'adulthood' (generativity versus stagnation) in middle and late adulthood (Brown and Lowis 2003; Erikson and Erikson 1997).

Generativity has been commonly associated only with parenthood and with 'establishing and guiding the next generation' (Erikson 1959: 103). Findings from studies examining generativity of parents and childless people are mixed. In the USA, Dan McAdams and Ed de St Aubin (1992) scale for measuring generativity found that young, midlife and older men expressed different levels of generativity. They also identified that fathers had higher levels of generativity than childless men did, although the same effect was not seen in women. McKeering and Pakenham's (2000) Australian study of 143 cohabiting parents found that parenting was more important to fathers' generativity than to that of mothers. By contrast, Jeong Shin An and Teresa Cooney's (2006) USA-based study of 1182 mid- to late-life parents found that non-familial generative experiences, such as civic and community engagement, were stronger predictors of psychological well-being. Likewise, Tanja Rothrauff and Teresa Cooney's (2008) USA-based study of 2507 mid- to late-life childless individuals (n = 289) and parents (n = 2218) also found that there were no significant differences between childless adults and parents regarding their generativity and psychological well-being. Indeed, Erik and Joan Erikson (1997: 67) highlighted that 'generativity … encompasses procreativity, productivity, and creativity'. Contemporary interpretations acknowledge that parenthood is just one of many ways of achieving generativity. Other ways include caregiving, community and civic involvement, mentoring, teaching, volunteering and actions that have a positive legacy (McAdams and Aubin 1992; McAdams and Diamond 1997; Moore, Allbright and Strick 2016).

The eighth stage, 'Old Age' (ego-integrity versus despair), involves the reflection on and acceptance of a life lived, and proximity to death leads to the Basic Virtue of Wisdom. However, failure to achieve resolution leads to despair or distrust (Erikson and Erikson 1997: 56–57). Nonetheless, as Joan Erikson (ibid.) experienced life in her nineties, she proposed the existence of a ninth stage for older people in later life. She argued that this new stage, contrary to the other stages, was age-specific, because 'Old age in one's eighties and nineties brings with it new demands, re-evaluations and daily difficulties' (ibid.: 105). Critically, Joan Erikson explained that people in 'The Ninth Stage' revisit the crises of all the other stages. To account for the increased range of challenge of everyday problems in later life, the ordering of syntonic and dystonic qualities is reversed. For example (and as mentioned above), at the Infancy stage, the conflict is between Basic Mistrust and Basic Trust, and at the Old Age stage, between Despair and Integrity. The basic virtue of the ninth stage is 'gerotranscendence'. Here, Joan Erikson draws on Lars Tornstam's Gerotranscendence Theory (Tornstam 1989), which focuses on the old person and the ageing process itself (Wadensten 2007). Tornstam (1989, 1992) argues that gerotranscendence is a meta-perspective shift from a rational materialistic worldview to a more cosmic and transcendent one. Conversely, Bugajska (2016) argues for the concept of the ninth stage, but with the crisis stage – Integrity versus Despair – of the eighth stage and the Basic Virtue of Wisdom. Bugajska outlines that it is the eighth stage that is reformulated to a crisis stage of Involvement versus Resignation, with a basic virtue of Courage.

Erikson's psychosocial 'Life Cycle' model is founded on the concept that the 'Individual and society are intricately woven, dynamically interrelated in continual exchange' (Erikson and Erikson 1997: 114). Members of the 'boomer' generations have lived through periods of economic uncertainty, the rise of neoliberalism, and 'new' lifestyle identities of mid- and older life (Arber, Davidson and Ginn 2003; Gilleard and Higgs 2000, 2005). Sara Arber, Kate Davidson and Jay Ginn (2003) contend that these representations are not based on the understanding of older people themselves but are extrapolated from large statistical datasets and the general media. Ginn and Arber (1995: 1–3) argue that ageing and gender need to be understood not only in relation to social change and age-related life course events, as above, but also through biography, social history, class and race (Heaphy 2007; McMullin 1995).

Ageing and Gender

A major limitation of ageing research in the mid- to late twentieth century was the invisibility of gender (Arber and Ginn 1991; Arber, Davidson and Ginn 2003; Ginn and Arber 1995). Carroll Estes (2005) has argued that gender is fundamental to both individual agency and social structure over the life course:

> Gender is a crucial organising principle in the economic and power relations of the social institutions of the family, the state and the market, shaping the experience of old age and ageing and the distribution of resources to older men and women across the life course. (Estes 2005: 552)

Raewyn Connell (2009: 11) defines gender as 'the structure of social relations that centres on the reproductive arena, and the set of practices that bring reproductive distinctions between bodies and social processes.' Candace West and Don Zimmerman (1987: 130) conceptualized that although people have many social identities, men and women are 'doing gender as an ongoing activity embedded in everyday action'. Therefore, 'doing gender is unavoidable' (ibid.: 145) and is continuously evoked and shaped through the interaction between the individual and their social environment. Although gender had been increasingly acknowledged in research between the 1970s and 1990s, it tended to be 'added on' as a variable without being incorporated into any theoretical perspective (Arber and Ginn 1991; Kohli 1988; Krekula 2007; McMullin 1995). Since the 1970s, most social relations and identity theories have been dominated by structural and post-structural theories. The former influenced the theoretical perspective of critical gerontology to concentrate on how structural disadvantage was produced through political and socio-economic factors. For example, retirement or reduced access to economic resources in later life result in losses that shape social relations and identity (Bury 1995; Vincent 1995). Nevertheless, critical gerontology has been criticized for concentrating on larger structural forces that shape ageing and missing its cultural and symbolic dimensions. The post-structuralist approaches theorized that ageing, gendered and sexual identities and relationships were formed more through discourse than social structure (Butler 2004a, 2004b; Simpson 2011). A central theme was the negotiation of the heterosexual/homosexual binary (Butler 2004c: 34), which privileged the former identity and occluded the latter. However, such a perspective risks minimizing actors' agency by not acknowledging their capacity to form gender identity through experience and 'critical thought and practice' (Simpson 2011: 24).

In recent decades, 'late modernist' theories have proposed that in post-industrial societies, the life view has changed to one of 'individualization', wherein people shape their own biographies through an emphasis on self-actualization (Beck 1992; Brannen, Moss and Mooney 2004; Giddens 1991; Morgan 1999). In this perspective, both the socio-economic and the discursive are seen as resources for the constant redefinition and expression of identity and ways of relating. Chris Gilleard and Paul Higgs (2000: 4) highlight the increase in longevity and affluence across all classes that has resulted in highly distinct 'cultures of ageing' which challenge the idealization of youth and the stereotypical view of mid- and later life as periods of increased social withdrawal. The concept of different cultures of ageing reflects involuntarily childless men's different experiences of ageing: the pronatalist norm for heterosexual men, the heteronormative for gay men, and from each other's individual experience. This perspective opens up the possibility of fluidity in the way actors reconfigure their identities and ways of relating as they age. Importantly, however, Simpson (2011: 51) highlights that this approach neglects those without the economic or cultural capacity to engage in life choices. Consequently, I view gender as the relationship between social context and the individual, and not the sole property of either: 'We make our own gender, but we are not free to make it however as we like' (Connell 2009: 74).

One aim of my doctoral study was to understand the interaction of structural (socio-economic), cultural (post-structural), and reflective (late-modern) elements and the effect that these have had on the participants' ageing identity and relationships. This approach is supported by recent arguments in the field of critical gerontology. Martha Holstein and Meredith Minkler (2007: 18) have argued that critical gerontology's focus on 'sociostructural forces' has ignored the experience of individuals, stating that 'Agency unnoticed is agency denied.' They went on to recommend the use of different perspectives and methodologies in ageing research. Taking such an approach would acknowledge the way social actors perceive the organization of their social world, and hence the subjective experience of the individual (Blaikie 2010: 171). The approach suggested by Minkler and Holstein (2007) informs this study by drawing my attention to how the interaction between social structures and individual agency informed the participants' experience of ageing as involuntarily childless men. In addition, I also drew on the life course and biographical approaches, and I also acknowledge the influence of feminisms in the methods used. These are discussed in the following chapter.

Sociological theories since the Second World War were much influenced by functionalism (see Parsons 1942, 1943, 1949, 1956). This perspective viewed people as individuals that fitted institutional roles: work for men and domesticity for women. The transition that retirement brought for men was seen as problematic, whereas women's roles were not seen to change significantly with age. More recently, the influence of the political-economic perspective and feminist approaches led to a shift in the 'problem of old age' (Russell 2007: 176), from an androcentric viewpoint in the mid-twentieth century to an almost exclusive focus on women in the late twentieth and early twenty-first centuries. One effect of this shift was to portray older people, the vast majority being women, as a problem group that placed an increased demand on resources because they lived longer, had high chronic comorbidities, received more state benefits and occupied the majority of the home care sector (Arber 1991; Fennell and Davidson 2003; Arber, Andersson and Hoff 2007). The greater population of older women, and the faster reduction in female mortality, led Arber and Ginn (1991: 9) to postulate the 'feminisation' of later life. In addition, Deborah van den Hoonaard (2010: 27) argues that widowhood has become a feminized space associated exclusively with women due to men's lower age of mortality, widowers' high rate of remarriage and the prevalence of widows following both World Wars (see Nicholson 2007, 2012). Ageing was therefore essentially an experience of women (Leontowitsch 2012, 2013). Diane Gibson (1996: 434–36) argued that older women had been seen as disadvantaged and that the strengths they bring to later life had been missed – for example, forming and maintaining social networks over the life course and experience of the informal economy. Feminist scholars recognized that men and women's experiences of ageing were shaped in relation to each other as well as intersecting with the power issues of other social categories, such as sexual orientation and class (Calasanti and Slevin 2001: 3).

The absence of older men in both ageing and gender research literature in the late twentieth century was exacerbated by three dominant views: first, that older men tended to die at a younger age than women did; second, that older men were reticent in accessing health professionals when ill; and finally, that partnerless older men were more likely to be placed in residential care compared to lone older women (Arber, Andersson and Hoff 2007; Arber, Davidson and Ginn 2003; Perren, Arber and Davidson 2004). Furthermore, John Knodel and Mary Beth Ofstedal (2003: 677) suggest that the 'misery' perspective has become embedded in policy as a 'one-sex view of gender'. For example, the 2002 'World NGO on Aging' (Global Action on Aging 2002: 4) emphasized that 'elderly women must be given special protection in order to defend their rights', with no explicit reference to men (Suen 2011: 73). Consequently, embedding of the 'misery' perspective towards women into conventional understanding of later life helps add to the invisibility of older men. Yiu Tung Suen (ibid.: 74) argues that Knodel and Ofstedal's (2003) research demonstrated the means by which men are absented from policy and resource recommendations.

Masculinity and Ageing

The recent focus on older women in ageing research has highlighted the paucity of contemporary research literature on men's experience of ageing and later life (Leontowitsch 2013: 226). For example, the *Handbook of Studies on Men and Masculinities* (Kimmel, Hearn and Connell 2005) has no reference to age, ageing or grandfatherhood, and only one small paragraph on infertile men by Don Sabo (2005: 337). The absence of men and masculinity from ageing research was first raised by Edward Thompson (1994). He suggested that not only were gerontologists and social scientists not interested in older men, but biomedical researchers were only interested in the causes of older men's early mortality (Russell 2007: 176). Furthermore, Thompson (1994: 8) contended that gerontologists had 'inadvertently homogenised elders to make older men genderless'. Similarly, Jeff Hearn (1995) argued that:

> Older men are also defined by virtue of their earlier death than women. Older men are constructed as pre-death. They are relatively redundant, even invisible, not just in terms of paid work and family responsibilities, but more importantly in terms of life itself. (Hearn 1995: 101)

Thompson (1994, 2006) identified several reasons for older men's invisibility in research literature. He noted that sociology generally tended towards researching the disadvantaged, with the political-economic perspective focused on disadvantage and ageing as residual categories. The assumption of the relative comfort of older men's lives – being economically stable, typically married with no mortgage, recipients of spousal care – led to men not being considered as worthy of investigation or as a group in need of emancipation (Calasanti 2004; Leontowitsch 2013). Significantly, critics of the political-economic approach have pointed out that important changes, such as the increase in occupational pensions, women's employment, improvements in health and social care and the increase in men's life expectancy, had not been taken into account (Gilleard and Higgs 2005; Leontowitsch 2012, 2013). Nonetheless, the effects of exclusion, inequalities and poverty are still prevalent in later life (Leontowitsch 2012, 2013). Moreover, there are other reasons that contribute towards men's absence: Suen (2010) proposes that older men are socially reticent and therefore difficult for researchers to access. Cherry Russell (2007) and Miranda Leontowitsch (2013) suggest that the purposeful selection of participants (theoretical sampling) contributed to the absence of men in research. For example, recruitment is often from settings such as residential care facilities that are heavily populated by women, and subsequent findings are frequently presented as the experiences of 'residents' (Russell 2007: 187). The relative absence of men from ageing research reflects both developments in sociological and gerontological research and the tradition of researching the disadvantaged (Leontowitsch 2012: 105).

Jeff Hearn (1998: 768) has highlighted that in both social theory and everyday life, 'men are implicitly talked of, yet rarely talked of explicitly. They are shown but not said, visible but not questioned.' David Morgan (1981: 93) reflected on how, in sociological studies, researchers adopted the view that 'men were there all the time but we did not see them because we imagined that we were looking at mankind.' Feminists subsequently called for 'naming men as men' (Hearn 1998: 783): as gendered social objects, not gendered objects (Hearn 2013: 31). Acknowledging that 'men are both a social category formed by the gender system and dominant collective and individual agents of social practices' (Hearn 2004: 59) is a key conceptual framing in this study's examination of men's expectations, and experiences, of living through a period of great cultural, social and economic change.

The notion of naming men as men arose from the feminist movement of the 1960s and 1970s. Early theories of masculinity were based on sex role theory (Connell 1995: 22), which linked social behaviour to biological sex (biological determinism). Theories of masculinity based on sex role models, such as Robert Brannon's (1976), were criticized for their reductionist nature and failure to account for social categories such as age, class, race and sexuality (Connell 1995: 22). Michael Kimmel (1994: 120) challenged the biological determinism of such male sex role models and emphasized that 'Manhood does not bubble up to consciousness from our biological makeup: it is created in culture.' He argued that masculinity was a dynamic set of meanings that changed with the relationships men had 'with ourselves, with each other, and with our world' (ibid.). Kimmel also addressed a major criticism of sex role theory: the issue of power. He proposed that the Western hegemonic masculine ideal rested on men being 'in power', 'with power' and 'of power' (ibid.). Kimmel (ibid.: 125) defined manhood as attributes of capability, control, reliability, success and strength. Conversely, as only a fraction of men achieve the dominant ideal, most men 'often feel *powerless* rather than *powerful*' (Bennett 2007: 350, original italics). Michael Kaufman (1994: 144) argues that gender is the 'description of actual social relations of power between males and females and the internalization of these relations of power'. Connell (1995: 26) emphasizes that sex role theory has difficulty in accounting for the dynamics of, and power in, social relations and gender identity, because of its reliance on differentiation. Connell (1995, 2000, 2009; Connell and Messerschmidt 2005) suggests that the gender order consists of hegemonic, subordinated, marginalized and complicit masculinities. He defines hegemonic masculinities as:

> the configuration of gender practice which embodies the currently accepted answer to the problem of the legitimacy of patriarchy, which guarantees ... the dominant position of men and the subordination of women. (Connell 1995: 77)

On the other hand, the notion of 'hegemonic masculinities' has been criticized for essentializing men into a static and limited typology and not accounting for 'the ever-changing social strategies' (Inhorn 2012: 45) of men's performance of gender. Michael Moller (2007: 266) contends that the idea of hegemonic masculinities restricts the understanding of masculinity to a specific framework of 'domination, subordination, and oppression'. For example, studies reporting on 'hegemonic masculinities' have focused on power and structure and have not accounted for the ways physicality and embodiment interact with gender practice over the life course (Atkinson 2011; Calasanti 2004; Calasanti and King 2005; Inhorn

2012). As Kaufman (1994: 152) explains, 'there is no single masculinity or one experience of being a man'.

Anna Tarrant's (2010, 2012a, 2012b) examination of the intersection between masculinities and the change in roles from midlife
onwards highlights that although men attempt to discursively
achieve the masculine 'hegemonic ideal', they seldom do so. Toni
Calasanti (2004) argues that this dominant 'ideal' – associated with
aggressiveness, competitiveness, independence, virility, wealth and
physical strength – is confounded by the construct of old age as
associated with loss of control, independence and strength. Consequently, older men are viewed as 'other' even if in every other
aspect they reach the masculine ideal (Calasanti 2004: 307). Gabri-
ela Spector-Mersel (2006: 78) proposes that older men in the West
'struggle to construct legitimate personal identities' because the 'hegemonic masculinity scripts' – the culturally specific life narrative
key-plots that provide men with a framework to draw on – have
been truncated by the focus on youth and middle age. As Kenneth
Gergen (1992: 132) noted, 'each gender acquires for personal use
the repertoire of potential life stories relevant to their own gender.'

A central theme of ageing is how an individual perceives themselves and in what manner they view themselves in relation to
other people and social institutions (Barresi 2006; Hendricks 2010).
The intersection of a person's differences and similarities with
others, and their relation with the social environment, directly
influences their experience of the self. Sense of self comes from
social participation, experiences and social resources: no aspect of
personal agency is isolated from social practices, group membership or structural conditions. Moreover, social resources such as
class, gender and education are essential to how people perceive
themselves and how others perceive them. Although these sources
may benefit self-identity, they may also constrain, deny, exclude
or isolate (Hendricks 2010: 256). Self-identity is fundamentally a
social construction gendered within behaviours governed by social and cultural processes (Arber, Davidson and Ginn 2003: 4). As
the societal environment in which ageing occurs changes, so will
expectations of self, by self and others, regarding self and self-concept (Hendricks 2010: 255). For example, the transition from being
employed to being retired has been seen as a challenge to a man's
masculinity due to the removal of the breadwinner or provider status (Phillipson 1999).

In a world where the configurations of self change over time,
identities are not fixed but are self-gained from experiencing

relational networks and self-appraisal compared against paradoxi-
cally fluid and normative expectations (Barresi 2006). Simon Biggs
(2004) argues the case for the use of both 'masque' and 'narrativity' in the understanding of self-identity (Biggs 1999; Estes, Biggs
and Phillipson 2003). Images and roles of ageing are increasingly
diverse, ranging from the stereotypical labels of decrepitude to
the denial of old age through commercialization, medicalization
and technology. Therefore, the performance of identity is negotiated (Biggs 1999) between fixed and fluid states: being and doing
'being'. The performance is related to the present through the utilization of existing societal scripts and images (personal history and
experience) to adapt both social and self-identity. The 'mask of
ageing' (Featherstone and Wernick 1995: 7) describes the contrast
between an ageing physicality and an 'inner' younger voice. The
fixity of the body and fluidity of social change require a 'masque'
in order both to allow social engagement and to appraise, and allow adaption to, self-identity (Biggs 1999: 80). Narrative provides
control over how we present what we are, what we may become
and how we are represented in any given situation. The ideas of
'narrativity' and 'masque' bridge the gap between the negative social construction of old age and the positive potential in later life.
Thus, ageing identities are layered between the inner and outer self,
with different ageing narratives at different levels of the psyche,
and appropriated for operating in diverse settings (Biggs 2004: 57).
Nonetheless, Spector-Mersel (2006: 78) argues that Western men
do not have the social scripts that 'take into account the elemental
and inevitable human fact of aging', and as a result struggle to construct legitimate personal identities. However, Thompson (2006)
describes young American adults as reporting a positive perception
of older men related to grandfatherhood and sagacity. That positive view of later life is an important challenge to Spector-Mersel's
(2006: 68) argument that Western male cultural life course scripts
end in late middle age. In addition, the association between the
positive role and grandfatherhood indicates a continuation of the
heteronormative pronatalist ideal.

The contemporary focus on the young body has challenged the
value of older men as experienced and powerful (Hearn 1995; Calasanti 2003; Heaphy 2007). The image of older people and old age
is frequently constructed through stereotypes of frailty, ill health,
dependence and shabbiness (Featherstone and Wernick 1995;
Hearn 1995; Shirani 2013; Tarrant 2010). Older people have been
viewed as sexless, with older men reduced to genderless status and

generalized as 'old' (Thompson 1994; Spector-Mersel 2006; Nilsson, Hagberg and Grassman 2013). Walz (2002: 100) has suggested that older people are not presented as attractive, with older men frequently viewed as 'sexually driven, but also sexually inappropriate and/or sexually impotent'. Bill Bytheway (1995, 2005, 2011) has long argued that chronological age does not necessarily equate with subjective health or age, but much research suggests that there is a cultural perception of old age as associated with decline in physical and mental functionality (Gullette 1997; Shirani 2013). With older men viewed as less masculine than younger and middle-aged men, Magnus Nilsson, Jan-Erik Hagberg and Eva Grassman (2013: 59) have reasoned that 'To age is to change and this also relates to how masculinity is performed.'

Theories of masculinity have unswervingly highlighted income generation as a central feature of masculine identity (Connell 1995; Mann 2007; Morgan 1992). A systematic review of forty-two studies from fifteen (mostly Western) countries identified that men were at greater risk of death following unemployment than women: 78 per cent compared to 37 per cent (Roelfs et al. 2011). Significantly, the authors demonstrated that the relationship between unemployment and risk of mortality had remained constant over the past fifty years: the highest risk occurred in the ten years following the first episode of unemployment. Moreover, the risk was greater for those in their early and middle careers, with greater risk for those aged under 50 (75 per cent) compared to those aged 50 and above (25 per cent).

For older men, roles that help define their sense of identity may switch from the activities associated with traditional provider role and public interaction to involvement with closer family ties (Arber, Davidson and Ginn 2003: 6). For example, in the late 1980s, Michael Young and Tom Schuller (1991: 130) found that older working-class men in London, on exiting the workforce, became more involved in the home, as women increasingly worked outside the home. The change in roles had given rise to a 'new kind of family' that 'stood apart' from the economy and centred on the importance of grandparenthood (Young and Schuller 1991: 140). Young and Schuller capture the significance of kith and kin relationships for men in the transition from the traditional provider role. Moreover, empirical studies report that older men's needs focus on actions and activities based on 'doing something useful' (Davidson, Daly and Arber 2003b: 84). For example, in one study, American solo-living men aged over 65 viewed part-time work as providing both financial gain and 'something to do', as well as countering the keenly felt loss of work-based friendships (Rubinstein 1986: 17). In retrospect, this was not seen as a severe loss, as the men's working life achievements were then deployed in their post-work identity (ibid.: 19). Similarly, Nilsson, Hagberg and Grassman (2013: 67) found that retired, unmarried and childless Swedish older men identified themselves through their midlife working-life skills and experiences: 'what I have done is who I am.' Significantly, Young and Schuller (1991: 146) observed that men who had exited work and recently lost their partners, whether through divorce or bereavement, found the 'double bereavement' difficult to adjust to.

Bereavement

Loss of a partner is a highly gendered experience: widowers tend to remarry quickly following bereavement, whereas widows are more likely to live alone for many years (Bennett and Soulsby 2012; Davidson 1998; Ray 2000). The timescale for the effects of bereavement has often been seen as two years, with effects after that period frequently not associated with spousal loss (Bennett and Soulsby 2012: 322). Kate Bennett, Georgina Hughes and Philip Smith (2003: 413) identified that both widows and widowers believed bereavement to be harder for men. Men believed that widows coped better because they had better domestic and social skills and were confident in expressing their feelings – something the men had difficulty doing (ibid.). In her study of twenty-five widows and twenty-six widowers aged 65–92, Kate Davidson (1998; 2001, 2002) outlined the different experiences of men and women. Davidson's (1998) study, framed within symbolic interactionism, involved participants born before 1930, and the attitudes they expressed reflect the normative roles of the time. For example, women learned in childhood that looking after men was a key factor in being a 'good wife' (Davidson 1998: 36), reflecting the criteria of the nuclear family. Widowers did not see bereavement as 'freedom' but were lost without the routine of married life – demonstrated in the reduction of external activities such as shopping and gardening, and the increase in domestic activities such as housework (see also Bennett and Morgan 1993; Bennett 2005). Widows tend not to re-partner due to intrinsic factors: the irreplaceability of their dead spouse, their freedom from a permanent carer role or their reluctance to lose autonomy (Bennett, Arnott and Soulsby 2013; Davidson and Fennell 2002; Lopata 1981, 1996). Conversely, widowers see a new partner not as a 'replacement' but as someone they could love and care for 'in addition to' their previous relationship (Davidson 2002: 55). Davidson (ibid.: 45) has identified living apart together (LAT) relationships as a pragmatic response to the different needs of widows and widowers. LAT relationships have increased in popularity from the 1970s, with Jenny de Jong Gierveld (2003, 2004) arguing that for older adults, the benefits are twofold. First, older adults may be reticent in forming a new joint household following their previous experience. Second, older adults prefer to retain existing social networks and close relationships (de Jong Gierveld 2004: 242). Widows tend to view bereavement as a form of liberation, while widowers view it as a loss (Davidson 2001: 309). Davidson (ibid.: 315) highlights that traditional roles, where men were socialized to be independent and women to be nurturing, are reversed in later life. However, this is associated with older parents, who, as their children mature into adults, can reclaim the repressed aspects of themselves (Davidson 1998; Huyck and Gutmann 2006: 29; Inhorn 2012).

Davidson's (1998; 2001; 2002) work is significant for three reasons. First, she demonstrated the gender differences in widowhood. Second, her findings contested the dominant narrative of decline and misery associated with widowhood. Finally, she highlighted the challenges and rewards that moving from 'coupledom' to 'singledom' entails. On the one hand, there is the challenge of taking on unfamiliar tasks, and on the other, there may be a sense of newfound freedom. Before Davidson's ground-breaking work, most material regarding widowhood and bereavement in later life had focused on women and concentrated on how people adapt to their bereaved state (Bennett, Hughes and Smith 2003; Chambers 2005; van den Hoonaard, Bennett and Evans 2012). The overall focus of research on women's experience of later life highlights the few studies that explore men's experience of later life. Two researchers have recently published studies on men's experiences of widowhood: Deborah van den Hoonaard (2007, 2010) and Kate Bennett (Bennett, Arnott and Soulsby 2013; Bennett, Hughes and Smith 2003; Bennett 2005, 2007). Both researchers' findings supported Davidson's (1998) conclusions. Additionally, both identified their participants' performance of masculinity as central to their judgements. Both van den Hoonaard (2010) and Bennett (2005, 2007; Bennett, Arnott and Soulsby 2013) found that widowed men initially drew on traditional masculine scripts of success in control, independence, provider status, and strength, in respect to their public actions (see also Calasanti 2004; Meadows and Davidson

2006). In private, the widowers struggled to resolve the power-lessness of their emotional experience with their understanding of the masculine staples of 'control, strength and capability' (Bennett 2007: 349). Bennett argued that older widowed men 'reconstruct their sense of manliness through emotional expression', using different narratives in public and private locations (ibid.: 355). The men's emotional struggle connects to Biggs's (2004: 54) concept of 'masque', where the presentation of an outer identity facilitated a difficult process of adaption to form an acceptable inner self-identity. Van den Hoonaard (2010: 6–7) proposed that her participants followed Tony Coles's (2008) post-structuralist concept of 'mosaic masculinities'. In this understanding of masculinity, men adapt parts of ideal hegemonic masculinity to form their masculine identity (Coles 2008: 238).

Grandfatherhood

The complexities involved in negotiating ways of being a man in mid- and later life were highlighted by Davidson, Daly and Arber:

> An important and potentially paradoxical new role for older men is that of grandfather. It is paradoxical because, on one hand, men may be exhibiting a 'gentler', more nurturing relationship with a grandchild than they had with their own children but, on the other hand, may still be viewed and view themselves, as having the traditional role as 'sage' or 'wise man'. (Davidson, Daly and Arber 2003a: 178–79)

In contemporary families, grandparents increasingly occupy an important role in providing care, and on average, there is a greater number of older adults (typically in their early to mid-fifties) being grandparents, for longer, and to fewer children (Timonen and Arber 2012: 3). Mann (2007: 286) argues that there has been a 'matrifocal tilt' in family studies, with the 'maternal grandmother-grandchild dyad' viewed as central to the family. Evolutionary biologists have postulated a 'grandmother hypothesis', asserting that the reason why women survive past their reproductive years is to care for younger children (de Medeiros and Rubinstein 2018).

The familial dynamic has supported the 'emotional' and 'instrumental' gender role models. As a result, the little work on grandfatherhood has reinforced the marginalized status of men as distant and not interested in grandfatherhood. Conversely, contemporary studies have highlighted the contradictory and complex role of grandfatherhood. Anna Tarrant's (2010, 2012a, 2012b)

UK-based qualitative study of thirty-one men aged between 51 and 88 highlighted a fluid and diverse range of grandfathering practices. Tarrant's (2012a) participants demonstrated 'soft' and 'sage' characteristics and indicated that they performed more care and nurturing activity than they had with their own children. Furthermore, family restructuring, for example through divorce, highlighted how grandfathers were proactive in maintaining and developing intergenerational relationships (Ando 2005; Chambers et al. 2009; Davidson, Daly and Arber 2003a; Tarrant 2012a, 2012b). Tarrant's study (2012a) demonstrated the importance of both relationships and roles for men in mid- and later life and followed both Michael Young and Tom Schuller (1991) and Kate Davidson and Sara Arber's (2004) research. Additionally, the fact that the men drew on their accumulated experience and knowledge to perform their role links to Nilsson et al.'s (2013) reflection that retired childless men identified themselves through their former working identity.

Family and Social Relationships

The functionalist concept of the nuclear family was the accepted model of family relationships until late in the twentieth century. In this model, each family member had differential but complementary duties inside and outside the home, with men in instrumental (breadwinner) roles and women in 'emotional' (housewife) roles (Allan and Crow 2001; Mann 2007; May 2011a, 2011b; Parsons 1949). As a result, the 'conjugal bond' (Haralambos and Holborn 2008: 475) – the strength of the relationship between husband and wife – was central to the functionality of the family and, therefore, society. Marriage was the only form of legitimized union and bestowed social status, acceptance, parenthood, commitment and reinforced heteronormativity: other types of relationship were judged on a continuum from inferior to deviant (Chambers et al. 2009: 39; Holden 2007). Same-sex relationships were cast as a threat to heterosexuality and the family idyll by political and religious authorities. Many gay men and women fashioned their relationships with family, friends and colleagues by 'passing' as heterosexual (Rosenfeld 2003a: 2–3). The stigmatization and discrimination experienced by non-heterosexuals resulted in the invisibility of their relationships (Chambers et al. 2009; Porche and Purvin 2008; Rosenfeld 2003a, 2003b). The 1960s and early 1970s are seen as one of the most important times in lesbian and gay history, as this period

marked the transition from 'passing' as heterosexual to an openly
public and political homosexual identity (Rosenfeld 2003a: 9–10).
Based on his mixed-methods study of gay people aged over 50,
Brian Heaphy (2007, 2009) highlighted that inequalities in class,
gender, race, economics, and social and cultural resources meant
that intimate and wider social relationships were complex and
'unevenly reconfigured' in later life (Heaphy 2007: 208; Simpson
2013). On the other hand, some found that their self-made communities and networks provided mutual support and a strong sense
of belonging and commitment (Heaphy 2007: 205).

Marriage

A person's level of social interaction in later life is important because isolation and loneliness are related to poor health and
well-being (Baars et al. 2013; Davidson 2006; Phillipson 2004;
Scharf and Bartlam 2008). An analysis of the UK General Household Survey of men and women aged 65 and over has explored
how gender and marital status interact with material and social inequalities (Arber et al. 2003). The authors found that older men
and older married women were the most advantaged in terms of
both material capital and social interactions. Widows were found
to be materially disadvantaged compared to married women in respect to mobility, as the majority of the latter had access to a car
(ibid.: 164). However, widows and married women had similar levels of social interaction with friends, neighbours and relatives. In
comparison, widowers were shown to be less likely to either visit
or host relatives or friends, or to speak with neighbours. The loss of
a partner through death or divorce highlights the 'protective effect'
of marriage. Nonetheless, the level of reciprocity is an indicator of
satisfaction, not marital status in itself (Hank and Wagner 2013:
649). Divorced, older and never-married men were disadvantaged
both materially and in terms of social contacts. Although divorced
women were also materially disadvantaged, they had strong social
links with family, friends and neighbours, comparable to those of
married women and widows. Arber et al. (2003: 165) concluded
that divorced, older and never-married men were more susceptible to social isolation and, because of their lack of social resources,
were vulnerable to early entry into residential care.

   Arber et al.'s (2003) analysis did not provide data on the effect
childlessness had on material and social inequalities. A recent European survey on older people's well-being found that generally,
the childless did not fare worse than parents either economically,

psychologically or socially (Hank and Wagner 2013). On the other hand, the importance of adult children in the provision of support in later life was demonstrated in the SHARE European study (Dykstra and Fokkema 2011). Most European later-life families are characterized by having a child nearby, being in frequent contact with at least one of their children, having strong family care obligations, and regular exchange of help in kind from parents to children (ibid.). Although daughters are widely seen as the main sources of care, some studies report that sons give as much emotional and financial support and help in accessing services. However, they are less likely to assist with 'hands-on' situations (Chambers 2005; Davidson 1998). Phillipson (2004) has highlighted that older people generally have small personal networks that consist of a few very close, or significant, support contributors. Although many of the networks are categorized as family-centred, they consist of couples (ibid.). This supports the contention that there has been a historical shift away from the family as 'the site of intimacy' to the norm of the 'good relationship' of coupledom (Jamieson 1998: 136). In addition, men are more likely to have very small networks of one person or less: 5 per cent, compared to 2 per cent of women (Phillipson et al. 1999; Phillipson 2001). It has been argued that the reduction in network size is because men switch from ties that provide instrumental support in their adult years to ties that provide emotional support in their later years (Carstensen 1992; Thompson and Whearty 2004: 7).

It is now widely accepted that older women, irrespective of marital status, are more likely to have a wider range of kith and kin in their network than older men are. Older men especially see their partner as a primary source of care and support (Wenger et al. 2007: 1449). Childless married men are particularly dependent on their wives' social networks (Knipscheer et al. 1995; Wenger, Scott and Patterson 2000; Wenger et al. 2007). Additionally, women have reported receiving more support and benefiting from personal interaction (Chambers et al. 2009; Davidson 2004; Scott and Wenger 1995). De Jong Gierveld found that loneliness differs between men and women who live alone: the former were more likely to be lonely than the latter. Never-married men reported the highest rates of loneliness, while never-married women had the lowest, with the difference attributed to relationship history and social and socio-economic resources (de Jong Gierveld, 2003: 107). In a study of older people's networks in the Netherlands, Knipscheer et al. (1995) found that excluding partners, kin were the most important, with children the foremost, followed by daughters and sons-in-law, brothers and sisters-in-law, siblings, cousins, nieces and nephews. In terms of non-kin, the most important relationships were neighbours, followed by friends, and then fellow associates of organizations, acquaintances and former work colleagues (Phillipson 2004: 43–44). Many researchers report that after the spouse, adult children are the most likely to provide care and support to older people (Campbell, Connidis and Davies 1999; Connidis and McMullin 1993; Phillipson et al. 2001; van Tilburg 1995; Wenger et al. 2007).

A recent cross-country European study (Deindl and Brandt 2013) found that extended family and non-kin frequently provided informal help for childless older people, but that intense care was provided by public service providers. Consequently, childless people are likely to experience a lack of help consisting of non-personal and less intensive support (Albertini and Mencarini 2011; Deindl and Brandt 2013). Marco Albertini and Letizia Mencarini (2011: 20) have highlighted that the older childless are not disadvantaged when their health is good, but as health deteriorates with age, the informal support declines and the formal care does not compensate for the shortfall. Echo Chang, Kathleen Wilber and Merril Silverstein (2010) analysed the US Health and Retirement Study to determine whether there were any differences in care needs and well-being between older disabled childless people and parents (aged 75 and over and non-ambulatory). Of the 1,456 community-dwelling respondents, 14.3 per cent were childless (not biological parents), 71.4 per cent were women and 28.6 were men. The authors found that there was little difference between the care received and psychological well-being of the groups. However, the childless received less informal care, with unmarried childless women more likely to live in institutions and have higher mortality rates than their married or parent counterparts. The equivalent data for men was not reported – possibly due to the sample size.

Generally, older childless people have been viewed as socially vulnerable compared to parents because of the lack of contact with adult children. Conversely, there is also much literature showing that childless people are not social isolates, but form strong ties with lateral kin and non-kin (Albertini and Mencarini 2011; Connidis 2001; Dykstra 1995; Townsend 1957; Wenger et al. 2007). Childless people develop close relationships with 'siblings, cousins, nieces and nephews over the life course' (Wenger 2009: 1244). Furthermore, when siblings die, relationships with nieces or nephews strengthen, whereas parents tend not to have formed that type of relationship (Wenger 2009). This reflects the concept of weak bridging ties that extend to wider networks with possible access to increased resources, and dense ties that remain in the close network (Borgatti and Halgin 2011; Granovetter 1973, 1983; Phillipson, Allan and Morgan 2004a). Taking into account that women live longer than men do, the studies may be more reflective of older women's social networks.

Recent technological developments such as the mobile phone and the internet have had a huge impact on social networks. Benefits include the ability to stay connected with kin and non-kin across long distances, for example via Skype. John Urry (2007: 198) proposes the concept of 'network capital', which is 'the capacity to engender and sustain social relations with those people who are not necessarily proximate.' However, such interactions are different to embodied experiences. Hannah Marston (2019; Marston et al. 2016; Marston et al. 2019; Marston, Musselwhite and Hadley 2020) has identified intergenerational differences in how technology is utilized in relationships and in health and social care.

Family Relationships

The reduction in family size stemming from increased life expectancy and lower fertility rates has resulted in a change of family structure, with Vern Bengtson (2001: 6) highlighting the increased length of intergenerational relationships. A European Commission survey (2009) found that there were inadequate community-based opportunities for older and younger people to meet and socialize. The change in demographics during the twentieth century has led to a 'beanpole' (Bengtson, Rosenthal and Burton 1990) family structure (also known as 'verticalization'), with a 'long and thin' (Bengtson 2001: 5) shape that consists of increased 'vertical' (grandparent–parent–grandchild) ties and reduced horizontal or lateral (siblings, cousins) ties (Dykstra 2010; Meil 2006). This has implications for care in later life, as the traditional reliance on informal care or familial support will be reduced (Phillips 2007: 67). The demand on formal care will increase not only due to the growing number of childless individuals, but also because adult children are not always available. Sociologists have postulated that demographic changes in Western society over the last few decades have resulted in an ideational shift from the 'fatalistic' to 'individualism' (Beck and Beck-Gernsheim 1995, 2002; Dykstra 2004); this is also known as 'the individualization thesis' and the 'de-traditionalization thesis'

(May 2011a). The 'individualization thesis' proposes that Western societies have undergone a seismic shift, with traditional social structures such as class, gender and family losing their significance. Ulrich Beck (1992) and Ulrich Beck and Elisabeth Beck-Gernsheim (1995; 2002) have proposed that the loss of these traditional norms has led not only to choice but also to risk and danger: individuals had operated in structured traditional kinship, familial ties or commitments, but are now constantly required to choose, and negotiate how to live through self-reflexivity (May 2013; Morgan 1999; Smart 2007). Individualization theory has also challenged the importance of chronological age and suggested that age is progressively fragmented in late modernity (Mac an Ghaill and Haywood 2007). Critics of the individualization thesis have highlighted that it lacks empirical data to substantiate its claims, portrays society and self as separate entities, diminishes relationality and has only a narrow definition of the family (Jamieson 1998; Mason 2011; Pahl and Spencer 2004; Weeks, Heaphy and Donovan 2001).

In contrast to functionalist family theories that viewed roles as structured by social determinants, Finch and Mason (1993) promoted the concept of 'negotiation' as a frame for understanding familial interactions (Chambers et al. 2009; Morgan 1996; Silva and Smart 1999). Finch and Mason examined the relationships between adult children and their ageing parents to see how decisions concerning care and support were reached. They found that obligations, roles and responsibilities were developed over time to form commitments. Familial commitments were formed, moulded and maintained via the reciprocal parent–child relationship, with each commitment being unique between the parties. Cultural rules and social structure may influence familial interactions, but the degree to which they did so was variable, not fixed. David Morgan (1996, 1999, 2011) has proposed that familial interactions are inherently agentic, flexible, fluid, multifaceted and interwoven with moral and normative kinship beliefs. Contemporary family relationships are defined more by 'doing family' than 'being' family' (Finch 2007: 66). Contemporary relational practices of non-heterosexuals have been conceptualized as 'chosen families' formed by a combination of friends, lovers and family of origin, where 'family relations, responsibilities, and obligations are increasingly open to negotiation' (Heaphy 2009: 122). Morgan (1996) contended that the interaction between the agency of the individual, gender, economics, politics, policy and ideology were seen in 'family practices':

> Practices are often little fragments of daily life which are part of
> the normal taken-for-granted existence of practitioners. Their sig-
> nificance derives from their location in wider systems of meaning.
> (Morgan, 1996: 190)

This viewpoint expanded the concept of familial structures from
the traditional biological and marital forms, to include reconfigured
kin networks, same-sex families, fictive kin and 'personal community networks' (Wellman and Wortley 1990: 559). The concept of
personal communities indicates how people draw on a convoy of
relationships at different points of the life course (Allan 2008; Antonucci and Akiyama 1987; Antonucci 1986). Throughout life, every
individual has a 'social convoy' that consists of a network of relationships that provide significant resources of support – for example,
social, emotional and financial help. As people age, the morphology
of their social convoy is influenced by 'major determinants', such
as employment, finance, gender, location and relationship status
(Davidson 2004: 38). Parenthood provides increased opportunities
for network building through the bridge children provide to other
social arenas.

Social Networks

The complex and fluid nature of contemporary family structure
is reflected in the blurring of roles between 'kin' and 'non-kin'
(Bengtson and Lowenstein 2003; Hall 2008; Morgan 1996). Family, partners, friends and non-kin relationships are integral to social
engagement in later life. Absence, dissatisfaction and low social
participation or engagement adversely influences quality of life,
with relationships and social support shown to be as important as
physical health for personal development (de Jong Gierveld 2003;
Scharf and Bartlam 2008; Victor et al. 2005). Social support is an
important dynamic in social networks and is enacted through different forms, for example as emotional support through love, trust
and friendship (Phillips, Ajrouch and Hillcoat-Nalletamby 2010:
199). The composition and functioning of an individual's 'social
embeddedness' (de Jong Gierveld 2003: 95) depends on their network of social relationships and resources. Gerontological research
frequently highlights older adults' embeddedness in dense, kin-ori-
entated networks. Typically, dense networks include frequent
contact, companionship, emotional and care support, monitoring
and access to resources, and produce social capital (Adams 1987;
Cornwell 2011). Although beneficial, such strong bonding ties can

also be oppressive by limiting autonomy, restricting privacy and increasing dependency through pressure to comply with social norms and group expectations. Conversely, informal acquaintanceships, random links, non-kin or associates of friends form weak ties that 'bridge' across communities to diverse networks and to different resources (Coleman 1988; Cornwell 2011; Granovetter 1973, 1983; Urry 2007). Personal community networks are social relationships that provide meaning, routine social capital and structure, and are viewed as a more accurate way of portraying the contemporary diversity in the ties between family, friends, and intimate and wider relationships (Collins 2011; Phillipson 2003; Spencer and Pahl 2006). Liz Spencer and Ray Pahl (2006) describe the dynamics of personal communities over the life course as follows:

> Personal communities provide a kind of continuity through shared memories, and help to develop a person's sense of identity and belonging; although their composition may alter as an individual moves through the life course, a core part of their reality does not change. (Spencer and Pahl, 2006: 45)

As such, they are integral to 'social capital' (Bourdieu 1986; Coleman 1988): resources that are available through connections, group membership, interactions, formal and informal networks, and relationships.

Although most research has concentrated on traditional family ties, more recently attention has been focused on non-family ties, or 'fictive kin'. Much of the early work on fictive kin examined relationship dynamics in non-majority families, for example working-class families in England (Townsend 1957), homeless American youths (McCarthy, Hagan and Martin 2002), gay and lesbian relationships (Friend 1989; Heaphy 2009; Weston 1991) and older adults (Allen, Blieszner and Roberto 2011; Litwin and Landau 2000; MacRae 1992). In a study of American family structure, Katherine Allen, Rosemary Blieszner and Karen Roberto (2011: 1164) found that a process of 'non-kin conversion' occurred, where 'friends, students, or work colleagues' were attributed the same status as biological kin. Allen, Blieszner and Roberto extended the concept of 'fictive kin' to all forms of family. However, the study's sample was limited to those with a minimum of one grandchild (adoptive, biological or step) and comprised thirty-four women and eleven men aged 56–88. A limit of cross-sectional research is that no data is available to show any changes in the dynamics of the fictive kin over time. This raises the question of what social networks look like for people with no adult children, grandchildren or siblings. How familial and other relationships intersected with my participants' social networks is discussed in Chapter 7.

Clare Wenger and colleagues have carried out one of the most widely cited British studies of the social networks of older people. Across several research projects, Wenger examined the dynamics and structure of older people's social networks in rural and urban settings (Scott and Wenger 1995; Wenger 1984, 1992; Wenger, Scott and Patterson 2000; Wenger et al. 2007). Across all the studies, a strong relationship was reported between people's well-being and the levels of support that their social networks provided. A longitudinal study found that most family-based social networks remained stable over a long period (Wenger 1990). Researchers have noted that within the flux and fluidity of social networks, there are some relationships that are closed, negative, truncated or disrupted (Burholt and Wenger 1998; Collins 2011; Phillipson 2004). Network studies have shown that kin supply the majority of intimate relationships and support for older people. Equally, older people are the 'donors and as well as recipients of aid in their network' (Phillipson 2004: 44).

Discussion

In this chapter, I have shown how the study of ageing has evolved since the Second World War, and the importance of the intersection of social categories such as gender and class. I have outlined how sociological research has been criticized for being 'blind' to both age and gender. Furthermore, critical gerontology has focused on structural disadvantage and neglected people's lived experience of ageing. This led to an exploration of the life course and lifespan, and the links between sociological and psychosocial approaches. I have highlighted that the childless have only recently begun to be acknowledged in ageing research. Through examining the literature, I have demonstrated the effect childlessness has on social networks with age. Critically, the focus of many studies has been on women due to the earlier age of male mortality and the pronatalist normative association between motherhood and women. As a result, the implications of childlessness for men as they age have been neglected. I have demonstrated how men were hidden in sociological research generally and, until recently, lagged behind in ageing and gender research. I highlighted the impact of the feminist approach to research and reflected the huge effect it has on the understanding of gender and ageing, and the resulting increase in both empirical and theoretical knowledge. The structuralist foundation of critical gerontology was challenged by the theoretical developments of the post-structuralists and postmodernists. Consequently, critical gerontology has started to examine how people interact with, and respond to, wider socio-economic factors.

The paucity of material on older men's experiences of ageing was exemplified by the recent focus of studies on the later lives of women. I have drawn on literature from demography and family studies to show how the shape and form of families has changed in Western societies across the last century. Although all terms are contested, family structures are now generally viewed as diverse and complex and have been variously described as 'extended', 'nuclear' and 'choice'. Factors such as the political and economic climate; the increase in the mobility of adult children, divorce and step families, same-sex families, solo living, and internal and external migration; and shifts in social policy have all impacted on the dynamics of family life, practices and structure (see Allan and Jones 2003; Chambers et al. 2009; Lowenstein and Katz 2010).

Summary

The literature reviewed in Chapters 1 and 2 has highlighted the lack of qualitative research exploring the lived experience of involuntarily childless men as they age, thus providing the justification for, and relevance of, this book. The demographic literature has shown the worldwide decline in fertility levels and increase in age of mortality. This has implications across the micro, meso and macro levels of social systems. An increase in older childless adults has consequences for health and social care for both institutions and individuals, as much informal care is centred on family. The collection of data on women's fertility intentions and behaviours allows the population level of women with and without children to be accounted for in future policy. Significantly, as there is no equivalent collection of male data, it is not possible to judge the population level of childless men in the UK.

There is good evidence that life course factors influence people's fertility choices. For example, the timing of entry into and exit from education, employment and relationships effects reproductive intentions and outcomes. Equally, structural categories such as sexual orientation and class also affect procreative intentions. This suggests that childlessness is much more complex than is suggested by the generally held belief that people either do or do not want to become parents. Therefore, this raises questions on how personal agency and structural factors influence people's reproductive lives. Much of the research concerning involuntary childlessness relates to the fertility intentions, behaviours and experiences of couples in ART treatment. The majority of such work reports the women's experiences and reflects the fact that the vast majority of ART treatment centres on women's lives and bodies. The negative impact that infertility has on identity, mental and physical health, social status, and well-being for women has been thoroughly documented. Recent research indicates that infertile men suffer comparable levels of distress. However, childless people who have not accessed treatment are not included in any statistics or dataset. Therefore, the unrecorded childless are invisible to policymakers and other stakeholders. Likewise, their life history and experience is not heard.

The stigmatization of those who do not comply with pronatalist and heterosexual norms has been acknowledged in infertility literature and other research into those who challenge social norms. The majority of infertility research is clinic-based, and this raises questions concerning the power dynamics and the relationships between researcher and participant. In addition, many studies report only the women's experience: men have been portrayed as not interested. Feminist researchers have highlighted the paucity of material on men's *lived* experience of infertility. The few studies that report on male infertility and involuntary childlessness show that men have deep emotional responses to not fulfilling the 'natural' father ideal. Childlessness affects how men view themselves and how they are viewed and judged by others. Infertility and unwanted male childlessness is a direct challenge to traditional, ideal-type, virility-proved-by-fertility masculinity. Yet masculinities theorists and researchers have failed to acknowledge this significant population of men.

Over the past decade, there has been a slow increase in research examining childless older people. The literature surrounding familial and social networks has successfully demonstrated the importance of adult children in the networks of older people. Frequently, it is 'childless' adults who are seen as 'available to care' (Beth Johnson Foundation/Ageing Without Children 2016), and are 20 to 40 per cent more likely to provide support than equivalent adults with families (Pesando 2018). Although it is widely reported that adult daughters provide the majority of informal care for ageing parents, in the UK 58 per cent of carers are female and 42 per cent male (Carers UK 2015). While adult daughters are seen to provide 'hands-on' support, adult sons are described as providing both emotional and instrumental support (Davidson 1998), such as aid in accessing services and financial assistance (Chambers 2005). In addition, Veronica Wallroth (2016) argues that there is a gender bias in academic and policy family caregiving literature that views women as ideal carers and excludes men's experiences. Comprehensively reported in this body of literature is the fluidity and adaptability of who is included as family, with non-biological members often having the same status as biological kin. The change in family size and morphology has been well documented, and there is good international evidence that older childless people are likely to have poorer health and social and economic positions than those with children. Recent research has highlighted that healthy childless older people have comparable social network sizes to those with children. However, when they need critical attention, they are moved to appropriate residential state services earlier and for longer than those with children.

In the middle of the last century, the sociological theoretical focus shifted from older men (and a resulting invisibility of women) to the reverse situation in the late twentieth and early twenty-first centuries. As a result, the majority of ageing research started to focus on women's experiences, because older men were viewed as structurally (economically) privileged. The research literature clearly shows the impact of feminist scholars' work in establishing the significant influence of gender in ageing. It is only recently that scholars have highlighted the lack of examination into men's lived experience of ageing and the impact that economic and relational transitions have on their sense of identity. Social gerontology literature saw midlife as time related to the third Age, and this was widely seen as an identity related to post-parenthood, and before the decline associated with the fourth Age. The assumption that midlife was related to parenthood reflected the dominance of the heterosexual pronatalist normative mandate and the importance of adult children in older people's social networks. Structural research viewed the issues for men in midlife as negotiating the change in identity from external provider to an adapted role within the home. Feminists, post-structuralists and postmodernists questioned the legitimacy of such a limited view of identity and suggested that the relationship between ageing and gender had a nuanced and unstable effect on identity. These theoretical developments led critical gerontology to adapt its political and economic perspective to a viewpoint that acknowledged actors' experiences over the life course. For example, the different gendered reactions to bereavement have been well established, including men's difficultly in adapting to that status.

The literature reviewed in Chapters 1 and 2 provides detailed insights into the issues surrounding both childlessness and ageing. Regarding the experiences of involuntarily childless men, the following issues were highlighted:

- The embeddedness of the heterosexual pronatalist norm in individual agency and all levels of sociocultural structures;
- The non-collection of data on male fertility intentions and history;
- The near invisibility of men's lived experience of involuntary childlessness;
- The absence of men's experiences of ageing;
- The effect of involuntary childlessness on men's intimate and wider relationships;
- The long-term influences of demographic change on the provision of health and social care services.

The literature examined demonstrated the absence of men's experiences of ageing and involuntary childlessness. Consequently, conducting a qualitative study of older men's lived experience of involuntary childlessness was not only a unique project but one which would also deepen the understanding of men and ageing. Significant life events and disruptions affect the arc of a person's expected life trajectory in respect to their interpretation of sociocultural norms and their structural environment. In order to understand older involuntarily childless men's lived experience, I framed my study using a pluralistic approach. Critical gerontology has proved how important it is to acknowledge the intersection between wider structural factors and individual agency. An understanding of the life course allows an understanding of the interaction between the timing of events and expected social norms. In order to capture and comprehend men's understandings of their life experience, the biographical approach, as used by Chambers (2002) in her study of widows, would be appropriate. By taking this pluralistic approach to explore involuntarily childless men's experiences over the life course, I hoped to gain an in-depth understanding of their experiences of mid- and later life. The gaps in the literature gave rise to the following research questions, as discussed in the Introduction:

Research Question 1: What are men's attitudes and behaviours in relation to their experiences of involuntary childlessness?

Research Question 2: How do men describe the influence of involuntary childlessness on their quality of life and relationships with close, familial and wider social networks?

Research Question 3: What are involuntarily childless men's expectations of the future?

Research Question 4: What are the policy and service implications of the findings in relation to the above?

Chapter 3

METHODOLOGY, METHOD AND ANALYSIS

Introduction

This chapter discusses the methodological underpinnings of the study, the method used and the process of analysis. Many books based on research studies do not include a detailed description of the methods used or the reasons for the approach. Anthropologist Marcia Inhorn (2012: 18) argues that not to include this reduces the credibility and trustworthiness of the research. This chapter starts by examining the background to the qualitative approach I employed to address the research questions posed in the Introduction and Chapter 2. I then describe the methodology and the pluralistic framework used. I follow this with a consideration of the ethical issues of my research, including a discussion of my own involuntary childlessness and my counselling background. This is followed by a description of the study, from the design and planning stage to the fieldwork. This stage included developing recruitment strategies to access and interview a hard-to-reach group. The penultimate section describes the processes surrounding the transcription of the interviews and the inductive latent thematic analysis used to examine the data (Braun and Clarke 2013). The final section gives an overview of the chapter and a brief description of the following four chapters and their findings.

Why a Qualitative Approach?

Qualitative inquiry is a 'reflective, interpretative, descriptive, and usually reflexive effort to *describe and understand* human action and experience' (Fischer 2006b: xvi, original italics). It is concerned with the exploration of social contexts, changes, experiences, processes and the 'situatedness' of social lives 'over time' (Mason 2006: 16). Mason (2002) proposed that:

> Qualitative research aims to produce rounded and contextual understandings on the basis of rich, nuanced and detailed data. There is more emphasis on 'holistic' forms of analysis and explanation in this sense, than on charting surface patterns, trends and correlations. (Mason 2002: 3)

In general, qualitative analysis follows a homogeneous thematic method that, in its most basic form, entails collecting of and familiarization with the data, coding, integrating themes and categories, analysis, and concept development. Taking an interpretative approach (Denzin and Lincoln 1994; Holstein and Gubrium 2005) to the analysis requires not only sensitivity to context but also an appreciation of the most suitable discourse (Mason 2006: 18).

The literature review chapters (Chapters 1 and 2) highlighted the need for a methodology that revealed the interactions between involuntarily childless men's life experiences and their cultural, economic, political and societal contexts (Letherby 1997; Portacolone 2011; Wright Mills 1959). To understand the actions and experiences of my participants, I utilized my knowledge from the disciplines of ageing, reproduction, health, and sociology and economics, as well as sources such as media and personal experience. A quantitative methodology was rejected for three main reasons. First, there was a lack of data to form the measures and instruments typically associated with this approach. Second, such approaches tend not to reveal the depth of understanding of the subjective and contextual dynamics of lived experience (Denzin and Lincoln 2008; Mason 2006). Finally, selection of the most appropriate method to address the purpose and nature of the research questions is central to research (Mason 2002; Teddlie and Tashakkori 2003). Consequently, a qualitative approach using semi-structured biographical narrative interviews was chosen.

Why Interviews?

Interviews give access to how people experience their social world through their ideas, memories, thoughts, relationship dynamics and views (Merrill and West 2009; Roberts 2002; Yow 2005). Steinar Kvale (1996: 37) declared that conversation was a 'basic mode of constituting knowledge'. Given the paucity of research concerning male involuntary childlessness, it was important for the interview method to allow the participants to talk about their experiences and the analysis to be shaped by their experiences and opinions. Given that men's personal experiences over time were central to the study, the Biographic-Narrative Interpretive Method (BNIM) was chosen as a suitable foundation for the interview structure (Wengraf 2001; Wengraf and Chamberlayne 2006). An important feature of the BNIM approach is 'its focus on eliciting narratives of past experience rather than (just) explicit statements of present' (Wengraf and Chamberlayne 2006: 4). Central to the BNIM method is that up to three interviews with each participant are possible before the participant becomes exhausted (Jutla 2011; Wengraf 2001; Wengraf and Chamberlayne 2006). The point in having at least two distinct interviews is to ensure that the first interview is uninfluenced by the focused enquiry of the second interview (Wengraf and Chambelayne 2006: 6). The follow-up interview clarifies and develops material arising from the previous one. The format and questions that guided the interview were developed from the BNIM model and the 'storyboard' interview template, as recommended by Catherine Riessman (1993: 55).

The biographical approach offers a method of capturing both the individual and social context of the participants' experience. Narrative interviews allow individuals to talk about their experiences of 'childlessness' and ageing. Taking this approach dovetails with the life course perspective, in that it reveals the social contexts of particular events, norms and ageing, of a particular period. Moreover, an in-depth examination of an individual's biographical narrative enables all the close and wider contexts of their experience to be understood. Accordingly, the differences and similarities between people's lives become integral to the analysis and help the researcher understand life in relation to the past, present and future (Chambers 2005; Fox 2009; Jutla 2011). Such an approach, in addition to exposing the richness and complexity of life stories, acknowledges that 'somewhere behind all the storytelling there are real active, embodied, impassioned lives' (Plummer 1995: 170). Consequently, this approach allows for the account of the dynamics and interaction between researcher and interviewee to be included in the analysis (Wengraf 2001). The biographical approach using narrative interviews has been noted as a suitable way of reaching and understanding the experiences of individuals in marginalized groups (Chambers 2005; Fox 2009; Jutla 2011). It does this by adding context through acknowledging the settings and dynamics of familial structures and all forms of relationship environments. Involuntary childlessness is a sensitive topic because any inquiry may cause feelings of distress, risk, deep emotion or unease, prior to, during or post-contact (Dickson-Swift et al. 2008; Lee 1993). Nonetheless, it has been observed that research participants often report a therapeutic benefit from the interview process (Etherington 1996, 2004, 2007). Tom Wengraf (2001: 125) stresses framing the meeting as 'a research interview' with the focus on the biographical narrative by keeping within the participant's frame of reference. My reflections on the interview process are presented in the conclusion chapter.

Methodological Foundations

In seeking to find out the meaning and significance of older men's lived experience of involuntary childlessness, a theoretical approach was required that acknowledged the interaction between the 'macro' of social and cultural contexts of reproduction and ageing, and the 'micro' of individual agency across the life course. The methodological approach that guides my study was derived from the framework developed by Pat Chambers (2002, 2005). In her study of the lives of widows, her framework was founded on life course, biographical and feminist perspectives. From Chambers (2002), I have derived a methodological framework formed by auto/biographical, biographical, feminist, gerontological and life course perspectives and methods.

Theoretical Framework

The contention that individuals have capacity in the construction of their own social worlds invites the use of qualitative methods and an 'interpretivist' framework. Melanie Mauthner and Andrea Doucet (1998: 125–26) suggest that a relational ontology is consistent with interpretivism in understanding how social actions and social structures enable and constrain each other (Marshall and Clarke 2010: 295). Qualitative research is primarily concerned with how people's social worlds are constructed, experienced, interpreted and understood, and has its foundations in the philosophy of 'interpretivism' (Denzin and Lincoln 2005b; Guba and Lincoln 2005; Mason 2002). Interpretivism seeks 'culturally derived and historically situated interpretations of the social life-world' (Crotty 1998: 67). Similarly, George Mead (1934: 162) has contended that 'a person is a personality because he belongs to a community, because he takes over the institutions of that community into his own conduct'. This highlights the embeddedness of people in a complex web of social relations ranging from the intimate to the wide (Gilligan 1993). Access to the lived world is through both the participants' and the researchers' subjectivity: actions, background, behaviours, beliefs, consciousness, concepts of self and the world, decisions, experiences, interactions, interpretations, reactions, reflections, values and views (Fischer 2006a; Jutla 2011). The following four findings chapters show how the participants are involved in the construction of meanings in, and of, their social worlds. Recently, there has been a focus on 'the sociology of the personal and the everyday' so as to see the relational dynamics between the microsociology of the individual and the macrosociology of social structure (Mason 2011; May 2011a, 2011b; Smart 2007). However, Vanessa May (2013: 63) contends that this approach has a limited viewpoint if it remains at the level of the everyday. Consequently, sociology must also aim to understand the larger context.

I view interpretivism as reflecting the core interest of this study, in understanding the interactions and dynamics between the actions and meanings of individual involuntarily childless men within their sociocultural context. Interpretivism holds the paradigms that developed in opposition to positivism. It reflects the myriad forms of examining and understanding human reality that have developed, and are developing, particularly over the past half-century. These include: social constructionism or constructivism, critical realism, cultural studies, feminisms, ethnomethodology, phenomenological discourse and symbolic interaction (Charmaz 2006; Denzin and Lincoln 2005a). Although the terms 'social constructionism' and 'social constructivism' have been used interchangeably (Burr 1995: 19), they are distinct. The two share a commonality in that they are perspectives on the perception and construction of social reality that is formed by human interactions and practices, contextualized by social engagement (Crotty 1998: 42). Michael Crotty (ibid.: 58) defines constructivism as 'the meaning-making activity of the individual mind'. Social constructionism highlights that human perception and experience are located culturally, historically and linguistically (Willig 2001: 7). Crotty (1998: 58) contends that constructionism fosters 'the critical spirit' while constructivism resists it. At its simplest level, 'constructionism' occurs in front of the nose and 'constructivism' behind it. In this study, I drew on constructionism. My aim in taking this stance was to explore how men negotiated between their own belief systems, hopes, thoughts, expectations and desires, and the wider social and cultural environment. One of my aims was to explore the interactions and intersections between the participants' personal meanings and structural norms.

I view reality as socially constructed by social context, interaction and discourse, and in terms of this study, by the researcher and the researched (Crotty 1998; Denzin and Lincoln 2005a; McLeod 1994). Donna Haraway (1988, 1991) contended that knowledge is not completely objective but situated, partial, political and located within the positions adopted through sociocultural practices, institutions, values, perspectives, power and experiences (Nightingale 2003; Stoetzler and Yuval-Davis 2002). This position leads to the proposal that there are multiple realities created by the evolving interactions between social actors in situated cultural and historical contexts (Bryman 2001: 15). This emphasis on constructionism in the generation of knowledge links directly to the interaction between the participant and the researcher. It also draws attention to how the dominant constructions we experience impact on how we situate ourselves within a wider social context (Swan 1998: 31). I bring into this study material from my past, including my upbringing, class, previous career, childlessness and research experience. Due to my working-class background and work experience I strongly identify with the pragmatic and 'what works' (Creswell and Garrett 2008: 327). Many of the experiences reported by the participants (Chapters 4 to 7) give credence to the interpretivists' perspective that the everyday social interactions of people are socioculturally complex and subject to multiple interpretations (Christians 2005; Lynch 2000; Simpson 2011).

Constructionism is central to critical gerontology: Chris Phillipson and Alan Walker (1987: 12) have argued that the aim of critical gerontology 'is not just to understand the social construction of ageing, but to change it.' Critical gerontology is a value-based approach concerned with equity and social justice across the life course. It draws on the critical, dialectical, reflective, interdisciplinary and emancipatory precepts of critical theory (Benton and Craib 2001; Osborne 1992; Ziegler and Scharf 2013). It centres on ageing, rather than old age, and is heavily associated with the political-economic perspective. However, it has been criticized for focusing on the impact of macro structural forces on older people's lives and neglecting actors' agency and experience (Holstein and Minkler 2007: 18). In response, critical gerontology has widened its remit and now examines ageing from a viewpoint which includes biological, cultural, demographic, psychological and social elements. The demographic element of critical gerontology is rooted in the life course approach – a perspective that examines the context of biographical experience of social events over time (Phillips, Ajrouch and Hillcoat-Nalletamby 2010: 140).

Chambers (2002) demonstrated that the assets, choices, constraints, deficits and opportunities available to social actors (widows) change across their life course. The life course approach recognizes that as an individual ages, their life experience is contextualized by cultural and social institutions, and shows how social ties are influenced by the circumstances of others (Elder, Kirkpatrick Johnson and Crosnoe 2003). The life course perspective has been seen both as a valuable element to approaches that foreground individual developmental properties and a method of assesing the impact of policy and socio-economic conditions on different generations (Lowenstein and Katz 2010; Melville 2013). Moreover, Paul Roodin (2004) has highlighted how the life course approach shows how sociocultural values affect individuals over their life course. The life course perspective has been criticized for not accounting for historical time or the unpredictability of role transitions (Bengtson, Elder and Putney 2005; Elder 1999). However, Glenn Elder et al. (2003: 11) stress that ageing, human development and adaption are lifelong processes that intersect with the key life course principles of human agency, historical time and place, the social contexts of transitions and timing, and linked or independent lives. Robert Atchley (1989, 1999) found that many older people successfully negotiate change through using, or adapting, past experience (Chambers 2005; Laceulle 2013). By using the life course approach in combination with the narratives of the participants' experience, the relationship between micro experience and macro structures would be understood (Dannefer and Settersten 2010; Grenier 2012; Hutchison 2011). Moreover, the use of biographical methods, with their premise that social processes can be understood through analysing people's experiences, is compatible with the 'interpretivist paradigm' (Giddens 1977: 168).

Insider–Outsider Research

Acknowledging the position of the researcher, and their power, through their 'knowledge, culture, and experience' (Ramazanoglu and Holland 2002: 119) has become central in much qualitative research. Ann Oakley's (1981) pioneering work led to the recognition of the importance of power and gender dynamics in research scholarship (Broom, Hand and Tovey 2009: 51; Finch 2004). The power and diversity in the dynamic between the researcher and the researched places the former as either an 'insider' or an 'outsider' (Kanuha 2000; Sixsmith, Boneham and Goldring 2003). Yvonne Jewkes and Gayle Letherby (2001) proposed that the insider–outsider relationship is located in 'interactive sites of meaning-making' (Järvinen 2001: 280). As a self-defined involuntarily childless man, I have to be aware of the effect my own experience and background has on the research in general and in the interview in particular. There are both advantages and disadvantages to the insider position. My insider status may be considered to add to the validity of the study through a shared understanding of our experience of involuntary childlessness (Jutla 2011; Kanuha 2000). Equally, through familiarity, I may have missed 'the subtle aspects of the data' that 'are vital in qualitative inquiry', and which an 'outsider' may have acknowledged (Green et al. 2007: 479).

Research into sensitive subjects – such as fertility disruption – entails emotional work for all parties involved in the research process (Carroll 2013; Malacrida 2007). Anne Gray (2009) has argued that any work involving contact with other people is emotional labour. The terms 'emotional labour' and 'emotional work' were developed by Arlie Hochschild (1983), with the former referring to emotional management in waged work and the latter to management in private. However, 'emotional labour' is now used to the describe the regulation of feelings, and 'emotional work' refers to 'dealing with other people's emotions' (James 1989: 16). Emotion is immanent in all social interaction, to a greater or lesser degree, and the significance of the emotional context involved in research interactions has been driven by the feminist approach (Collins 1998; Dickson-Swift, James and Liamputtong 2008; Duncombe and Jessop 2002).

As explained in the Introduction, this study draws on the auto/biographical approach, which is widely associated with the feminist perspective. The auto/biographical approach situates the biographies of 'the researcher and the participants as data and as an inextricable part of the research process' (Carroll 2013: 457). Consequently, carrying out research into sensitive topics requires the researcher to be attuned to both the participants and their own emotional labour (Dickson-Swift et al. 2009; Liamputtong 2007). Steinar Kvale and Svend Brinkman (2009: 101) discuss the 'emotional dynamics of an interview journey'. Their focus is on the researcher's emotional relationship with the interview project, with which I can associate. Furthermore, Helen Sampson et al. (2008: 930) highlight that emotional risk and harm does not end with data collection, as there are other risks 'associated with leaving the field, analysing sensitive data, and fulfilling commitments to research participants in the delivery of research findings'. How I managed the contextualized and multifaceted emotional subtleties of the interviews, analysis and writing are described in the 'Risk Management' section later in this chapter. To acknowledge interview dynamics, I followed the accepted method of keeping field notes and a research diary as part of a reflexive process. I also drew on my supervisor's knowledge and experience, and accessed personal counselling (see Etherington 2007; Sampson et al. 2008; Dickson-Swift et al. 2009). Reflections on interview interactions and my experience of undertaking this study are explored in the Discussion chapter (Chapter 8).

Validity and Trustworthiness

One of the criticisms of qualitative research is that it is not generalizable to the wider population because it does not fit the criteria of verification through objectivity, reliability, repeatability and validity of traditional natural sciences (Mason 2002; Punch 2005). In most qualitative research, this option is generally not available or feasible because of small sample sizes. Qualitative research has instead developed criteria of 'trustworthiness' through the demonstration of plausibility, credibility, dependability and 'confirmability' (Patton 2002: 93). One of the most common methods of establishing plausibility is by demonstrating the transparency of the research process (Flick 1992). Typically, this involves providing an audit trail to indicate how findings were formed, prolonged engagement in the field, thick description (Geertz 1973), transcripts of interviews, a research diary, reflexivity and peer debriefing (Hammersley and Atkinson 2007; Lincoln and Guba 1985; Webb 1970). Moreover, Deirdre Davies and Jenny Dodd (2002: 288) argue that ethical processes such as attentiveness, empathy, awareness, openness, context, respect, honesty and reflection add to the internal validity of qualitative studies. The qualitative approach used in this study can be viewed as supporting its validity, as it encompasses the subjectivity of the lived reality of older involuntarily childless men (Collins 2011; Denzin and Lincoln 2005c).

Ethical Considerations

I have based my ethical approach on the ethical guidelines of the British Sociological Association (2004) and the British Society of Gerontology (2008). Both guidelines emphasize the importance of confidentiality, research integrity and the safety of both participant and researcher. From these guiding principles, I understood the main areas of concern in this study as:

- Trustworthiness
- Confidentiality
- Risk management
- Ethics in action

Trustworthiness

The ethic of trustworthiness is needed in order for participants to feel safe and that it is worth their while to have participated in the study. The process of trust building began in the initial contacts with participants and continued as the project progressed. Central to building trust was the transparency of motivations for the study. This was established in the invitation to participate letter and the information sheet every participant received before the first interview. The information sheet described the background to the study, interview details, right to withdraw, benefits and risks of participation, the complaints procedure, informed consent and information on data handling.

Confidentiality

Confidentiality was central to the ethics of the study. The procedures I adopted for maintaining anonymity included the use of pseudonyms for the participants and people the participants referred to (Dickson-Swift, James and Liamputtong 2008; Ellis 2007). Locations were also disguised in order to prevent any participant in a particular area being revealed. Company names have been similarly coded, and the nature of their trade broadened. This strategy was implemented at the transcription stage of the first interview in order to 'build in' anonymity at the earliest opportunity. The protection of the participants' personal information is of paramount importance. Complying with the Data Protection Act (1998) and ensuring the safe handling of personal information, including password-protected data and secured storage for hard copy material, is essential. Participants also had the opportunity to stop the interview or withdraw part or all of their narrative as stipulated in the 'informed consent' form. One participant took the option to withdraw from the second interview, but gave permission for the first interview to be included in the study.

Risk Management

A fundamental ethical duty is the avoidance of harm. The identification of, and response to, such risks was critical to the ethical position taken from beginning to end of the study. Involuntary childlessness is a sensitive subject and care was taken to minimize any distress or harm. Integral to this aim was my approach to, and style during, the interviews. Mindful that the interview may be viewed as an environment where masculinity is both displayed and under threat (Schwalbe and Wolkomir 2001: 91), I drew on my counselling background to be authentic and genuine (Etherington 2004) in all my contact with participants. Awareness of how people react when disclosing deeply personal information, and the acknowledgement of the difficulty in disclosure, were areas where my counselling background and experience were drawn on. Therefore, details of organizations that could offer support were included in a 'support sheet' that was supplied to each participant. Kvale (1996: 172) has noted that participants may experience 'a sense of shock' when reading their interview transcripts. In anticipation of such a reaction, I drew the participants' attention to it as part of the first interview exit strategy and in the letter accompanying the transcript. As an 'insider', I had to be aware of the impact of any distress that I may experience. To minimize that risk, I drew on my experience and training as a counsellor in 'processing' emotional reactions, recording my reactions in my research journal, accessing support from my supervisors and accessing personal counselling. The ethical position of the study was constantly reviewed as part of the regular supervision process. At the completion of the study, participants were sent a letter thanking them for their involvement and a summary of my findings.

Ethics in Action

The relationship between researcher and participant is of critical importance to any research study. Keele University's Ethical Review Panel approved my study in October 2011. Central to the ethical concerns is the notion of informed consent: 'the right to give or withhold consent to participate in research is a basic human and civil right' (Bond 2004: 6). Two types of consent were collected: first, consent to participate, and second, consent for the use of quotes. In addition to obtaining signed consent before any interview, a 'rolling consent' system was employed: consent was reconfirmed at every contact with the participant. Additionally, I was concerned with minimizing harm to participants, although Bryman (2001: 118–20) notes that there are limits to how much a researcher can plan to avoid emotional distress. Due to the sensitive nature of the research, I used two separate semi-structured interviews in order not to 'exhaust' the participant. In a number of interviews, I sensed that the participants were becoming emotional, and some became so. For example, one participant recounted his experience of the long illness and death of his partner. At these times, I offered to stop the interview or move on to another topic. None chose to do so, and it is significant that participants continued to tell their stories. Mindful of minimizing harm, one interview was conducted via email to reduce any distress and enable the participant to retain control.

In the next section, I will discuss the recruitment and data collection strategies, and then demonstrate the procedure I used to analyse the data.

Methods Employed

Pilot Study

A small pilot study was conducted to evaluate the interview schedule and check that all communication material was clear and acceptable. The interview schedule was based on my knowledge of the literature and my research questions, and although the interviews were semi-structured, they were open to follow the direction of the participant. Both interview schedules are reproduced in Appendices 2 and 3. The size of the pilot study was limited to one individual drawn from my personal network in order to prevent 'using' any potential participants that could form part of the main study. Two learning outcomes were drawn from the pilot study. First, the inadvisability of interviewing someone known to the researcher became clear: the dynamics of the interview may affect either the analysis or the relationship (or both) in a positive or negative manner. Second, the running order was changed: the demographic questions were relocated to appear later in the schedule in order to avoid 'blocking' the next section of the interview. This had two advantages: first, it gave a lead into the debriefing by moving the participant from the emotive to the cognitive. Second, it provided a form of internal validation, as most of the participants revealed their demographic background earlier in the interview.

Design

On first contact, a 'Respondent Fact Sheet' form was opened that recorded details such as name, address and preferred contact method, and listed every further point of contact with the participant. It also included a space for my reflections. With the participants' agreement, all interviews were recorded and then transcribed verbatim. A copy of the transcription of the first interview was sent to the participant. Once confirmation of the receipt and reading of the document had been received, arrangements for the second interview were made. The first interview consisted of five sections, with the first and fifth sections related to administration and introducing and ending the interview respectively (see Appendix 2). The second section had a dual purpose of relaxing the participant and locating his thoughts on his experience. The third section was aimed at uncovering the men's attitudes and experiences of involuntary childlessness. The fourth section consisted of questions drawn from research on ageing and related to how men viewed their present and future health and social networks, as well as demographic questions (Amieva et al. 2010; Crystal et al. 2003; de Jong Giervéld 2003; Wenger 1984). The rationale for including these questions was to explore men's health practices and the significance of social relationships. The second interview comprised three elements, with the first and last having the same administrative functions as in the first interview (see Appendix 3). The second section was centred on the participant's response to reading the transcript of the first interview. This gave the participant the opportunity to edit and correct the transcript and confirm that he had been represented accurately. Clarifications and any issues arising could be discussed, and any themes that had developed during the ongoing analysis could be addressed at this stage.

The Sample

The full criteria for participation were given in the information sheet, but briefly *excluded* men who considered themselves biological fathers or who were presently occupied in any form of social fatherhood, such as being a stepfather. The initial age range of 50 to 70 years was selected to cover the increase in live births in the UK between the Second World War and the early 1960s (Goldstein 2009: 9). Difficulties in recruitment led to a loosening of the age criteria, and the final participants' ages ranged between 49 and 82 years, with a mean of 63.5 years. The sample was not stratified by other criteria, such as ethnicity or social class, as having such classifications may have impeded recruitment. Table 3.1 summarizes general information about the participants, including their age, relationship status, education, occupation type, qualifications and employment status.

Pen portraits of the participants, and a brief account of my reflections on each interview, can be found in Appendix 1. Each portrait is a reflection of the men's narratives and the interview dynamics, location and quality of our interaction. The intention in supplying these vignettes is to enable the reader 'to have a grasp of the person ... if anything said about them is going to be meaningful' (Hollway and Jefferson 2000: 70). The pen portraits are drawn from my experience of the interview process before, during and after each contact. The descriptions are relatively brief, as the participants' narratives are used extensively throughout the findings chapters. The aim in providing these short accounts of the participants' history, their situation and the interview environment is not only to 'flesh out' the representation of each participant, but also to indicate the events, people and attitudes that may have influenced their life narratives. Although Chambers (2002: 177) argues the case for pen portraits to be located within the main body of the text, I have located them in the appendices for convenience. Moreover, the location our pen portraits – mine in the Introduction and the participants' in Appendix 1 – negates any criticism of the study being 'self-indulgent' (Letherby 2002c; Merrill and West 2009). Reflections on the interview interactions, and my experience of undertaking this study, are explored in the Discussion chapter. Further details of the men's financial situation (Table 7.1), quality of life and health can be found in Chapter 7. After I had been given ethical approval, the fieldwork was conducted between January and November 2012. Interviews were conducted with fourteen self-defined involuntarily childless men: thirteen from urban and rural communities across the UK and one based in Thailand.

TABLE 3.1. Participants' demographic information. Hadley, Robin A. 2019. "It's Most of My Life – Going to the Pub or the Group": The Social Networks of Involuntarily Childless Older Men', *Ageing and Society*: 1–26. Reproduced with permission.

Name	Age	Ethnicity	Relationship status	Sexual orientation	Faith	Education level	Occupation	Location
Stephen	49	White British	Single	Heterosexual	Spiritual	Higher degree	Professional	South-east England
Russell	55	Anglo-Celtic Australian	Single	Heterosexual	Non-believer	Higher degree	Professional	Central England
Frank	56	White British	Single	Heterosexual	Other	Degree	Unskilled	Wales
Colin	59	White British	Partnered	Heterosexual	Other	HNC	Professional	Central-southern England
John	59	White British	Partnered	Heterosexual	Non-believer	HND	Skilled	Central-east England
David	60	White British	Married	Heterosexual	Christian	Degree	Professional	South-east England
Edward	60	White British	Partnered	Heterosexual	Non-believer	Degree	Professional	South-east England
George	60	White British	Married	Heterosexual	Christian	Higher degree	Professional	North-west England
Michael	63	White British	Single	Heterosexual	Other	Higher degree	Professional	Thailand
Harry	64	White British	Widower	Heterosexual	Non-believer	None	Semi-skilled	South-east England
James	65	White British	Partnered (LAT)	Heterosexual	Atheist	City and Guilds	Skilled	North-east England
Martin	70	White British	Married	Heterosexual	Spiritual	Degree	Professional	Wales
Raymond	70	White British	Widower	Gay/Homosexual	Non-believer	GCE	Manual	North-west England
Alan	82	White British	Single	Gay/Homosexual	Christian	Degree	Skilled	North-west England

Recruitment

There is a vast amount written on participant recruitment (sampling strategy) in the social science literature (Butera 2006; Hadley 2014b). However, there is very little work on how to access participants for research on sensitive and deeply personal matters. Moreover, the majority of that work examines 'respondent resistance', interview dynamics (Adler and Adler 2001) and the emotional labour of dealing with sensitive research (Dickson-Swift et al. 2008, 2009). As described in the previous chapters, men's experiences are virtually absent from research on ageing and reproduction. Moreover, men are viewed as difficult to access and not interested in research. Consequently, I anticipated that participants would be difficult to recruit for a number of reasons:

• the sensitivity of the subject
• the lack of records on men's fertility history
• the view of childlessness as a loss
• the fact that I was not an 'insider' to any organizations that dealt with involuntarily childless men

Robert Miller (2000: 76, 79) advises researchers to exercise 'ingenuity' and 'presence of mind' in order to access dangerous or difficult-to-reach groups. As this study required access to a hidden population, the 'snowball' method was selected, because it is viewed as one of the best approaches to accessing such populations (Bryman 2001; Miller 2000). This approach requires respondents to become recruiters by encouraging others to follow their example of engagement in research. Likewise, the use of third parties, such as acquaintances, colleagues, family, friends and partners is also viewed as a particularly effective means of recruiting male participants (Butera 2006; Oliffe 2009; Oliffe and Mróz 2005).

First Recruitment Phase

In the initial recruitment drive, I employed a variety of approaches to promote my request for participants. Leaflets and posters were posted on Keele University campus and in cafés, libraries, charity shops, hairdressers and theatres of Newcastle-under-Lyme, Manchester and around my home location (Wythenshawe). Recruitment emails were sent to my personal and professional contacts and to Keele University distribution lists. Other networks were also accessed, such as the Valuing Older People (2013) programme of Manchester City Council. My personal networks included my family, friends, former colleagues, and social and trade union organizations. Strategic institutions such as Age Concern, Age UK, Beth Johnson Foundation and University of the Third Age (U3A) were contacted at national and local levels. My professional network included bodies specializing in involuntary childlessness and infertility: More-to-Life (MTL) of the Infertility Network UK (2014) and Mensfe (2008). MTL agreed to circulate details of the study in exchange for a piece written for their newsletter (Hadley 2012b). The professional associations the British Association for Counselling and Psychotherapy (BACP), the British Society of Gerontology (BSG) and the British Sociological Association (BSA) all circulated details of the study on their respective websites. However, after six weeks the only respondent had withdrawn, and I was feeling the pressure of time: the study was racing away from me. I was surprised by the lack of interest: when I had spoken to people, they were interested in the subject and often told me their own reproductive experiences. I was also disappointed by the absence of attention from organizations associated with Keele University and those I had connections with. I had hoped these would lead to successful recruitment, but as Wright Mills found out, 'this turned out to be an illusion' (1959: 210). A progress review was held with my supervisors. Consequently, the decision was taken to refresh and increase the recruitment campaign.

Second Recruitment Phase

A significant element of the review was the gathering of feedback from 'critical friends' (Koo 2002): peers, friends and field notes taken following contact with potential respondents and recruiters. Consequently, a number of creative strategies were put in place.

First, I was fortunate that Dr Elena Portacolone (2011) gave a guest lecture on her doctoral study, which had involved interviews with older people living alone in San Francisco. Elena kindly gave me the benefit of her experience of difficulties in participant recruitment, and advised me to change the tone of the text in my material and to include a photograph of myself. The original recruitment material had been framed by the institutional diktat of a scientific research agenda. For example, the original leaflet was dominated by the University logo, was titled 'Male volunteers needed for a research study' and used the word 'Father' throughout. Moreover, there was a large section of text detailing the ethical protocol. Consequently, the design and wording of the leaflets and posters were adapted to 'de-power' and 'humanize' the material without misrepresenting the purpose of the study. Although Karl Nunkoosing

(2005) identified power issues in research, he was referring to the seeking of consent. However, power is also held in the symbols and words of the material promoting the study (Cameron 1985). The redrafted material received positive feedback – including unsolicited favourable responses to my photograph.

Second, in order to reach a wider audience I promoted the study across different media platforms: print, radio and social. Since there was no financial support, I could not follow Ives et al. (2008) and advertise in a national newspaper. Therefore, I paid the costs of advertisements in three local newspapers and a magazine for people aged over 50: *The Sentinel* (11 April), the *Manchester Evening News* (1 May), the *West Midlands Metro* (25–29 June) and *The Oldie* magazine (May and June editions). Only *The Oldie* was successful, providing three participants. I contacted, and was interviewed, on BBC Radio Manchester (Hadley 2012a). In order for listeners to easily contact me, I set up a website with a simple title that would be easy to write down: www.wantedtobeadad.com. I designed the website as a 'virtual' shop where interested parties could find out about the study and access the information sheet, my background, the ethical protocol and contact details. No participants were recruited either through the interview or through the website. Significantly, the majority of the respondents viewed the website before joining the study in order to check out the validity of the study. In addition, the website received very positive feedback from participants, academics and particularly journalists. To support my online and social media presence I set up a Twitter account linked to the study's website. Twitter was chosen because approximately 20 per cent of users are aged between 35 and 60 (Cheng and Evans 2009). Compared to Facebook and other social networking media, Twitter fitted the demographic criteria of the sample. Although no participant was recruited through this method, the study's profile was raised and several contacts requested posters for display.

Third, the approach to recruitment was adapted to a more direct face-to-face style in dealings with individuals and organizations. For example, I would offer to help when distributing publicity material, particularly with charities. In order to build a wider network of 'recruiters', I attended a local over-50s keep-fit class. I also disseminated posters and leaflets at academic seminars, conferences and workshops. This approach generated one participant. I increased the range of local venues at which I distributed leaflets and posters to include barbers, churches, health centres, libraries, shops, social clubs, sports clubs and the University of the Third Age (U3A). Regrettably, most of the local groups contacted failed to reply or to see the relevance of research. For example, one U3A coordinator responded that her group were all widows aged over 70 'and not at all likely to be interested in hearing about your research'. In addition, I tried to recruit local 'recruitment champions' to promote the project. This was only successful with the staff of the Valuing Older People (VOP) programme. VOP organizes and coordinates local and national activities that bring together older people with business, charity, education, health, social care and housing organizations. VOP staff helped promote the study by distributing leaflets and posters, and regularly including an advert in their 'E-bulletin' newsletter. I attended their events and was able to meet end-users, field workers, managers and policymakers from a wide range of organizations. Through VOP, I was able to recruit two participants from an LGBT support group.

Figure 3.1 shows the most effective recruitment strategies. Out of twenty-eight respondents, fourteen suitable participants formed the sample of this study (for more details on this topic see Hadley 2014).

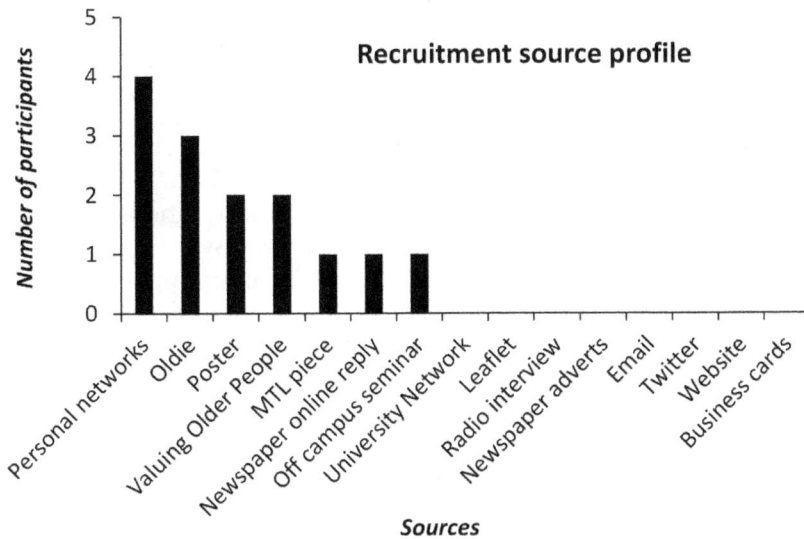

FIGURE 3.1. Profile of the recruitment strategies. Hadley, Robin A., *Methodological Innovations* (13, 2). pp. 1–11, © 2020 Robin A. Hadley. Reprinted by Permission of SAGE Publications Ltd.

Data Collection

As the recruitment progressed, the main fieldwork of interviewing and transcription of the interviews took place. Informed consent was gained at the start of the first interview and the end of the second interview, and was confirmed verbally at all other points of contact. All audio interviews were digitally recorded and transcribed as soon as possible. The interviews took place at the preferred location of the interviewee – the majority in the participant's home. One advantage of individual face-to-face interviews was the privacy it gave (Kvale 1996; Roberts 2002). There were four exceptions: email interviews with Colin, computer-to-computer interviews (via Skype) with Michael, interviews held on Keele University campus with Russell and mobile telephone-to-computer (via Skype) interviews with Stephen.

Due to his motor neurone disease, Colin preferred the use of email for our 'interviews', as he experienced emotional distress and physical reactions when talking about sensitive subjects (Motor Neurone Disease Association 2012). In line with the ethical principle of respect (of not harming the participant), I decided to send the interview schedule as an email attachment and then conduct a 'live' synchronous 'e-interview' (Bampton and Cowton 2002) at an agreed time via email. One disadvantage to the email interview was the lack of visual cues. Many of Colin's replies were short and, in an attempt to deepen the response, 'probes' were used in the second 'interview'. Skype was used as the means for interviewing two of the participants: Michael, who was based in Thailand, and Stephen, who preferred to be interviewed by mobile telephone. In the interviews with Michael, there were also occasions when either the image or sound was lost or cut out altogether. However, the shared experience of those glitches helped build a good rapport between us. Stephen preferred to be outside to prevent his mother overhearing his conversation (Chapter 6). Consequently, there were occasional losses of signal and constant background noise.

Data Analysis

Transcription

Transcription is an interpretative practice that involves a degree of decontextualization, abstraction and loss from the original conversation (Kvale and Brinkman 2009; Langdridge 2007). Transcription of the audio recordings took place as soon as possible after the interview and a copy of the first interview's transcription was sent to the interviewee. The period between first and second interview was framed by the participant's availability, and as a result varied between ten days and eight weeks.

The interview transcripts were uploaded to NVivo 9 and initial coding of the first interview was undertaken. As well as being iterative and informing the timing and content of subsequent interviews, at this point the analysis became concurrent with the data gathering. NVivo 9 software was used for the management, storage and analysis of the recordings, transcripts, fact sheets and field notes. The software allowed organization of material into folders, such as participants' first and second interviews, contact sheets, field notes and research diary. As the analysis progressed, I used the memo facility to record notes and ideas, and I linked these with nodes, participant folders and memos. In addition to the software's 'model' facility, I also used freehand graphics to help visualize the concepts and links between data. NVivo 9 cannot 'decode the meaning of the text' but is 'a mechanical aid' to manage and support a project (Joffe and Yardley 2004: 65). Moreover, Hammersley and Atkinson (1983: 198) suggest that software-based coding procedures are 'no different to "manual" techniques'. Furthermore, they have the advantage of combining codes and 'nesting' codes within one.

Thematic Analysis

Data analysis involved the use of a broad thematic analysis. I drew on Virginia Braun and Victoria Clarke's (2006: 84) latent thematic analysis, which fits with the constructionist paradigm and in which 'the development of the themes themselves involves interpretative work'. This method of analysis 'aims to identify and describe the contents of an individuals [sic] perceptions, ideals and values' (Luborsky 1994: 205) and discovers and contrasts themes and patterns (Braun and Clarke 2013; Collins 2011). Thematic analysis works both to reflect reality and to unpick or unravel the surface of 'reality' (Braun and Clarke 2006: 81). The analysis in this study was contextualist, as it was interested in understanding the participants' individual experiences in relation to the 'broader social context' (ibid.). Furthermore, the thematic analysis was inductive, as the identified themes were thoroughly linked to the data (Braun and Clarke 2006, 2013). In conducting the analysis, I followed Braun and Clarke's (2006: 86) six phases of analysis:

1. Familiarization with data;
2. Generation of initial codes;
3. Search for themes;
4. Reviewing of themes;
5. Defining and naming of main theme(s);
6. Compilation of final report.

Analysis started after the first interview and involved listening and relistening to the interviews, reading and rereading the transcripts and field notes, and coding the data. Familiarization is a common process in qualitative analysis and involves engaging with, and becoming immersed in, the emotions, feelings and meanings within the narratives. It is a dual process of consumption and engagement, reflecting the individual in relation to wider contexts (Braun and Clarke 2006). This process 'begins to sensitise the researcher' to creating themes and contexts and also provides background for following interviews (McLeod 2001: 72).

The initial codes were generated through a line-by-line 'open coding' analysis of the transcripts. This challenges the researcher's preconceived ideas and directs them to 'open' up to different elements and theoretical possibilities (Braun and Clarke 2006; Charmaz 2006). 'Codes are tags or labels for assigning units of meaning to the descriptive or inferential information compiled during a study' (Miles and Huberman 1994: 56). During this phase, I kept asking of the data, 'What is happening here?' 'Where does this belong?' 'Is this different?' 'How so?' These initial codes were the foundations of the analysis and indicated the possible concepts within the data. Codes were generated inductively through engagement with the participants' narratives (en-vivo codes), established criteria, previous studies and sources of literature. A node is the place where NVivo 9 stores labelled codes, text and associated data such as the transcript line number. The ease of coding at the click of a mouse button entails the potential for over-coding. To manage this, I regularly reviewed the nodes and their relevance and examined if they could form, or fit, another theme. However, as many qualitative researchers have stated (Ray 2000; Chambers 2002, Ballinger 2012), I found the analysis of 'rich, thick data' time-consuming, confusing, frustrating and 'messy'.

The next phase focused the analysis on a deeper level by examining the relationship between codes and the data to see possible themes. 'A theme captures something important about the data in relation to the research question' (Braun and Clarke 2006: 82).

Therefore, prevalence is not a criterion for theme creation, but 'keyness' is. Individual nodes were grouped into further nodes that represented provisional, candidate and main themes (ibid.: 89). I explored the relationships and links between themes and codes by considering how codes may combine, and by making comparisons, modelling, memo writing and transcript annotation. The initial open codes form provisional themes and these are then analysed to shape the candidate themes and structure the main theme. Braun and Clarke (ibid.: 92) suggest that the 'defining and naming' phase concerns the identification and refinement of the essence of the analysis. Although their method of analysis is presented as a linear process, in practice the boundaries between the stages were blurred, as the analysis involved constant movement between the different phases. For example, while writing up the study I found myself re-engaging with the recordings and transcripts. In addition, I found that moving from the 'micro' level of the analysis to the 'macro' level of the compilation of the findings for the audience was another form of analysis, and influenced the interpretation of the data. As a result, codes and themes were re-engaged with and revisited throughout the analysis and writing-up stages of the study. Braun and Clarke (2013: 225) stress the active, creative and organic process of analysis.

Summary

In this chapter, I have described the rationale for using both a qualitative approach and a theoretical framework that drew on biographical, gerontological and life course perspectives. The use of biographical interviews was justified as the most appropriate method for an in-depth exploration of the experiences of involuntarily childless older men. I have highlighted the significance of ethical practice and have documented the research process in order to fulfil the criterion of trustworthiness. As I experienced a number of issues relating to recruitment, a wide range of strategies were developed in order to recruit the sample. Key lessons in accessing hard-to-reach groups included:

- Appreciation of the sensitive nature of the subject matter;
- Creativity and flexibility: although the website did not directly generate any respondents, the majority of respondents had

visited it before contacting me, and as such, it supported the recruitment process;

• Persistence: recruitment improved in the latter half of the study.

This chapter included my evaluation of the different processes encountered during data collection, analysis and management. The
findings from my latent thematic analysis are presented in the next
four chapters.

The first of the findings chapters, Chapter 4, describes the different influences that contributed to pathways and routes taken by the
men that led to them being childless. The beginning of the chapter
describes the social context that influenced the participants' expectations regarding parenthood, and goes on to describe the diverse
influences on how they became, and remain, childless. Chapter 5
examines the effect that being childless has had on the men and the
intersections of cultural, social and economic norms that interact
and effect reproductive beliefs and behaviours. The third findings
chapter, Chapter 6, explores temporality and the hierarchy of relationships, social networks, stereotypes and social heirs. Chapter 7
describes the participants' economic and health characteristics and
their view of the future. Throughout all four chapters, quotations
from the participants are used to support the presentation of the
findings. The transcription process involves the translation 'from an
oral language with its own set of rules, to a written language with
another set of rules' (Kvale 1996: 165). In order to 'keep the human story in the forefront', the transcripts have stayed as close to
the participants' speech as possible (Charmaz 2006: 107). Although
most of the participant quotes used have been 'cleaned' of para-
verbal elements and pauses, some have been retained to provide a
clearer understanding of the participants' meaning. Words stressed
by the speaker have been underlined, and actions and relationships
such as [laughs] or [partner] have been included to aid the understanding of the participants' meaning. The use of '...' indicates that
a section of narrative has been removed to avoid confusion (Bailey
2008; Davidson 2009; Miller 2000).

Chapter 4

PATHWAYS TO INVOLUNTARY
CHILDLESSNESS

Introduction

This chapter demonstrates the intricacy and diversity in the factors that influenced the participants' involuntary childlessness. It answers the question, 'How did these men become childless?' by uncovering how issues as diverse as economics and partner selection can influence the participants' reproductive outcomes. Pen portraits of the participants are located in Appendix 1. The chapter comprises six sections and begins by inspecting the background from which the men's beliefs, and subsequent behaviour, developed. Inherently connected with that influence was the form of upbringing the men experienced: in effect, the incubator of the accepted, and expected, rules, values and roles that formed the men's attitudes to parenthood. The movement into adulthood and associated relational and socio-economic events, and their timing, is then considered. This leads to an exploration of issues in relationship formation and dissolution, followed by a description of attitudes to parenthood and childbirth. The experience of those who, by varying degrees, investigated ART is then examined, followed by a view of the different transitions into childlessness. The final section looks at the attitudes towards, and awareness of, fatherhood.

The majority of men in this study defined themselves, at least in agreeing to participate, as involuntarily childless – that is, men who, at some point in their lives, had wanted to father children. The exception was Alan, who, having experienced the role of 'adopted' grandfather, wanted to repeat that relational experience. From a pragmatic perspective, the participants had some commonalities. Until proved otherwise, they held the assumption that they were fertile and therefore expected that they could biologically father a child. The two gay men made it clear that they could not have had sexual intercourse with a woman, as evidenced by Alan's statement, 'As I say, I certainly didn't want the physical way of getting that end product.'

Becoming a parent was an assumed element of the life course for all the other participants. However, other factors, including upbringing, relationship dynamics, fertility, economic factors, age and sexuality, influenced their reproductive outcomes. Some had considered alternative modes of parenthood, such as adoption, but these had either been discounted or withdrawn from. Although some of the participants had been more motivated than others to pursue fatherhood, the majority did not indicate that they were desperate for parenthood. The men described a range of responses to their non-parenthood, including acceptance, regret, loss and a nuanced non-acceptance.

Background to Beliefs and Behaviour

In order to understand the inherent differences between the participants in their routes towards involuntary childlessness, it is helpful to locate the dominant sociocultural attitudes and beliefs towards parenthood. As Phillipson (2013: 82) noted, the baby boom of post-Second World War Britain was divided into two 'spikes': one in the late 1940s and the other in the early 1960s. The demographic profile of this study follows that pattern, with most of the participants having been born in the 1940s and 1950s (along with one, Stephen, who was born in 1963). The exception was Alan, who was born in 1930. John and Martin both noted their childhood relocation to post-war New Towns, and this highlighted the degree of renewal and change in which the country was involved in the post-war period. That period also saw an increase in the promotion of traditional norms and values, including the importance of marriage, and the role of motherhood and nurturing for women and that of father and provider for men (Holden 2007). The universal opinion of the participants was the assumption of marriage and parenthood as the social norm, and therefore the re-entrenchment and maintenance of heterosexual pronatalist customs. Martin and David respectively described themselves as working and middle class, and showed similar assumptions regarding their cultural inheritance.

> I think if you're in your teens and twenties, you know you're having a good time and, gradually your peers start to get married, in those days, because we didn't have partners, you think that's the way you're gonna go along. ... I guess you expect there to be a natural progression without even really thinking about it, this is the way it's going to be, you know, you meet a girl, you get married, you have children, and that's the way it is. (Martin)

Despite having a similar trajectory to Martin's, David's middle-class life course arc included attending university as taken-for-granted: 'I expected to leave school, do university, get a job, get married and have a family.' Martin's comment also highlighted two other elements: first, the 'social clock' relating to peers getting married, and second, the generational change in values from marriage to 'partners'. In their responses to the question, 'Was that actually verbalized by your parents or was it just ...?', Martin and Stephen further highlighted the embeddedness of the essentialist heterosexual pronatalist normative assumption. Martin responded: 'No, no, it's a, it's a social thing. ... It's a social norm isn't it? ... I mean, but whatever your religious views are, we're here to procreate that's, you know, that's why we're here, no there wasn't anything spoken.' Stephen reflected the commonly referenced order of the 'Package Deal' (Townsend 2002): 'I'd see, you know, having a child is very much part of being in a relationship, and so for me, first would be the relationship and then the child would follow.'

The dominance of the traditional pronatalist norm was also reflected in the attitudes and actions of the two gay participants, Raymond and Alan. Raymond reflected on the social conventions of 1950s Britain: 'I think from about like fifteen years old I knew I was gay, so in my mind even then I knew I would never get married. So, I suppose I didn't even think too much about children because you don't get married them days you didn't have children.' Likewise, Alan revealed the differences between generations that social (equalities legislation) and technological (ART) advances had brought: 'I could never have been a father, I don't think so. Might've worked if it had bin in today's time and place, you know.' Raymond and Alan highlighted their awareness of the change in values from their formative years. For example, the UK Equality Act (2010) protects certain characteristics from discrimination:

age, disability, gender reassignment, marriage or civil partnership, pregnancy and maternity, race, religion or belief, sex and sexual orientation. As homosexuality was a criminal act in the UK until 1967, Alan had to assume a heterosexual identity – 'passing' as a heterosexual man (Rosenfeld 2003a: 2) – from his teenage years until his late thirties: 'There are certain rules and regulations you 'ave to live with. ... You work ways to get round the rules. Ways to keep the awkward questions away – but I got rid of two of my ex-girlfriends at my twenty-first birthday party: introduced 'em to two lads. And then went on to be best man at both weddings.'

Conversely, George, who had a middle-class upbringing in north-west England, had an attitude influenced by the dynamics of the familial environment. The lifestyle of his uncle made a deep impression on George.

> He had this life, he had his own sports car, open-topped sports car, he had his own boat, he sailed, he skied, and he was always tanned and he had always to be out. ... I think I had some sort of role model of what to be. And you know in a funny way that is what I became. ... So, most of my life was focused, you know, it was a lot of fun; it was great.

George's narrative demonstrated the different influences that combined to form his perception of how to be in the world. However, Stephen's attitude to the pronatalist norm was to reject it while engaging in what may be seen as a form of hyper-masculinity in his adulthood.

> I had spent most of my thirties, and even into early forties, living a lifestyle ... which was very much a day-to-day lifestyle, chaotic. ... Lots of drinking, lots of womanizing, and in fact, I only worked in order to get money to fund that lifestyle. ... I used to see men in families living that kind of stable life as something that I didn't want to be.

Stephen acknowledged an awareness of the pronatalist norm with reference to his lifestyle not being suitable for the 'responsibility of children'. Moreover, compared to those that assumed they would, for the most part, marry and become fathers, he rejected that norm, and this may be related to his upbringing.

> So my early childhood experiences were, you know, very, well not positive in terms of, you know, there being any kind of positive role model for family life at all. ... So certainly, I'm quite sure that, you

know, I didn't have any expectation of having or aspiring to having anything that I'd experienced in terms of, family life because I'd never really experienced it.

Parenthood was a deeply embedded social structure for all the participants. The almost-unconscious expectation that fatherhood would happen at some point was set in each participant's view of self and view of others, and in their cultural, economic and social contexts. It is from that perspective that the men's attitude to fatherhood was shaped. The men wanted to become parents, with the exception of Alan and Raymond; many had been hesitant or fatalistic about their opportunities for fatherhood. Michael contextualizes his view: 'I think it's always been in the background, but, of course, I don't think that desire to have children has been so desperate that I've, you know, made myself marry.' Similarly, George stated, 'If it happened it happened, if it didn't it didn't.' Nonetheless, both Michael and George and their partners accessed ART. Moulet (2005: 104) suggests that the men in her study provided a form of biographical ambivalence with such terms as 'lack of readiness' and often related to their experiences of childhood. Russell expressed the effect of being diagnosed with paranoid schizophrenia in his mid-teens, which added to his anxieties regarding fatherhood.

> One of the reasons I think I'd make not a very good father is because I'm too anxious about it because I've got too much baggage. … I've got, possibly, I carry a gene for schizophrenia or some other form of mental illness, you know? … I was really scared about becoming a father. … Now I was very concerned I'd not fuck up some other person.

Russell's disrupted and violent childhood contributed in a number of ways to his attitude towards fatherhood. He was afraid of repeating his father's behaviour, and his childhood experience of institutional care added to his insecurity concerning parenthood. In addition, he feared that there was a genetic legacy to his (misdiagnosed) mental health. Once he fell in love and married, he and his wife agreed that once their child was born, the child must be brought up in a financially and emotionally stable home. Consequently, strategies were put into place to achieve their aim of building a secure family environment. Contraception was used to avoid unplanned pregnancy and at the same time items were bought in readiness for the baby's arrival. However, poor economic conditions in Britain led the couple to move to Australia.

> Both of us wanted to ensure that it was a so-called planned birth, from a financially responsible sort of viewpoint, as well as from an emotional one. So, we were extremely careful about conception. ... An indication of how seriously we took family planning was that we used to buy an item for the baby each week, which we had a trunk for. So that if the baby did happen, even though we were having protected sex ... if it did happen by accident that we would be prepared sort of thing.

The importance of relational experience in childhood and formative years was demonstrated in John's description of the dynamics that influenced, and continue to influence, his relationships with others. A dispute with his partner regarding parenthood intentions not only challenged John's procreative plans but also his self-concept. As part of his self-assessment, John employed a cost-benefit analysis combined with a risk assessment of his options, leading him to stay in the relationship.

> I should have just said, 'Okay, we'll sell the house and we'll go'. ... The background stuff and the damage to my self-esteem and any self-confidence that I may have had, had stopped me from doing that because I was afraid – that things would be worse. I mean, if this was bad then being out there on your own, in your mid-thirties, not thinking that you're particularly attractive, you know, somewhat overweight and all that stuff, you're going to end up on your own all of the time.

John's 'aversive' childhood experience influenced the view he held of himself and how others viewed him. Consequently, fear of not being in a relationship, and of being alone, determined that he remained in a situation that would not satisfy his desire for fatherhood. The effect of poor parenting continued to influence how John negotiated his self-identity and his intimate and wider relationships: 'Because you ain't going to find somebody, and if you do find somebody, you're not going to find somebody who hasn't already got children so you've got to pick up somebody else's kids, somebody else's hang-ups, and baggage. And I thought, "How the hell is that better?"' John's vision of himself was balanced against his age, and the age, life stage and familial status of any potential partner. Moreover, he highlighted a negative opinion not only regarding any potential partner but also about any potential partner's children. The undertone of the comment paralleled opinions expressed regarding adoption and fostering: the view that the child may have needs that the participant cannot meet or that are too demanding.

Stephen had had many sexual encounters from his late twenties until his early forties. As he had always used condoms, he was confident that he was not a father.

> Self-preservation was important to me – if for no other reason than to carry on living like it. Yeah, it was very much around the era of HIV and AIDS. ... So, I was very, very, very, careful, yeah, which is why I also know that I've not, by default, ever become a father that I don't know about it because I always did.

During that period of his life, contributing factors to Stephen's childlessness included his attitude to family life, parenthood, women and the HIV-AIDS awareness campaigns of the 1980s and 1990s. The relational undercurrents between partners were also seen to change over time and affect reproductive intentions. Frank highlighted the dynamics surrounding sex and contraception: 'Sex was a problem because she wouldn't – my ex was quite irresponsible; she forgot her contraception quite regularly. So that, as you can imagine, that didn't help with sex and I gradually sort of, went off it.' Stephen's and Frank's accounts show the different elements that may affect parental aspirations and expectations, from internal relationship breakdown to global health issues.

All the participants, with the exception of the three men who had had infertility treatment, responded 'No' to the question, 'Have you ever had sex with the intention of getting someone pregnant?' Of this group, the two gay men would not contemplate any form of sex with a woman and had not been asked, formally or informally, to donate sperm. The heterosexual men stated that they wanted to be fathers at one time or another during their lives. However, with the exception of the men who had accessed ART treatment, none had had 'baby-making-sex'. All confirmed that they had never had consensual, or non-consensual, sexual intercourse with the intention of becoming a parent. Therefore, they had contributed, either consciously or unconsciously, to their childlessness.

Stephen and Frank are two participants who became aware of their position towards fatherhood in their mid-forties, exemplifying 'late awareness'. Stephen acknowledged that his behaviour and attitude between his late twenties and early forties had led to his current position.

> So the slow process of, kind of, coming out of that life, coincided with the realization that I was single, not married, not in a relationship, and more importantly, haven't had kids and, you know, I

realized that that was probably the most significant impact on me of living in that way, which, on reflection, I wished I hadn't.

Frank became aware of his desire for parenthood as his ten-year relationship was ending, when he was approximately 44: 'It was losing the relationship and maybe, perhaps, substituting it with ... with a child and maybe, okay that child would have a mother.' He had shown a growing dissatisfaction with his partner. Although he had not had a strong drive for fatherhood at the beginning of the relationship, as the relationship deteriorated he increasingly saw his partner as unsuitable for motherhood, and took control of contraception to ensure that there was no pregnancy. However, he had not found a partner in the twelve years since the break-up of his only long-term relationship. Additional factors influencing attracting a suitable partner included his poor health, unemployment and living in a rural location.

Both Stephen's and Frank's late awareness of potential fatherhood were responses to transitional points in their lives. Frank had radically changed his view of himself and his behaviour, while Stephen accepted that he was exiting one phase and entering another. The attitudes shown by the men highlighted how social norms influenced their ways of being in the world and influenced their relationships, beliefs and actions at the individual, familial and wider social levels. John's account demonstrated how his attempt to fulfil the heteronormative interconnected with his past, his view of himself, his being in the world and being with others, and his perception of his social world.

The different outlooks shown by the participants demonstrated the social and cultural environments that each man occupied, and point towards how these were then interpreted in both thought and deed by the participants. The internalization and transmission of how to be in the world by the sociocultural construct of 'relationship followed by parenthood' was so embedded that it was difficult for the men to reveal its origins. This was indicative of the individual perspectives of parenthood held by the men. For some, this agentic direction was not fully accepted, or legitimized, until it had to be negotiated in later life. The change in social and cultural attitudes was evident through the participants' reference to the differences between the social values and duties of their upbringing and those available today. For example, Raymond and Alan highlighted the change in the social and cultural norm, in attitude and practice, with regard to fostering and adoption, with specific reference to Elton John and David Furnish (Pidd 2010). Furthermore, George and Stephen's experiences indicated how upbringing influenced their views of the world and their interaction within it.

Having described the normative narratives available, and how these were inculcated into the participants' ways of seeing and being in the world, the following sections demonstrate how different elements contributed to the individual participants' childlessness. In the next section, the focus shifts from sociocultural structural values of marriage and parenthood to an exploration of the participants' early and familial experience, and how different experiences had varying degrees of impact on the men's attitudes and aspirations regarding parenthood.

Familial Context: Upbringing

The strong expectation of conforming to the heterosexual norm towards relationship formation, marriage and parenthood affected all participants. The initial interview question asked the participants to say a little about themselves. All the men began by referring to their childhood, although the amount of time spent on this topic varied greatly. The experiences expressed ranged from the very good to the turbulent. Those expressing the former did not draw any connection between their upbringing and childlessness. The latter group indicated various effects on their attitude, ambitions and behaviour towards parenthood.

> Only child, loving parents, great upbringing, you know working-class upbringing, honest and, and, stable, I suppose. None of the horrors that kids apparently go through today. (Martin)

> I suppose perhaps one of the most significant things was growing up, only realizing later on, growing up in what was probably called a lower middle-class family ... So, it was a very, sort of, I can only call it, sort of, mediocre. ... I say, there wasn't the being ferried around in cars to various clubs, and friends and that sort of thing like nowadays. (Frank)

> My childhood recollections of parents are of turmoil, arguing and subsequently learning that my mother attempted suicide, which led to her incarceration ... I have very distant memories of being in care homes, some sort of local authority care homes. (Russell)

Alan, Stephen, Russell and John indicated that they had had disrupted childhoods. Alan had been adopted from an early age. His narrative highlights a tension between morals of the time: the choices available to the birth parents, the attitude of the birth mother's parents and social policy that facilitated the removal of the child. For Alan, aged 13, his adopted mother's death could have resulted in him being returned to 'care'. However, the wider social context, dictated by the Second World War, led to his adopted family of two brothers and a sister taking over his care.

> Yes, I was born in 1930, out of wedlock. ... The usual thing, an unmarried mother, 'er parents weren't prepared to take full responsibility for the child so 'e was – baby was taken away shortly after she came out of hospital. ... You know, mum was 51 when she adopted me – with a grown-up family.

Although Alan described a happy and supportive upbringing, he also retained a connection with his birth mother and a strong interest in her lineage. He made clear his long search for a 'dad' but not a 'father'. He described the importance of the absence of an 'ideal' father–son relationship, where the 'dad' was non-authoritarian and the imparter of skills and knowledge. Alan's longing for a father–son relationship reappears later on his life, as the desire for the role of a grandfather. This is discussed in Chapter 6.

> Alan: I was adopted by the family. And that's where me surname comes from. The 'B' in the middle what I sign, was mother's maiden surname; funnily enough, not the surname of 'er parents. ... But I say, I went through my life and until I was 50, I think I was still going round looking for a dad. Din't want a father.
>
> R.A.H.: Tell me what you ... ?
>
> Alan: Well, a father is the 'ead of household. He's the 'ead; he lays down the law on things. ... A dad is the one you go and ask, 'How do I shave, dad?' ... The one who shows you how to bowl a googly, whatever your sport is. The one who – that was the one that was missing.

Stephen also referred to himself as being 'born out of wedlock'. The use of this term by both the oldest and youngest in the study demonstrates the strength of the cultural embeddedness of the link between marriage, procreation and family. Stephen highlighted his lack of 'living a family life':

> I was an only child, born out of wedlock, father unknown, never asked her one question about my father, so ... I've never actually addressed the issue with her, so, didn't have any, experience of being fathered at all. ... I didn't experience a family in the sense of my mother and father living a family life, no.

Stephen had no curiosity regarding his father or a need for any paternal relationship. Another participant, John, was the eldest of three brothers. Although he described how his father would sometimes put him 'over his knee and give me a bleedin' good hiding', he did not feel his was an abusive childhood: 'If I were to look back on my childhood, I think in some respects – I was not abused as such, but it was aversive in ways. You know, I didn't get the nurturing that a three, four, five-year-old should have had.'

The childhood environment has an important influence on people's ability to face adversity and problems across the life course (Machielse and Hortulanus 2013: 128). John, aged 9, was diagnosed with psychological issues. Consequently, he was sent to a 'Boarding school for what was termed being maladjusted children.' There, he was physically and psychologically bullied, and reprimanded through corporal punishment. After five years he was diagnosed with a medical issue, successfully treated and returned to the family home. Likewise, Russell's childhood was one of multiple disruptions.

> Much of my childhood was, firstly, in foster care and then in an orphanage. ... But despite being extremely violent, and me being a so-called abused child, there was a considerable feeling, father–son, thing, even though it was a very short space of time that I ended up with him. ... He, very reluctantly, agreed to relinquish custody so that my mother could take me out to Australia. ... It had an enormous impact, on the way I regard fatherhood.

John's and Russell's experiences demonstrated the tension involved between policy and parenthood located in a particular time and social context. Out of the fourteen men interviewed, four specifically drew attention to their childhood. The reaction to the different forms of disruption was seen in the range of participants' attitudes to fatherhood, from rejection by Stephen to control by Russell. Additionally, their childhood experience was reflected in their relationships and demonstrates how social morals and codes are incorporated into each individual's interactions within their respective micro-level environments. As the men moved from childhood and the familial environment into adulthood, they also moved into different social environments. The transitions involved occurred over different social, cultural and psychological levels, including biological (puberty), social (school to work/university), identity (child to adult), social networks (familial to peer), economic (unearned/earned), and different types and levels of relationships (hierarchical, peer, romantic, sexual).

The period that covers this transitional period is typically associated with a drive for autonomy and exploration of identity, in parallel with age-related markers such as legal standards and socially symbolic rites and roles. All the men referred to this period in the context of their ability to relate to others and the wider world. After the death of his adopted mother, and with the Second World War still being fought, Alan, at 14, decided to leave school, start work and contribute to the family finances: 'I got this complete teenager angst in me ... – I wanted to earn my own money. I was paying; you know, bring 'em my wages and give them. That was a, you know, this was the mental thing up 'ere [taps side of head with finger].' Others expressed an awareness of inhibition in forming friendships and in social situations. This was reflected in the men's self-assessment of lacking social skills, resulting in few friendships. Frequently, the latter was measured by not being in the popular group at school. The 'popular' group was defined as the boys who had girlfriends and claimed to have had sex. Moreover, these participants revealed that their social reticence – from awkwardness to shyness – had never been fully overcome. David did not have a problem forming relationships. However, he had noted a pattern that as they progressed to the stage of marriage, he became distressed and ended the relationship: 'I had already started calling it "girlfriend phobia" m'self because if I got too close and things got like, you must commit, the level of psychological upset and distress became extreme.' Consequently, this conflicted with the 'package deal' (Townsend 2002) ideal of marriage-then-parenthood, which is one element of the pronatalist heteronormative remit.

The majority of the participants placed themselves in a subordinated group, at a time of many forms of transitional events in terms of personal agency and sociocultural constructs. The effect of delaying intimate and sexual relationships on childlessness was noted in Chapter 1, as was the level and timing of leaving education and the type of career. Edward's biography encapsulates all these elements. Throughout his life, his shyness had influenced the number of relationships that he had formed, with men and women.

> Looking back I don't think as a kid I was – I wasn't that sort of gregarious, you know, as now, I suppose. I was always a little bit shy and a little bit withdrawn. ... So, I think that, you know, looking back it doesn't surprise me, you know, to be looking back at my life and thinking, 'Oh, you know, I've gone through all these stages and not really known many women and not known many men either.'

As with most of the participants, Edward recalled a difference at secondary school between himself and other boys who were at ease with girls: 'I think as a teenager I wasn't that sociable really; you know. ... It was a small circle of friends and an even smaller circle of girls that I knew.' Edward went on to study architecture at university, a course that lasted longer than most and was populated mainly by men. The professional experience criterion meant that he did not leave university until his late twenties. His social reticence and choice of course contributed to the timing of his first and current intimate relationship, which began when he was nearly 30 years old. Edward hesitantly described the dynamics involved in negotiating the movement into a sexual relationship.

> I mean it was very lucky really, 'cos it isn't as though I'd had a lot of experience in forming relationships with women, but, she was the first, yeah. ... She didn't want me to be too reticent. ... I may have been a bit shy in, sort of, initiating the physical side of our relationship. And I think that she was [laughs], she'd made her mind up, she was not gonna let me be too shy about it, you know.

Edward's attempt to fulfil social and cultural standards had to be negotiated through a cost-benefit risk assessment of his social skills and social interaction. Edward's example links together a number of elements, including the ability to form intimate relationships and the timing of those relationships. Economic factors also combined with interpersonal skills to influence relationship building. For example, David's experience illustrates the pressure between personal agency and socio-economic environment: 'I was very, very busy at work, I moved, for the job, occasionally and I think I worked jolly hard. I think I was also quite shy; I don't think I was very good at generating new social circles wherever I went.' David summarizes the tensions and difficulties in balancing the expected norm of family, economic security and social skills. Interestingly, each time David had to relocate, he bought a three-bedroomed house, not only because that type of accommodation would be easy to sell, but also to account for any future family.

David and Russell had held senior management positions in international companies with concomitant power. As such, they held a status that, when viewed from a stereotypical masculine position, imbued them with privilege that could be used to attract a partner. Both were very aware of not abusing their responsibility and their ethical duty with regard to forming relationships with employees or colleagues. David forcefully made his attitude clear: 'I moved back into manufacturing – by this time I was a production superintendent in a factory full of women. Well, you can't mess with the women working under you; I wasn't going to do it. To me it's unethical, completely out of order.' Meanwhile, Russell found being pursued because of his position a challenge, both personally and professionally.

> I've never seen myself as being attractive to women anyway. I actually was concerned about a 'come on', whatever, and I actually spoke to HR. I said, 'You know, I'm very concerned about this.' I'd run a mile, and it would interfere in my ability to give advice, sort of thing; I don't think I'd be objective.

This section has highlighted how the men's early experiences affected their transition from childhood to adulthood. The different experiences in family, education, and building and maintaining relationships had varying degrees of impact on the men's attitudes and aspirations regarding parenthood. The majority of the men positioned themselves, in their late school years, as separate from the 'popular boys' and socially reticent to varying degrees, with small social networks. The transition into early adulthood demonstrated that the skills to form and maintain relationships varied from individual to individual, and intersected with other factors in affecting the men's childlessness. Relationship skills formed during the formative years affected the timing of role transitions. Childhood interactional style is therefore active throughout the life course: this is known as 'interactional continuity' (Caspi, Elder and Bem 1988: 826; Hadley, Newby and Barry 2019). The following section describes the significance of relationship formation and dissolution to fertility intentions and outcomes.

Relationships: Formation and Dissolution

The heteronormative narrative that the majority of participants attempted to fulfil dictated a specific order of events, including marriage followed by parenthood. Elements of that ordination were formed by the women's biological clock – the acknowledgement that the older a woman was, the less chance there was for children. Age is a determinant of infertility treatment, as the success of IVF declines for women aged 35 and over (HFEA 2009a). Recent research has shown that semen also declines in potency at around 35 years (Cohen-Bacrie et al. 2008; Kidd, Eskenazi and Wyrobek 2001; Siristatidis and Bhattacharya 2007). Men have identified that their desire to become fathers peaked in their mid-thirties to forties, citing their concern regarding being too old to have a full interactive relationship with their children (Hadley 2008a). For the heterosexual men in the current study, the selection of a partner who was willing to become a mother was fundamental to fulfilling the pronatalist norm of fatherhood. For example, Edward met his partner when he was approximately 30 and she was 24 years old. However, they delayed trying for children until he was in his early forties and she was in her mid-thirties:

> So you know, I was getting on towards 30 before my partner and I did get together. ... She certainly wanted to delay it until she was settled. ... There was a mutual desire. The age thing, at the time when we felt ready, didn't bother me because, you know, being with my parents both in their forties when I was born, I thought it would just be like falling off a log.

Consequently, in addition to the age of the participants, the timing of relationship formation and any subsequent dissolution was a critical element in the opportunity to become a parent. That Edward's parents were in their forties when he was born was significant in his attitude to the timing of fatherhood. Edward's and his partner's experiences match life course timing criteria that are known factors influencing childlessness: education level, establishing careers and buying of first home. As David aged, his desire for fatherhood had not waned, and he married a woman twenty-three years his junior who was aware of his desire for fatherhood. David highlighted the significance of the biological clock:

> So we got married and she, at the time, had said that her number one ambition was to have kids. ... So, four and a half years of marriage, not a hint of pregnancy. ... So, I've ended up having married a nice intelligent, interesting person but we haven't come up with the kids, which is disappointing. Which is not to say it won't happen but you know every year that ticks by the probability is getting less.

Becoming a parent was a shared goal for Edward and David and their respective partners. However, a significant difference between Edward and David is their age and life stage, with David having the socio-economic capital to consider parenthood almost immediately. By comparison, Edward and his partner had agreed that they needed to 'settle down' – for example, establish their careers and acquire suitable accommodation before starting a family. John and his partner, who were in their mid-twenties when they became a couple, had a common aim to have children:

> It was not if we had children – it was how many. I said, 'You know, two would be pretty good' but she said, 'Yeah, but four would be better, though.' And I thought, 'Bloody hell, cor, I don't know how I'm gonna deal with four' but I certainly wasn't alarmed or, you know, frightened by the prospect. I just thought, 'Christ, I didn't think life could be this good.'

John and his partner had bought a four-bedroomed house in anticipation of having children. However, two factors affected their plans. First, the country suffered a recession and the mortgage interest rate increased, leading them to delay starting a family.

> You know, we've been working together, you know, to find a suitable place, you know, to be our nest, find a suitable place, get moved in. And then just after we moved in, you know, interest rates, the bloody interest rates hit 13 per cent or whatever it was. So, it needed the two of us to be working and getting in all the overtime that was going just to survive it. So, you know, you weren't pressing somebody to be having a family under those sorts of circumstances, so that, so that made me delay, you know, overtures in those directions.

Second, John's partner became focused on her career. Consequently, it was a few years post-recession, at which point both were in their mid-thirties, when John's awareness of the 'biosocial' clock led him to address the subject of parenthood: 'I said, "C'mon, we really need to make a decision, you know, we just don't want to let time go by and let nature take the decision for us". And so, she said, "Well, I never thought you are responsible enough to have children." Which, I guess, is the time I started drinking seriously.' John's account highlighted his reaction to the complex intersection of events between the macro-level events of national economics, including the increased opportunity for women to develop careers; the micro dynamics of his partner changing her view of him as a potential father; and the biosocial dynamics.

Frank's experience also revealed the significance of the relationship to reproductive outcomes. 'I did quite like her. ... But, you know, I obviously made a mistake there because I misjudged her character completely.' At that time, Frank was 34 and ten years older than his first intimate girlfriend was. They prioritized achieving a stable socio-economic position before considering starting a family. However, the relationship deteriorated over the ten years they were together. Because of the changing internal dynamics of the relationship, Frank felt that he had to take control of the contraception: 'She was on the pill. So, once we were living together, she, you know, she'd suddenly say halfway through sex, "Ooh, I forgot". She just wasn't responsible like that.' Frank and his partner ended their relationship after ten years and it was a further ten years before he started to look for another relationship. During that time, Frank's awareness of not being a father steadily increased: 'It's just something that's gradually increased in my mind, thinking, "Oh, time's running out" and thinking – well one of the reasons I'd like to meet someone younger is because they might have children who might need a father, you know, whoever, might want children, I don't know.'

Frank's experience highlights how the social and biological clocks may apply differently to him compared to any new or younger partner. One aspect of any potential relationship is the possibility of having to negotiate between biological and social father roles. Furthermore, Frank's narrative centred on the timing of relationship forming, dissolution and a new relationship beginning.

Frank was not the oldest man in the study to form a significant relationship. George met his wife when they were 40 and 30 years old respectively.

> I met her when I was 40, so she was 30, and we married a year or two later. But up till, well certainly up till my thirties, I was keen, very keen to find a partner, but never seem to be able to find anyone that it quite worked with until Joan came along and it's been very good.

The participants' experiences highlighted how different factors influenced their childless state, for example, the timing of relationship formation and the choice of partner. Colin had formed an intimate and meaningful relationship with his first wife in his mid-teens, married her and subsequently divorced in his early thirties.

> At age 26, I married my childhood sweetheart after courting for ten years. We were both excellent at sport and both had successful

careers. My first wife did not want to give up work and at the time did not want children (although she went on to have two with her second husband who she left me for). When I was 22 to 33, I would have particularly loved to have children.

One effect of the relationship ending was the long delay until Colin's next intimate relationship. The period between his first and second relationships was critical because it encompassed the biological clock of peer females and increased the significance of the social clock.

> I was devastated by our divorce and went twelve years before I had another serious relationship, aged 45. I married for the second time when I was around 48. I hadn't realized until she told me when we were first intimate that my second wife had previously had surgery to prevent her having children (after having three in a previous marriage).

Alternatives: Relational, Medical and Adoption

The previous section demonstrated how interrelational couple dynamics might lead either partner to change their opinion of the other. John later speculated that his partner's fear of pain had also influenced her view of childbirth. James and Martin's partners also expressed a fear of childbirth (tokophobia). Tokophobia has only relatively recently been classified as a medical condition, and with the dominant pronatalist discourse surrounding women and motherhood at the time, non-compliance would have probably led to stigmatization and exclusion. The lack of a socially acceptable alternative narrative would support non-disclosure of any non-compliance ideation (Hofberg and Brockington 2000; Marcé 1858; Scollato and Lampasona 2013; Zar, Wijma and Wijma 2001). James became aware of an urge to become a parent in his late thirties.

> James: So really it was late thirties when I might've started havin' those inklin's. ... She didn't want children. ... She was very petite; it was just the thought of it – she found quite scary.
>
> R.A.H.: Was that ever said?
>
> James: Yeah. I think it was said, yeah. Yeah, I'm sure she said that.

James's partner made it clear from before they lived together that she did not want children and as a result, he put his considerations aside.

> I think it was when I was gettin' together with Meg and, the fact that she stated that she didn't want children, it sort of concentrated my mind that it was something to think about then. ... And I think that's probably when I first, sorta – by her puttin' a negative, I started givin' it a little bit o' thought, you know? ... I just quickly put that to one side because it had been broached as a subject: I don't think it had ever been broached before, as a subject, with anybody else.

James had stated that he had not been conscious of the pronatalist dominant norm. Conversely, his statement relating to life stages, felt age and awareness of parenthood indicates some level of acknowledgement of it. The relationship ended when James was aged around 50. The ranking of an adult relationship over parenthood may reveal some of the relational dynamics of people classed as 'watchers and waiters', as per Cannold's (2004) categorizations. Moreover, James's reaction to the articulation of the subject highlighted how the option not to have children was taboo. Others were often unaware of their partner's fear of childbirth. For example, Martin only became cognizant of his partner's fear when the relationship was ending.

> We had a good relationship, we spoke a lot to each other, but she never really articulated the fact, until quite later on, that she was just terrified of the thought of childbirth, you know. ... Anyway, that relationship ended in '85. I married my wife in '90 and then we'd tried to have children and that's really, where I've found medically that, yes – you're definitely infertile. (Martin)

The reticence of the partners in declaring their fear of childbirth, with the exception of James's, supported the dominant pronatalist social dynamic. Therefore, it is understandable that the women did not, or could not, express their fear but 'passed' as conforming to the norm. Additionally, they may have believed that, over time, the desire for children would override the fear of childbirth. This was emphasized by James's declaration that he had not previously heard the subject spoken about. Moreover, James referenced both his age and stage of life, and thus drew attention to the relationship between social context and parenthood: the social clock. Martin's experience illustrates the importance of the timing of events: divorce (aged 43) and remarriage (aged 48) followed by a diagnosis of infertility, culminating in acceptance of biological circumstance. Two other men, George and Edward, and their partners also sought help in trying to conceive. Both George and Edward were in their mid-forties to early fifties, and their partners in their mid-thirties to early forties, when accessing infertility treatment.

> When we got to the point of the next stage of the IVF, we just felt, 'I don't think we want to do this' you know? If it happens it happens, if it doesn't, it doesn't. ... We spent a lot of time talking about it because we wanted to be clear what decision we were making and why we were making it. (George)

George and his wife withdrew from treatment early in the process and he emphasized the deliberations surrounding the decision. The influence of their Christian faith on their decision was not directly referred to, but may have given some support during their contemplations.

The impact that IVF treatment has on women and couples has been well documented (see Chapter 1). Men are often distressed by the effects the treatment has on their partner and are frequently the initiators of the decision to end it (Brian 2009; Moulet 2005). As Edward explained, 'We discussed various options but we didn't feel happy about adopting, or perhaps trying fostering, anything like that, and the IVF was very stressful for my partner. The injections and the hospital visits were, were not particularly easy for her so after two cycles we called it a day basically.' Edward and his partner were diagnosed with unexplained infertility and withdrew from treatment after two cycles. Between 30 and 40 per cent of couples in infertility treatment have this diagnosis (Siristatidis and Bhattacharya 2007: 2084). Martin and his second wife discovered that he was infertile after unsuccessfully trying to conceive.

> At that point, I had to think to myself, 'Do I want to have another man's children?' And it took me a while to sort of – get round that. I used to say, 'Well is it better to have none at all, than to have a child you know is not, not yours' ... I think it took a while to accept that but I did, and I thought, particularly for my wife more than anything ... because basically she'd need to fulfil her need to be a mother. So, we had a couple of goes at IVF, donor IVF. But what she went through from the drugs and the playing around with the hormones. And financially we just couldn't afford to do it more than a couple of times. And then we just sat down and said, 'Well if this is the way it's meant to be, then so it is.' I think then everything became very clear and easy. ... We'd have both been very happy if it had worked.

Martin struggled with the thought of donor insemination, and his view of the eugenic hierarchy against what he believed to be his wife's maternal right. His attitude reflected the dominance of the heterosexual pronatalist norm: the primacy of biological fatherhood was set against Martin's view of a woman's 'need to be a mother'. I view this as a negotiation between Martin's sense of self, the societal and cultural norms, economics and the age-related policy of ART treatment. However, at the beginning of the second interview, Martin revealed the emotional complexities that ART involves. Navigating between one's own need and the 'natural' pronatalist norm of parenthood exposed the embeddedness of the latter within the social and cultural structure.

> I made a comment in there that we tried for children artificially and that, you know, I wanted that because of her. And she said, 'Well, it wasn't a big deal for me, I wanted it because of you' [laughter]. So, I said, 'Well, we could have spoken to each other more clearly at the time and saved a lot of money' [laughter]. But that was an interesting, you know, that neither of us at the time, I don't think, realized that was the situation, but there you go.

The importance of parenthood and awareness of the predicted needs of the other is clearly shown in this exchange. Moreover, it highlights how sensitive the subject of parenthood is for both the individual and the couple.

Martin and his wife felt they were too old to be considered as suitable adoptive parents. Only one participant had applied to adopt children. Harry and Helen lived together; he was divorced and she separated from her husband. In the early 1980s, she had been told that she was very unlikely to conceive, and they applied to be considered as adoptive parents.

> We looked at one point many years ago at adoption. ... It was obvious they felt we weren't what they wanted. ... We didn't fit the criteria. I mean they even hammered it down to, they said, 'Do you go to church?' I said, 'No' and they said, 'Well, your partner's very religious' and I said, 'Yes' and they said, 'Well this is, you know, a problem that we find, you're sending a mixed message.'

Harry's experience reflected the societal infrastructure of the period: the difficulty in negotiating a social system that delivered the dominant perspective of marriage. Therefore, neither the relationship nor his partner's health was acknowledged. Frank was attracted to the notion of adopting, but his view of his health and accommodation prevented him from applying:

> I know that they're allowing single men to foster now. Again, there can be problems and I'm aware of the fact that they can be palmed off with some difficult child without 'em knowing it. But I think if my health had been better and I'd had a bigger house, I would've probably looked into the possibility of doing that 'cos you can get paid quite good money for fostering. ... So, it might sound very, very, what's the word, cynical, you know, but I mean if it pays the bills and some child gets looked after, why not?

Frank's speculation demonstrated the changes in policy that have taken place in the UK in the past two decades. For the two gay men, Alan and Raymond, the change in policy and equality legislation highlighted a generational difference between older and younger gay men, with the latter having the opportunity to adopt children.

> Then after he died, I started to think more, I wonder, you know, wouldn't it have been nice to have had children. But, nowadays of course, two men could adopt a child, but then they couldn't. ... I don't say now I'd want children around me every hour of the day now, because I'm nearly seventy and you haven't the patience. ... I wish it was in an enlightened day when me and Paul could have maybe adopted a little child. (Raymond)

Bereavement had caused Raymond to revisit his attitude towards having a family, and there was a sense of regret that the adoption policy changes had arrived too late for him and his partner. This illustrates a generational difference between older and younger LGBT people in the potential identities and roles that are now available. Similarly, Alan noted that if he was younger he might have adopted. 'I think if it could 'appen now, you know, like I say, a young person, obviously not at the age I am now, but if I was in my forties now and I was with a permanent, proper relationship, you know, then I think, yes, I would. I think one could be 'elpful.' Alan also saw his age as a barrier to being an adoptive parent. Conversely, as part of a local school intergenerational project he had experienced being an 'adopted grandfather'.

> Alan: I thought, you know, why, wonderful being granddad, I like that, yes. I could live with that 'cos you didn't have 'em 'ome with you. ... But they still always talk; he always comes down, the young one that still goes... he still comes down, or 'e waves, yells, and 'e always yells 'Granddad'.
>
> R.A.H.: How does that make you feel, when he yells 'Granddad'?

Alan: Erm, make me feel belonged. Makes me feel I'm part of something.

While Alan and Raymond were aware of the recent changes in policy regarding adoption, Michael reflected a different belief. His statement highlighted that the association between parenthood and women was ingrained in policy and meant he was not eligible to adopt: 'Us men can't even adopt. ... I would be quite happy to adopt. ... Of course, I'd want to adopt amazing children. You know, there's a few kids that are just born under a bad sign. ... So, I would want some assurance they weren't.' Michael draws on an idealization of 'amazing children' against those that are 'born under a bad sign'. Consequently, for him, being an adoptive parent was not fully an altruistic proposition. The indication was of a cost-benefit risk analysis that accounted for Michael's awareness of his needs in relation to that of any potential adoptee. George also highlighted the poor experience of a member of his social network who had adopted: 'We discussed adopting and decided we wouldn't. I think Joan was probably more keen than I was but I wasn't that keen. ... We didn't take it very far at all. We had a discussion between us.' George and his wife had withdrawn from IVF in the early stages of treatment. George's view of himself as not having the personal reserves required for adopting a child that needed more than the expected resources was at odds with the confident, self-assured person that otherwise came across during the interview.

> I think we talked with some very old good friends of mine who had had one child and adopted a second child. And there were a lot of big problems and I thought, 'I don't think I want that.' ... I'm not sure I'm a big enough, strong enough, loving enough person to cope, you know? Having seen it at close hand what was going on there, and the pain and the difficulty. I thought, 'I don't think it really is me.'

David's preference not to adopt highlights the different dynamics between couples in similar situations. Moreover, the former couple's decision appeared directly related to the stress of IVF treatment. Furthermore, both men were in their mid- to late forties when this issue was being discussed. David highlighted his preferences for a biological child and the reasons for not adopting:

> I don't know that I would feel the same adopting a child as I would about having one of my own. ... I think, for me, it's more about having our own kids and creating our own family and that is what appeals most to me. ... It's still very important and I'd rather do the

whole job than pick it up half done. Particularly if you're picking up somebody else's kid half done, you'd probably pick up a lot of trouble ... I think it's fair if we have kids of our own but I would not ask her to embark on more than two and I think she might feel one was enough. ... I don't think we would adopt, I don't think we would go for IVF – I don't know, unless my wife suddenly said, 'I'm broody. We must do IVF.'

David's position emphasized his view of the central primacy of the relationship in relation to the biological and social familial forms. This highlighted the reciprocal interconnectedness between individual agency and structure. Stephen, a single man, located adoption firmly in the context of a relationship: 'I'd see, you know, having a child is very much part of being in a relationship, and so for me, first would be the relationship and then the child would follow. ... But the idea of me independently embarking on parenting outside the context of a relationship isn't something I'd consider, no.' Stephen's view was linked to his experience of working with young adults in the care sector. In Russell's case, both his biographical experience and social awareness influenced his perspective: 'You must remember I was fostered. ... Because I was a youth worker, I'd seen a lot of adoptions go wrong. ... I think because of my experiences, I would be very wary about taking on the responsibility of adoption because I know that it's even more stacked against you ...'. Russell's reactions drew on the experiences of others and his view that his desire for fatherhood was limited, and reflected the primacy of the biological imperative. The different views on adoption indicate that although it may seem a logical 'next step', the issues involved connect to deeply personal viewpoints of self, others and social elements.

Summary

This chapter examined the participants' paths to their involuntary childlessness, and highlighted the different elements that influenced it. Following a brief overview of the analysis, the different influences on the participants' childlessness were drawn from their biographical narratives. The interconnection between different elements, such as relationship forming, partner selection, biology and economics, was explored. The chapter has demonstrated the relational dynamics between the men's attempts to negotiate individual desires and beliefs in the context of sociocultural expectations. This

was shown in the interaction between the men and their upbringing, sexual orientation, relationships, age, and social and political
environments. The recognition of the complexity and diversity of
their experience is one of the keys to understanding the experience
of involuntary childlessness. Against the generally held view that
people choose childlessness, the participants' narratives revealed
the different elements that influenced their childlessness: choice of
partner, attitude towards parenthood, economic factors, relationship issues and the timing of transitions.

The dominant pronatalist heteronormative was so pervasive
that of the thirteen participants born post-Second World War,
none could express where their assumptions regarding parenthood
originated. The norm was seen as repeating the example set by
parents: work or university, marriage and children, with the participants occupying the role of breadwinners and providers. While
some happily followed the normative pathway, others were unsure. For example, the normative directive of marriage followed
by children meant that the two gay men, at a relatively early age,
put aside any thoughts of fatherhood. Although the majority had
good familial experiences, the experiences of those who did not
influenced how they viewed themselves and their relational interactions throughout their lives. The timing of transitions such as
entering the workforce and starting and leaving university were
shown to affect relationship formation. The skills needed to facilitate social interaction were demonstrated as having a lifelong effect
on how some of the participants entered and maintained relationships. Moreover, the internal relational dynamics between partners
led to previous agreements to start a family being changed by both
males and females. Furthermore, the age at which men and their
partners attempted to start a family was influenced by both career
choice and opportunity, particularly for female partners, as well as
economics. Some female partners were scared of childbirth, but so
great was the norm for women of marriage and childbearing that
they could not express their fear. However, one woman did make
her tokophobia clear at the start of the relationship, and James set
aside his 'inkling' for parenthood.

Three participants and their partners had to varying degrees accessed Assistive Reproductive Technology (ART) services. All three
men were in their forties when they entered treatment with their
partners, who were in their mid- to late thirties. The two couples
who elected to continue and access IVF treatment both withdrew
after two cycles of treatment. Both men cited the deleterious effect

treatment had on their partner. In addition, the ART treatment was mostly self-funded, and this highlights contemporary issues surrounding access to treatment. In the UK, this relates to the difference in the levels of service offered by health authorities. For example, different acceptance criteria are applied in neighbouring regions regarding age, weight and reproductive status (Fertility Fairness 2018). The age-related policy of access to ART treatment reflected the relationship between an individual's desire and health and social policy. The definition of agency and structure that Ingrid Connidis and Julie McMullin (2002) have proposed did not fully account for the multivalent levels that appeared in participants' narrative. The three participants who accessed fertility treatment were the only men in the study who had had sex with the intention of conceiving a baby. Therefore, one factor in the childlessness of the remaining eleven men in the study was that they did not have sex with this intention.

Some of the men, as they aged, had become aware of the role of grandfatherhood. The role of grandfather had been experienced through four routes: latent, adopted, surrogate and proxy. Others held alternative views on grandfatherhood – for example, that it was a position achieved only through fatherhood, and that not gaining that status was a source of difference and loss (grandfatherhood is examined in Chapter 6). The next chapter will explore issues related to the impact that childlessness had on the men's behaviours, beliefs and relationships.

Chapter 5

Negotiating Fatherhood

Introduction

In this chapter, the influence of childlessness on the participants' lives is examined. Parenthood has been shown to be a complex transition that generates change on many levels, including identity, close and wider relationships, finances, health and social life. I will demonstrate the different positions that the men held with regard to fatherhood and non-fatherhood. My argument supports the view that childlessness should be viewed as a continuum on which individuals may locate themselves at different points and at different times (Monach 1993). By taking account of the life course, I explore the contingencies, differences and similarities of how male involuntary childlessness is experienced. The following sections show the variety of ways in which the men related to not being a father, and how childlessness affected their senses of self and their lives. One of the themes that emerged from the analysis was that while some participants desired to be parents, others were unsure if parenthood was possible, or desirable, while the remainder had rationalized that they were not going to be parents. A pen portrait of each participant, and a short reflective account of each interview, can be found in Appendix 1. The chapter begins by examining the men who wanted to, and believed that they could, be fathers. The second section explores the participants who were contemplating accepting the idea of not being parents, and the third describes the men who have accepted that they will not be fathers.

Aspirational: Fatherhood Wanted

The analysis showed that the men viewed their involuntary child-lessness differently at different points across the life course. The participants' attitude to parenthood ranged from those who wished to be a parent to those who accepted that they would not become biological parents. Table 5.1 shows how the men related to parent-hood in three discrete types. In the first, 'aspirational' group, three men stated the desire to become a father. For example, David detailed his plans on how to negotiate being an older father. Two men formed the 'uncertain' set: both had doubts over the possibility of becoming a father. With the exception of David, the men in these first two groups were single and solo living. The nine remaining participants formed the 'mediated' type. These men had accepted that they were not going to become biological parents and had a 'mediated' perspective based on their experience of different contingencies at different times in their lives. Six of these men were in relationships: this is significant because older men in relationships have better health and well-being than those who are not (Davidson and Arber 2004). Table 5.1 illustrates how it was older men who held a reconciled position to their childlessness.

The 'aspirational' men – Stephen, Frank and David – were some of the younger men interviewed. All three men expressed the desire to be a father, and the impact of this wish was balanced against an awareness of a number of factors: age, relationship and their view of the future. David was the only one of the three in a relationship and had married when he was 55. He had considered the consequences of becoming a father: 'If it really became impractical to juggle even limited part-time work with looking after a baby … I would say, "Right I will stop working, look after the kid", and that becomes my focus.'

David's view highlighted his adaption of the traditional male 'provider' role by drawing on recent discourse surrounding involved fathering. Within his strategy was the acknowledgement of his wife's change in role to become the main breadwinner. The birth of any possible children also had implications on how future age-related social transitions, such as starting school, would impact on David's role in later life: 'You think, "Well, if I produce kids at the age of 61 then by the time they're off to university I'll be 80." That means that all of my retirement will be spent bringing up kids. And if I make it beyond 80, which I hope I will, I mean to fund them through university.'

The focus on adapting the traditional role of breadwinner reflected the association between ageing and decline. David's narrative exposes the theoretical view of the third age as one of freedom from parenthood as grounded in the pronatalist norm. David acknowledged that there was a time limit on the possibility of having children, and how adapting his role as provider and breadwinner took account of his possible death: 'My wife says we don't put enough effort into conception, ... everybody says men's fertility tends to decline, you know, when much past 30. So, we're probably on a ramping down of fertility.' The biological aspects of ageing were reflected in the disclosure of intimate details of the relationship. The effect of ageing on virility and fertility drew on wider media discourse, where the global decline in sperm potency has had wide coverage (Inhorn 2012: 303). Conversely, the decline in sperm efficacy after the age of 35 has only been fleetingly acknowledged in the media.

The non-transition into parenthood also means not accessing the associated social relationships, roles, scripts and status. David went on to express that being childless led to a sense of loss in terms of experiencing the parent–child relationship and the opportunity to share skills and experience: 'It just seems to me that's one of the

TABLE 5.1. Participants' attitudes to fatherhood. Reprinted with permission from Emerald Publishing Limited, reproduced from *Working with Older People*, vol. 22 no. 2 by A.R. Hadley DOI: https://doi.org/10.1108/WWOP-09-2017-0025. © Emerald Publishing Limited, Publication date: 11/06/2018.

Attitude	Participant	Age	Relationship status
Aspirational	Stephen	49	Single
	Frank	56	Single
	David	60	Married
Uncertain	Russell	55	Single
	Michael	63	Single
Mediated	Colin	59	Long-term relationship
	John	59	Long-term relationship
	Edward	60	Long-term relationship
	George	60	Married
	Harry	64	Single/Widower
	James	65	Long-term relationship
	Martin	70	Married
	Raymond	70	Single/Widower
	Alan	82	Single

central experiences of human life and I'm missing out and I think I have something to give and it's a pity. It's one of the challenges of life, which, somehow, I feel I've missed out.' As noted in Chapters 1, 2 and 4, David's views reflected how children are viewed as a focal point and give continuity to life in three ways: first, by continuing the genetic line; second, via the experiences of the child–parent bond across the life course; and finally, through the passing on of one's own experiences, heirlooms and significant items, skills and stories. Consequently, the acknowledgment of ancestry, through the passing on of treasured items, adds to familial, cultural and socio-economic capital. As such, the narrative of previous lives is inherited, not only through the genes but also symbolically through material artefacts. The impact of not having children not only left David in limbo regarding what role he was to take in later life, but also had consequences for hereditary possessions of both form and genetic substance. Therefore, having children liberated a way of being in the present and an acknowledgement of being in the future: 'I think having kids is a way of producing a sense of continuity. Otherwise, death feels very final. If you're leaving kids, you've left something of yourself. ... It's just the sense that you've contributed to their values and their formation and they carry on.'

David's negotiations of the present, and the future, related to his wife's reproductive choices. Stephen and Frank were both single. Therefore, their need was to be in a relationship with a partner willing to have children, or one who had children already. Stephen and Frank's awareness of fatherhood related to their cognizance of the biosocial clock. Stephen only became aware of the impact of his involuntary childlessness in his early forties, when he changed his lifestyle because of its deleterious effect on his mental and physical health. Subsequently, he reviewed and regretted his earlier style of life.

> So that lifestyle was very connected with drinking and, so in terms of my health, it was taking its toll. The slow process of coming out of that life coincided with the realization that I was single, not married, not in a relationship, and more importantly, haven't had kids. So, the concept of being fatherless is a new phenomenon to me, only that it's happened in the last five years or six years, but it's been significant, and, you know, quite devastating really.

Stephen compared himself against the 'package deal' social ideal, with the realization of the importance of *not* being a father having a significant impact. This order of relationship preference goes against the generally expressed view of the primacy of the adult-to-adult relationship. The bearing of his adult lifestyle led Stephen to look for a partner that would be interested in settling down into a long-term relationship and starting a family. As demonstrated in Chapters 1 and 2, the biological and social clocks are equally important to reproductive intentions and desires. Stephen's age had affected at least two other recent intimate relationships with younger women:

> I only want to meet people who I can have a relationship with. And I've found that they see my age as a deficit. ... I met someone last year, but she indicated that she'd go back to her ex-husband, rather than pursue something with me. She definitely implied that there was an age factor in that decision as well.

Stephen's experience highlights the complexity in negotiating age, biological primacy and social mores. Not being in a relationship with a possibility of reproduction influenced his intentions and plans regarding becoming an older father.

> How do I see the future? You know, it's not looking favourable in terms of having children now unless I got very, very lucky, I'd say. ... Not because biologically that'd be a problem because I could still, you know, father a child. Being an older father wouldn't necessarily bother me, although I'd wonder what the impact of that might be on the child when they're getting older and I'm then getting much older. But it's less about that and more about whether, you know, I could find a viable partner who would even want to have children with someone of my age.

Stephen did not acknowledge the link between age and decline in sperm potency. However, he demonstrated age-related awareness that any partner would have to be younger than he was – the 'bio-social' clock. Although Stephen recognized that his age could have an effect on any future child, there were no plans or strategies regarding any future father role. His focus was on the immediate and near future.

Whereas David had always expected to be a father, it was only as Frank reached his mid-fifties that he became aware of a desire for fatherhood. Being 'on' or 'off' time, with regard to social expectations, has significant implications in social contexts and for the well-being of the individual (see Chapter 2). All three men articulated an awareness of missing the parent–child relationship, as exemplified by Frank:

> I've become, sort of, more aware then of how nice it can be to have children, you know, from the families and the people I know. ... It's just something that's gradually increased in my mind, thinking, 'Oh, time's running out.' ... So that's probably one of the reasons I feel I've sort, over, twelve, fifteen years, I've missed out.

The timing of the dissolution of Frank's relationship, and the length of time before he realized that he was 'off time' compared to peers, were critical in influencing his attitude to fatherhood. It is not only the timing of entry and exit of relationships that has an effect on procreative outcomes; other structural factors, such as finance and location, do too.

> It's because 35, 40-year-old women tend not to want a 56-year-old man. ... I'm trapped on benefits, with the lack of jobs, and first of all you think, 'Well, okay, I'll get something.' ... My health problems got worse and you realize everything's against you. ... But as I say, just living in a rural village in Wales, you know, I'm not gonna find them very easily. (Frank)

Stephen and Frank both expressed similar views regarding the biosocial clock in terms of finding a suitable partner because of their age. In addition, Frank reflected on other factors that he felt had contributed to his lack of success in finding a partner. Economic status, health and geographic location all influenced Frank's perspective on his ability to find a partner. Stephen, living in a city, did not see location as a problem in accessing potential partners. Frank was also positive about managing his health and being a father. In this way, he negotiated the social clock that related age to age-appropriate roles (at the time of the interview, he would have been 71 in fifteen years' time): 'Also, with my health, you know, there again, I wouldn't let that put me off. I mean, you don't have to play football, you know, with your child until he or her is 15.' Frank's attitude ran counter to the general view expressed by the participants that at an unspecified, age-related cut-off point, the role of father was deemed unsuitable and that of grandfather became more appropriate. Frank's awareness of his position as an older single man was reflected in the challenge involved in becoming a father.

> Maybe it's a really stupid idea to want to be a father; maybe there's just so much hassle with it, so I don't know. All I can do is try it. I'm not gonna know unless I try it, am I? ... And I'm also aware that if

I had loads of money and I was famous, I probably would easily be able to have a partner and father. All these celebrities, you know, women seem to get in touch with these men who are a lot older than themselves.

Frank's dialogue reveals a perception of modern culture that located both men and women as following traditional heteronormative roles: women were attracted to men who displayed virility in economic or social environments and therefore reflected a successful breadwinner or provider identity. Frank highlighted the challenges he felt in forming a new relationship and alluded to not quite knowing how to be in the world: 'I don't know how to approach women; I'm always wary about … putting a foot wrong 'cos it all seems so sensitive nowadays. I'm thinking about writing an article now about how is a man supposed to be a man.' Frank viewed himself as being different from his contemporaries, based on the projection that having procreated and been socio-economically successful, they would guarantee their continuity by becoming grandfathers. In taking this view, Frank highlighted the future discontinuity that not being a father would bring. The potential of a role and relationship in later life was an additional difference between Frank and his peers: 'I see myself in such a different category as other people that it's hard to imagine that the people I was at school with are grandfathers and have completely different lives really to me and they're coming up to retirement from good jobs. … You know, if you don't have children, you're not gonna have grandchildren.'

The different perspectives of these three participants highlight the influence of their relationship status on their opportunity to become fathers. Only David was in a relationship where there was an agreement regarding parenthood. Both Frank and Stephen were seeking suitable partners, but they were both conscious of their age and expressed a sense of time being limited. Similarly, David also indicated that time was a dwindling resource. All three men had acknowledged age as a factor that would affect their roles as a father, with David replacing the 'hands-on' provider role with a 'facilitator' role. Frank had rationalized the physical interaction with children to a particular age: 15 years. Conversely, Stephen had noted, but not articulated in depth, that there may be implications in being an older father.

Uncertain: Fatherhood in Limbo

Two single men, Michael and Russell, held no active views on becoming a father, but neither did they state that they would definitely
not become fathers. Michael was employed full-time as teacher in a
school in Thailand, and Russell, a former business consultant, was
seeking employment. Both men expressed that they were missing
the uniqueness and importance of the father–child relationship.
Michael touchingly envisaged the quality of such a relationship
and suggested that his position as a teacher provided a form of
that interaction: 'To have that sense of unconditional love and
that unfathomable sense of that paternal feeling that only comes
with having a child. The child that hugs you, leans against you, sits
on your knee, looks at you, holds your hand, all those things, the
sense of trust.' Consequently, his employment, and the relational
context that it brought, may have affected his motivation to seek
fatherhood: 'If I'd worked in a job that was completely bereft of
children, then my desire to enjoy their company might have been
much, much more, and led me to get married and have children.'

Michael expressed his awareness of the biosocial clock in his deliberation on the negotiation of his present position. He did not
know whether his opportunity to become a father had receded, or
whether there was still a prospect of fatherhood: 'If my mind does
wander to what might have been or what might be then it is still
with that one thought: can I have a child at my age now?' In relating his uncertainty to his age, Michael also questioned his fertility
and how, consequently, potential partners and others viewed him.
In addition, he made the importance of his relationship with students, and his fear of losing that interaction, very clear. As such, his
work with the pupils provided him with a fundamental relationship which, should it cease, would severely affect how he located
himself and his being in the world: 'I've been saying to people that
the children give me oxygen and I still love their company. I'm ter-
rified of not having that teacher–student relationship.'

Thailand is viewed as a country that is very tolerant of non-heterosexuals, and it has an established sex tourism industry. However,
the majority of the population is both Buddhist and strongly con-
servative (Research Directorate 2008). As a result, Michael felt that
as an older, single, solo-living man, he had to defend himself from
being viewed as a sex tourist. Consequently, in social situations, he
felt that he had to explain first that he was not gay, and second that
he did not have a wife or girlfriend. He speculated that if he were

seen with a woman and children, he would then be viewed with the respect that came from fulfilling the patriarchal norm.

> If I was to walk down the street with a Thai woman that would be immediately seen as she must be a prostitute. If I walk down with a Thai woman and with two children, then I'm suddenly elevated to, 'Ah, wonderful!' You know, he's a father. ... I relax people by letting them know that I'm not gay when they ask where's my, you know, am I married?

Michael's narrative highlights subordination, as determined by hegemonic masculinity. The hierarchy within the subordinated set was such that determining his heterosexuality gave him more approval than being judged gay. Russell also raised the aspect of isolation, with particular reference to older men. Loneliness in later life has been strongly connected to being vulnerable to poorer outcomes in mental and physical health, well-being and social interactions (see Chapters 1 and 2). The paucity of information regarding involuntarily childless people was emphasized by Russell not knowing of anyone else having his experience. The successful compliance with the dominant pronatalist discourse was seen in commonplace exchanges.

> People with kids just have got no conception of how alienated people like me, presuming there are people like me, feel. Obviously when couples get older they have a whole raft of experiences, you know, first day at school, whooping cough, or whatever it is that bonds them, and that shuts out all sorts of other stuff from their lives. If you haven't had those experiences, you're shut out along with everything else. ... People just talking, you know, at work, they talk about their kids; they talk about their experiences raising their family. ... All this stuff that you don't know about, but you're on the fringe, you haven't experienced, that is alien to you.

Russell highlighted how the difference between parents and the involuntarily childless was underscored in everyday social interaction. Not being privy to the experience and subsequent shared social bond affected Russell's identity. His experience fits with research that shows involuntarily childless people as having a sense of 'outsiderness' (see Chapter 1). The pronatalist ideal places great emphasis on the role of women as maternal and nurturing. Accordingly, caring, emotional roles have not been associated with men, and the concomitant impact of childlessness on men has not been recognized. This was demonstrated by Russell's anger at the lack of recognition of the impact of his childlessness. He went on to argue that although sociocultural infrastructure regarding family was changing, for instance concerning recognition of paternity leave, it was still weighted towards women.

> I think it is easier for a woman to have a family than it is for a bloke. ... But if a woman wants a bloke, she can go out and get one. ... There is still a societal support mechanism for women to have a family, you know, it's the women that get custody. Okay, it's changing, but it ain't changed that much. ... It's laughable to suggest that the same options are available to men as they are to women.

Russell's comments point towards the degree to which the pronatalist agenda is embedded within the social system. How an individual perceives themselves in relation to such an environment was demonstrated by Russell's view of his present and future situation. One of the impacts for Russell of not becoming a parent was frustration based on not knowing how he would have performed as a father. The potential father element of the self remains unexamined, but is contextualized by the reported experience of an ideal type. 'I'll never know whether I could've done it or not. You don't know. I mean men that I've known that are very macho change.' The awareness of the social clock was also evident in Russell's rationalizing of his own situation regarding fatherhood, as well as the wider discourse on older biological fathers:

> Now I'm 55, fifteen years have gone and, in the back of my mind, the candle's been going, or the light's been getting dimmer and dimmer and dimmer of me ever being a father, to the point now where as I say, it's probably not gonna happen. ... I think there does get to be a point of no return. It's not just women that have got biological clocks. You hear about John Humphreys having had a child in his seventies, or whatever, and it does happen, but that's very much the exception.

A consequence of Russell's social withdrawal following his divorce was that he only recently acknowledged that one of the implications of his behaviour was the consideration of not becoming a father. Nonetheless, he was objective about both the possibility of his becoming a father and the media celebration of older fathers. The latter can be seen as the promotion, and maintenance, of masculinity, through the patriarchal privilege of virility being proved by fertility.

Russell evaluated the influence of not becoming a father and re-flected on the well-being of people close to him. In contemplating his future, he had realized that with the legacy of non-fatherhood came an additional layer of grief: the loss of grandfatherhood. 'First thing is that, my own demise is becoming more real. More importantly, the very few people that are significant others to me are very close now to their demise and that makes me extremely anxious. ... I'm also grieving that, just as I won't have the paternal role, I won't have the grandfather role either.' Russell's assessment of his position reveals the complex intersections between how one locates oneself within a social network and one's view of oneself as one ages. The disenfranchised grief of involuntary childlessness was compounded by the loss of a future role and highlighted the loss that may surround ageing.

Michael and Russell highlighted a sense of loss surrounding be-ing involuntarily childless, and showed how not being a parent contributed to various feelings, particularly 'outside', 'different' and 'alienated' lives. In addition, there was an indication that the legacy of childlessness was accessed in the present and in the future ways of being. With parenthood comes the knowledge of continuity, and with involuntary childlessness comes the knowledge of non-con-tinuity of genetic legacy, role and identity. Russell's last statement indicated the grief involved with beginning to accept non-father-hood. I propose that he was on the cusp of the beginning of the journey into the mediated phase. He argued that older fathers were the exception and that men had biological clocks, and expressed his regret over the likely loss of father and grandfather roles.

The next section examines the impact of involuntary childless-ness on the men who had indicated acceptance that they were not going to be fathers.

Mediated: Fatherhood Negotiated

Nine men formed this group, and all suggested that they accepted they were not going to become fathers. The elements surrounding that decision, and any subsequent effects, will now be explored. Three of the men related their acceptance of their childlessness to unsuccessful infertility treatment and three related it to a particular age. As discussed in Chapter 4, Alan and Raymond assumed at an early age that they would not be fathers due to the sociocultural dynamic regarding homosexuality. Harry related his decision both to his partner's health and to their withdrawal from the adoption process. For Harry, the impact of being childless was connected to his grieving over his partner's death some two years previously: if they had had children, then he would still have a connection with his partner, Helen. Furthermore, the sense of loss was compounded by the disenfranchised grief of involuntary childlessness. Although the loss of his partner was acknowledged through ritual and ceremony, the loss of future parental roles remained less visible and unacknowledged. One of the consequences of childlessness for Harry was that he was aware of the loss of social capital:

> I always imagined I would have children. ... It became something that we accepted, we didn't fight round it. The biggest regret based on that that – and it's not from what might happen to me down the road – is that I would have liked some part of Helen to still be here. ... The real loss is – there is nothing of her, you know, if you have a child there would be a part of Helen still walking the streets. ... And I – that really, that sits there: that sits in my heart and my head. ... I mean if we'd had a son and a daughter I could say, 'Well look, there's a part of Helen walking about.' ... You know. I'm never going to be able to say this is my grandson, am I?

The effect of his partner's death was reflected in Harry's experience of his interactions with his friends and neighbours. Although Harry had been well supported after his loss, he now believed that as an older single man, he had to change his behaviour with children. During his partner's lifetime, children were welcomed freely into the home, but now he feels he has to guard against being viewed as a paedophile. Harry's story demonstrated the depth of the association between 'women and nurturing' and the heteronormative. Moreover, it highlighted a concern that the majority of the men in the study alluded to: the fear of being viewed as a paedophile.

> I've got a couple of really good mates. Wonderful neighbours in this street. ... Now, there's loads and loads of really young children along this street. ... some like to come in and play with the dogs. And you have to say, 'No! Look go and get your dad.' ... It's things that bother you – I'd hate someone to look saying, 'Watch that old man, always got kids round him.' ... And I don't want anyone looking at me thinking that.

Harry's mediated view of his childlessness had occurred as a combination of timing, reaction to medical diagnosis and the failure in the attempt to adopt. The loss of his partner disturbed his preferred order of events: that he would die first and leave Helen and any children provided for. In addition, he viewed his future against loneliness, poor well-being and a society he did not recognize:

> And, always at the back of my mind was that ... that I wasn't going to leave her a mess, when the heart attack took me and I was gone. ... The one concern I have in life is longevity. I don't want to, to be old. ... The thought of modern-day Britain and being that old person living all on your own is not where I want to be.

Harry's experience highlighted the hierarchy of relationships, as noted in Chapter 4, wherein the most valued was one of an intimate adult nature, followed by children. Therefore, the loss of the prime relationship compounded an awareness of loss, with the absence of children accentuating that loss.

Three other men and their partners had sought medical assistance in their attempts to become fathers. In all three cases, the decision not to continue with treatment was a joint one that was thoroughly explored. As George got older, he noticed that being childless had made a difference in his work environment, on three levels. First, the social environment: he did not feel that he fitted in with the social activities of his younger teacher colleagues. Second, he did not 'fit' with his peer cohort because he was not a parent. Finally, he wondered if the experience of being a parent would have given him some deeper insight into the parental world.

> As I got older I no longer belonged to this younger group of teachers. I couldn't do all the things that they wanted to do, and I didn't want to, but I also didn't belong to the families group. ... It would have added to my ability to be a teacher if I had had the experience of being a parent because I would see where parents were coming from.

For the involuntarily childless, the sense of grief and loss was compounded by the lack of societal acknowledgement, and the absence of social rules that governed what constituted legitimate grief.

> We actually decided to have a little ceremony to create something between us to symbolically mark the fact that we were not going to pursue this any further. ... We created a box where we put together all the stuff about the IVF and the whole thing and we painted it together. We did a little ceremony with some very close friends of ours.

In contrast to most of the participants, who found difficulty in legitimizing their childlessness, George and his wife Joan marked their joint decision not to pursue IVF treatment with the joint creation of a 'memory box'. The end of the pursuit of parenthood was acknowledged by the performance of a ceremony that was witnessed by two close friends. That ending was recognized by the construction of a customized ritual that was both intimate and shared. The acknowledgement of the ending of the pursuit of parenthood places George in the mediated group. However, as George aged, he had become increasingly aware of the difference between himself and parents:

> You know I would see the relationship between a father and son, or a father and a daughter, and I was thinking, 'Ah! I'm never really going to get that.' I knew, you know, I miss that. So, lots during the last fifteen years or so they'd be more little experiences like that where – sudden sort of painful experiences – that I'm missing out on: I'm not having that.

Although George had accepted that he was not going to have children, there was an indication of an ongoing loss that was drawn from appreciating the relationship and interactions between adults and children. George's reflections identify the loss of the child–father bond and the experience of fathering. The latter may reflect the increased discourse that surrounds contemporary fatherhood (Dermott 2003; Doucet 2006; Letherby 2016). George's narrative illustrates that how an individual reacts to their childlessness varies across time and is influenced by internal and external events. This supports my contention, made in regard to the 'mediated stage', that self-identity is negotiated through a complex process involving not only what one is but also what one is not.

Edward was also firmly in the mediated group, having jointly decided with his partner, Lois, to end IVF treatment. This was followed by a period of grieving, which included the loss of many friends who were parents from their social network. However, forming relationships with people in similar circumstances through joining the 'More-To-Life' (MTL) infertility support group helped strengthen their wider social contacts. Consequently, the reconstruction of their social infrastructure involved both unintentional and intentional change: 'It is noticeable that friends who have children drift away; they get into other circles of other friends who've got children and that's been very marked. ... Through More-to-Life, we have met people who are in exactly the same situation, and so we're similar and we come together.' Edward highlighted that his own emotional reactions to peers who became parents led him to feel anger, envy and jealousy. His experience highlighted the value placed on fulfilling the pronatalist norm and how integral this is to one's identity. Edward's reaction demonstrated the depth and the complexity of social loss:

> One of my friends, who was the same age as me and had his family at the same time we would've, perhaps, had ours. ... I was hugely jealous of him. I just shut him out, you know, I didn't wanna see him. ... He is probably who I see most of all, now, after that period of not wanting to see him.

The degree of emotion he felt led him to withdraw from some close relationships, although in some cases the relationship was later re-established. However, the process was mutual in that some people withdrew from his circle, or he withdrew from theirs. The lack of any social framework or acknowledgement meant that Edward had no vehicle to help him rationalize and negotiate the depth of his reaction.

The use of the term 'involuntarily childless' is generally associated with those whose infertility treatment has been unsuccessful. Edward defined himself as involuntarily childless through information he received from the support group More-To-Life. In addition to providing support through facilitating contact with similar others, MTL also supplied the means, through language, for an individual to adapt their identity. As Edward's experience illustrates: 'The phrase "involuntarily childless" has really been in our minds since More-to-Life because it is a phrase that they use in their material. ... The description of involuntarily childless still goes back to your original intent of wanting parenthood and it being denied.' Edward stressed that he felt it was important for others to know of his desire for fatherhood and the loss associated with not becoming a parent: 'When they ask me if I've got children of my own, or if I'm a dad, or whatever, I normally say, "Regrettably, no." I do let people know who've asked me that I would've wanted children, but I don't have them.' Interestingly, both Edward and Michael used a similar social strategy of identifying themselves by what they are not.

Following unsuccessful donor insemination treatment, Martin accepted that he was not going to become either a biological or social father. In line with the cases of George and Edward, the decision to stop treatment was a joint one with his wife. Martin highlighted two factors that contributed to that decision: the medical process

and his wife's fertility. He also drew on the social clock, which reflected a social norm of age, capacity to parent and role of carer:

> We accepted that that was the way it was gonna be, but we found
> a happy way of life. ... Once you get to a point in life where there's
> nothing you can do about it anyway. If somebody said to me you can
> have a child today, my thought would be, 'Well do I want a 20-year-
> old to have a 90-year-old father?' And the answer is no because
> that's just screwing up someone else's life, you know.

In his description of his 'coming to terms' with not having children,
Martin highlighted three elements of the process. Two were opera-
tionally related, as one is the consequence of the other: denial and
acceptance. Martin saw these as key in his reaction towards not
becoming a father. The third was a form of 'bargaining': rationalizing his emotional response against a fatalistic scale. As a result, the
sorrow of childlessness was used to map his emotional position:

> You've gone through the process of accepting that you won't have
> children, and that's a bit of an emotional tempering, if you like.
> What's the worst thing that can happen? Not having children – that's
> pretty bad. What's worse in comparison? Perhaps it gives you an
> emotional benchmark. ... So, once you've got over the denial bit,
> 'Yes I'm, I'm really not gonna have children.' ... Then you can get to
> the acceptance bit and, eventually, you can come out of the other,
> the other side of it. It's something I will never stop regretting. You
> know, it won't go away.

The eventual acceptance, nuanced in the context of the paradoxical
legacy of not being a father, was one of both acceptance and lament.
This reflects the contemporary view of grief as a challenge to identity, which involves reconstruction and change to form a post-loss
position. All the participants who related their involuntary childlessness to ART treatment went on to describe that although they
could identify a reason for their decision, one of the impacts of not
being a father was an ongoing negotiation of that loss. Therefore,
although parenthood gave a legacy in the present, and tangibly in
the future, the legacy of involuntary childlessness is in the present,
and involves the negotiation of the missing relationship between
self, possible self and other.

Common between all the men was an awareness of the social
norms surrounding the appropriate age for parenthood. For example, Martin had highlighted the inapposite position of being an
'old-old' father to a young child. Three men correlated their age and

the dynamics of their intimate relationship as the point of acceptance of non-fatherhood. For example, Colin knew that he was not going to become a biological father when his then spouse informed him on their wedding night that she had been sterilized. The effect of not being a father was expressed as a deeply significant core regret: 'Since I was about 47, I accepted that it won't happen. ... When I realized my second wife couldn't have children. ... You think you have missed the most important part of life.' All the participants shared a similar sense of a fundamental remorse.

Awareness of the 'biosocial' clock influenced James and John's acceptance of not becoming fathers, regarding their specific age, their partner's reproductive capability and the dynamics of their respective relationships, as outlined by James:

> I met Liz [partner], who has a grown-up family and plus which she was no longer able to have children anyway 'cos she was kinda 51 then, you know. ... So that was the end of that in a way, you know. ... The alternative would 'a been to, you know, look for a younger woman 'cos I was 52 so it would be somebody not in my age group, you know. Then there's the consequent possibilities of problems, you know, with women in their late forties, you know.

James's decision to accept involuntary childlessness was based on four considerations: first, his age – 48 when his previous relationship had ended. Second, age and generational differences were considerations against seeking a younger, fertile partner. Third were the risks involved with pregnancy in older women. Finally, his current partner was post-menopausal and already had biological children. James's views reflected both the heterosexual norm surrounding pregnancy in later life and the fertility and virility-based assumption of lifelong fertility. James's experience also shows both the importance of the timing of entry and exit of relationships and partner selection. John related the impact of his childlessness directly to his poor health. He started drinking heavily after his partner decided she did not want to consider parenthood with him. His behaviour can be linked to the denial and anger stages of the grief model: 'Just, you know, felt so devastated that, you know, I just drank to anaesthetize myself.' The consequence of John's drinking was several related medical conditions, including Type 2 diabetes and the associated problem of erectile dysfunction (ED). John built a mediated perspective that balanced his partner's refusal to have children with him, his low self-esteem and the lifestyle that his partner's status provided. In addition, he supported his position by counterpointing the masculine ideals of virility and risk-taking, highlighting his lack of virility and fear of exacerbating his position:

> You have to try and accept the situation for what it is. I mean, she earns a very good amount of money, so in that sense I have a very good life. You know, I'm not going to get involved in a serious relationship with anybody it just ain't going to happen, is it? I mean for a start off this ED is not really much of an advantage is it? ... You know, you'd have to be pretty bloody sure to not make your own life even worse.

The sexual orientation of the two oldest men, Raymond and Alan, ran counter to the heteronormative diktat that was dominant at the time of their upbringing. During their formative years (see Chapter 4) they dismissed any thoughts of fatherhood and moved into a mediated position. Their experience was an example of the different timing for moving into the mediated period. The death of Raymond's long-term partner, Peter, some eight years ago led Raymond to reflect on his life and debate his reasons for wanting to have a parental or grandparental relationship. Raymond reveals a similar narrative to Harry in that the loss of his partner emphasized the loss of other possible relationships.

> I don't know whether I missed as much at the stage not having any because I had what I wanted and I had somebody and I was quite content with life. Then after he died, I started to think more, wouldn't it have been nice to have had children. ... Am I being selfish or am I thinking because I get fed up or I'm being lonely, is that why I want children, somebody of my own to love and little grandchildren to come pottering round to see me?

Raymond felt that he did not have the patience or energy to be a full-time parent, but did regret not interacting with children. Moreover, he was aware of an age-related reduced capacity to deal with children. However, his workplace provided not only adult social contact and money, but also a form of intergenerational relationship:

> I don't say I'd want children around me every hour of the day now, because I'm nearly seventy and you haven't the patience. ... I think in a way of the two little ones in the pub as the grandchildren I've never had. ... I don't say that in the pub to anybody, I don't even let them know it, or their dad. Their dad wouldn't mind, but I don't want people saying, 'Oh, he's a bit of a paedophile, this one, looking at the kids.' You know?

Raymond's narrative revealed the complexity in the relationship between an individual's interpretation of their place in society, and the societal parameters formed by accepted and expected behaviour, age appropriateness and gender role. Alan had never wanted to be a father, but an experience in the recent past drew his attention to the possibility of a role as social grandfather. Although both men had from their teenage years been excluded from the role of fatherhood, in later life they had been alert to alternative roles available to them. The cognizance of roles such as that of social grandfather will be discussed in the next chapter. The men in the mediated stage highlighted the complexity of their experience of involuntary childlessness. The effect of childlessness was uniquely felt, in varying intensities and at different times across the participants' life course. Moreover, it may have accentuated other losses, as the central loss, or the focus of grief, varies in relation to time and circumstance.

A view widely expressed by the participants was an awareness of age and its impact on fatherhood: many of the men noted that a child would not want to be associated with an 'old' father. David's awareness of time meant considering that in the next five years, he would have to accept that he was not going to become a father: 'Well the future is fine. I might make it until 95 but, or even 100. ... But, you know, it will be another five years it would be fairly clear we're not going to have kids.' Moreover, Martin's observation was typical and pointed towards a relationship between how age and role are viewed, indicating a demarcation between father and grandfather in the phases of the social clock: 'And once you get to 50 then it ceases to be tenable because nobody wants a 70-year-old father when you're 20. You know, that's grandfather age when you're 20.' Conversely, Frank's statement earlier in the chapter highlighted that conformity to social norms was dependent on individuals' interpretation of, and adaption to, those strictures. The two different positions taken by Frank and Martin to age-determined criteria surrounding the role of fatherhood may be seen as integral to their aspirational and mediated standpoints, respectively. For the gay men, the changes in equality law and social mores over the last few decades gave them an opportunity to consider their roles in later life. Therefore, the timing of wider social change – for example, gay men being able to adopt – meant that alternative narratives in later life, such as grandfatherhood, could be considered. Continuity was seen in the passing on not only of knowledge and skills, but also of heirlooms. However, this was seen as reinforcing an element of loss of connectivity between generations. The breaking of the link between the previous generation and the next was another node of loss, not in only in terms of paternal beneficence and possible economic gain, but also in highlighting discontinuity.

Summary

This chapter has examined the participants' relationships to fatherhood. The analysis found evidence in the men's narratives to support the notion of negotiation between the individual and the ideal of fatherhood and its concomitant roles and status. But the acceptance of childlessness was shown not to be linear: each participant's response was influenced by interpersonal, intrapersonal and wider social factors. The change of state was divided into three categories: 'aspirational', 'uncertain' and 'mediated'. The aspirational group consisted of three men who still desired to be fathers. All three had different concerns regarding their desires and intentions towards fatherhood. All were aware of the social expectations concerning the age appropriate for parenthood. Similarly, those in the second group were concerned about their age and the factors that influenced their relationship with fatherhood. The final, and largest, group had negotiated a nuanced acceptance of involuntary childlessness. This group demonstrated the contingencies that influenced their viewpoints and the many and complex intersections between the individual and wider social relationships and processes. Underpinning all was the negotiation of the self in relation to the dominant norms of heterosexuality and pronatalism.

The intersection of social and biological factors, in addition to the primacy of an adult relationship over a parental type, highlighted the complex arena that encompassed the relationship to involuntary childlessness. The concept of the 'third age', as a time of freedom between the end of parenthood and the 'decline' of the 'fourth age', was seen to reflect the unquestioned pronatalist norm. A key element of the process was the participants' view of their age in relation to social expectations. The majority of the men indicated a social-clock element to their view of fatherhood. For example, there was an age when fatherhood was deemed inappropriate, and when grandfatherhood was the more appropriate role. Moreover, the men spoke of 'missing out' on, for example, the father–child relationship. Even those who had gone through infertility treatment tended to use the word 'missing' rather than the vocabulary of loss, bereavement or grief. Although infertility research places men as not being as emotionally affected as women, I would suggest that men do have an emotional and long-lasting reaction. As with disenfranchised grief (Corr 2004; Doka 2002), there is a lack of recognition of men's loss of identity, role and emotional experience. In addition, there were few societal resources available for the men to draw on as an aid to reconstructing their view of self.

The majority of infertility literature highlights a trajectory of grief that ends with a sense of completeness. Conversely, this study highlighted the complex and enduring nuances of loss and loneliness that all the participants expressed. All the men expressed a fear of being viewed as a paedophile; the widowers and single men expressed this most strongly. One of the themes that emerged from the analysis was how the participants negotiated their relationship with the fatherhood ideal, from desiring parenthood to recognition of not being a parent. Older men in relationships have been shown to have better health and socio-economic outcomes than solo-living men of equal status (Dykstra and Keizer 2009; Keizer, Dykstra and Poortman 2009). This study revealed the complexities of intra-relationship dynamics and how they both influenced and were influenced by procreative desires and intentions. The current discourse surrounding older men highlights a number of issues: discrimination, health, loneliness and relationships (Cruz 2003; Davidson and Arber 2004; Guasp 2011). However, specialist support groups for both the involuntarily childless and older LGBT people have been seen to have positive effects in 'closest', 'inner' and 'wider' circles. The following chapter explores the intersections between age, relationships, social network and well-being.

Chapter 6

RELATIONSHIPS AND SOCIAL NETWORKS

Introduction

The focus of this chapter is on an exploration of the relationships that form the participants' social networks. The social 'embeddedness' of individuals is concomitant with their social capital and the dynamics that influence the formation, maintenance and continuance of their social networks (de Jong Gierveld 2003; Victor, Scrambler and Bond 2009). Communities formed by kith and kin are extremely important in lived experience, giving a sense of conscious connectivity between past, present and future, in addition to place and role (Arber, Davidson and Ginn 2003; Davidson 1998; de Jong Gierveld 2003). Moreover, the composition of social networks reflects the interaction across time between age, gender, sexual orientation, class, economics, employment, religious activities, leisure, health, location and relationships at all levels. The terms 'vertical' and 'horizontal' are used in this section to represent the participants' family networks (Bengtson, Rosenthal and Burton 1990; Bengtson 2001). The former refers to grandchildren, children, parents and grandparents, and the latter traditionally refers to siblings and cousins, although I am extending the concept to include all other relationship ties. For the purposes of collecting the experiences of the different dynamics of people's relationships, I used three categories of relationship: 'closest', 'inner' and 'wider'. 'Closest' indicates a relationship of complete trust, typified by a long-term intimate adult relationship where, for example, complete trust is assumed. The 'inner' circle is one where trust is a priority, and there may be a formal aspect or duty involved, such as that of a godparent. The last category, 'wider', incorporates those with informal connections, such as people with a shared interest.

In the previous chapter, I demonstrated how the participants' attitudes to parenthood changed over time and in response to individual circumstances. For example, choice of partner, timing of and reaction to relationship dissolution, health and the decision to end IVF treatment contributed to each participant's involuntary childlessness. Similarly, the opening section in this chapter highlights the factors that shaped both the formation and quality of the participants' social networks across the life course. The following section examines the different constructions of social networks of those with and those without partners. The section after that explores the 'fictive' relationships that were in operation. This chapter reveals the complex structure, dynamics and interactions involved in forming, and maintaining, different types of relationships. The sample divided equally into two groups: seven with partners and seven without. The results record some similarity with previous research, in showing the centrality of the partner for those in adult intimate relationships (Bennett 2005; Davidson 1998; Davidson and Meadows 2009; Gabb et al. 2013; van den Hoonaard 2010). As Brian Heaphy (2007: 202) has noted, the mediation of male heterosexuals' relational and emotional connectedness through their partners or wives highlights the situation of non-heterosexuals in later life. Figure 6.1 illustrates the participants' social networks by 'closest', 'inner' and 'wider' categories.

Family Practices and Social Relationships

The analysis highlighted a number of factors that influenced the social networks of the participants across the life course: familial structure and relationship quality, location, and entry to and exit from employment. The influence of the participants' familial circumstances had an important effect on all levels of social relations, but more so on the 'closest' and 'inner' relationships. John was the only member of the seven men with partners not to nominate his partner as his 'closest' relationship. He had been living with Sue for approximately thirty-six years; however, as discussed in Chapters 4 and 5, John felt that their relationship had lost its core. At the time of the interview, in addition to a number of chronic health conditions, John's mobility was restricted because he had cellulitis in his lower left leg. Due to his poor health, he was not available for employment. John's health had directly influenced his ability to socialize, and consequently his social network was formed by his

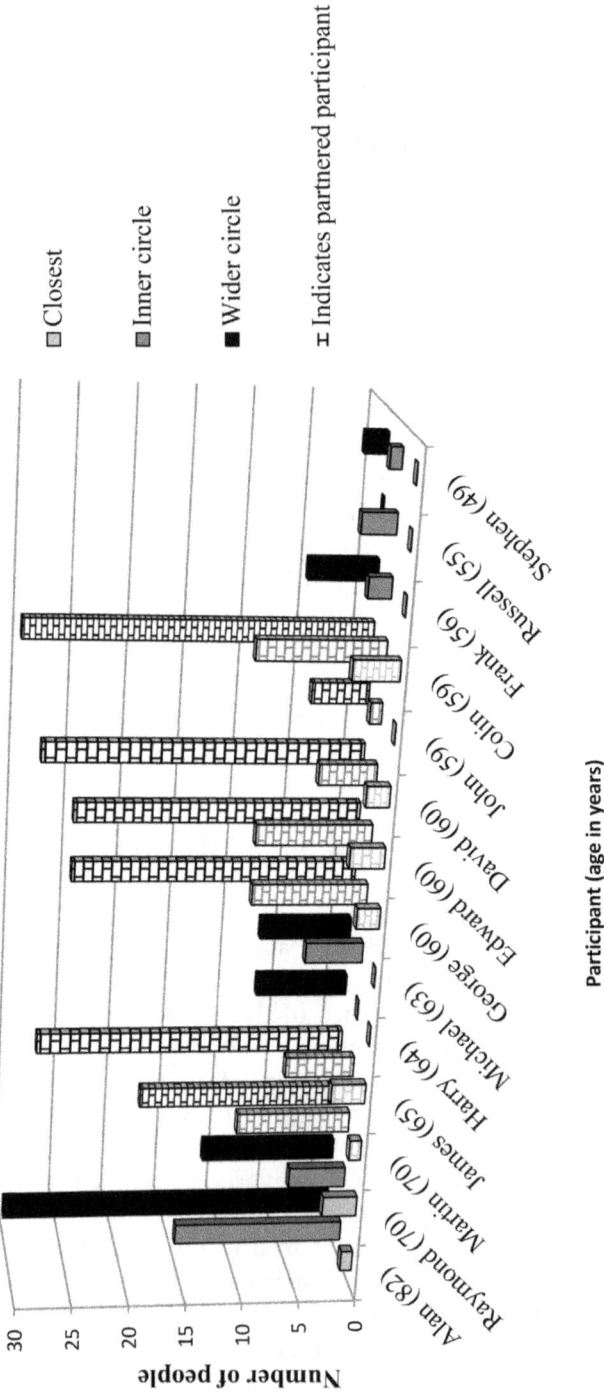

FIGURE 6.1. The participants' social networks categorized by 'closest', 'inner' and 'wider'. © Robin A. Hadley

relationship with Sue and occasional contact with his family and a few friends.

> In terms of the actual quality of the relationship, the communication, the closeness, it ain't there. I'm not working and all that sort of stuff, I sit here in this house on my own all day. ... I've not been out of the house on my own since. Once it's sorted, and it's getting close, then I'll have independence and freedom of movement.

Although John and Sue live together, their poor intimate relationship had also led to reduced access to each other's familial networks. John's familial vertical ties were reduced, as only his mother was still alive. His relationship with his mother reflected his experience of ambivalent parenting in his early and formative years. John had disassociated from one brother and his children, thus reducing his horizontal ties. Additionally, location had influenced the more distant familial networks, and again reduced John's horizontal ties.

> Even now, my mum, it's still a bloody monster. ... My middle brother I can't have any respect for him at all. He doesn't deserve any. ... I'm in contact with me [youngest] brother. ... Cousins and all that stuff, I guess 'cos I moved away, I would be hard-pressed to recognize; it's been so long. So now relative strangers.

In later life, siblings become significantly more important in social networks than friends are (Chambers et al. 2009; Davidson, Warren and Maynard 2005). However, the familial experience of two participants, Colin and John, highlighted the diversity and complexity of the dynamics surrounding family practices and the effect they have on social networks. For example, Colin highlighted mutually supportive familial experience: 'I have a great relationship with my partner and my brothers, they are most important. My family was, and is, extremely close. ... Very happy, and fun, childhood.' Colin's vertical ties were deprived, as his parents were no longer alive, but his horizontal ties were strong, with his brothers and partner in the 'closest' category. Moreover, his family had always been a close one and his positive view of his upbringing reflects the view that close bonds in childhood continue, or rekindle, in later life (Burholt and Wenger 1998; Chambers et al. 2009). Of the seven participants who were partnered, Colin had the largest social network and John had the smallest. Colin and John have a number of similarities: both were aged 59, both self-defined as working class and both had serious medical issues. Figure 6.2 shows the difference that the quality of their respective intimate and sibling relationships had across their social networks. Colin's 'closest' and 'inner' network gives him access to additional forms of support compared to John. His 'convoy' of long-term acquaintances, from his employment and sporting activities, forms a larger 'wider' network. John's 'wider' network reflected his upbringing, self-confidence, employment history, health, location and the withdrawal from his main social activity. His poor formative experience had resulted in ambivalent relationships with his partner and family. Both the number of siblings and the quality of the relationships between siblings affected the participants' social relationships.

Three participants, Martin, Harry and Stephen, were only children, and consequently their horizontal ties were reduced. Figure 6.3 highlights the difference between their 'closest', 'inner' and 'wider' circles, from all being filled to only the 'wider' being populated. Martin and Harry's social networks were vertically sparse, as both their parents are no longer alive. Although Stephen lived

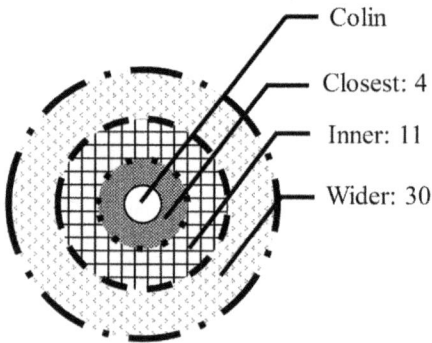

Colin

Closest: 4

Inner: 11

Wider: 30

FIGURE 6.2. The social networks of Colin and John, highlighting the difference between those with close relationships and those without. © Robin A. Hadley

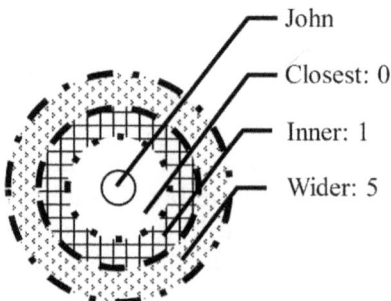

John

Closest: 0

Inner: 1

Wider: 5

with his mother, the quality of their relationship led him to place her in his 'inner' circle. Martin's wife's family accounted for his large social network and his wife, Pat, was the 'closest' in his social network. His large network was a consequence of his extended in-law family contact and active social endeavour. The centrality of their intimate relationship forms the mainstay of Martin's social world, with his horizontal ties significantly weighted by Pat's family (Martin's reference to a grandchild is discussed later in this chapter): 'I think my wife and I are very much for each other, so we tend to be our own social field. How do we socialize? Family. Of course, it's my wife's family, 'cos I've not got any. And that's really just her siblings saying, "Let's visit", whatever, and particularly the, I say, the surrogate grandchild.' Martin divided the members of their network into those with whom they had direct contact and those they were in virtual communication with. Furthermore, although social media was used to keep in contact with the extended family, Martin was a passive recipient of information: 'Now we've got Facebook … Physically, it'd be family. … So, the social network we've got is, apart from family, is relatively loose and thin. So, we've still got that loose network of cousins: it's never been a support group.'

Martin's social network highlighted the importance of fictive family: he saw the distant parts of his own family as insubstantial. This indicated that Pat's biological family had precedence over his distant biological relatives, as he located his cousins on the periphery of the social network. Moreover, in reflecting on his social network, Martin used the pronoun 'we' and thus indicated a collective view of his and Pat's social resources. This supports previous studies which indicate that in long-term heterosexual relationships, women generate and maintain social connections and men benefit from those social interactions (Davidson 2004; Davidson, Warren and Maynard 2005).

The importance of in-law relationships in the shaping of social networks (Figure 6.3) was highlighted by Harry's experience following the death of his partner, Helen, some two years ago. He had no siblings and, as his parents were dead, his familial ties were drawn from Helen's siblings and their children. Consequently, his 'closest' and 'inner' circle was vertically deprived and horizontally reduced: 'She'd employed a lawyer and the mere fact that she was Helen's sister, and I'd only lived with her for thirty years, meant that she was entitled to this house! … I can't have the family conversations with them, "Your mum did this", "Your mum

did that", because I don't think I was ever really uncle to them.'
Harry's experience highlighted how events influenced the fluidity of family formation with subsequent implications for isolation
and exclusion. Helen's death had reduced Harry's interactions with
her family. This was due, in part, to disputes over Helen's funeral,
their house and how Harry then saw himself in relation to Hel-
en's extended family. Not only was Harry disconnected from the
family structure, he was also disconnected from any social scripts
he could have drawn on. The primacy of biological lineage was revealed in the discourse concerning inheritance and the legal rights
embedded in the institution of marriage.

The life experiences of Martin and Harry demonstrated how important partners were in terms of social network, and revealed the
dynamics within familial structures. However, as Stephen's experience demonstrated, having a vertical tie did not necessarily mean
that a participant's personal community was particularly stronger than those with no vertical ties: 'She's got a nasty little habit

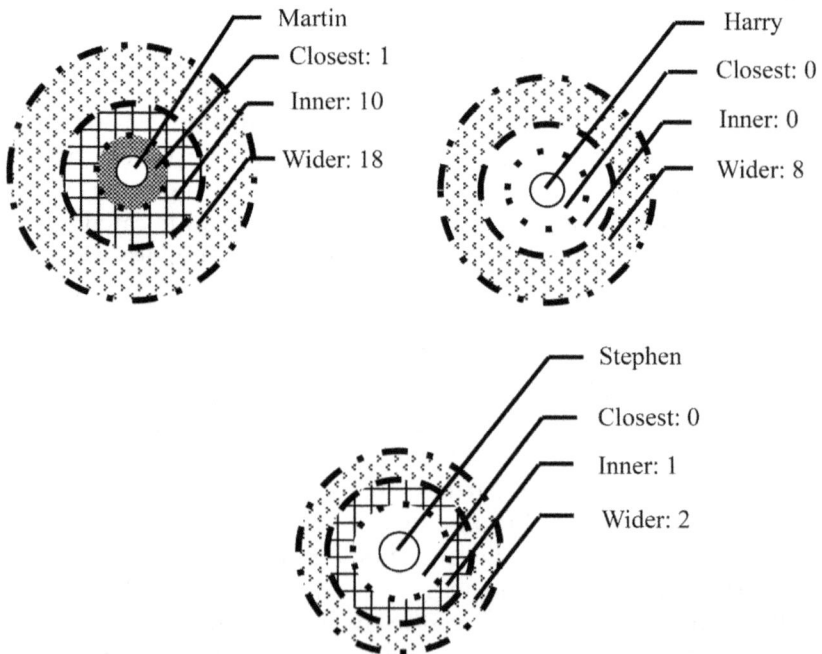

FIGURE 6.3. Social networks of only-child participants with (Martin) and
without partners (Harry and Stephen). © Robin A. Hadley

of opening my mail. ... It'd depend on the problem. I wouldn't ask her.'

As indicated by this statement, Stephen had an ambivalent relationship with his mother. For example, he wanted all communication between us to be by telephone or email, as he felt his mother would open his post. Moreover, although he has lived with his mother for the past twenty-eight years, he would not turn to her if he had a problem. Although Stephen was in full-time employment, he had little social contact with his colleagues, and described himself as having few friends, spending a lot of time on his own. The significance of work-based relationships for men has been well documented (Davidson, Daly and Arber 2003b; Fairhurst 2003b; Phillipson 2004).

> I'm not a particularly sociable individual. ... I have one or two good friends. ... I don't feel the same level of discomfort at being on my own. ... I do think it would be nice to have somebody to share my life's ups and downs with. ... Whereas now, if I can't travel with someone who I'm in some kind of relationship with, I can't be bothered to go away.'

Stephen did not consider himself lonely, but he noted that there was an absence of sharing day-to-day experiences. Furthermore, he had recently changed his view on solo travelling, and now would only travel with a companion. Stephen's change of perspective with regard to relationships and family norms influenced his outlook on his identity. His reflexivity was indicative of a common view of midlife adaptation to one's internal and social scripts (see Gutmann 1987; Biggs 1999; 2004: Simpson 2013).

Michael compared the significance of the merits of solo living against those of being in an intimate relationship. He saw that one of the advantages of being in a relationship was the status it gave – for example, the fact that married people were socially accepted and recognized by the wider community:

> When you're on your own, you have to decide all these things – it's not a shared decision. So, it's tougher, I think, much tougher to know when you don't know what to do. ... So, if I was married and had a child, I probably would fit into their world and not be seen as a threat or as odd. ... I would not be this, sort of, figure who's black and white where everybody else is in colour, you know, sure.

Michael identified that not having a partner or family led to a reduction in opportunities to access a larger social network. Again, this participant's benchmark involved defining himself against the sociocultural ideal. Not achieving that ideal contributed to the feeling of alienation: that he was 'outside'. Moreover, the social construction of the accepted norm of heteronormativity also informs the construction of the subordinated 'outsider' position. Likewise, Michael believed that not being in a relationship required an additional effort to maintain social contact: 'I think when you're single you work hard in keeping up friendships.' Conversely, when this was suggested to Alan, he argued that it was probably more reflective of the heterosexual community than the LGBT community. The latter, he indicated, was more supportive and protective, and less suspicious, than the heterosexual community: 'I think in the LGBT community I don't think it's quite the same. … Mainly because our community is like all communities: they look after their own. You look after your people – your own tribe first.' For

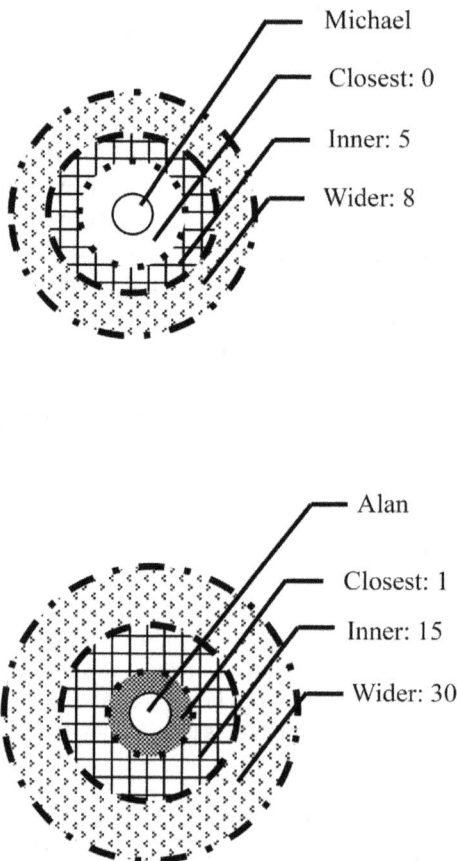

Michael

Closest: 0

Inner: 5

Wider: 8

FIGURE 6.4. The difference membership of a social support group made on social networks of solo-living men. © Robin A. Hadley

Alan

Closest: 1

Inner: 15

Wider: 30

example, both Alan and Raymond were members of the same LGBT over-50s support group. Significantly, both Alan and Raymond recorded support-group members in all their three social network categories. Raymond included two members of the support group in his 'closest' circle, while Alan had a number of its members in his 'inner' circle. Figure 6.4 shows the difference between Michael and Alan's social networks.

The participants' narratives demonstrated how familial structure and dynamics influenced different levels of social networks across the life course. The quality of the relationship was a major factor in how people were positioned in the social network, with biological hierarchy not having the prerogative it had with regard to parenthood. For people with no siblings, their horizontal ties were dependent on either their own distant relatives, such as cousins, or fictive kin. The intricacy of social networks and familial ties was therefore complex and diverse. For example, Martin, as a single child, had no direct horizontal ties, but included members of his wife's large family in his 'inner' and 'wider' categories. Inclusion of non-familial members in the 'inner' and 'closest' zones was not limited to partner networks, and circumstantial associations may be included – for example, having to move due to a change in personal circumstances (Allen, Blieszner and Roberto 2011; Kamo, Henderson and Roberto 2011; Reid and Reczek 2011). Although people with siblings had the capacity for support through their horizontal ties, this was dependent on the quality of the relationships. The quality of both enduring and family relationships also had a great influence on the personal network, as highlighted by the internecine dynamics of John's familial relationships. John's narrative also highlighted the effect that location had on social networks, and this will be the focus of the next section.

The Influence of Geographic Location on Social Networks

Geographic location had a significant effect on the participants' social networks in terms of maintaining established ties, forming new relationships, building networks, participation in social activities, loneliness and isolation. With the exception of Colin, all the men had at some time relocated for employment-related reasons. Two of the participants, Michael and Russell, had travelled overseas from their countries of origin for employment. Both were non-partnered and had no one 'closest' in their network (Figure 6.5). Michael was born in England and has worked and lived overseas since his late twenties. He had worked in a major city in Thailand for the past two years, where he taught drama. He had no one in his 'closest' category, and although he had five people in his 'inner' circle, due to his geographic location contact with these was typically by telephone and the internet. Face-to-face contact with these associates was planned, and while Michael had built up a large group of friends over the world, access to them and his relatives was limited. For example, compared to his 'inner' Thailand network, when Michael returned to England, he had a much larger community of people he could contact: 'Friends in south-west England – I think I can count on about fifteen or sixteen that I could ring up and say, "Let's have a pint." … Friends around England, I would say, there's about fifty people I feel I could say, "Can I come and stay the night?"'

The impact of geographic location on Michael's time outside school hours meant he often spent evenings and weekends alone. Although he was comfortable with the situation, he noted that the lack of social interaction was probably not good for his well-being:

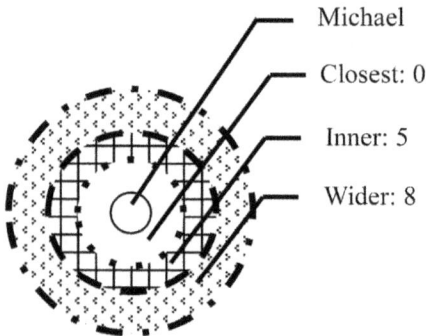

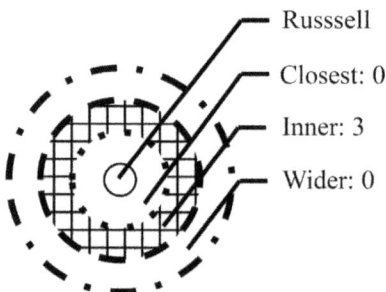

FIGURE 6.5. The effect of employment overseas on Michael's and Russell's 'closest' and 'inner' social networks. © Robin A. Hadley

Michael
Closest: 0
Inner: 5
Wider: 8

Russsell
Closest: 0
Inner: 3
Wider: 0

> I spend a lot of time being quite alone during the week, and some Saturdays alone, on the whole, comfortably. I'm not sure if it's completely healthy. ... So, as I get older, I am aware of the fact that it's great when you're fit, but if you are fatherless, there is no son or daughter checking up on you, phoning you, knocking on the door, or saying, 'You look terrible – go to hospital.'

As a childless, solo-living man based overseas, and one whose parents were dead, Michael's vertical network was deprived and his horizontal network of support reduced. The importance of proximate family in supplying support in later life has been well established (Phillipson 2004). Michael related how with his retirement due in the next few years, he was unsure what the future held: 'I'm, sort of, in a state of, do I carry on working? Do I stop? Where do I go when I stop? Who will I be with? If I'm alone, what is my network and so on?' Moreover, he speculated on declining health in later life, and the consequence of having no familial support. Considerations around the transition from work to retirement had raised anxieties surrounding role, location and relationships.

Russell lived in a small city in the Midlands and was actively seeking employment. In the meantime, he was living off his own financial resources. In the mid-1990s, he had moved to the UK from Australia for relationship and economic reasons. Russell believed that he was indebted to the support he had received from two older female friends, with whom he lodged. His appreciation of them was evident, although the manner and tone he used when he referred to them counterpointed his lack of 'closest' and 'wider' social circles: 'I live with two sisters, retired sisters, pensioners, and we are very happy. ... I am very worried that I get more out of the relationship than they do, because I am so cossetted, so looked after.' Although Russell had both a surviving birth mother and birth sister, as well as many half-siblings, they were all in Australia, and he only had regular telephone contact with his mother. He had not maintained contact with ex-colleagues, fellow students or family. Consequently, he had no 'convoy' of people collected over the life course that could facilitate social participation in any form. Figure 6.5 shows that his social network consisted of an 'inner' circle formed by his mother, with the two sisters given equivalent status. Russell's social capital was low due to a number of factors, including the geographic location of his extended birth family, the absence of in-law relationships and the lack of any maintained relationship with friends or relatives.

> So, social network, I haven't got any. I'd say there wasn't really any-
> one that I could call a friend now. Such friends as I had, I've not
> maintained contact with. ... But I don't have any family contact ei-
> ther. My birth father is dead. I no longer have contact with either
> of my stepfathers, or stepbrothers and sisters; there are thirteen of
> them in all.

Russell was one of five men who did not have anyone in the 'closest'
relationship category. However, he had a relationship that supplied
trust, support, understanding and safety. Russell had created a small
accommodating network from a non-familial source and, as such,
had developed a 'fictive' family. Significantly, the majority of Russell's birth and stepfamily were absent from all of his relationship
categories. This counters the traditionally held view that family are
available to support their members, and supports contemporary
research highlighting the diversity in familial dynamics. However,
poor experience of parenting in childhood and geographic distance
meant that his birth mother was included as an 'inner' type rather
than a 'closest' type (Figure 6.5). Both Michael and Russell's transnational locations related to employment and influenced the shape
and dynamics of their social networks.

Change and exit from employment also influenced how participants felt about their location and their personal communities.
David had moved to his current house in the commuter belt fifteen years ago and, following early retirement, he now worked
part-time from home. The change in situation had brought matters
concerning social connectivity to his attention. He and his wife,
Cathy, found that the opportunities to form friendships in their
suburb were limited, not least because of the time available for
socializing while working full-time. Moreover, David identified
himself and his wife as introverts, reticent in social situations such
as parties.

> I've moved places because of the job and maybe embedding myself in
> the community is a skill I don't have. ... I have been in this area since
> 1997 but being a commuter place it is not easy to put down roots. ... I
> think actually there are a lot of folk in about their sixties, about here,
> and have been here a long time, but how you get into the social circle
> they're *in* – I don't know.

David's narrative highlighted the effects of a geo-economic transition from office to home-based worker and a subsequent change in
available networks. Furthermore, interactions with neighbours are

a marker of social embeddedness: poor or no contact is an element of social isolation. In contrast, Martin and Pat retired to their home in rural Wales three years ago. Both the retirement, and the change of location from a commuter community to a rural one, had an impact on the social networks of both Martin as an individual and Martin and Pat as a couple.

> You lose the social aspects of work, which I, I found one of the most difficult things actually. ... But going to work every day isn't just going to work every day. It's a whole social structure that you're no longer part of. But that, you know, that builds up again, you build other structures ... One or two of the guys that used to work for me are still in contact.

Martin experienced retirement as a form of bereavement after the realization of the loss of multiple social connections. Following their relocation, he and Pat had actively sought to build networks in their new locality in addition to their established friendships and activities. For example, they had run an international vintage marque motorcycle club for over twenty years. It is interesting that Pat had the greater diversity in her local interactions, and that Martin's volunteering role related to his career in engineering: 'The motorcycle club – they tend to be social events. We've made a few friends around here, since we've been here, through us trying to learn Welsh. Pat has more than I because she's involved in running a local charity shop, and knitting circles and the WI. ... I've just started doing some work at the local heritage railway.'

The importance of the workplace as a resource for social relationships for men has been well documented (see Chapter 2) and, as Martin described, exiting employment truncated those relationships. However, the quality of relationships with colleagues and peers is variable and dependent on many factors, such as class, education, gender, location and relationship skills (Spencer and Pahl 2006). For example, Stephen identified how colleagues labelled him:

> I tend not to socialize with the people I work with anyway. I tend to try and avoid it. I'm not aware that I've been excluded. ... I've definitely had people saying to me things like, 'Oh, I thought you were gay', once I've got to know them a bit and we're talking on that level, they've actually said it. ... They've definitely very strongly alluded to the fact that it has to be because I'm with my mother.

Stephen reported that he rarely participated in work-based social activity. This was his choice rather than being through alienation. However, he had found that living with his mother had led him to be frequently categorized as both her carer and gay. Stephen assessed this practice as a strategy used to assign people to a category. This labelling of him was only challenged when a certain level of social interaction had been established. Because he did not fit the expected social norm for his gender and age, stereotypes were applied that attempted to position him in a known social category. Although Stephen had displayed a form of hyper-masculinity earlier in his adult life (see Chapters 4 and 5), his current lifestyle positioned him as 'other' in the way peers regarded him.

The majority of the partnered participants lived with their partners, with the exception of James, who was 'Living Apart Together' (LAT) with his partner, Liz. They lived approximately 130 miles from one another and accessed each other's local social network: 'We've, sort of, incorporated each other's friends now. ... Because they're geographically distant, they tend not to meet each other, the two groups.' James's vertical ties were deprived due to parental bereavement and his horizontal ties were centred on his brother and his brother's children and grandchildren. However, his relationship with Liz gave him access to her familial networks of her children and grandchildren. As with five men from the partnered group, James's 'inner' circle comprised his partner and a family member. Furthermore, James also included a longstanding friend in his 'closest' circle. His dearest friends were from his early twenties and were mainly based in the area he was raised in and had lived near for most of his life. Consequently, he had a convoy of friends that he could access while he remained in that location:

> Liz's the one closest. ... I'm quite close to my brother. I think we're quite alike and it's not just a blood tie: we probably would be friends if we weren't brothers. And then, after that, it's a woman friend who I've known a long time. ... My close friends now are from 20 onwards, you know.

Likewise, Edward's network also highlighted the nuances of family members being included in the 'closest' section of a participant's network. Edward was the youngest of four children, and although the family was close, he had a particularly strong connection with his brother, Roy, who was nearest in age to him. As with all but one of the partnered men, John being the exception, Edward's partner was the 'closest' to him. Although Edward's vertical ties were deprived, his horizontal ties were strong. Edward did not allude to any particular bias towards his own or his partner's family in terms of contact: 'I'm closest to Lois, then it would be my brother and his wife. ... Next brother to me, he lives nearby, so we see a lot of each other, I'm very close to him. ... It would represent a bit of a downturn in my life if my brother wasn't just three or four miles away.'

The complexity of the intersection between place, socio-economics and different levels of relationships were highlighted in this section. The importance of securing work meant that the vast majority of men had had to move, and this had influenced their enduring intimate and familial relationships. The workplace has been shown to be important to men's social networks, and access to employment dictated residential location. On exiting employment, the issues surrounding the building of new local networks become apparent. This was evidenced in Martin's narrative around the losses linked with his retirement. Conversely, not everyone finds that their personal network is formed by colleagues, or wants it to be. Autonomy, therefore, in what constitutes personal networks is complex, diverse and contrary. The next section examines the effect of, and responses to, loss on social networks.

Loss and Bereavement

The cessation of an enduring, intimate relationship, or a hoped-for relationship, had a deep effect on the participants and their social relations. The effect of the change in status led to adaption and negotiation of new relationships at all levels. Both Harry and Raymond became widowers in their early sixties when their respective partners died. Alan broke up with his long-term partner, Carl, when he was in his mid-seventies. The reactions of these participants to these changes highlight the complex interactions and subsequent negotiation of relationships at all levels that bereavement brings.

The death of Harry's partner, Helen, had significantly reduced his social network. Her loss had devastated Harry, as well as confounding his expectation that he would be the first to die. His being a single child meant that there were no siblings to access for support. He had assumed that Helen's extended family, for example her nephews and goddaughters, would provide succour in his bereavement. However, the significance of a gendered biological hierarchy was apparent, in that Harry had bequeathed to Helen's nephews rather than her goddaughters:

My plans were to leave Helen as comfortable off as I could. ... Had I gone, I think there'd be the missing of me, or something, but Helen would have had steps to take. ... Because there's no one to leave it to, I've arranged that if something happens to me this [house] is to be left jointly to her nephews.

Harry's main interactions were with two old friends, two neighbouring families and one person he knew from walking his two dogs. Contact with ex-colleagues had reduced in the two years since Helen's death, but Harry testified that he had also not maintained contact with them. He occasionally saw his 'nephews' and an honorary godson – the son of a neighbour – who helped with his cars, but these visits were irregular and on an ad-hoc basis. In addition, he felt that he did not have an 'inner' circle, and indicated that he had become wary of, and withdrawn from, social functions because of having to attend without a partner. Harry had no 'intimate' or 'closest' relationship, and it appeared that he had no immediate support network. Nevertheless, Harry stressed that he could call on his old friends and his neighbours. Significantly, Helen's family were not included in that support system. Furthermore, the support he referred to had been established through time and neighbouring locations, and there appeared to be no recent additions to his network:

> There's no inner circle, no. ... Loads of activities around here from people we knew. I've dropped out of that because I hate going on my own. ... A problem – I'll solve it. I'm the only one. I don't know anyone. ... There's two mates that I got, that have been buddies for a long time, that if I rang would come at a click. I also have neighbours that if I rang would come at a click.

A number of factors affected Raymond's personal social network: his sexuality, his small family network and the death of his long-term partner, Peter. They had worked as waiters in the hotel trade and 'passed' as stepbrothers to account for their relationship. Seeking employment in low-paid areas has been a common strategy for non-heterosexuals (Dunne 1997; Heaphy 2007). Advantages of this choice of occupation included accommodation and the freedom to choose the location and duration of employment:

> Me and Peter just were me and Peter, we went out together, we worked together, we did everything together, we had friends, but not what you call close friends who we met up. ... We didn't really go to gay places we just, just lived an average, well I suppose what you'd call like most couples do.

The unsocial working hours affected the size of their social network, both as a couple and as individuals. Consequently, they did not socialize or participate in the gay community to any great degree. In addition, Raymond's mother died two years before Peter, and the combined loss of those close relationships led to a period of deep mourning. The bereavement affected Raymond's behaviour and mental health, leading to heavy alcohol consumption and suicidal thoughts. However, he changed his lifestyle, initially for social contact, by taking a job as part-time bar staff at a local pub. In the eight years he had worked in the pub, the relationship Raymond had with his employer had changed from one of social support to financial necessity.

> Me mother died two years before Peter died and that were bad enough. And then when Peter died I thought, 'Well that's it, I've lost the lot now', nothing mattered. ... So, I were just getting sloshed every night thinking, 'Oh, tek all your tablets' an' all this, but then I thought, 'No, this isn't the way to progress.' So, pulled meself together, and I got the job at the pub and, you know, built up from there. ... When I first went it was for company. Now it's for the money as well!

Raymond's adjusted lifestyle had led him to new social contacts, and beyond those in the workplace, he started looking for a relationship. He joined a local LGBT over-50s social group. Both arenas, the pub and the group, have had a significant impact on Raymond's social network. Members of both the pub and the group were included in his 'inner' circle, and two members of the latter were, with his sister, 'closest' to him. Moreover, both the pub and the group had become central to Raymond's life, the former providing economic and social resources and the latter giving social and care support.

> I've the people at the pub and I've got the group. With the group, if you're not well ... I ring and then they know I'm not just, sommat's happened, I've not gone. I had a couple of phone calls back, see if I were alright, you know. You think, 'Well somebody cares' you know? ... It's most of my life – going to the pub or the group. So, I mean, you take that away from me and just sit here forever? Then might as well curl up and die now, you know?

Raymond had found, in common with many widowers, that the loss of his partner profoundly altered his life. However, he had built a social network through employment in a job that brought him into direct contact with people, and via a group that reflected his lifestyle choices. The importance of both groups to Raymond's sense of self was apparent, to the degree that he considered that life would not be worth living if the opportunity to socialize was withdrawn.

Alan had the strongest network in terms of 'inner' and 'wider' categories in the group. Adopted when a baby, his nearest adopted sibling was twenty-one years older. His adopted brothers and sister were now dead, and although he had contact with his extended kin network, they were geographically distant and on the periphery of his social network. As such, his vertical ties had been severed very early in life and the adopted vertical ties were now deprived. His horizontal ties, through his adopted family, comprised great nieces and nephews, and were extended but weak; contact was intermittent:

> I've got, I don't know 'ow many great, great – my niece, 'er children are my great, so they're great, greats, aren't they? My great, great, all of 'em 'ave children, all four of 'em 'ave children. I enjoyed, you know, the kids. I didn't want kids o' my own. ... Polly [niece] and Ivan [niece's husband] were 'ere visitin' last month. ... They were planning to goin' to Aussie.

Alan felt that the relationship he had with a friend, Simon, whom he had known for fifteen years and who was twenty-four years younger than him, was his most important relationship. The depth of the relationship was shown by Alan's nomination of Simon as his power of attorney, and as such, he was the 'closest' in Alan's network. Therefore, through the legitimization of 'fictive' kin, Alan had created his own vertical network: 'As I say, same as Simon he's probably the only real family I 'ave now. All right, I 'ave my family, niece and nephew. ... But they're distant, you know, they're peripheral. 'E was the most closest to me, I'd say, Simon. He's my power of attorney.'

Two significant events in both Alan and Simon's lives appear to be fundamental in the transformation of their relationship status: firstly, the ending of Alan's relationship with Carl a few years after moving back to his birth town, and secondly, the friendship that Alan and Carl had formed with Simon following Simon's father's death: ''Is dad died. ... And 'e needed a little bit of advice on things so we became 'is dads, you know, as it were. ... Where 'e could come to and say wanted, you know, 'elp, kind 'o thing.' The relationship between Alan and Simon had changed from friendship to one of an agreed form of father–son surrogacy following Alan and Carl's sepa-ration. The elevation of friends or non-relatives into equivalent kin status – 'non-kin conversion' (Allen, Blieszner and Roberto 2011: 1167) – had enhanced Alan's social network and quality of life.

> I said, 'You know, you're like the son I never had.' ... 'You do things for me, don't you, like a son would for a father', I said, 'So you might as well be, like, you know.' ... Alright, 'e's gay. We've gone to saunas together. But I could never 'ave anything sexually to do with 'im. You know, incest if I did it, you know, it wouldn't be right, no way. ... If somethin' really went wrong, Simon would get 'ere.

Since the early 1950s, Alan had been a gay activist, and when at-tending meetings, he had used a pseudonym to avoid discovery. This was indicative of the attitude to homosexuality at the time: 'The original one was the Homosexual Reform Society. That evolved into the Campaign for Homosexual Equality. You put an assumed name in the book. Different. Well, I couldn't have let 'em know I were in Navy, you know, you just dare not get caught out.'

Alan's 'inner' circle comprised a mix of relationships between relatives, longstanding friends and researchers with whom he had shared details of his life experience. Alan did not detail which members of his extended family were included in his 'inner' cat-egory. Those whom he had historical links with included founder members of a local LGBT over-50s group:

> There is a core of people that is my relatives and some o' the closer people from the group. The ones that 'ave been there probably from the beginnin'. There are one or two who know me very well and there are also one or two other people, who I know from other things: Professor Plum – I'd met 'im through being in his research of elderly LGBT people.

One difference between solo-living older women and men is that the former regularly invite friends into their homes as a social net-work activity, whereas men tend not to. Moreover, widowed men in later life are more likely to be members of an informal group than partnered men (Perren, Arber and Davidson 2003). Both Alan and Raymond (see also Chapter 7) emphasized the importance of being able to socialize outside the home and the adverse effect of not being able to do so for any significant period. The support pro-vided by the LGBT over-50s support group has been significant in helping both Raymond and Alan mitigate the loss of their intimate life partners:

> I am a volunteer with Age UK, I'm involved with football, you know,
> member of Supporters' Club and go to things to do with that. I am
> 'eavily involved in things like the Lesbian & Gay Foundation and
> PRIDE. ... I'm a member of the local Writers' Group and local BASE
> [a group for LGBT youth]. ... In fact, I'm on the Church Council,
> Parochial Council. ... 'When it rained like it did yesterday – when I
> can't get out like that, then I'm stuck and you don't see anybody. ...
> I'd become very, very morose and bored. (Alan)

The importance of social activity was highlighted by Alan's reaction to recent poor weather preventing him from attending a group meeting. His experience indicated the local environmental issues that may affect the day-to-day interactions that inform quality of life. The positive effect of support groups on Raymond and Alan's 'closest', 'inner' and 'wider' relationships was indicative of others' experience of support from outside family norms. Moreover, a strategic facility, such as the LGBT over-50s group, illustrates the interaction between structure, policy and individual agency. As with Alan and Raymond, accessing a group of people who had shared a similar experience had been important to both Edward and Lois.

> I think it's very important because, you know, there is a bond, which
> is unspoken. We know that there is one thing that we all share, and
> that is quite important. I think there is a little core; there is just a
> small number of couples, through More-to-Life, that we have be-
> come very close to and that's been very gratifying. (Edward)

The significance of the help that support groups gave was reflected in the membership of the 'inner' circle of the participants' social networks. The ending of unsuccessful infertility treatment has been viewed as a form of complex bereavement, and as noted in Chapters 1 and 6, Edward and Lois's infertility treatment led them to become involved with the More-to-Life support group. In addition to More-to-Life forming part of Edward's 'inner' and 'wider' circles, he also viewed his business as a conduit for social interaction:

> My business now that I've set up – there are meetings to go to. ... It
> is a social event 'cos, you know, you always start the meeting with a
> bit of chat and you finish it with a bit of chat. ... Without interludes
> like that it would be a very depressing thing to be at home all the
> time, on one's own.

Edward ran his business from home and believed that not having face-to-face social interaction would have been debilitating. In that regard, he reflected the opinions of both Alan and Raymond. In addition to the social capital that family and employment brought, voluntary work also added to Edward's 'wider' social network: 'It is, sort of work, because I'm doing something for the benefit of somebody else, but it's certainly a pleasure; I enjoy it very much. But it is leisure because I can say, "I'm not doing this anymore" whenever I want.' Not only had this enabled him to meet fellow volunteers and members of the public, it also linked to his architectural practice. Moreover, he was in control of his commitment and had the option to leave at a time of his choosing. With regard to 'wider' social communities, John had observed how the evolutionary nature of groups had formed, adapted and dissolved over time: 'My circle was based on my local Labour Party. ... It became defunct, you saw people less and less, you know, these groups always just break up, it's normal. ... I've asked people that I worked with to come over for a meal, for a drink, and that. None of them bloody reciprocated!' John's experience demonstrated the relationship between the evolution of social groups and the concomitant fluidity in individual social networks. As with a number of the participants, John's ex-colleagues had not maintained contact, contradicting his expectation of relational mutuality. Contrary to the social etiquette he had expected, in attempting to build social relationships he had experienced a lack of reciprocity. John's attempt at managing the transition from work to home-based social activity had been unsuccessful and had left him frustrated.

Colin's management of the loss of social contact associated with a terminal illness had a different outcome. One of the effects of Colin's condition was that if he became emotional or stressed, he would lose some degree of cognitive or motor functions, or both. Consequently, in order to manage any trigger events, he used email and Skype to keep in contact with others.

> I have about ten to twelve close friends and thirty to forty casual friends. ... I wouldn't describe myself as outgoing or particularly sociable. I socialize mainly by the internet, hospice, MND groups and lunch meetings with family and friends. When I was younger, I made most of my friends through sport. ... I see my partner and Facebook friends daily, brothers weekly, art class weekly. Ex-work colleagues regularly but less often.

Colin divided the 'inner' and 'wider' constituents of his social network between friends for the former and associates for the latter. The members of his 'social convoy' (Antonucci and Akiyama 1987) were historical relationships drawn from work and sporting activities, and were spread geographically, both locally and further afield. The motor neurone disease (MND) support groups and activities associated with his treatment – for example, art classes – provided an additional form of social network and support. Although Colin held Christian beliefs, he did not refer to any faith-based activity or support.

The attitude to spiritual matters of the majority of the men in the study was vague and did not involve any commitment to any specific organization or practice. Alan, David and George did practise a faith and noted its effect on their 'closest' and 'wider' networks. Research studies have indicated that in retirement, spirituality and organized religions become an important element of older people's social networks and sense of well-being. Alan had returned to the church following an absence of over thirty years, having directly encountered homophobia there in the past. However, he had recently found a place of worship where non-heterosexuals were welcome, and this had positively affected his social network and given him a sense of inclusion:

> I went back in a church again on the eleventh September, two – three years ago. And I went to our local church 'ere. The Vicar at the time was a gay man. ... A new family. I 'ave people I can talk to and go to if I need any help. Personally, I can do my little theatrical bit. I can read the lesson, can't I, on a Sunday. ... I enjoy it.

Alan's experience highlighted the change in attitude in some religious organizations (a historically deeply embedded social structure) and the effect that it had on his agency. David and George and their partners also held religious beliefs and were active participants in their respective churches. Both David and Alan had reflected on the sense that church provided a form of family:

> I am also a member of the church, which is always a small minority thing. ... The churches I've been a member of provided a certain sense of familyness [sic] ... Quality of life involves, well for me, it is also about being a member of a church where you feel you can get together with like-minded people. (David)

David positioned attending church as a minority activity, and this comment may reflect the decline in England and Wales of people who define themselves as Christian (ONS 2012a) and the reduction in Church attendance (Archbishops' Council 2013) across the nation in the past few decades. David's narrative indicated that being an active member of his faith positively affected his quality of life through giving a sense of family and compatible company, but that it also had a positive effect on his social network. Alan, David and George had held their beliefs from childhood and, although all referred to active involvement in their local churches, only David specifically included both his local vicar and family in his 'inner' circle.

The church community generally seemed to provide a pool of support that could be drawn on in times of need. But not all experience of the church community had been unanimously positive. George had noted that after moving to their present home four years previously, it had taken a few years for he and Joan to feel accepted in their local church. In addition, the church had a school attached to it, and he indicated that being childless might have affected people's attitude towards them. As such, George and Joan's social capital was reduced in an area where parenthood and children were embedded into the institutional structure:

> The secondary school choice is very tied into church attendance. So, you get this rather skewed effect on the local church and of course, we're out of that. There's a group of people who sort of, know each other through their children ... we're not excluded from it, but we don't really belong. ... Our experience, for nearly two years, was this is really hard work. ... Sometimes we had people round for a meal and it wasn't reciprocated back.

George's experience highlighted the geopolitical intersections through the interaction of parenthood, children and the structural hegemony that reinforced the subordination of those without children.

The participants experienced loss not only through the death of loved ones, but also through infertility, social etiquette and social hegemony. The consequence of their actual or perceived loss was the negotiation of social relationships at all levels. For example, shared experience support groups had filled not only the participants' 'wider' social circles, but also their 'closest' and 'inner' requirements. However, access to and acceptance within a new social community was not always easily negotiated, but was seen to take time and perseverance. This highlights the potential difficulties involved in forming friendships in later life. The importance of external social engagement was reflected in the participants who noted how not being able to access activities outside the home would have a negative effect on their disposition. As a result, a gamut of activities were viewed as sources of interaction, including business meetings and volunteer work. The participants drew on a diverse range of resources that were outside the familial norms typically associated with 'closest' social networks. As such, the concept of 'fictive kin' in the social networks of the participants was apparent. A different form of fictive kin – 'fictive grandfatherhood' – will be examined in the following section.

Grandfatherhood

Due to demographic factors, studies of grandparenthood have historically focused on grandmothers. However, with the life expectancy of men in Western societies now predicted to reach the same level as that of women within the next two decades, there has been an increased focus on the role of grandfatherhood. Recent research has shown that the dominant perception of grandparenthood fails to account for the complexity in modern family relationships. The nuances of the role of grandfatherhood have been misrepresented through the mutual construction of women as central kin keepers and men's downplaying of their role (Arber et al. 2003; Mann 2007; Tarrant 2012b). The men in this study demonstrated a range of attitudes to grandfatherhood, from seeing it as something that naturally followed fatherhood to actively seeking a role as grandparent.

The experience of 'fictive' grandfatherhood for the men in this group ranged from the covert to the overt. The four participants who highlighted grandfatherhood were Raymond and Alan, who were not partnered, and James and Martin, who were partnered. All four had members in their 'inner', 'closest' and 'wider' network categories of their social networks. In this section, I have followed the participants' attitudes to fatherhood developed in Chapter 5, to demonstrate how they both intersect and vary within and between the different phases. For those in the 'aspirational' group, their attention was on becoming a father, and although grandfatherhood would be a natural consequence, it was not of importance. As David noted: 'Now? I don't really want to think of myself as a grandparent but a lot of people my age are grandparents.' David identified how disruption from the ideal life course trajectory for the involuntarily childless continues across the life course.

Of the two men in the 'uncertain' group, Michael reflected the aspirational attitude of the natural order of the primacy of biological fatherhood: 'I cannot recall having any thoughts about being a Granddad because there was or is no possibility of it.' The dominance of the importance of the father–child relationship leaves little or no room for consideration of alternative roles, in the present or the future. On the other hand, Russell was conscious of the connection between the roles of father and grandfather, and acceptance of the former led to the latter being viewed as a loss: 'There's also a sudden realization that I'm not gonna be a grandfather either.'

The nine men in the 'mediated' group ranged from those who had not considered grandfatherhood following their acceptance of involuntary childlessness to those that actively pursued a grandparent-type role. Those that had not considered grandparenthood included Harry, John and Colin. Harry's assumption of fatherhood had ended when he became a widower. Similarly, John did not consider grandparenthood following his partner's refusal to consider him as fit for fatherhood. Colin's acceptance of not becoming a father was the consequence of his then wife's medical history and his age: 'No. I didn't get around to even thinking about missing out on being a grandfather. So *no*, I haven't missed it really. The only time I ever think about what I might have missed out on is when I see people putting comments or pictures of their grandchildren on Facebook.' Colin's attitude followed the primacy of the genetic legacy, therefore accepting non-fatherhood and automatically dismissing any form of grandfatherhood. Nonetheless, Colin was aware that his peers had a different experience to his.

Two of the participants, Edward and George, held different views on their roles within their family structure. Edward was the youngest of four children and his siblings were all grandparents. He enjoyed a close relationship with different generations, with the effect of balancing any regrets about not becoming a parent or grandparent:

> So you know, all my siblings are grandparents. ... I'm uncle and great uncle to youngsters and babies. So, that is a role that brings great joy. I relate pretty well to my nephews and nieces. ... It doesn't fill me with any great sense of regret because I've always been quite an active uncle. ... It is almost as good a way of engaging with the generation that, sort of, one beyond yourself, you know.

Interestingly, Edward saw intergenerational interaction as an opportunity to connect with future generations. This reflects the continuity of strong familial bonds. He went on to differentiate between the roles of grandfather and uncle, with the latter viewed as the 'next in importance' to biological parenthood. Edward's testimony highlighted the primacy of the biological imperative in social roles in later life, and the kudos reinforcing the masculine norm of virility proved by fertility: 'It's not as important as being a grandparent but, you know, in terms of socializing and just having a family, not quite as good as your own children.' Moreover, because of the inclusive family interaction from their birth onwards, Edward believed that his nieces and nephews recognized him as having high status within the family network. Edward's role of uncle was an important part of his biological family identity and reflected the primacy of the biological connectivity in many families: 'I think they look up to me and accept me as a, sort of, senior member of the family, not like a dad. ... Being an uncle has never, sort of, had that role of, not a substitute parent – that would be far too grand – but as a, sort of, crutch in times of need.'

In locating his position in the familial infrastructure, Edward was careful to establish what the role of uncle entailed; he was not an ad-hoc parent but an available support when needed. George's interactions with younger generations were through Joan's extended family and with the children of friends. 'On my side of the family, I only have my sister. ... Although we have got nephews and nieces, it is through Joan's side and not through my side. I do feel that increasingly there's not many people left that I belong to as a blood relative.' Being conscious of his limited family network drew George's attention to the importance of the connectedness that blood relatives give. The awareness of ageing without children also highlighted an underlying mindfulness of the end of the familial line and an absence of future familial support.

> I'm going to grow old without having children around or grandchildren. ... You know, the family is not carrying on, I haven't got that relationship. ... There is nobody going to be around for me, as I get older. ... I don't think I would really want children in order to make me feel better when I got older. So, you realize it is all quite mixed.

The complexity of the issues surrounding a childless later life highlighted the common narratives of not being a 'burden' to one's children, and the need not only for close relationships in later life but for the reassurance of knowing one is not going to be alone. George's reflections also illustrated the caring roles he and Joan adopted in caring for his parents before their death: 'I mean both my parents have died now but I and my sister were around as they got older and supported them and we are supporting my wife's family now. ... 'Cos they're now getting older. ... We're the main support and we don't have children. The other two children, Joan's brothers, have children.' The family dynamics surrounding the care of Joan's parents positioned Joan and George as available to care for a number of reasons. Care of parents has commonly been associated with daughters, and they were geographically near and seen as free to attend because they had no child commitments. Thus, George and Joan's experience reflected the social norm that associates women with care and the childless with being free to care (see Chapter 2 and Pesando 2018). Conversely, George's narrative also revealed that caring for his ageing parents was part of his role as a son. George's position in the familial network seemed nebulous: although he took pleasure in the interactions with Joan's family, he did not refer to himself in terms of any familial role, for example as an uncle. Moreover, he specifically saw one aspect of later life as missing: both the parental and grandparental relationship.

The four remaining members of the mediated group all displayed a means of accessing intergenerational relationships. The experiences of fictive grandfatherhood for the men in this group ranged from the covert to the overt. I have divided them into four categories – latent, adopted, surrogate and proxy – to reflect the different dynamics of their experiences.

Latent

Since Peter's death, Raymond had reflected on his reasons for wanting a grandparental relationship and questioned his own motives. He reflected on the emotional and practical benefits that an intergenerational familial relationship would help provide:

> I've never totally sorted it out in my mind whether it's because Peter 'ad died and I were on my own 'cos I felt more lonely. ... I could do with 'em comin' 'ere really, they could do all me things – when my computer doesn't work fo' me, and me television plays me up. They'd sort it out where I can't.

Raymond's view of what a supportive family might offer reflected an 'ideal' portrayal of intergenerational familial relationships that did not acknowledge that some older people have estranged familial networks. Raymond had stated that he saw the children of his employer as his grandchildren. However, he believed that being a gay man meant he could not declare his grandparental feelings or views towards the children. His age, he felt, had prevented him considering a parental role: 'I wouldn't want, now, obviously, well at my age, no.' In addition, the family had relocated and as the children had grown up his contact with them had reduced. As such, his role had been hidden (latent), and does not appear to have been acknowledged by others:

> They don't live in the pub now. ... But I always give them Christmas and birthday presents. ... You know, they used to sit in pub and they'd read out o' their book, 'Do you want me read yer a story?' I'd say, 'Yeah, go on then', things like that. I mean now they've grown up a bit, so there isn't really anybody, in that sense, I am particular close to, no.

Raymond did not indicate if his gifts were reciprocated, and neither did it seem that his relationship with the family was acknowledged through any form of name, such as 'uncle' or 'granddad Ray.' The construction of his personal social networks meant that there were no obvious means of obtaining the relationship Raymond wished for:

> Sometimes I sit 'ere when I'm in on me own, I think, 'Ohh, bit fed up and I wish Peter were 'ere', and then I'd think, 'You're lucky Raymond because you've got the group, you've got the pub, there's a lot of people don't 'ave as much company as you do.' ... That's why I'm always out.

Raymond's main social network consisted of those in his work-place and the LGBT over-50s support group. These two arenas provided support and, in particular, a means to avoid being lonely, which he strongly associated with having to remain in his flat.

Adopted

Following the end of his relationship with his long-term partner, Alan moved from their home to a privately rented one-bedroomed ground-floor flat. Local authority housing policy dictated that people over 70 had to be housed in sheltered accommodation, something he was not prepared to accept: 'He said, "We do not cover 70s on their own." I was a bit irate. ... He said, "You might get some help with your rent." So, I did. And I do. I get two-thirds of it paid. So, they can't let me live in one of their places but they'll pay me two-thirds of this.'

Alan's experience highlighted the age-related gateways that are embedded in society. His encounter can be seen as an example of the tension between individual agency and social structure. More-over, it demonstrated how age-based policy reflects the view of older people being at risk and in need of managing.

During the transition into solo living and singledom, Alan was approached at a local football match by the father of two teenage boys to fill the role of 'adopted' grandfather for a school project. Reflecting on his experience of discrimination, Alan clarified that his homosexuality was not an issue:

> They said, 'Will you be our granddad for this?' So, I looked at the fa-ther, 'e said, 'It's all right, there's no problem.' And 'e knew I was gay. ... I became their honorary granddad. And that lasted three years. ... As I say, I'd do it again. ... I've got lots of nieces and nephews, but, you know, grandkids I would've loved.

The experience of grandfatherhood had expanded Alan's percep-tion of potential roles in later life from just that of being an uncle. Alan located his role as being secondary and supportive to the role of a father. He defined a 'dad' as someone who was available and supportive, whereas a 'father' represented authority. Alan viewed his position as one that supplied historical depth to issues, but was aware of the primacy of the boys' father: 'I think if you're a fa-ther then you're committed to being – especially father, not dad, in charge. ... I thoroughly enjoyed it being there if they wanted it, but not committed to being there 100 per cent of the time. ... As I say, with grandkids, you can send them back to their parents.'

In exchange for his life narrative, Alan gained a sense of inclu-sion and a desire to repeat the role of grandfather. He also noted a major difference between the position of parent and grandparent: the full-time responsibility and role of parenthood compared to the grandparents' negotiation of any contact. The contact between Alan and the two boys, now men, has continued but takes place on an informal and ad-hoc basis: 'But they still always talk; he always comes down, the young one that still goes [to the football match], Bert, he still comes down, or 'e waves, yells, and 'e always yells, "Granddad". ... That makes me feel belonged. Makes me feel I'm part of something.' The relationship between the 'boys' and Alan had formed a bond that lasted beyond the duration of the scheme. Alan had been very clear in his attitude of not wanting to be a father when he was younger and entering middle age. However, as he got older, and events unfolded, he had negotiated the role of 'surrogate' fatherhood, and had accepted the role of 'adopted' grandfatherhood. The difference between the two roles, apart from how they originated, was related to the depth and mutuality of the relationship and the suitability of contingency support. The basis of the relationship was adult–adult for the former and adult–child for the latter: 'The two young lads who, as I say, I became adopted granddad for, they don't do anything like Simon does. ... Well, the thing being, you see, it means I know at the other end of a phone, ... I can ring up if I've got a problem.' Both Raymond and Alan had to adapt their lives following different forms of loss: the former through bereavement and the latter through the end of an intimate relationship.

Proxy

Alan's experience of unsought grandparenthood provided a sense of intergenerational integration. James also experienced an un-asked-for grandparent role, although his was via his partner's children. James and his partner, Liz, had been in an intimate relationship for approximately twelve years. James's social network was mainly made up of friends, with some ties reaching back to his childhood and early working years. The people dearest to him were his partner, followed by his older brother and his two daughters, and then two childhood friends of some twenty years standing, one female and one male. Contact with his nieces and nephew and their children was limited by their various and distant locations around the country. Likewise, his partner's two children lived quite a distance away: her daughter, Sonia, in South America, and her son, Tom, some 250 miles away in the UK. However, it was through Sonia's baby daughter, Myriam, that James became aware of not experiencing the parental relationship:

> Her sons had a little boy and her daughters had a little girl, you know, so they're all great, you know, and that's lovely. ... Myriam, the little girl who's eighteen months now, like, and we interacted wi' her a lot. I have particularly spent more time wi' her than, as a baby, than I even did with my nieces, funnily enough. And that's kinda re-awoken that, I thought, it would'a been nice, you know.

Familial support for Sonia through the perinatal period was negotiated by each spending time in both countries. The logistics involved in complying with sociocultural practices surrounding pregnancy demonstrated the tensions between traditional duties, roles and transnational mobility. For James, this led to his experiencing the intricacy of family intergenerational practices at first hand: 'It's complicated 'cos, Sonia and her partner, the parents of Myriam, live in South America. She was here for three months, so I was kinda around this pregnant woman a lot as well, which was interes'in' and strange. ... Liz and I went out to South America

when Myriam was seven months and we spent three weeks there.'
A combination of circumstances led James to experience a period
of caring for Myriam during their stay in South America. After
hurting his ankle, James spent a significant amount of time with
Myriam, during which he formed a deep attachment to her: 'I
couldn't walk, so I was actually with the baby for most of the time,
you know. They would go off and I just, you know, left with this
baby, and she's lovely, you know. So, that was quite a bonding
thing.'

In contemporary familial environments, fictive kin are often
absorbed into the family network, using the dominant hierarchal
kin structure: 'We're tryin' to work this out: Liz's ex-husband, he's
granddad, you know, and there's a South American granddad. ...
So, because we go to Greece a lot, I says, "Oh well I can be the
Greek word for granddad, 'Pappous', we'll just use that". So, we
just started to use that.' James's increased involvement in Liz's
family was legitimized and recognized as grandparental, through
naming him 'Pappous', from the Greek for grandfather. As a result,
both the hierarchy of the bloodline and the inclusion of James's
role were acknowledged: 'No. It's just recently, it's just like Liz's
grandchildren appeared on the scene that I discovered what a pleasure that is, you know. ... I'm keenly interested in them, as I would
be if they were my genetic grandchildren, I think.' The experience
of 'grandfatherhood' had given James an insight into a role that he
had not been conscious of before Myriam was born. Furthermore,
James equated the relationship with his 'grandchildren' to that of
being biologically related. Moreover, his status and experience as a
proxy grandparent had an effect on his 'wider' social relations:

> I'm, sort of, much more aware of how they must feel now towards
> their grandchildren, yeah, which I just 'adn't thought about it really,
> you know? ... I can, sort of, feel what's happenin' with them and
> how they must be feelin' toward their grandchildren now, yeah. ...
> Yeah, we do talk now, yeah, sort of, a new topic 'as entered the con-
> versational gambit, you know?

James's experiences and status as 'Pappous' had an effect on him
in a number of ways. First, he was able to appreciate, and empa-
thize with, the bond between parent and grandchild, and between
grandparents and parents. Second, his grandparenting experience
allowed him to engage on an equal level with the section of his peer
group that were grandparents. Finally, James had noticed that the

experience he had gained had also influenced his behaviour in the wider social world:

> A young woman along the street had a baby about three months ago. ... I would see 'er pregnant, you know, in the streets, and have a good chat and so on. ... And since then, she comes along sometimes and she'll say, 'Oh yeah, come and see baby', or I'll call in. ... This little baby's, sort of, she's lovely, you know. So yeah, I probably wouldn't 'a done that.

Noting that a near neighbour was pregnant, he formed a relationship with her and her partner that had continued once the baby was born. The influence on James's social network of a change in his fictive family had affected relationships at all levels. James had rationalized that his and his partner's age meant that he would not be a father. Furthermore, he had not considered the consequential loss of any grandparental role. However, circumstances led to him experiencing a role similar to that of a genetic grandfather. James's experience reflects the fluidity in family formation and the flux in the boundaries between kin and fictive kin.

Surrogate

In contrast to Raymond, Alan and James's happenchance entries into grandfatherhood, one participant actively pursued the role. Martin had accepted that he was not going to be a father following the diagnosis of his infertility and his subsequent withdrawal from donor insemination. It was through his wife Pat's family that Martin had successfully pursued the role of surrogate grandfather. On finding out that one of Pat's nieces was pregnant, and in order to prevent anyone else claiming the role, he quickly sought permission to fulfil the role of grandfather. Generally, fictive kin has been seen as referring to non-blood-relation individuals who have been 'adopted', through mutual negotiation, into a family:

> I said to the parents, because her father is dead, 'You know, this baby when it comes, hasn't got a paternal grandfather. Can I be a surrogate grandfather?' Which I am. ... We arrived at the hospital just after she was born and I – they handed me this tiny little thing; it was, what, six hours old? And I was just smitten, and, I'd never understood the bond between a parent and a child, until that moment, you know that was, I just looked at her and said, well that, 'If I had been a father ... I can, you know, nurture you for the rest of your life.'

Although Martin was accepted as surrogate grandfather-in-waiting, it was through his efforts that the role was established. Paralleling James's experience, Martin's interactions with his surrogate granddaughter Heidi had given him insight into the emotional bond between parent and child. The experience also drew Martin's attention not only to the absences he associated with involuntary childlessness but also to the difficulties of parenthood:

> But then I understood what the parenthood bit was, really. So, that's really, why she's so important to us. ... But God, I can see what parents go through, suddenly this cute little thing starts to grow and have a mind of its own and a will of its own and, and you're not allowed to hit 'em!

Martin's narrative reflected his awareness of a generational change in the culture of raising children compared to his own experience. In particular, the challenges in caring for an inquisitive child highlighted the change in culture from Martin's childhood to the present time. The intergenerational connection between Martin and Heidi, although rewarding, also challenged the suitability of the resources available for Martin to draw on. Martin reflected on his experience – and appreciation of the emotional depth between the parents – to distinguish between men who were childless and those who were not: 'And maybe that's what men who don't have children don't realize because you can see what you're missing physically. You know, social connections and all the rest of it, but you don't know what you're missing emotionally.' Martin identified the understanding that fatherhood is limited to the visible, external and tangible elements of the parental relationship. The emotional element of the parent–child relationship was intangible and could only be appreciated through experience. The grandparental role undertaken by Martin and Joan had expanded their social network: the acceptance of Martin in the role of surrogate grandfather had led to the development of the role as one of support to the biological parents. Additionally, the role was equated to that of biological grandparents. The inclusion of the role of surrogate grandfather had thus seen an adaption of the family structure to accommodate the demands of the fictive kin member, in an example of the fluidity within family practices: 'And particularly, I say, the surrogate grandchild, is a big part of the social thing. Because it's convenient for her parents to leave her with us and do other things, 'cos they're in their early forties. So, we are acting as, as you would treat a grandparent really, in that respect.'

The change in family structure to accommodate Martin's role also meant that as with James, the demarcation between blood kin and fictive kin had to be acknowledged. In Martin's case, the name was derived from the combining of the words 'surrogate' and 'grandpa'. However, his wife, Pat, retained her familial salutation, albeit with a slight alteration that acknowledged and reinforced her positional lineage to Heidi. The acknowledgement of the blood kinship therefore took precedence over fictive kin: 'They call me "sgrampy", which is an 'orrible word, but it's surrogate grandfather, surrogate grampy. Anyway, that's the nearest we could get to – granddad wasn't appropriate because it's not a real relationship. Not a hereditary relationship, shall we say, so "sgrampy". ... It's on a mug somewhere. ... Pat is "Gruntie" because she's actually a great aunt.' Martin drew attention to one aspect of being a surrogate grandfather that had not previously been alluded to – an ambition to live to see Heidi become an adult. Martin acknowledged that the certainty of his death was counterbalanced against uncertainty of his health in later life:

> To be quite erm, brutal, death is the future, I mean that it's, I reckon I've got, if I've got fifteen years, that'll be alright. ... You don't know what life's gonna throw at you do you? I may not have a choice about that. ... I'd like to see the, my surrogate granddaughter grow up, she's 3, fifteen years will take her to 18. So, that's about right, you can see them be an adult then, can't you?

The men's experiences highlighted the flux and fluidity in both the social and relational environments surrounding them. Two of the men, Raymond and Martin, wished to be grandfathers, but Raymond did not feel he could risk losing the latent fictive kin role he had developed. Martin seized the opportunity to fulfil his wish, and this had given him an insight into the emotional and physical world of parenthood. Neither Alan nor James had sought grandfatherhood, but had experienced it through association. Martin and James's experiences were directly connected to their partners' extended family ties. Raymond and Alan's experiences were related to social environments and independent of their family ties.

Summary

The relationships and social networks discussed in this chapter highlight how the different intersections between agency and structure over the life course are performed through roles, personal life, social networks and relationship dynamics. Factors such as familial background, quality of family relations, socio-economics, personality, geographic location, relationship status and desire to relate all intersected in the creation and maintenance of the participants' social networks. The biological imperative, prevalent in the ordering of family hierarchy, was negotiated by the use of fictive kin to build vertically, as in the case of surrogate fatherhood and grandfatherhood, and the use of social networks to build horizontally. Moreover, the actions of the participants highlighted the complexities in navigating between the 'closest', 'inner' and 'wider' relational environments. Location was a significant factor in the construction of social networks, with the transnational participants highlighting the difficulties involved in maintaining and forming social communities. The majority of the men had changed location for employment reasons and had lived within commuting distance of their work. Change of circumstance, for example exiting employment, led to an examination of the character of an area and its suitability to fulfil the participants' needs. Likewise, workplace friendships tended to fall away once participants had exited the work environment. Some men went on to build new networks while others did not.

This chapter has supported a number of concepts relating to social networks over the life course. The impact of events linked to the life course, such as bereavement, retirement, and entry into and exit from relationships, was reflected in changes to the structure of individual social networks. The size of vertical and horizontal ties was useful in highlighting those who would be seen at risk of social isolation and exclusion. Having no children automatically reduced the vertical structure, and for those whose parents had died, the vertical ties were further reduced. However, observing the size alone could not account for the quality of the relationships or the influences that shaped any given network. The configuration of the participants' 'personal convoys' altered with Davidson's (2004: 38) 'major determinants': age, employment, gender and relationship.

The impact of major life course events and non-events had implications for how the participants reflected and performed their social and self-identities. Personal social networks were seen to reflect the continuity of both positive and negative personal competencies that can affect all forms of relationship. Both positive and negative sibling relationships were seen in this study. The former has been viewed as an important resource, giving a sense of connectedness and a barrier against loss of autonomy. The latter have been seen as contributing to social withdrawal and avoidance, with a concomitant increase in the likelihood of social isolation (Chambers et al. 2009; Connidis 2001; Machielse and Hortulanus 2013). Continuity was seen in the membership of organizations that reflected work skills, sexual orientation and experience of ART. All relationships involved negotiation of challenges such as family friction, health and role loss or adaption across the life course. The participants' narratives supported the views of 'doing family' (Finch 2007: 66) and 'family practices' (Morgan 1996: 190). Consequently, the complexity and diversity involved in their 'personal community networks' (Wellman and Wortley 1990: 559) recognized the concepts of fictive kin and adapted family networks. The next chapter will explore the participants' views of the future and examine the different factors that affected that perception.

Chapter 7

AGEING WITHOUT CHILDREN

Introduction

In this last findings chapter I address the research questions concerning the participants' quality of life and views of the future. Later life has often been viewed in the context of a loss of agency in all environments: economic, health, social and identity. The age range of the participants covers the transition through the third age, which is commonly associated with competence before the decline linked with the fourth age (see Grenier 2012; Grenier and Phillipson 2013). Laslett's (1989) concepts of the third and fourth ages have been the source of much discussion, with the latter associated with limitation, vulnerability and loss of agency. Brief accounts of the participants' life history in the form of pen portraits are given in Appendix 1. The framing of old age has moved from of one of loss and decline to one of 'successful' ageing measured by objective indicators. However, older people with poor health have nonetheless rated themselves as ageing successfully (Strawbridge et al. 2002). Older people have also reported that in addition to their own health, and that of kith and kin, finance is an important element to their quality of life (Gabriel and Bowling 2004).

This study took place at a time when issues surrounding provision in later life, including pensions and the delivery of both health and social care, were the subjects of much media attention. The key themes in this chapter relate to ageing and health. The first section links the critical gerontology element of economics to ageing, with older people reporting that finance is highly significant in the maintenance of independence and autonomy (Gabriel and Bowling 2004: 29). Furthermore, the timing of the exit from employment to retirement not only has fiscal consequences but also connotations for social and personal identity (Phillipson 1999, 2013). Although both 'Quality of Life' and 'Health' were covered separately in my interviews, the analysis highlighted that the participants saw health as central to quality of life. The second section of this chapter begins with a broad examination of the participants' economic environment and their views of the future. The following section explores the participants' experience of ageing and health in relation to involuntary childlessness. The men's concerns relating to access to care and health resources are also explored. The fourth section examines the participants' reflections on legacy and finitude, and the final section provides a brief summary of the chapter.

Economics

Later life has often been viewed in the context of a loss of agency in all environments: economic, health and social care, and sense of self. The childless, whether voluntary or involuntary, have often been seen as 'other', with one assumption being that they are 'free' because they do not have the financial cost of parenthood (Connidis and McMullin 1999; Deindl and Brandt 2013; Kohli, Künemund and Lüdicke 2005). Conversely, it is fathers that have been shown to have higher average incomes than their childless counterparts (Dykstra and Keizer 2009). Table 7.1 details the participants' self-defined occupational statuses and financial resources. This table is ordered by age in order to account for the mandatory state retirement age, and highlights how the participants were subject to policy rooted in age and stage constructions surrounding functionality, productivity, contribution and liability. Eight of the participants cited some form of pension as part of their main income, with five in receipt of both state and employers' pensions. Of those five men, none had exited employment at the statuary retirement age of 65, but had left due to ill health or as part of a severance scheme.

Alan retired early with a full pension as part of an industrial injury settlement: 'I retired on me sixtieth birthday. ... I got repetitive strain injury. Have you ever seen somethin' like that [holds up hands]? ... Lost the use o' me thumbs. ... They said, if I dropped any claims, they would pay me full pension at 60.' Table 7.1 illustrates the influence that partners have on the financial resources available. Consequently, men whose partners were employed had

TABLE 7.1. The participants' occupational status and financial resources. © Robin A. Hadley.

Participant	Age	Occupational Status	Financial Resources
Stephen	49	Employed, full-time	Salary
Russell	55	Seeking employment	Own resources
Frank	56	Seeking employment	State support
Colin	59	Retired	Employer's pension, partner's income
John	59	Temporarily unavailable for work due to illness	Disability Living Allowance, partner's income
David	60	Self-employed, volunteer	Salary and employer's pension
Edward	60	Self-employed, volunteer	Salary
George	60	Seeking employment, volunteer	Employer's pension, partner's income
Michael	63	Employed, full-time	Salary
Harry	64	Not seeking employment	Own resources, widower's pension
James	65	Retired	State and employer's pensions
Martin	70	Retired, volunteer	State and employer's pensions, and partner's income
Raymond	70	Retired, part-time employment	State and employer's pensions, part-time salary
Alan	82	Retired, volunteer	State, armed services and employer's pensions

an 'economic dividend' to add to the 'health caretaker' associated with men in relationships (Davidson and Arber 2004: 131).

The men illustrated that for some of them, the transition from full-time employment to retirement was to their advantage. For example, David explained his position: 'I also felt that if I was to leave the company, I would be abandoning my final salary pension scheme. ... The period of my career from 53 to escaping was quite uncomfortable and was mostly going downhill. ... I stayed there until one day when they said, "Opportunity for voluntary redundancy".' David's experience of the latter years of his career highlighted the intersection between individual needs and the wider economic environment. Early retirement from the workforce has been widely used in the last half-century (Phillipson 1982, 1999, 2013). It also necessitates negotiation of an expected life course event. David's experience exemplified the tensions between an individual's future economic capital and his everyday social capital.

Two of the eight men who were in receipt of pensions, Raymond and David, described themselves as being in part-time employment, while a third, George, described himself as looking for employment (Table 7.1). As such, their narratives reinforced the fluidity and flux for those in the third age, and challenged earlier concepts of mid- and later life as being a period of reduced activity and control. Of the three, Raymond was the only one who referred to his employment as an economic necessity as well as a social resource (see Chapter 5). Raymond's former occupation as a waiter was typical of the low-paid careers that many LGBT people held in order to 'pass' in a heteronormative society (Dunne 1997; Heaphy 2007; Rosenfeld 2003). As a result, the only employer pension he had was from the few years he had spent working in the NHS before taking early retirement. Both David and Raymond had had their socio-economic status influenced by the macro-structural institutions of the stock market and government policy. David's experience was in the private sector and related to the former: 'It was not the time to be going looking for a new job in my field. ... Now we were post-dot-com boom. ... The need for the day was ruthless cost-cutting.' On the other hand, Raymond's post in the NHS was lost in a change of strategy and practice: 'It was across the board, thousands went. ... It was a mental hospital, and they'd got people out into the community.'

David and George both self-defined as having had a lower-middle-class upbringing. Both had attended university and had professional careers in management and teaching respectively. Both David and George, in discussing the transition from their careers, had referred to their partner only, and no other downward or horizontal relational connection. The period between the age of 50 and 60 had been one of great change for David: his career had peaked, declined and ended, and he had married. Following the exit from his professional life, David now viewed his time as divided into four main areas of activity: part-time business consultancy, voluntary work, domestic life and hobbies, such as running and sailing. As such, his lifestyle fitted the remit of 'successful ageing', although he had not been referred to any specific health programme or advice. George had left teaching after twenty-six years to pursue a doctorate in his late forties; however, the teacher's pension scheme had a strict policy of paying the pension on the contributor's sixtieth birthday. This had disturbed his sense of self and how he was viewed: he strongly resisted being labelled a pensioner. The imposed nature of the transition had directly determined George's perception, and his viewpoint reflected the normative discourse of decline surrounding the status of 'pensioner'. He described the powers inherent in the structured transition of receiving a pension and their effect on available identities.

> I think it sends all the messages that you're moving into a different phase of life: you're getting older. ... There is a sense of which the way the system works could easily shape me into seeing myself as a retired person at 60 in a way that I wouldn't if I was in a different context. ... Shaping me into someone who's getting older, less able to do what he were able to do, who is retired with all the connotations that that means. ... That will happen again when the state pension kicks in at 65 [laughs].

Furthermore, the different timings of the transitional events of qualifying for the workplace or state pension heralded 'multiple transitions' (Fairhurst 2003a, 2003b) and challenged the participants' present and future identities. The men's transition from full-time employment involved a renegotiation of their identities, and an examination of the meaning of activities and their associated values. Many of the participants, who considered themselves either full-time or part-time retired, noted how pursuits that had previously been viewed as leisure time were now seen in a different light. As George noted, 'I enjoyed gardening but you could say that was work and sometimes it does feel like work when there is a task to be done, and at other times it feels relaxing.'

Although there have been changes in the gender profile of the UK workforce, typically it has been women who disrupted their employment in order to care for children (Arber, Davidson and Ginn 2003; Davidson 1998; Mayhew 2006). Additionally, from 1997 to 2011 there was a 25 per cent increase in adults aged between 20 and 34 living with their parent(s) (ONS 2012b). A number of the participants, particularly those in the mediated group, noted the difference that children had on the finances of peers who were parents. For example, Martin observed: 'If I'd had children, I could have been in a position of having to fork out to buy properties and, as a lot of my friends have, have taken big lumps of their life savings to help kids out of situations.'

In addition to the benefits of partnership highlighted in Chapter 6, an additional aspect for the partnered was that of the partner's financial contribution. Six of the seven partnered men expressed the importance of the financial contribution their partner brought to the household economics. One aspect of childlessness for partnered participants was therefore the possibility of being in a relationship or a household consisting of two full-time-earning adults. James was the only partnered participant who did not allude to any financial interaction in his LAT relationship with Liz. The maintenance and control of economic independence has been shown to be one of the attractions of LAT-type relationships (Borell and Ghazanfareeon Karlsson 2003; Chambers et al. 2009). The nuances within John and Sue's complex relationship were exemplified by his reflection that although his benefits contributed to the household costs, Sue was the primary source of financial income. As noted in Chapter 4, John had considered the financial aspects of having children and summarized that for both financial and personal preferences, he would have become the main provider of childcare: 'That's her indoors. ... She earns a load o' money. So, we don't want for anything. ... So, in that sense I have a very good life.'

The participants' views of their future economic positions related to their assessment of their present positions, contextualized by experiences. The 'childless' have been viewed as economically advantaged (Bulcroft and Teachman 2004; Connidis and McMullin 1999; Deindl and Brandt 2013) and some of the participants acknowledged that compared to their peers, they had possibly had greater material benefits. However, they also noted that this did not compensate for the sense of loss associated with not being a father. Of the three aspirational participants, David, Stephen and Frank, only David referred to the socio-economic difference a child would have made: 'I think we would get by. ... It doesn't need a big salary to take us back to a reasonably comfortable financial position.' Stephen and Frank did not refer to any future financial implications of becoming fathers, focusing instead on concerns regarding finding a partner (see Chapter 5).

At the time the interviews took place, the UK government had applied a number of substantial reforms to the state pension provision. For example, the age of access to the state pension had changed from 65 years of age to being raised progressively dependent on date of birth (DWP 2014). The changes reflected issues surrounding the increase in life expectancy, the funding of pensions for the 'boomer' cohort, and employment in later life. As such, macro age-related strategies directly influenced an individual's perception of the future. For example, Stephen's view of his future was influenced by the political discourse regarding provision in later life. As one of the aspirational men, Stephen's attitude did not account for any possible future family that may have offered some level of care. Like the other participants, Stephen had resisted the view of children as duty-bound carers in later life: 'Yeah, it's scary in terms of, you know, not being able to rely on the state to necessarily meet your needs as an older person if you haven't already made provision for yourself.'

Recent government policies had influenced Stephen's thoughts of his future existence. Nonetheless, he was aware of the impact of his past economic choices on future economic capital. Stephen's lifestyle and economic choices had not only affected his relationship status but also his finances. He expressed concern for his financial post-retirement future: 'I'm in shit street when it comes to retirement because I've never paid into a pension and I'm 49. So, assuming I work 'til I'm 65, if I'm lucky enough to stay in work 'til I'm 65, I've got sixteen years left to try and salvage something that'll mean I won't be on the breadline when I'm 65.'

Stephen had not demonstrated any awareness of either the actual and proposed change to the single-tier state pension system or the increase in the age when he would become eligible for the state pension.

Frank had been in receipt of state support for twelve years, and was in dispute with the Benefits Agency regarding his chronic fatigue syndrome (myalgic encephalomyelitis, or ME). He supplemented his income through various cash-in-hand odd jobs. In addition to ME, his ability to obtain permanent employment was also restricted by a chronic health issue of a bad back. The combination of solo living, poor health and unemployment had led him to a stark assessment of his future: 'If she [his mother] died tomorrow, I'm not gonna suddenly be really well off; I'm only gonna get a third of the price of a small house, so it's not gonna solve my financial problems in the future. So, you know, things are quite bleak for the future. ... There's no money gonna come from anywhere.'

Frank was the only participant to refer directly to his surviving parent as part of any future economic capital. The participants' economic futures reflected a complex negotiation of background, class, macroeconomics, policy, roles, relationships and health across the life course.

The actions of both commercial and governmental policymakers following global economic events, and the anticipated increased demand for social and healthcare related to demographic change, was shown to have a significant impact on the youngest participants' views of their financial resources in later life. Of the remaining men, most had exited their main career, with some considering themselves retired while others viewed themselves as available for work but in receipt of a pension. For those in relationships, there was the added benefit of their partners' financial resources. For the older men, there was a concern regarding the cost and provision of care in the future; the latter, along with other aspects of health, will be examined in the next section. The effect childlessness had on the men's economic decisions has not been identified to any extent. What can be said is that had the men become fathers, any decisions would have had additional considerations, depending on the individuals' economic, cultural and social capital.

Health

The increase of an ageing population and life expectancy, combined with medical advances and increased health and social care costs, have led many governments to advance policy promoting ways to age 'successfully' (Bowling and Dieppe 2005: 1548). 'Successful ageing' is measured by the absence of disease or disability, the presence of high cognitive and physical function, and an active engagement with life (Rowe and Khan 1997; Strawbridge, Wallhagen and Cohen 2002). This approach uses objective scales to measure 'quality of life' and has been criticized for not representing older people's subjective experience of ageing. Older people have defined a good quality of life as including good social relations, health, finance and independence (Bowling et al. 2003). The importance of partners and adult children to the levels of personal satisfaction and quality of life in later life has been firmly established (see Scott and Wenger 1995; Burholt and Wenger 1998; Wenger et al. 2007; Bowling et al. 2003; Grundy and Read 2012). In Chapter 6, I showed the intricacies of the participants' social networks and the impact that these had on their identity, family practices and personal communities. As people age, their social networks reduce, with both older childless and solo-living people shown to have smaller social networks than parents and partnered older people. Moreover, within those networks the importance of sibling relationships is significantly increased (Grundy and Read 2012; Kendig et al. 2007; Wenger 1992, 2009; Wenger, Scott and Patterson 2000).

The participants' views and definitions of their quality of life illustrate the importance of both health and relationships in their lives. Those with partners, with the exception of John, rated their quality of life highly and all, including John, defined quality of life as good health and relationships. For the most part, the single rated their quality of life negatively, but they also defined it by health and relationships. For example, Harry's quality of life was determined by the death of his partner. The men's views of their quality of life reflect the significance of people's subjective experience (Strawbridge, Wallhagen and Cohen 2002; Bowling 2009). Health, at any age, is produced through a complex interaction between individual life history and biological, behavioural, physical, psychological, economic and social environments (Alley and Crimmins 2010: 91).

Biological ageing reflects the changes in physiological functioning and physical structures that lead to increased risk of mortality, disease and disability (Alley and Crimmins 2010: 76). The perception of decline in function in later life was prevalent among the participants. However, these views could be ascribed to other people and not specifically associated with childlessness. How the participants rated and defined their health status and how they accessed healthcare, spotlights the intersection between subjective agency and objective norms. For these men ways of 'doing health' were linked to their subjective experience of control and functionality.

The participants strongly associated their quality of life with health issues, often highlighting how an improvement in health would improve their quality of life. As a result, decline in mental or physical health (or both) was often cited as a disadvantage to ageing. The combination of personal bereavement, macro environment, care issues and loss of independence contributed to Harry's concerns regarding later life. The death of Helen had a significant effect on Harry: his view was influenced by bereavement and the media reports of abuse of older people in health and social care settings. He associated ageing with potential loss of autonomy due to the loss of physical capacity and well-being. Harry's opinions highlight the interaction between an individual's fears surrounding ageing (and consequent loss of agency) and the available public discourse. His views reflected a popular and distinct theme in the participants' views: health and care structures for older people as limiting and repressive.

> The one concern I have in life is longevity. I don't want to be old. ... Old people that are laying in hospital beds being beaten up by people that don't care for them. ... I don't want to be that man laying in that home, you know? While I can get out and drive and get about and do stuff. ... Life as an invalid or in poor health – I don't want any of that. ... I don't mind going tomorrow. I'm not looking for it or desiring.

The speculation on moving into residential accommodation included not only loss of identity through reduced autonomy but also the loss of material that helped form the participant's identity. John suggested that a reduction in independence and autonomy would challenge the continuity of identity located in items of significance:

> You know when you go in these sheltered bungalows there's not room for six guitars. You know and the bloody computer and, you know, 1200, 1500 CDs. There ain't room is there? So, something has to change. It's all that stuff that kind of defines you – you end up in one room and a television. And I just think 'No.'

Dignity for older people has been much in discussion in the media, academia and in practice settings (Baars and Phillipson 2013; Neuberger 2009; Scambler 2009). All the participants expressed issues surrounding dignity in later life. Martin framed his view of later life through the experience of caring for his mother and the dementia she lived with in her later years. Martin's experience highlighted the issues surrounding 'who cares' in later life and reflected the opinions of many adults whose older relatives live with dementia. Martin's narrative also revealed a subtext alluding to not repeating the experience of his parents, but also his own experience as the only child of increasingly ill parents. Consequently, one legacy he would not be passing on to any children was one of 'duty of carer':

> My mother's last five years were of no value to her at all. ... I think if you knew you were in that situation and you were still that mentally astute to plan it, it's not something I would rule out, particularly if

I was impacting other people's lives to the point that was unacceptable to me.

Martin reflected the views of other participants, who had ventured that there was a point when the decline–dependency balance would lead them to take control of their death. Anxiety surrounding possible future illness was linked to social embeddedness. Michael raised the concern of how a solo-living older person would access health and care services in later life: 'My Swiss, single, fatherless, gay friend said to me, "Who's gonna take us to the hospital? Who's gonna push us, when we fall on the floor, who's gonna pick us up?" ... So yes, I'm aware of that.'

The loss of control through failing health brought a number of scenarios from the participants regarding their fears and solutions. As noted in Chapter 6, Alan had arranged a power of attorney and a notice of advance decision (formerly a living will) regarding medical treatment. With regard to later life, Raymond had anxieties surrounding his capacity to care for himself and being both injured and isolated. Although Raymond had a strong relationship with his sister – who had power of attorney – he viewed residential care as preferable to being a burden to her. The drive to maintain an identity and autonomy was not so much disengagement but adaption and negotiation of self and being in the world.

I've accepted the fact that if I have to go into an old folks' 'ome, I'll go. 'S'nothing else 'cos I certainly won't go and live wi' me sister or with anybody else 'cos, I don't think it's fair to put a burden like that on somebody else. ... The only thing I worry about now is if I fall or anything like that.

For those with no partner, or with a nominated power of attorney, there was also anxiety regarding loneliness in later life. For Michael, who was both geographically and emotionally distant from his family, the end of life was an issue that was difficult to acknowledge. In referring to his solo status, Michael tacitly recognized the connection between the lack of close relationships, including childlessness, and isolation at the end of life: 'I think it's a dilemma and I don't think there's an immediately easy answer to it. ... And I'm sure a there's lot of people who don't need care but die alone. ... Yes, it's something I think we put to the back of our mind, those of us who are single.'

The attitude the participants displayed towards residential care in later life highlighted a difference between the heterosexual and non-heterosexual men. The former, as demonstrated by both Harry and John, did not refer to any anxieties regarding their sexuality in accessing any form of residential setting in later life. Conversely, both Alan and Raymond raised concerns regarding discrimination against non-heterosexuals in residential settings. Raymond observed the increased awareness of homophobia in the care sector:

> Housing associations now are certainly having to train their staff and open their doors to taking in gay people. Not just men, women too. … To be the only man sat in a room full of women is a bit daunting. … I'd feel really at a loss then, I wouldn't know what to, how to join in. Where if I say, equally men and women, then it's not so bad, you know.

Alan and Raymond's concerns reflect an ongoing debate on housing options for older LGBT people: the fear that their sexual orientation will result in inadequate treatment, discrimination or isolation (see Cruz 2003; Heaphy 2007; Guasp 2011).

Age and health influence sexual activity, with many studies highlighting the reduction in sexual behaviour in older age groups. A number of factors are seen to influence sexual activity: relationship satisfaction, physical and mental health, medication, self-image, diet, social network, social skills, moral values and well-being. As noted in Chapter 6, the biological clock and social age appropriateness of parenthood, both strongly associated with women, were also issues for men. For example, Russell noted the link between older men's sperm and genetic birth issues: 'I've become more aware that infertility increases with age and also that congenital abnormalities increase with conception, the sperm degrade. … In that sense my biological clock is I'm more aware of it.'

Scholars of masculinities have often placed sexual performance as central to men's identity, and one challenge of ageing for the participants was the negotiation of reduced libido. Not all the participants referred to their sexual activity. However, seven men directly or indirectly spoke about their libido. For example, Frank indirectly alluded to his ability to reproduce through viewing his sperm: 'I bought a microscope a year or two back, and just out of interest, I looked at my semen, it was fascinating to see these sperm wriggling around. I've no idea, obviously an expert would know, what the quality was and how many are swimming in the right direction, fascinating, you know.'

The importance to older men of being in an intimate relationship has been shown in a number of areas, including health, social network and well-being. However, as John's narrative suggests, the dynamics within a relationship are not always positive or healthy. David, who had married Cathy, twenty-three years his junior, described the subtleties within a relationship. David initially labelled the decrease in his libido as a reduction in his health; consequently, an increased libido would have increased his quality of health. However, he also drew on both ageing and the maturing of his marriage relationship as affecting his libido. Whereas Michael drew on age and medicine to explain the change in his reduced libido, David drew on age and discourses taken from the wider social network: 'I don't think I'd quite have the level of libido that I used to when younger. I think my wife would be like to be jumped on more enthusiastically for longer [laughs]. ... So, that is an issue which, I assume, is to do with the mixture of ageing and marriage.'

The decline with age of the men's libidos was often related to the question in the third section of the interview schedule regarding what had changed after the age of 50. The connection between health and sexual dysfunction was clearly demonstrated by John, whose circulatory, heart and diabetic conditions all contributed to his erectile dysfunction (ED). Both diabetes and hypertensive medication are known to cause impairment in sexual function. John's health and social profile fitted those that Weitoft, Burström and Rosén (2004) and Kendig et al. (2007) described in their studies (see Chapter 1). John linked his ill health to his reaction to being rejected as a suitable father by his partner (see Chapter 4) and subsequent poor health behaviour: 'My neurophia damaged nerves in my extremities, with my feet and my hands, erectile dysfunction I've had for a number of years, a common diabetic problem. ... We ceased having sex, so, bloody hell, probably about 1988 or '89.' John's experience demonstrated the link between illnesses, cognitive processing and sexual functioning. He also revealed the relational dynamics inherent within sexual relationships.

The acceptance of a reduction in libido has usually been associated with older men, as one of the elements in the transition of moving from the third age into the fourth age (Gott and Hincliffe 2003). Michael viewed the decline in his libido as a natural part of ageing. Moreover, a parallel was drawn with the menopause, and although it was not referred to, this may indicate media attention regarding a possible 'andropause', as suggested by Michael:

> My libido has reduced, yes, I'm aware of that. ... The hardness of one's erection does decrease, yeah, without feeling, interestingly,

without feeling – it must be a natural flow because I don't wake up at night bitterly disappointed or do anything about it. Women apparently get very depressed about the menopause but men have a sliding and slow menopause.

Michael had rationalized the change in his sexual identity; he also drew attention to the possible effect reduced sexual performance might have in a relationship. The nuances of sexual identity in later life involved the navigation between the physical, desire, individual preference and performance. Although Alan was twelve years older than Raymond, he located his response to his reduced libido within a framework that emphasized both choice and control.

It doesn't disappear, no, no, no. I think you're more discerning in what you're looking for, you know. ... I wouldn't want a younger man sexually, not much younger, but, you know what I'm sayin' when I say younger: under, say, 40, no way. ... But that dun't mean that I can't appreciate the beauty of a younger man under the age of 40 and say, 'Ooh 'e's a nice lad', you know? Eye candy! ... You can look at the menu but you don't 'ave to eat.

The acknowledgement of the social clock as an element of identity performance was juxtaposed between the rationalization of the lived self, duration and embodied effect. Moreover, Alan located himself in relation to his peers as younger, and highlighted the complex relationship between social identity, age and performance:

The thing is I 'ave always thought of age as a state of mind. ... It's 'ow many years' experience you've got. It's not 'ow many years you've lived or 'ow many years your body's lived. ... I know an awful lot o' people are a lot younger than me, who be'ave like 80-year-olds. I don't think I be'ave like an 80 year old.

The narratives explored above show that the participants strongly associated their quality of life with health issues, often highlighting that an improvement in health would improve their quality of life.

The effects of biological ageing and related health issues interacted with the participants' social and psychological identities. In terms of hegemonic masculinities, men are constantly attempting to subordinate everyone else or avoid being dominated in order to fulfil the patriarchal ideal. One consequence of an aged identity was the sense of liberation from having to conform to social hierarchy, and, possibly, an acceptance of childlessness.

> Being more settled in terms of accepting life conditions as being, as being *it*. Rather than always feeling you've got to make change and fight, you know, resisting all the time. I think, as you get older, you tend to resist less. ... And that can be pleasurable somehow. (Stephen)

The advantages of growing older were also associated with sagacity, maturity, contentment and freedom. The identities of 'wise man' and 'sage' are traditional patriarchal roles and connect with an 'ideal' masculine identity, as well as being typified by the role of 'grandfather', as seen in Chapter 6. Associated with the role of grandparent is a socially sanctioned caring and nurturing facet of masculine identity. The criteria the participants used to formulate the 'sage' identity acknowledged their experience, knowledge, empathy and fairness. For example, Alan saw a reward in his way of being: 'Advantages to ageing? It makes you a bit more patient. ... You're more understanding. ... You have, hopefully, the gift of wisdom and experience.'

Contrary to the widespread promotion of everything 'young' and the denial of ageing, no participant indicated that they wanted to return to their younger selves. Although liberation from the both the previous self and social norms were acknowledged, there was a tension between the present and past selves. In Russell's narrative, there appeared a retrospective bereavement for his younger self: 'With age comes some understanding. ... It's the freedom aspect of it for me. I'm freer now to be who I am more than I've ever been and that's come about through age, I think. I wish I could've been who I am now when I was young 'cos I would've been much happier.' The patriarchal ageing dividend that promoted sagacity and accepted nurturing, however, also demonstrated hegemonic tendencies with retrospective subordination of the younger self. Subordination also framed Edward's view of young people today and highlighted the link between view of self and view of other: 'The knowledge and experience that I've built up, I do sometimes think that I wouldn't want to exchange that for my young self. ... I do sometimes think I actually would rather be older and not so silly, rather than being youthful but with all that, sort of, the callowness of youth, yeah.'

Images of older people range from that of the obstreperous older individual, for example from such programmes as *Grumpy Old Men*, to adverts that promote the freedom of retirement and 'the good life' that the purchase of a particular product brings. Although the examples above seem separate, they all view being older as being different to the current domination of the beauty and non-aged agenda. Both are examples of the neoliberal marketization of the individual. The participants noted that with age, their attitudes had changed. For example, Frank contended that he challenged the status quo rather than being compliant with the social norm. He compared the timing of his changed identity with peers who now fitted the heteronormative pronatalist ideal: 'They went from rebel to settled – I've gone the other way. ... I was quiet and fairly timid then, and fairly conventional outwardly, and I've become more of a rebel as I've got older.' George, as with all the other participants, feared the loss of physical or mental capacity. His concern was founded on his experience of his parents' dementia, and expressed a transformation from an outward-looking to an inward perspective: 'I do fear – a stroke or cancer, dementia, both my parents had dementia. ... I fear that if restrictions of those sort come along – that I will become self-centred, obsessed with myself, and all the things that are wrong or afraid because I can't cope.'

Spirituality has been shown to have a positive effect in old age. Although the mechanism of how faith influences subjective well-being is not fully understood, the combination of social and emotional support, shared beliefs, community, safety and structure through ritual provides coherence and meaning in a changing world. Three participants, George, David and Alan, indicated that their belief would provide, in addition to social continuity and support, spiritual sustenance and a way of being in the world. David highlighted how faith was fundamental to his world and his actions in it. Consequently, he foresaw greater commitment to the spiritual aspect of his life: 'I would like to improve my contribution to church and I would like to spend more time on my own spiritual growth and, actually, that probably ought to be the number one focus, because that naturally feeds through into improving the quality of everything else.' George expressed the notion that the age-related reduction in external performance and health-resource capacity would ideally be countered by an inversely proportional spiritual growth. George's 'ideal' transformation counters the fears he expressed regarding ill health and becoming 'self-obsessed' in later life:

> I would like to be able to age gracefully. ... In terms of my health or my ability to do things, I hope I will make the adjustments as they come along, to those, to that new space. And I can be as big, as large a person, even though my horizons might be coming in, there is a

sense of which other things can open up. ... I hope as, and when those come, I can make the adjustments, gracefully, and find an inner freedom even though I haven't gotten an outer of freedom. Or have less of an outer freedom.'

The participants' concerns regarding health and ageing ranged from those that were not specifically related to men, or involuntary childlessness, to those that were. Martin described the essential management of his heart condition as juxtaposed against good health: 'I've got a pacemaker. Had that for twenty-odd years, doesn't do anything to me other than keep me alive. No, my health's pretty good, you know, for my age I suppose. I still dig gardens. ... I comfort myself by looking at the average statistics and saying well for, for my height, I'm about the right weight.' Martin drew on the available-to-all institutional health discourse of 'successful ageing' that promotes health as a personal issue to support his individual agency. The effect of age on health was often expressed by the decline in eyesight or hearing, accompanied by an acknowledgement that health would worsen in the future: 'I'm overdue for an eye test. I'm conscious that my eyesight is deteriorating. ... I've had the hernia for ten years. I'm sure a doctor would say to me, I should get it fixed – it'll get worse.' This statement of Russell's highlights two issues concerning health and ageing: first, the physiological degeneration that applies to all over the life course, and second, an attitude to health that is mainly associated with men. Men are typically seen to have an ambivalent attitude to health and to accessing health services (Davidson and Meadows 2009; Robertson 2007; Williams 2010).

Men's health behaviours have often been linked with the hegemonic masculine ideals of stoicism and risk-taking. The stereotypical constructions surrounding men and masculinity entail men being independent, virile, assertive, strong, emotionally restricted and robust. These traits are often associated with poor social and health behaviours, with older solo-living men reported as demonstrating similar 'macho' attitudes to health as young men. However, compared to lone older men, older partnered men are advantaged by their health being monitored by their partner (Arber, Ginn and Davidson 2005; Davidson and Arber 2004). As such, the stereotypical masculine ideal of 'independence' has been viewed as conflicting with the 'independence' and 'interdependence' of successful ageing (Arber, Davidson and Ginn 2003; Bowling and Dieppe 2005; Smith et al. 2007). The participants' view of attending health services indicated a range of responses, from the stereotypical masculinity espoused by Russell to Edward's self-definition as a hypochondriac: 'I am a bit of a hypochondriac, I will go and see him if, her, sorry, I should say, if something starts that worries me, or if I can't explain.' Contrary to the widespread association of avoidance of the health services, most of the men viewed attendance at the GP's as common sense. With the exception of John, those men with partners would often discuss any issue with their partner, thereby confirming the well-being support dynamic of a relationship.

The maintenance and dominance of patriarchy, through the practice of hegemonic masculinities, has been much discussed in sociological and health research (see Chapter 2). Conversely, recent studies have highlighted the complex dynamics in the relationship between the structure of healthcare institutions and the agency of individuals. Studies of staff in healthcare settings show that male patients have been viewed as not fulfilling the traditional norms of invincibility and bravery associated with the masculine ideal (Gough and Robertson 2010; Watson 2000). For example, healthcare providers and receivers in IVF clinics have both performed hegemonic masculinities (Dolan 2013). Consequently, health and care settings are locations where the performance of hegemonic masculinities is embedded within the structure of the institution and in the agency of the individual (Robertson 2007; Williams 2010). For example, James found that his embodied experience was not acknowledged before being diagnosed with a chronic heart complaint: 'I had to keep on at the medical establishment before I could get the checks and tests that I needed, I felt I needed, you know. I was quite, I mean I didn't want to have it, but I was glad to be proved right.' Interestingly, James also noted that not only did he have to negotiate the norms embedded within the social structure, but also the social norms he used that framed his being in the world. The stoicism James displayed was associated with a cohort value and reflected the ethic of his working-class background. However, that value position conflated with his needs and highlighted an internal conflict between conforming to the normative social narrative and individual agency: 'I don't like to bother the doctor, you know, I'm still of that generation. But, also I think, "Well I've only got this one chance" you know? And bugger 'im if he doesn't, you know, he doesn't wanna see me again. He can't not see me again.'

The overall view the participants had of their future was a fear of deterioration in physical and mental health. Therefore, the views they expressed were similar to those of ageing people generally. The major difference was the absence of any reference to the role of children or grandchildren in their lives.

Individuals and institutions have often referred to the male body in a mechanistic fashion. This reflects the Cartesian duality of body and mind, and provides the masculine discourse through which men see their bodies as controllable and controlled. Martin used the metaphor of a motor engine to describe the function of his pacemaker: 'It's like putting an electric, electronic ignition on your engine.' In doing so, he drew on his background in engineering and interest in motorcycling, but also reflected a discourse that has been popular in the promotion of good health behaviour for men (Gough 2010). However, the notion of the body-as-machine forms a paradox with the knowledge of the decline of the body with age. Negotiating the transition from the 'body infallible' to the 'body fallible' challenged the participants' perception of control and raised questions surrounding age and self. John summarized the effect his comorbidities had on the reflexive gaze by which he now viewed himself in the context of his age: 'So having the health stuff having gone a bit like this [points to leg], just makes you more vulnerable – because you're suddenly aware, you know, you're not, you're no longer invincible.'

One of the consequences of ill health had been to challenge John's sense of his body's indomitability, with a resultant difficulty in rationalizing the change in the mind–body dynamic. Although few of the participants saw themselves as 'invincible', they certainly had not viewed their bodies as fallible. Colin highlighted an age-related change in his perspective of later life: as a young man, not only was he extremely athletic, but he also viewed old age as something to be avoided. After being diagnosed with motor neurone disease (MND) in his early fifties, he now viewed his future health in terms of negotiating the desire to live as long as possible, against the increased need for care as he ages: 'Before I had MND I saw the doctor very, very, rarely. ... I wouldn't say invincible but I was a fast runner and super fit. When I was younger, I had no desire to live beyond 70. Now I do.'

All the participants associated later life with a decline in functionality, with the fear of loss of either physical or mental capacity evenly distributed among the sample. Studies that report differences between the health of parents and the 'childless' tend to be based on census, health and mortality records, and have high-lighted the poor health outcomes for the latter (Kendig et al. 2007; Weitoft, Burström and Rosén 2004). Only John conformed directly to that 'problem' typology. The other participants' concerns regarding ageing and involuntary childlessness were more nuanced. Martin reflected on the balance between the physical and emotional differences between himself and his long-time friend. Counterbalancing Martin's greater health capital was the relational depth between the father and his adult children and grandchildren.

> I went to a seventieth birthday party of a chap I went to school with. ... Physically, he's, well, pretty well nearly crippled with back problems and knee problems. ... It was quite stark for me then to look at that – I'm physically very well. ... And he is opposite of that, but emotionally he's very rich: it was evident how much he was loved by all these daughters and granddaughters. And that was a bit painful.

Finitude

Death is integral to the process of life, and the cessation of biological function is held within a wider social environment of relationships and rituals. Death in old age is viewed as 'normal' and part of the natural cycle of life, with the result that in the period before clinical death, older people may be subject to a degree of social death. Social death has been associated with healthcare settings where older patients received poorer care than other patients, by a process that progressively excluded them from their social environment. In this way, the older person lost both functionality and social identity (Kellehear 2007: 12; 2008). Another element of social death occurs when individuals withdraw from their social world, by relinquishing their roles in preparation for death. Death typically involves the social engagement of others: relatives, friends, health workers, administrators, morticians, funeral staff and others, depending on the individual and their social and cultural heritage (Corr 2004; Doka 2002). Death has a wide social impact and has been described as becoming an environmental norm for older people. As people age, death becomes more familiar as their experience of the morbidity and mortality of peers and contemporaries increases (Phillips, Ajrouch and Hillcoat-Nalletamby

2010: 67). For example, David described the funeral of a younger former colleague in pragmatic terms that demonstrated an acceptance of death and the dynamics of his wider social network: 'And I went with other colleagues who live in the next town, I gave them a lift up to the service and back yesterday. Nice to be in touch but we don't see each other that significantly.'

The change in the demographic profile of the UK is linked to the decline in fertility rates and the increased longevity of its population. Moreover, advances in treatment mean that there is a greater number of older people with comorbidities, with the result that there has been an increased demand for care. Consequently, health and social care for older people has had a great deal of media attention, with many health and care institutions, national and local, being heavily criticized. The participants reflected that debate in responses regarding later life and the end of life. The economic and existential future was closely related to, and highlighted by, the considerations regarding the participants' legacy. Martin noted that women live longer than men and saw their familial house and vehicles as assets that would be used to secure health and care for both him and Pat in later life. Furthermore, the same assets would also provide financial security for Pat should he, as he anticipated, die first. Martin's strategy may be seen as a continuation of the 'provider' role. His considerations may be typical of older people generally; nonetheless, he did not have to account for, positively or negatively, any vertical beneficiaries such as children or grandchildren:

> What I can't do is not leave some provision. And again, the buffer at the end of it, if all the money's gone and we're struggling along and I die, she's got the house, so she's got the roof over your head and the buffer of the bikes, she can sell those off and that'll give her a bit of cash.

As Martin had previously observed, many older people financially support their children or grandchildren (Albertini and Kohli 2009, 2017; Kohli 1999) and leave their estate to them (Legacy Foresight 2007, 2010). The majority of the participants nominated to their partner or biological next of kin any legacy in the event of their death (Kohli and Albertini 2009). Legacy was not only a concern over the future, but included the discontinuity that involuntary childlessness brought to other emblems of ancestry. The passing on of treasured material connects the familial culture from generation to generation. As such, the narrative of previous lives is inherited not only through the genes but also through physical items. David's narrative underlined that involuntary childlessness ended the passing on of the stories embedded in heirlooms:

> I have a bit of a sense of the way values and experience has been passed down the family tree, as it were, and people to pass it on to and I don't. ... My mother will eventually produce a large flood of mementos. ... Pity. There is a sort of richness of family history, which it's nice to pass on to people, again no one to pass it on to.

The increasing number of childless older adults has been viewed as an emerging market and is of particular interest for charity legacy bequests (Legacy Foresight 2010). On the one hand, the childless singleton does not have to negotiate kin dynamics; on the other, they do not have the blood-kin network to guide any decision. Both Harry and Martin (see Chapter 6) were the only children in their respective families. Harry had arranged for his partner's nephews to be the beneficiaries of his will. Similarly, Martin and Pat had nominated her siblings' children as the beneficiaries of their estate. Many older adults, parents, grandparents and other relatives often plan their financial legacy to directly support younger generations (Legacy Foresight 2007, 2010):

> So, when the last of us dies, then the estate gets broken up and goes primarily, well, solely, to the generation after Pat's siblings. ... So, it skips a generation on the basis that if they haven't made it by that time, then they don't deserve to be given any help and the next generation is going to benefit more from it.

As noted earlier in this chapter, the men associated ageing with a decline in health and functionality. However, their speculations regarding later life and death were age-dependant. The two youngest men did not want to consider their mortality, while the older men expressed an awareness of the proximity of their demise. Common to both statements was the awareness of time limited by mortality. However, the future held significantly different meanings for Stephen, the younger man – 'I prefer not to think about that, Robin. ... I want it to be as long as possible' – and Martin, the older man: 'To be quite brutal death is the future. ... Long term has suddenly become quite short.'

Government rhetoric in the UK over the past decades has emphasized the importance of the family in areas ranging from childcare to ageing. In the past, care of parents and older relatives has fallen mainly on daughters, with many women in a 'care sandwich' of managing both children and parents. Changes in the ways family operates, older people's concerns regarding 'not being a burden', economics and the delivery of social care have led to a shift in the availability of care in later life. The participants, as noted in Chapter 4, conformed to the widely held view that children were not to be conceived in order to provide care in later life. The participants' attitudes concerning their childlessness related to their age and views of fatherhood or non-fatherhood. The 'aspirational' men believed that becoming a parent would influence every aspect of life. The differences that fatherhood would bring were so fundamental to Stephen as to be unimaginable: 'I think if you've got children and family, then the way that you would view your life, and the end of your life, it's very different. I mean I don't know how different 'cos I'm not in that situation, but I would guess it would be very different.'

Both Stephen and Martin believed that having a genetic legacy, whatever the relational circumstances, would be qualitatively different between parents and childless people. Martin reflected on the continuity of difference between those ageing with children and those ageing without children. He saw the pragmatic reality of a childless old age, compared to an idealistic view that adult children would provide some level of support for parents in later life:

> You plan your life on the basis there's no one gonna look after you. Whereas, you could plan your life on the basis, I've got a couple of children who'll be there for me, you know, when I'm old and dribbling. ... Even as you come towards death, it does change your life. Yeah. Never thought about that, it's quite profound isn't it?

Children were viewed as a focal point and gave continuity to life, not only by being the recipients of experience, but also through the legacy of material items of previous generations. The acknowledgment of ancestry, through the passing on of treasured material, adds to familial cultural and socio-economic capital. As such, the narrative of previous lives is inherited not only through the genes, but also through physical items. The impact of not having children not only left David in limbo regarding what role he was to take in later life, but also had consequences for hereditary possessions of both form and genetic substance. Therefore, having children liberated a way of being in the present and an acknowledgement of being in the future: 'I think having kids is a way of producing a sense of continuity. Otherwise, death feels very final. If you're leaving kids, you've left something of yourself. ... It's just

the sense that you've contributed to their values and their formation and they carry on.' The rationalization of not having any
children was also negotiated through the meta-narrative of global
warming and the environmental issues of overpopulation against
loss of the parental dividend. For George, his individual loss was
set against the gain for the overall community: 'I don't have any
children to look after me in my old age. ... One way it feels like I'm
doing the right thing for the planet but in another I'm missing out.'

The acknowledgement of the finitude of life highlighted the
intersection between individual agency, social context, economic
status and health. The majority of the men did not have to consider
their imminent demise; however, John, like Colin, had comorbidities that were life-threatening. John had related the cause of
his poor health to childlessness. Nevertheless, in considering the
future, neither referred to the loss of any potential parental or
grandparental relationship. Both had different views on the end of
life that highlighted the interaction between health, social context
and relationship:

> I want to live as long as possible but that my partner and brothers
> outlast me. ... Due to the MND, I will need more and more help but
> don't want to be a heavy burden on my partner. ... I have told my
> partner I will probably go into to a hospice to die to relieve some of
> my partner's distress. (Colin)

Quality of intimate and social relationships had a direct effect
on the men's attitudes to end of life. Colin's attitude to his demise
involved elements of both altruism and control. Nonetheless, the
position that John occupied contained a powerful controlling dynamic. He did not acknowledge the effect of his possible death
on either his partner or family network: 'I've been an emergency
admission to hospital on eighteen occasions. Now, I keep getting
this cellulitis problem and it has occurred to me that, you know,
next time, you know, I just don't bother phoning the ambulance.
You know, I think, "Why should I bother?" Because all I'm going
to get is more abuse.'

Death and dying are often contextualized by biomedical and
social meanings, and the participants' narratives reflected the
complex existential interdependence between individual agency
and sociocultural values. The participants' accounts indicated that
planning for, and managing, ill health was agentic in itself. The
relationship between social structure and agency in later life was a
complex interaction that reflected the individual's past and present

experience. Future agency was of concern and dependent on how the participant identified himself. The negotiation of agency in the transition between the third and fourth age was an ongoing element of the participants' lives and indicated that the fourth age was an agented environment.

Within the interviews were both a legacy and an ending: the legacy of the first transcript and the ending of the second meeting (the exception being Harry who declined the second interview). Our first meeting had focused very much on the grief Harry felt after the death of Helen. The intensity of his pain was palpable, and it was with some relief on my part that he withdrew: 'I don't think I have anything left to say that I haven't already said.' The participants' treatment of their transcripts fell into two camps: those who were going to destroy it and those who were going to keep it. One participant who viewed the interview as a legacy was Russell. It seems appropriate to end this last of the findings chapters with his quote:

> I'm glad I've done it, because I will have done it, so it's on record. But having taken the opportunity, you know, I'm pleased that I've done it. Sort of a legacy in the sense that we were discussing Hirschman's [1970] comment at the end of his book, saying he'd hoped that someone would benefit from it. ... I don't know whether you've been aware of it, but I expect you are, there's also grief that this'll be the final session for us. You know, an awareness that it's ending.

Summary

The participants' views on finitude reflected the complex interaction between age, economics, health, autonomy, lifestyle, location, view of the past, present and future, culture, sexual orientation, relationships policies, state institutions, globalization and neoliberal politics. All the men's views of ageing reflect how they relate to who they are in the present, and how, who and what they will be in the future. The participants' attitudes were dependent on the complex interaction between their individual agency and structural factors, including the dominant sociocultural narratives that formed their worldviews and how they navigated their life-scapes (Hadley 2008a). Economically, the two youngest men were most uncertain of the future and highlighted the relationship between an individual's economic history and government policy. Concerning attitudes to health, the men did not all conform to the masculine norm of stoicism and non-engagement with health services. Instead, a complex set of interactions between health and age challenged the construct of the constant chase of the hegemonic ideal. Moreover, with age came a sense of release from that way of being a man, and the freedom to find a form of nurturing through the performance of sagacity. Those with a faith had the social support of ritual and a model of how to manage the transition from physical decline and loss of capacity to a spiritual worthiness. Approaching later life and the narrative of decline held many challenges for the participants, from the younger men not wanting to contemplate these issues to the older men's acute awareness of mortality. The ideas and beliefs surrounding later life reflected a structural condition that associates ageing with decline and dependency, and denies the potential galvanising and enriching capital of older people.

Conclusion

Introduction

This chapter completes my study on the lived experiences of involuntarily childless older men. In this chapter, I draw together my empirical findings, my earlier critical review of the literature and my analysis of the fieldwork into a discussion, conclusion and summary. I consider the findings in relation to the existing literature; this is followed by a conclusion section in which I appraise and evaluate the study by addressing its contribution to the knowledge base. I then move on to offer guidance for future research. The chapter concludes with my reflections on the study.

As discussed in the Introduction, this study arose from a combination of personal, academic and professional interests. I have had the privilege of interviewing fourteen older men about their experiences, thoughts and feelings regarding involuntary childlessness. The participants' narratives highlighted the complexity of their individual agency within social structures formed by social institutions, culture, class, economic and political contexts, and relationships. The key findings of the study support the concept of a 'continuum of childlessness' (Monach 1993: 5) in the manner in which the men negotiated the fatherhood ideal. I also contend that the patriarchal dividend further supports the pronatalist ideal types, by both stigmatizing and denying the existence of men who do not reproduce. The concept was extended to show how the men related to and managed non-fatherhood and the influence it had on their behaviours, attitudes and identity at different times and locations. The timing of events such as relationship entry and exit was very significant in the men's fertility intentions, outcomes and history. Elements of complex bereavement and disenfranchised grief, both associated with infertility, were evident and can be extended to those not receiving ART treatment. Losses included the roles and social dividend associated with parenthood, family status and grandparenthood. The social clock was significant in the participants' judgement of the appropriateness of actions, abilities and behaviours, with some men viewing themselves as too old for fatherhood. Consequently, I found that there was a desire for, and significance in, different forms of relationships, from intimate to intergenerational, across the life course. This finding supports the view that social relations are adaptive, creative, complex, fluid, important and significant.

This study drew attention to the contexts surrounding ageing in general and the nuances of ageing without children. The findings support the concept of ageing as a complex interaction between biological, economic, social and chronological factors. The participants' subjective experiences viewed health and relationships as the most important contributors to quality of life, with the single men broadly citing the former and the partnered men the latter. This finding demonstrates the importance of relationships across the life course. The positiveness of the continuity model was seen as not representing those whose poor formative experiences influenced their problem management and resolution across the life course. Consequently, a finding of this study is that involuntary childlessness brought a 'continuity of disruption' that fluctuated in importance relative to complex stimuli. I argue that the men adjust their ageing identities by utilizing available social scripts and other social resources, rather than blindly following the traditional ideals of masculinity. A significant finding was the fear expressed by all the participants of their being a threat to children. The absence of childless older people in policy was identified in the Introduction. Accordingly, the findings support the criticism of policy based purely on chronological age. This is particularly important in the light of the coronavirus (Covid-19) pandemic. For example, there have been reports that in the UK, access to medical treatment has been based on age (Hill 2020).

Central to the natural order of biological reproduction is the transition to parenthood. Disruption to expected continuity challenges people's resilience and sense of normalcy, as well as the expected trajectory of the 'package deal' for men (Townsend 2002) and the 'motherhood mandate' for women (Russo 1976). This study supports Allen and Wiles's (2013: 206) contention that the *'pathways and meanings of childlessness vary so much that it is unwise to assume that people have similar experiences of non-parenthood, especially in later life'* (italics in original).

Drawing on the evidence provided in Chapters 1 to 7, I discuss below the extent to which the aims of the study were achieved, and show how the research questions presented in the Introduction and Chapter 2 were answered.

Discussion

Events Influencing Childlessness

The paucity of research into involuntary childlessness was discussed in Chapter 1, where it was noted that the vast majority of infertility literature had, until recently, reported that infertile women experienced greater distress than men did (Culley, Hudson and Lohan 2013; Fisher, Baker and Hammarberg 2010). My research demonstrates the diversity in, and intersection between, events that contributed to the participants' childlessness. For example, John and Sue's delay in trying for children related to wider economic circumstances: the rise in bank interest rates forced them to focus on income generation. This was compounded by Sue's change of mind to not wanting to become a parent. Although frustrated in his expectation of fatherhood, John chose not to pursue another relationship, believing he could not risk not finding a willing partner. A major consequence of his reactions were the chronic comorbidities caused by poor dietary and health behaviours. This highlights the interweaving of factors that have consequences which not only disrupt reproductive decision-making but also have a subsequent effect on relationships, health, behaviour and identity. John's story adds to the claims of existing literature that indicate that the quality and status of the intimate relationship has an effect on both the health and social behaviour of childless men (see Dykstra and Hagestad 2007b; Kendig et al. 2007; Weitoft, Burström and Rosén 2004). Although not all the men responded in the same manner, John's story shows how not achieving the expected identity and status of the parental ideal exposes the lack of alternative, socially approved narratives one can use. In addition, the relationship between national economic factors and reproductive disruption adds to studies that have highlighted men's attitude to money as a factor in childlessness (Parr 2007, 2009). Conversely, John's experience was contrary to life course studies that have indicated the timing of entry into relationships as a predictor of childlessness (Hagestad and Call 2007; Morgan 2003; Simpson 2009). John's narrative highlighted how outside influences can influence intra-relational dynamics and any reproductive strategy.

The influence of their partners' views on fertility intentions and outcomes was very influential in some of the participants' procreative narratives. Partners delivered their views in different ways: Liz made it clear from the start of her relationship with James that she did not want children because of her fear of childbirth. John also thought fear of childbirth was an unspoken reason behind his partner's change of attitude. Similarly, Martin indicated that his first wife had hidden her fears surrounding giving birth until near the end of their marriage. Colin's second wife did not disclose that treatment prevented her from having more children until after they were married. The men's narratives exposed the dominance of the view that motherhood, and ergo childbirth, was central to the identity of women (Franklin 1997; Letherby 1994; Petchesky 1980). Moreover, Sarah Earle and Gayle Letherby (2003: 2) highlight that although reproduction is often assumed to be 'women's business', the majority of women make their reproductive decisions not in isolation but frequently in the context of intimate and other relationships (Cannold 2000; Heaton, Jacobson and Holland 1999; King 2003; McQuillan et al. 2003). The strength of the association between women and motherhood gave little resources or opportunity for the women to express their fears, or state their views, regarding not becoming mothers. This finding supports the argument put forward by Hofberg and Brockington (2000) that although fear of childbirth had been known since the mid-1800s (Marcé 1858), the severity it has on women's health and well-being had not been acknowledged in the medical establishment (see also Scollato and Lampasona 2013). The men's narratives also highlighted the effect of the dominant pronatalist norm in denying any positive counter-narrative for women who did not want to become mothers. Likewise, this supports the view that voluntarily childless women are viewed negatively (Gillespie 2000, 2003; Letherby 2002)

The findings in this study confirm the timing of events and attitudes as contributing towards the men's involuntary childlessness. The past influences the present and the future, and consequently influences a person's role within the wider social landscape. The actions and attitudes of the men, as they negotiated the movement from an aspiring to a mediated stance towards fatherhood, demonstrated the different strategies each adapted in order to negotiate their procreative remit. This study has shown the combination of events that can affect reproductive outcomes. Therefore, it supports previous research that cites events such as early divorce, timing of exiting education and leaving home, marrying late and employment history as contributing factors. In addition to the timing of formal and informal transitional events, men's upbringing and attitudes to family, health, leisure, money, women and work have also been noted as contributing to childlessness (Dykstra 2006; Hadley, Newby and Barry 2019; Hagestad and Call 2007; Morgan 2003; Parr 2009, 2010). Gender identity in particular shapes the trajectory of life course transitions through the timing of events, such as intimate relationships, sexual activity and parenthood (Connell 1995, 2009; Dudgeon and Inhorn 2003; Forste 2002). Fertility potential is a significant component in the majority of people's well-being, and distress levels in individuals who have strong procreative intentions increase for a period when they give up that desire (Heaton, Jacobson and Holland 1999; Quesnel-Vallée and Morgan 2003; White and McQuillan 2006).

The unquestioning assumption of the majority of the participants that parenthood would happen automatically demonstrated the depth and sophistication of the social constructs that embedded biological imperative within social structures. My research demonstrated that the men were all aware of the social clock that informed the criteria surrounding the 'acceptable' age for fatherhood. The men's reaction to, and negotiation of, the social criteria challenged the voluntary–involuntary binary found in infertility research literature. My findings support research showing that childless men's fertility intentions change with age, and that financial circumstances and their partners' biological clock and attitudes to parenthood increase in importance (Roberts et al. 2011). My research showed that there was an age-related change of attitude towards parenthood. Frank and Stephen only came to the realization that they aspired to fatherhood in their forties. Before that awareness, both had been ambivalent about fatherhood, with Stephen being contemptuous of the 'package deal' norm. The majority of studies have shown that heterosexual men hold a 'package deal' view of the order of the adult life course that includes work, marriage or a partnership, home and children (Townsend 2002: 30). The two gay participants highlighted how in their teenage years, they decided that becoming fathers was not achievable. My findings support the view that individuals relate to their childlessness in different ways at different times, dependent on their unique circumstances (Keizer, Dykstra and Jansen 2007; Kemkes-Grotten-haler 2003; Letherby 2002; Morgan 1991). Linn Sandberg (2009: 71–72) has postulated that there is a 'reproductive script' that de-termines the performance of masculinity in earlier life. Men with and without partners may feel lost, excluded or isolated with the loss of the script structure. Men in intimate relationships in later life may position themselves outside of that script, and are therefore free from the pressure to conform.

Social Practices and Networks

There is a large body of literature that reports on the social networks of older people, from the influential work of Townsend (1957, 1962) through to the longitudinal study of Wenger (Scott and Wenger 1995; Wenger 1984, 2009; Wenger, Scott and Patterson 2000). One finding of my research is that all the men demonstrated a hierarchy of relationships in which intimate adult relationships were desired more than the parental relationship. The social networks of the participants contradicted some of the established notions regard-ing personal communities. For example, the two oldest participants had larger social networks than the two youngest: all of these men were single and solo-living. Social networks are seen to reduce with age and people's ability to travel. Typically, older people with children have larger social networks than those without. Children, stereotypically daughters, are often both the main social contact and deliverer of care to parents (Burholt and Wenger 1998; Wenger 1984, 2009). Later-life families are characterized by having a child nearby, being in frequent contact with at least one of their chil-dren, having strong family care obligations, and regular exchange of help-in-kind from parents to children (Dykstra and Fokkema 2011; Phillipson 2013). Couples tend to have larger networks than solo-living or single people, while childless women tend to have smaller networks than women with children. Childless men have smaller social networks than childless women. A common theme emerging from research work has been the difference in the shape and size of social networks between men and women, those with children and the childless. In other ways, my data conformed to previous research, with the majority of the partnered men having the greater size of social network overall (see Arber, Ginn and Da-vidson 2005; Davidson, Warren and Maynard 2005). The quality and size of social networks in later life are viewed as important factors in well-being, as social networks provide support and help prevent exclusion and isolation (Bernard and Scharf 2007; Victor and Scharf 2005).

The continuity model (Atchley 1989, 1999) is often drawn on in gerontological studies to demonstrate how older people positively negotiate change – for example, through coping with an illness by drawing on their experiences of successfully managing ill health. Two men with small social networks illustrated the dynamics of continuity theory in action. John's experience highlighted how the poor quality of his interpersonal and familial relationships influenced his social networks. His experience of an 'aversive' upbringing, and issues in his relationship (see Chapter 4) led to ambivalent relationships with his family and his partner. As a result, he had little support with his health problems, for example in attending appointments. An example of the positive exploitation of existing resources was Russell's utilization of his wider social network when seeking accommodation. He had accepted lodging from two older women, who were sisters, with whom he had a very informal connection. Consequently, the two sisters had come to mean a great deal to him, and as he placed them in his 'inner circle' with his mother and birth sister, in effect the two sisters were his fictive kin (Allen, Blieszner and Roberto 2011; Finch and Mason 1993; Heslin et al. 2011; May 2011a; Morgan 2011a). The findings in this study point towards a more nuanced negotiation of problems than the positive approach widely associated with the continuity model. Some, with negative early experiences or limited resources to draw on, challenge the positiveness of the theory (Grenier 2012: 140). Others, however, highlight the creativity and adaptivity that people use in forming supportive relationships. This supports the literature that points to the fluid, complex and contradictory dynamics of both social relations and networks.

Research into formations of family and social networks has evolved from the views of post-Second World War theoretical functionalists – for example, Parson's (1951) much-quoted 'nuclear family' – to a more nuanced understanding (Bengtson 2001; see, for example, Finch and Mason 1993; Morgan 1999, 2011b; Phillipson, Allan and Morgan 2004; Smart 2007). Morgan's work (2011b) has shown the complexity in the flux and fluidity between, and across, kith and kin and other social relationships. The change in demographics following the fall in fertility and mortality is seen in the intergenerational structures that are more pronounced at the top than at the bottom. Vertical (grandparent–parent–grandchild) ties are increased and horizontal (cousins, siblings) ties are reduced

(Phillipson 2013: 112). Furthermore, the increase in the number of grandparents, and the role they occupy, may mean a sense of difference for those who are not grandparents. Although not all the participants were 'vertically deprived' (Dykstra 2010), meaning that they had no children, surviving parents or grandparents, those who had a surviving parent were, I suggest, 'vertically truncated'. The majority of participants did not have a surviving father, while five of the men had a surviving mother.

The majority of the participants had small convoys: typically one or two friends from their teenage years. Those that had exited their main careers followed the established pattern of having little contact with former colleagues, except on occasions such as attending funerals (Davidson, Daly and Arber 2003a; Davidson, Warren and Maynard 2005; Fennell and Davidson 2003). The interpersonal contacts that form personal community networks (Wellman and Wortley 1990: 559) are often referred to as an individual's social network or their social capital. Through an array of practices and strategies, this collection of contacts provides individuals with access to economic, emotional, health, practical and social support. The nature of the support available is dependent on the network ties with others and the quality of the relationship, as well as factors like availability, shared values and trustworthiness. The ties may be with biological or 'fictive' kin, partners or spouses, colleagues, friends, neighbours or those who hold similar interests. Sexual orientation, gender, class, location and type of relationship may influence the social support within a social network. Within social networks there may be significant others who support an individual over the life course. These convoys of social support vary with the individual and their circumstances, and may change over time, as demonstrated by Russell earlier in this chapter (Antonucci and Akiyama 1987; Davidson, Warren and Maynard 2005; A. Gray 2009; Litwin and Stoeckel 2013).

Letherby (1997) has argued, following Monach (1993), that there is a continuum encompassing the voluntarily and involuntarily childless on which people may locate themselves at different points in their life, dependent on their situation (Exley and Letherby 2001; Letherby and Williams 1999; Letherby 2012). The notion that events influence one's positioning on the continuum relates directly to the fluidity in social networks that has become widely acknowledged in sociology. For example, this can be seen in how the functioning of family relationships changes following a divorce. The findings of this study point to the extension of that continuum to encompass later-life intergenerational relationships, such as grandparenthood. It was noted that some of the participants held firmly to the primacy of biological lineage and, having rationalized that they were not going to become biological fathers, dismissed any thought of grandfatherhood. Increased longevity in conjunction with diminished fertility rates has, as seen in Chapter 2, led to there being an increased number of grandparents and a decreased number of grandchildren (Mann 2007; Timonen and Arber 2012; van Bavel et al. 2010; Van Wormer 2019). The majority of participants had noted the effect grandparenthood had on the lives of peers and family members. This was seen by some as another form of difference between themselves and contemporaries who were grandparents.

This study demonstrated that some participants negotiated a 'grandparental' identity through various routes, which I termed latent, adopted, proxy and surrogate. The first two categories applied to the thoughts and behaviours of Raymond and Alan respectively. As gay men, they had at an early age reacted to the dominant homophobic norm of the time. Their intergenerational roles were generated from different sources, and this highlights the relationship between agency and structure. Raymond's fear of revealing his role was another example of continuity – that of his experience of 'passing'. In contrast, Alan's experience of 'adoptive grandfatherhood' can be viewed, initially, as the continuity of his activism. Significantly, that he viewed the ending of that arrangement as a loss indicates the importance intergenerational relationships can have in later life. For James and Martin, the proxy and surrogate grandfather roles were directly accessed through the familial structure of their partner. As such, their experience underlines the notion of flux and fluidity in the boundaries between kin and non-kin. In order to acknowledge their roles in relation to their non-biological positions in the familial infrastructure, names were adopted: 'Pappous' and 'Sgrampy', respectively. This illustrates how the norm of the biological imperative is structured into the hegemony of the family.

Overall, the grandfather role was seen as one of providing nurturing and mentoring through the passing on of knowledge and experience, thereby linking the past to the present and the future. The four participants' experiences not only reflected the literature on the role of grandfatherhood, but also drew attention to a change in masculine identity with age: from provision of resources external to the home to emotional, family and associational ties (Davidson,

Daly and Arber 2003a, 2003b; Mann 2007). This finding not only adds to the small but increasing research on the role of grandfather-hood; it also highlights the different ways that relationships may be negotiated across the mid- and later life course. Meaningfully, the study shows that some older childless men have a strong desire for intergenerational relationships – a desire that, for some par-ticipants, underscored a sense of loss and difference, while others attempted to fulfil that wish. The study highlights the importance of relationships to men throughout the life course and emphasizes the significance of social networks.

The participants' narratives reflected the criteria of ageing capital (Simpson 2013: 285): all gave accounts of feeling that with age they were freer to express themselves. However, the men's views of their future were strongly associated with reduced activity and predicted decline in functionality. This indicates that the participants' views on later life had absorbed ageist social constructs that model old age as a period of decline, dependency and loss of dignity. The men's perspectives also accentuated concerns for later life regarding fur-ther reduction in physical or mental capacity, or both (Gabriel and Bowling 2004; Hussain, Marino and Coulson 2005). Specifically, Michael related a concern regarding how to access support if he fell ill or needed support in later life. Although none of the men viewed children as 'insurance' for later life, children often provide support for older parents. Some cultures place the intergenerational care of older people into the societal structure (Butt and Moriaty 2004; Phillips 2007). The midlife period has often been reported as one of negotiating individual and structural transitions: the acknowledge-ment of loss of youth and the inevitability of structural constructs, such as eligibility for a state pension that positions an individual closer to death, social or actual (Gilleard and Higgs 2000: 135). This period is typically shown on the one hand as a freedom, usually related to the end of parenthood (Dykstra and Hagestad 2007b; Gutmann 1987; Karp 2000), and on the other hand as the negoti-ation of social and inner identity through the adaption of available structural and existing individual scripts (Biggs 1993, 1999; Estes, Biggs and Phillipson 2003; Simpson 2013).

The study demonstrated that although health was a signifi-cant element in quality of life, it was not the sole influence, and its interrelationship with other matters should be appreciated. For example, the variety of responses surrounding the experience of ageing without children ranged from the shared to the uniquely individual. Three men agreed that health was an issue in later life, but placed other sources as being the causes of improvement. David indicated that becoming a father would be the one improvement in his quality of life; Stephen nominated an intimate relationship; and Frank believed that improved treatment would enable him to have increased social and economic status. A fourth participant, Harry, found that his thoughts and feelings around quality of life were dominated by the death of his partner. Widowerhood has been shown to have a significant effect on the health and well-being of men (Bennett 2007; van den Hoonaard 2010), as both Raymond's and Harry's respective experiences demonstrated (see Chapter 7). Quality of life research has been criticized for using quantitative instruments that have not accurately reflected people's experiences. This study shows the range and complexity of factors that individuals see as influencing their quality of life (Bowling 2009; Gabriel and Bowling 2004).

The findings indicate that the majority of men in this study did not conform to the stereotype of stoicism. Those in the poorest health felt older than their chronological age, whereas the other men rated themselves as younger than their chronological age. Matters surrounding felt age and health influenced all levels of relationships across the social network, as illustrated by the difference between Colin and John (see Chapters 6 and 7). Moreover, issues surrounding the appropriate age and ability to perform a parental-type role were measured by both the social clock and sense of self. This highlights the subjective experience of ageing and the interconnection between chronology, physiology and social relationships (Arber and Ginn 1995; Simpson 2011). It draws attention to the contexts of ageing in general and the nuances surrounding ageing without children. There was little difference in attitude between the partnered and the single men, and most accessed health services without being prompted. Older men and their health behaviour have received relatively little attention, with the persistence of the stereotypical idea that men do not access health services until forced to do so by their partner (Davidson and Arber 2004; Davidson and Meadows 2009). However, James found that healthcare professionals did not take his heart condition seriously. His experience gave some support for the case that the stoic stereotype of men was embedded in the delivery of health services.

Research has shown that male patients who do not conform to masculine stereotypes can be viewed negatively by health professionals (Dolan 2013; Robertson 2007; Seymour-Smith, Wetherell and Phoenix 2002). This highlights the relationship between individual agency and the institutionalization of ideal gender norms. The institutional embeddedness of ageism was highlighted in Alan's experience of attempting to access local authority accommodation. The local policy was that those over 65 had to be housed in sheltered accommodation. This finding shows how the association of ageing and decline is absorbed into the policy and practice of social establishments. Moreover, it supports the claim that basing policy on chronological age is limited and, rather than aiding autonomy, may steer older people into structured dependency. This highlights a well-established criticism of ageing policy generally, rather than ageing without children (Phillipson 1982, 2013; Townsend 2010).

'Outsiderness'

The study also confirmed other research which has indicated that involuntarily childless men have a sense of 'outsiderness.' Alan and Raymond, who were both gay, had to negotiate the dominant sociocultural heterosexual norm that dominated their formative and adult years, resulting in the unavailability of biological or any other form of fatherhood. Their experience highlighted how the political structure inherent in social pathways can determine personal agency. Both men's narratives supported the concept of 'passing' that Rosenfeld (2003) described LGBT people as adopting in order to avoid criminalization and discrimination. Dalzell's (2007) study indicated that her participants had struggled with an 'outsider' status in both heterosexual and non-heterosexual social interactions. The results demonstrated a form of double subordination that resulted in a sense of outsiderness. In my study, Raymond indicated that he did not feel able to raise his paternal feelings with his partner or wider social contacts. Furthermore, he did not feel that he could express his desire for a grandparental role. How individuals view themselves is related to their experience of self, their upbringing, how they feel they are viewed by others in their community of relationships, and the sociocultural setting they operate in. This sense of outsiderness has been related to being both part of, and yet outside, a group (Exley and Letherby 2001; Letherby and Williams 1999; Wolff 1950). As a result, people are connected in a range of networks, in some of which they will be central to the group, while in others they will be on the outside and only partial to the shared experience of the group. Therefore, they may be seen as 'othered', 'scapegoated' or otherwise stigmatized or excluded in the event of change within the group (Letherby 1999:

369). Stigma is defined by Erving Goffman (1963: 15) as 'undesired differentness from what we have anticipated.'

The men in this study reported very few instances of direct discrimination related to their childlessness. George indicated that not being a parent may have affected his career but could not indicate a specific instance, and Stephen noted that his living arrangements led to him being viewed as gay (see Chapter 6). Other participants noted that they felt excluded from conversations and from the social opportunities that parenthood supplies. However, I would argue that as parenthood is seen as 'natural' for women and 'learned' for men (Blyth and Moore 2001; Letherby 2010), the social scripts that the men have access to are limited. Additionally, the men may view their childlessness as a 'secret stigma' (Whiteford and Gonzalez 1995: 28) and something that may be seen as a discreditable attribute to the 'master status' of fatherhood – a prestigious status that 'overrides all other statuses' (Becker 1963: 33). Voluntarily and involuntarily childless individuals are stigmatized and subject to social disapproval both medically and socially because they challenge the dominant traditional and cultural norms of pronatalist societies. In addition, many infertility studies have demonstrated that both men and women experience stigmatization, exclusion and isolation from others (Blyth and Moore 2001; Miall 1986; Throsby and Gill 2004; Veevers 1972, 1980). As such, the findings give limited support to the view that men are overtly stigmatized because of their childlessness.

All the participants in this study reported concerns regarding being viewed as paedophiles, and this was strongest among the single men. The awareness of the subject ranged from Alan's remark on the automatic labelling of gay men as paedophiles to Harry and Raymond's fear of being viewed as a danger to children (see Chapter 5). This awareness of older men as a threat may have been related to the wide media coverage at the time of the case of the paedophile Jimmy Saville (BBC 2014). In addition, during the period of the fieldwork there was a widely reported case of a missing child in Wales (BBC 2012). However, the negative portrayal of older people has long been established, with lone older men critically being particularly viewed as 'dirty old men' (Bytheway 1997; Scrutton 1996; Walz 2002). Media campaigns such as that run by the *News of the World* in 2000 of 'naming and shaming' sex offenders multiplied the stereotype of the 'dirty old man' and reinforced the view of men as sexual predators (Gutmann 2009: 21). The ensuing 'moral panic' included reports of riots, arson, violence (Cavanagh 2007; Critcher

2009; Marsh and Melville 2011) and an attack on a paediatrician because of her job title (BBC 2000).

Reproduction and the 'Social Clock'

My research demonstrated men's awareness of the social clock with regard to the social mores surrounding the appropriate age of becoming a father (Hadley and Hanley 2011; Roberts et al. 2011). The social clock describes the societal expectations of the timing of formal and informal rites and roles, and has been strongly linked to women's biological clock (Cannold 2000; Neugarten 1976). Women's fertility intentions are often viewed in the context of a biological imperative driven by 'their maternal instincts/drives/hormones or biological clock', (Cannold 2000: 15). However, Cannold suggests that this construct does not account for the effect the social clock has on reproductive decisions (such as familial attitudes), partner selection, education, ethnic and religious beliefs, economics, and the behaviour of friends and peer groups. Furthermore, Cannold (ibid.) suggests that childless-by-circumstance women divide into three subcategories: childless-by-relationship, thwarted mothers, and watchers and waiters (see Chapter 1). The subcategories are not all completely applicable to the experiences of the participants in this study. This is due in no small part to the age range of Cannold's participants (28–42). Moreover, Cannold's categorization is dependent on the baseline orientation (Gerson 1985: 21) towards parenting established in early life. Cannold's taxonomy, to a limited degree, applies to this study. However, it does not account for other factors that intersect with childlessness – for example, health matters, relationship dynamics and economic issues. These factors may apply in different intensities, at different times and either singly or in combination, and can be seen in the different routes to childlessness that the men in this study have described. The temporal contexts of events have been seen to be critical to the participants' accounts of their thoughts, feelings, behaviours and actions. Letherby (1997, 1999) notes that the choice for women is not when to have children but when not to, and she argues the importance of societal expectations in influencing women's reproductive decisions. Men do not have the same choice as women, although they may face similar sociocultural and relational accords.

Much of the literature has pointed to the importance of the on-and-off time of the social clock, and the participants in this study have shown the significance of time and timing in their attitudes to achieving parenthood. The participants demonstrated a range of positions regarding the social clock, from those, like Martin, who were conscious of being viewed as an 'old' father, to Frank, who did not view his age as an issue for any future child. Martin also believed that an aged parent would be a source of embarrassment to any teenage child. David, who saw his role in pragmatic terms, took an alternative view: when the child was young, either he or his wife would work and the other would care for the baby. As the child aged, then his role would become one of financial provider. David's narrative followed the 'New Man' discourse that has been widely portrayed in the media and is under increasing academic scrutiny (Goldberg 2014; Lupton and Barclay 1997, 1999; Miller 2011; Wall and Arnold 2007). Within the narratives surrounding infertility is the assumption that men are fertile from puberty until death. A few of the men were aware of the decline in sperm efficacy from 35 onwards, and of the correlation between older fathers and babies born with genetic issues (Bray, Gunnell and Smith 2006; Goldberg 2014; Povey et al. 2012; Sartorius and Nieschlag 2010; Yatsenko and Turek 2018). Alan and Raymond had responded to the homophobic norms that surrounded their youth by rationalizing that they would or could not be biological fathers. However, the changes in equality legislation in the UK and advances in ART have seen a rise in LGBT people becoming biological or adoptive parents. For example, both Alan and Raymond referred to Elton John and David Furnish becoming fathers through surrogacy. They both commented that if they were young now, they would consider the options now available for a form of parenthood. Their reflections demonstrate how across the life course, change in different fields – in this case, technology such as IVF and political and social policy – as well as increased media exposure of reproductive diversity, can affect an individual's sense of being in the world. Consequently, the reoccurrence of random reminders may bring with them feelings of loss, difference and outsiderness.

Psychological studies of infertility are mostly based on those who have sought treatment, and focus on the early stages of adjustment to infertility (see Chapter 1). However, they do offer some insight into the variability of the adjustment process involved with infertility and, therefore, with involuntary childlessness. Part of that process of adjustment is the negotiation of the different options to parenthood, both medical and non-medical. The amount of resources used in that adjustment depends on the individual's attitudes towards parenthood and on their sociocultural environment. Christine Moulet (2005: 109) suggests that couples, following unsuccessful fertility treatment, negotiate the transition after crossing a threshold between disengaging from fertility treatment and accepting non-parenthood. She suggests that her participants experienced the transition in three ways, dividing into prompt acceptors, movers-on and battlers. This form of categorization would only apply to the 'mediated' men in my study. Moulet's typology is limited because it only applies to those who self-defined as involuntarily childless and were not seeking parenthood (ibid.: 66). Even so, none of my participants fully fitted her typology, and this is particularly true of Alan and Raymond. Because of the change in equality legislation and policy, they were aware that as gay men they would be able to adopt. However, they held the view that their age would prevent them from managing children for any extended period. George would have initially fitted the 'prompt acceptors' category; however, a decade after 'accepting' non-parenthood, he showed a growing awareness of both loss and difference regarding his involuntary childlessness. This highlights an important finding in my study and a limit of the transitional model. Two of my participants who had experienced infertility were certainly 'battlers'. Martin's experience demonstrated that the feelings, thoughts and behaviours surrounding involuntary childlessness are complicated and lifelong. Similarly, Moulet (2005) argues that the effects of unsuccessful infertility treatment do not end with the complete acceptance of involuntarily childlessness; instead, there is a continued, if mediated, bereavement. My study supports Moulet's contention that although a rational 'acceptance' of childlessness may have been negotiated, the reminders of not being a parent are ever-present and necessitate the continued negotiation of a complex discontinuity: a continuity of discontinuity. Therefore, the complex bereavement and distress reported in infertility studies (Lechner, Bolman and van Dalen 2007; Moulet 2005) was apparent in some of the participants' narratives.

Loss

The men in this study all indicate, to varying degrees, some form of loss associated with not being a parent or grandparent. Two of the three men whose partners had been through infertility treatment referred to the counselling each couple had received. Interestingly, both these men found that therapy was more useful for their partners than it was for them. These men's attitudes may reflect the stoic and unemotional 'ideal' forms of masculinity absorbed through the male socialization process that values detachment,

disconnection from feelings and risk associated with expressing emotions (Evans and Wallace 2008; Fischer and Good 1997;
Smith, Lad and Hiskey 2019; Wong and Rochlen 2005; Wong,
Pituch and Rochlen 2006). It could also indicate that counselling
favours the communication style of women (Boivin 2003; Malik
and Coulson 2008; Pleck 1987; Wong and Rochlen 2005). The acceptance of non-parenthood is viewed as a complicated form of
grief, as it involves negotiating issues surrounding loss, existential meaning, substantial emotional and biographical processing,
and relational dynamics (Daniluk 1988, 2001; Exley and Letherby
2001; Greil, Slauson-Blevins and McQuillan 2010; Lechner, Bolman and van Dalen 2007; Mahlstedt 1985). A number of stage
models of grief have been developed from Kûbler-Ross's (1970)
original theory. However, these have been criticized for being limited, for not reflecting the open-ended experiences of grief and for
not accounting for broader sociocultural context. Doka's (2002)
concept of disenfranchised grief acknowledges how social and cultural norms may deny support, ritual, legitimation, and public and
private recognition of a person's loss (Corr 2004: 40). A significant
element in complicated grief, for both men and women, is the lack
of social support.

One of the biggest losses was that of the potential relationship
and role not only of fatherhood but also of grandfatherhood. This
was demonstrated by Alan's experience of being 'adopted' as a
grandfather for three years. Other losses relate to exclusion from
the intimate parent–child–family bond, social scripts, and wider social relationships and communities (Letherby 1997, 1999, 2012).
Two men defined themselves as widowers, and contrary to general findings, neither saw domestic tasks as 'women's work', but
referred to them in pragmatic terms. Moreover, although one man
was still in deep mourning, the other had broadened his social network through taking a part-time job and joining an LGBT over-50s
social group. The importance of groups based on a shared identity
was noteworthy for Alan, Raymond and Edward in influencing the
membership of their closest and inner social networks (Bennett
2007; Davidson 1998; Davidson and Arber 2004; van den Hoonaard
2010). Although Harry had been well supported by his neighbours,
he saw Helen's death as being 'off-time' and against the natural
order. This may relate to the concept of masculine control and the
'norm' of widowhood in later life, reflecting the way in which the
expectation of earlier male mortality has been absorbed into social
and cultural discourse.

Masculinities

My findings highlight the fact that the participants of this study follow recent challenges to the model of hegemonic masculinity, and adapt their ways of being via the health, economic, social and emotional resources developed over their life course. The application of Connell's (1995) concept of hegemonic masculinity has become standard in both health and social science research. In the course of this research, I have come to the view that health researchers use Connell's hegemonic masculinity as a framework to expose the structure of the relationship between the individual and the institution (see Seymour-Smith 2002; Dolan 2011, Inhorn 2012). Those in social sciences and anthropology have recently assumed a more nuanced understanding of the relational element of men's experience. Gerontological researchers and theorists now suggest that masculinity is not fixed, but fluid and adaptive over the life course. Such a perspective, following feminisms, reflects the intersection of personal, social and cultural differences, leading masculinity to now be viewed as 'masculinities' (Coles 2009; Connell 1995; Hearn 2000; Spector-Mersel 2006). There is a growing weight of evidence from anthropological studies that men are challenging the concepts inherent within hegemonic masculinity in their day-to-day interactions (Dudgeon and Inhorn 2004; Inhorn 2007; Ranson 2012; Wentzell and Inhorn 2011). For example, Inhorn (2012: 59, 225) points to studies from across the globe which report that young men are challenging dominant hegemonic masculinities through emergent masculinities. She highlights Middle Eastern men as engaging with assisted reproductive and pharmaceutical technologies related to infertility and erectile dysfunction in order to fulfil the pronatalist social agenda. In doing so, they are rejecting traditional practices. Inhorn (ibid.: 60) states that 'Whereas hegemony emphasizes the dominant and ideal, emergence highlights the novel and transformative.' As a result, emergent masculinities encapsulate not only social history but also change over the life course, as social processes adapt to the local realities in the context of local, national and global forces.

Constructing Invisible Men

The lack of recognition by social science researchers of the diversity and variety of the life experiences of older childless people has been noted by Dykstra and Hagestad (2007a). The scarcity of research into both older men and men's reproductive lives has been increasingly recognized. With regard to ageing research, Leontowitsch (2013:

227) notes that older men's lives are still largely absent, despite their invisibility being highlighted from the mid-1990s (Davidson and Arber 2004; Suen 2011; Tarrant 2012b; Thompson 1994). This absence is due partly to the political economy approach that has concentrated on the disadvantage and marginalization of older women compared to older men (Calasanti 2004; Davidson, Warren and Maynard 2005; Leontowitsch 2013). Other influences include the sampling of participants from settings such as nursing homes that have a high female population; furthermore, as men die at an earlier age than women do, there has been a smaller population to sample. In addition, older men's smaller social networks and style of socializing make them hard to reach (Russell 2007; Suen 2010). However, as the recording and screening of people's lives becomes more and more widespread and acceptable, more men may make themselves available for research.

This study shows that men are interested in reproductive matters, and supports Inhorn's (2009b, 2012: 7) argument that men have become the 'second sex' in all areas of the scholarship of reproduction. This form of marginalization has been related to the vast bulk of sociocultural significance surrounding reproduction that is placed on women (Culley, Hudson and Lohan 2013; Daniels 2002, 2006; Marsiglio, Lohan and Culley 2013). Inhorn (2012) emphasizes that as a result, there has been an erasure of men's procreative remit in both scholarship and policy arenas. This is based on a 'widely held but largely untested assumption' (ibid.: 6) by those in anthropology, the social sciences, sociology, demography, health studies, gender studies, the media and non-academia that men are not interested in reproductive matters. In Cynthia Daniels's (2006: 6–7) concept of 'reproductive masculinities', four assumptions about men are postulated: that men are virile and can father children, that they are secondary to biological reproduction, that they are less susceptible to reproductive harm and hazards and that paternal biology and behaviour are less linked to health issues (such as genetic defects) in their children. As a consequence, Daniels (ibid.: 29) argues that culture distorts the role of men in reproduction and reinforces gender stereotypes. Furthermore, Lorraine Culley et al. (2013), Marcia Inhorn (2009, 2012) and William Marsiglio et al. (2013) have suggested that feminist scholarship has retained the theoretical and experiential spotlight on women's reproductive issues. Consequently, the meanings of male reproduction remain unexplored. David Morgan (1981: 96) highlighted the 'taken-for-grantedness' of embedded gendered social relations in sociological research. As a result, he suggested that men's gendered experience was hidden in plain view, and observed that: 'Thus taking gender into account is "taking men into account" and not treating them – by ignoring the question of gender – as the normal subjects of research' (ibid.: 95).

Historically, the experience of women was given prominence in feminist research, in order to explore the sexist bias generated through distortions, misrepresentations and women's invisibility within traditional 'malestream' research (Earle and Letherby 2003; Finch 2004; Haraway 1988; Woodward and Woodward 2009). Similar arguments have been raised within feminisms regarding men's experiences, and have led the way in examining the multi-layered meaning and sociocultural intersections that concern reproduction for men (Daniels 2006; Earle and Letherby 2003; Inhorn 2012; Inhorn et al. 2009a; Letherby 2003; Wentzell and Inhorn 2011). Furthermore, as part of the patriarchal dividend that controls, and depowers, women through hegemonic masculinity, the non-recognition of men that do not fit the virility-proved-by-fertility mandate would seem logical. For example, by only collecting female fertility intention and history data, the relationship between womanhood and reproduction is reinforced and the masculine ideal of virility unchallenged. The embeddedness of an essentialist dividend in structural institutions is demonstrated by Daniels's (2006: 109–56) analysis of the US Government's resistance to funding studies into the effect of toxins on sperm compared to similar studies on women's fertility. Tong (2009: 2–4) notes that all feminist perspectives hold a view on reproduction, from those who view reproductive technology as a means of liberation and control to those who see 'biological mother-hood [as] the ultimate source of women's power'. This reflects the wide-ranging debate in feminisms regarding assistive reproductive technologies, family, motherhood and non-motherhood (Franklin 1990, 1997; Oakley 2005; Woollett 1985). There is no such debate in masculinities.

Research in the field of masculinities has concentrated on younger men in education, crime and employment, and on the body and fatherhood (Arber, Davidson and Ginn 2003; Inhorn et al. 2009b). Although there has been an increase in material on fatherhood in recent years, infertility seldom features in masculinities research, including Connell's (1995) pivotal book. Conversely, studies have shown that during or after infertility treatment, men reported that the process had a profound effect on their views of their masculinity and their beliefs about themselves and their place in society (Fisher, Baker and Hammarberg 2010; Throsby and Gill 2004; Webb and Daniluk 1999). It could be argued that the two approaches parallel the dominant social heteronormative, with feminisms encapsulating the gamut of reproductive narrative while masculinities have only recently looked at fatherhood. However, that argument does not do justice to the ongoing debates in feminisms concerning the relationships between equality and difference, the status and representations of bodies and embodiment, and the continuing invisibility and visibility of women (Woodward and Woodward 2009). Given that much of the research described in this book illustrates how theoretical descriptions of masculinities do not fit men's experiences, a similar argument could be made about the absence of a comparable level of debate on those subjects. Daniels's (2002) sociopolitical examination of masculinity in relation to reproduction found that the 'ideal' types supported the denial of men as vulnerable to biological, economic, emotional, physical, political, psychological and social forces. Consequently, the social structures that determine women's oppression also support the mechanisms that view men as disposable. Martin Seager and John Barry (2019b: 88) hypothesize that there is a 'gamma bias' whereby women's positive achievements are magnified while men's are minimized. Conversely, men's negative behaviours are magnified while women's equivalent conduct is minimized. William Collins (2019) argues that an 'empathy gap' has developed concerning men's lived experiences. Using in-depth statistical analysis, he argues that men's experiences are ignored, demeaned or dismissed at structural and personal levels. For example, Collins (ibid.: 90–91) describes how in 2008, the NHS introduced a routine vaccination programme for girls aged 12–13 against human papillomavirus (HPV). HPV causes cancer and other serious diseases in both sexes. However, only after campaigns by health professionals and special interest groups was a vaccination programme for boys aged 12–13 started in September 2019 (HPV Action 2020).

The men in my research study were born at a time when the traditional package deal (Townsend 2002) of education, employment, relationship and children was the ideal for heterosexual men. However, the last forty years have seen a vast change in global economics, health, education, equal rights, reproductive technology, the welfare state and much more. Consequently, the participants have lived through a period of great change, from a social world that was very structured to one where the personal is now a site for neoliberal marketization. The normative roles of men as breadwinners and women as nurturers have been seriously confronted, although gender inequality is still very much an issue in home and work environments (Connell 2009; Gabb and Silva 2011; Kluwer and Mikula 2013; Martinengo, Jacob and Hill 2010). Additionally, research shows that young men are aware of their own emotional, relational and caring characteristics, although they expect to follow some elements of the package deal of becoming fathers by their mid-thirties (Koropeckyj-Cox and Pendell 2007a; Thompson and Lee 2011a). Therefore, later cohorts experience a different social context, with different pressures and different narratives available to them than the men in this study.

Summary

In this section, I evaluate and comment on the research and my learning more widely. First, I return to my research questions to briefly summarize my findings. Second, I consider what difference the findings have made to the knowledge base. In the third section, I highlight areas of possible further research in this field, and fourth, I offer considerations for future researchers, followed by suggestions for future studies. The penultimate part appraises the research study as a whole, and I finish this section by noting the limitations of the study.

Reprise of the Research Questions

Research question 1: What are men's attitudes and behaviours in relation to their experiences of involuntary childlessness?

The men's attitudes and behaviours depended on a complex negotiation of gender, sexual orientation, embedded social expectations, economics, relationship skills, class, health, social network, relationship status and location. A framework was developed that indicated the significance of the social clock in the men's decisions to 'accept' that they were not going to be fathers. There was a theme of grief in negotiating the 'loss' of the fatherhood role and the father–child relationship. The majority of the men who had considered adoption had rejected the notion for a number of reasons. These included reports of other people's poor experiences of social parenting and anxieties concerning any poor relational or social issues any child might have. One couple had withdrawn from the adoption process because of the stress of the assessment procedure. Two men classed themselves as widowers, and one participant associated the loss of his partner as the end of any fatherhood ambition. The other participant reflected on what could have been. Thus, bereavement was layered with the loss of a possible role and relationship. Although the majority of the men saw that one of the advantages of being childless was a material dividend (for example, not having to support adult children financially), they also acknowledged that this did not compensate for not being parents. Moreover, the majority of the men noted a concern in respect of being labelled as paedophiles.

Research question 2: How do men describe the influence of involuntary childlessness on their quality of life and relationships with close, familial and wider social networks?

The participants described a wide range of responses regarding the effect that involuntary childlessness has had on their quality of life, relationships and social networks. Quality of life was heavily influenced by the participants' health; those with chronic comorbidities felt older than their chronological age. While some intimate relationships had not been affected by involuntary childlessness, others had become very strained. Generally, men with partners had a larger social network than single men. Partnered men who were from 'only' child families were shown to be dependent on their partner's familial network. Conversely, against the general pattern of smaller networks in later life, the two gay participants, who were among the oldest in the group, had strong closest and inner social networks. This was due in no small part to their membership of a LGBT over-50s support group. Four men described themselves as having a grandparental role. One man enacted the role without telling the family involved for fear of being castigated. Another had been 'adopted' as part of a school project, and following the project's cessation, it was a role and relationship that he missed. The two other men had become 'grandparents' through their partners' families: one had requested to be a surrogate grandfather and the other had become one by proxy. Both received great pleasure from the relationship. There was a sense of outsiderness in the group compared to those who were parents that varied in depth and duration. Moreover, there was evidence of a separation from friends who had become parents. Friendships were resumed once the children had matured, but were then disrupted when grandparenthood arrived.

Research question 3: What are involuntarily childless men's expectations of the future?

The majority of the participants' views of the future associated old age with decline in health and functionality. The two youngest men were concerned with socio-economic issues, such as relationship forming and funding future pension entitlement. The older men's views related to their economic circumstances, with those in secure financial states concerned with fulfilling a variety of roles – for example, finding part-time employment, supporting their partner's career or volunteering. Their views of old age involved worry about losing mental or physical capacity, with subsequent loss of dignity.

Research question 4: What are the future policy and service implications of the findings in relation to the above?

The absence of the childless in policy and practice related to health and social care for older people is a significant issue. This is largely down to the childless being viewed as a 'noncategory' (Dykstra 2009: 682), with the result that their data is not routinely recorded in reports, surveys or other statistical data-collection events. However, as identified in Chapter 1, it is possible to ascertain the level of childless women because the fertility history of a mother is recorded at a child's birth registration, while the father's is not. A contemporary report by the ONS (2020), 'Living Longer: Implications of Childlessness among Tomorrow's Older Population', projected a more-than-threefold increase in the population of older childless women (aged 85 and over) by 2045. There were no comparable statistics for equivalent men. This structural exclusion – 'symbolic violence' if you will (Bourdieu and Wacquant 1992) – has significant implications for both individuals and the future provision of health and social care services.

The single men in my study tended to have smaller social networks than those with partners. Lack of social embeddedness is an indicator of social isolation in later life. Moreover, those men that lack social skills or draw on stereotypical masculinity scripts may also be vulnerable to social isolation and exclusion in later life. When considering social inclusion for minority groups, policy has an important place on the agenda. It is important for policymakers to take note of the differentiation of older men and not to treat them as a homogenous group (Davidson, Warren and Maynard 2005). This is especially important as it is predicted that there will be an increase in the number of older people living alone, the majority of whom will be men (Jamieson, Wasoff and Simpson

2009; Smith, Wasoff and Jamieson 2005). Research into healthcare settings has highlighted that stereotypical masculine ideals are not only performed by users but are also embedded in the providers' attitudes and policies. Men who do not conform to the assumed and expected gendered construction may be negatively labelled or may not have their concerns acknowledged. It is important for academics, policymakers, professionals and other stakeholders to be aware of how the sociocultural attitudes and standards surrounding men and masculinity may contribute to the exclusion, isolation and stigmatization of men who do not conform to those ideals.

Contribution to Knowledge

My research has contributed to the literature on ageing in four main ways. First, the study identified that involuntary childlessness would affect the individual agency of men, and their interactions in intimate, local and wider social relationships, as they age. Moreover, the study was unique in taking a life course approach to examine the lives of involuntarily childless older men, and the findings highlight the different factors that influence reproductive decisions. Second, my study also contributes to the knowledge on how to conduct research with hard-to-reach groups, and recommends the use of adaptive and flexible methods. Third, my research utilized a qualitative method that incorporated feminist, biographical, social-gerontological and life course perspectives (see Chambers 2002, 2005). Through such an approach, the wide range of factors that contributed to the participants' childlessness, and the impact of childlessness on their lives, was revealed. The men's negotiation of the embedded social construction of the 'ideal' of fatherhood was demonstrated. Finally, this research has been widely disseminated to the academic community via a number of invited papers and chapters, and to the wider population through various international news media outlets, including *The Times*, *The Guardian* and the *Daily Telegraph* (Bingham 2013; Gorman 2016; Hadley 2013, 2016b; Hodgekiss 2013; Marsh 2017a, 2017b). I have also participated in radio and podcast broadcasts on the topic of infertility and childlessness (Kafcaloudes 2013; Tracey 2015; Zevallos 2014).

The research reported in this book significantly contributes to the debate surrounding ageing and quality of life by adding to the call for research instruments to absorb data from people's experience into measurement items. Using a qualitative method to collect data on quality of life and health provided findings grounded in lived experience. The conclusions support the idea that quality of life is a complex intersection between multiple factors, including health, age, socio-economics and relationships. The impact of health on economic activity and the participants' sense of well-being, and hence their quality of life, was seen in Frank's negotiation of chronic comorbidities and the health and benefit agencies. The findings correspond to existing research and accounted for recent criticisms of quantitative measurements that are employed in traditional quality-of-life research instruments of health and functionality (Bowling 2009; Gabriel and Bowling 2004). The findings also give support to the continuity theory (Atchley 1989, 1999). For example, the importance of experience in successfully managing disruption that challenged the participant was demonstrated. However, Atchley's theory has been criticized (Grenier 2012; Phillipson 2013) for not accounting for negative experience, which may then stop people from moving beyond the disruption. In a recent self-funded study, I, John Barry and Chloe Newby (2019) found that anxious attachment was a predictor of childlessness in later life. Therefore, I argue that there is a 'continuity of discontinuity' across the life course concerning childlessness. This is related to the factors that influenced the men's childlessness, including upbringing, infertility, partner selection and timing of relationship formation and dissolution.

My research has demonstrated that contrary to a widely held belief, men are actively concerned about their reproductive status, as highlighted by their sense of loss over not experiencing the father–child relationship. Furthermore, disclosure surrounding relationships revealed that although the father–child relationship was valued, an intimate adult relationship was the most sought after and appreciated. The four oldest participants negotiated different forms of undertaking a grandparental role that allowed the performance of an intergenerational script. However, all the men indicated that they were aware of being viewed as a threat to children, and this finding highlights the depth and duration of negative stereotypes of older men. The importance of the social clock was central to reproductive decision-making, and the study exposed the complex interaction that affected the participants' reproductive actions. The participants in this research were all negotiating their reproductive decisions alongside other transitions and disruptions common to older people: retirement, ill health and bereavement. Quality of life was strongly related to health, with those in poorest health indicating that their 'felt age' was greater than their chrono-logical age. The nuances of class advantage across the life course were apparent, and the changing financial environment, for example regarding pension provision, was a source of consternation for the younger participants. My research findings provide insight into how the participants managed change in their status, health, finance, relationships and roles as they aged. It adds to the existing literature in terms of its methods of recruitment, relevance to men interviewing men (Hadley 2020) and findings. However, there is room for improvement and potential for further research, and these are examined as part of the following section.

Considerations for Researchers

This book has highlighted the lack of research on involuntarily child-less older men. There were a number of challenges encountered during the fieldwork, and I offer the following for consideration when undertaking research on hard-to-reach groups. What accounted for the sample size? Karina Butera (2006: 1274) suggests that difficulties in recruiting men into sensitive research are linked to men viewing such studies as a challenge to 'successful mascu-linity'.[1] The 'snowball' method of recruitment sampling is highly recommended for generating respondents from hard-to-reach groups (Merrill and West 2009: 109). However, feedback from both participants and third-party recruiters highlighted that they had great difficulty in broaching the sensitive subject of someone's fer-tility history. For example, a fellow PhD candidate informed me that although he knew three potential participants, asking them face-to-face would overstep a boundary of their relationship. Another third-party recruiter recounted another issue: they contacted the partner of a suitable candidate, which led to a personal disclosure that may have had a long-term effect on their relationship. This highlighted the difficulty in knowing the tensions and dynamics in the relationship between third-party recruiters and participants. One other factor in my recruitment difficulty was that I had no established links with any individuals or organizations that would have enabled me to access potential participants. In attempting to promote the academic worthiness of the study, the original word-ing of recruitment material was not engaging.

Awareness of the power of language and symbols was a signif-icant learning point. To aid recruitment, I had contacted relevant people and organizations, such as The Beth Johnson Foundation and Age UK, before commencement of fieldwork. However, their responses were not encouraging. One must be aware that some form of reciprocal endeavour such as volunteering, giving a talk or a regular commitment may be required (Adler and Adler 1987; Sixsmith, Boneham and Goldring 2003). A flexible recruitment strategy needs to be built into the structure of the research design, with regular assessments of which approaches are working and which are not. A social media presence is, I believe, going to be the default practice in the future and should be taken into account in any research design. A further lesson relates to this study's website; a series of issues meant that it has been difficult to update. Incorporating the cost of creating a basic website that can easily be maintained and updated into the research project is strongly recommended. A simple website that gives a clear summary of the research and contact details is very important, not only for recruitment but also for dissemination of results. Participants, academics and the media all visited the study's website. Although the use of 'snowballing' provided four participants, I did have some concerns regarding this method. These included not knowing how the research would be presented to the participants; if the participants were complying because of the dynamics of their existing relationships, how voluntary was their participation? While I do not consider this to have meaningfully compromised the study, it identified an opportunity to reflect and learn from the subtleties involved in the identification, approaching and enlisting of participants. The findings of my research suggest that the gathering of data on men's reproductive history would be of great benefit to policymakers, practitioners, service providers and stakeholders.

Suggestions for Future Studies

I earlier demonstrated the lack of response to calls for more research into the experiences of men in the respective fields of gerontology and reproduction. Therefore, proposals for further research are crucial. I suggest a number of projects that would help further develop this area, based on my experience of the work I have undertaken. I was very intrigued by Frank's question, 'How is a man supposed to be a man?' (Chapter 5). This led me to wonder if there was an existential difference between men and women. What other factors affect one's view of one's existence? The participants in this research project indicated that ageing gave a sense of liberation from social expectations. Thus, a study that examined the attitudes and experiences of men and women in midlife would show any impact of ageing on self-identity. A study that explored the circumstances and experiences of men who occupy a fictive 'grandfather' role and included the views of their kith and kin network would reflect the changing dynamics of 'family practices' (Morgan 1996, 1999, 2011b; Smart 2007). An alternative project would be to explore the reproductive intentions and behaviours of individuals and couples without biological children aged between 30 and 50. This would capture the effect of the social clock and the processes surrounding the decision of whether to have children or not.

A theoretical area worth further development would be the application of Pierre Bourdieu's (1986) concept of capital to reproduction. Capital (resources) is a combination of four forms: economic (material and monetary assets), cultural (prized style and practices), social (networks and groups) and symbolic (status). Bourdieu's theory also includes 'habitus', in which social structures are internalized to form deeply rooted, durable dispositions and subjective identities (Mullins 2018), and 'fields' (social arenas), where 'capitals' are operationalized. The notion of habitus has been much debated in sociology and psychology. Bernhard Wagner and Kenneth McLaughlin (2015) argue for its use as a valuable method of capturing how social world structures become internalized and embodied. They contend that mainstream psychology is focused on the individual and fails to account for structural inequalities and the impact they have on health and behaviour. Similarly, Helene Aarseth, Lynne Layton and Harriet Bjerrum Nielsen (2016) argue for viewing conflicts in the habitus through a psychoanalytic lens. The use of relational analytical theory and object relations would lead to a deeper understanding of the role of the conscious and unconscious in people's reactions to social change. Moreover, Diane Reay (2015) explains how the concept of the habitus illuminates the relationship between the individual's psyche, their inner emotional and structural world and the wider social world.

Bourdieu's early research explored the generational retention of power and wealth in the honour culture of the Kabyle (Nye 2013). In addition, Bourdieu wrote three papers on rural French communities that gave a piercing insight into interactions between class, economics, family, legacy, marriage, occupation, ownership, power and tradition. Those papers were collated in a book, *The Bachelor's Ball* (2008), in which Bourdieu captures how the complex relationship between cultural, economic, social and symbolic capital is embodied in individuals and social structures. For example, the effects of obligatory bachelorhood for eldest sons were beautifully captured in Bourdieu's description of the Christmas Ball (drawn from Bourdieu 1989). In this social microcosm, Bourdieu observes the differences in age, dress, behaviours and attitude between the 30-year-old bachelors and the younger attendees. The bachelors are both insiders and outsiders, ruefully accepting of, and bonded in, their role. Bourdieu's arguments embrace legacy and the embodiment of 'capital' in life as lived.

Contemporary health researchers have offered the concept of 'biological capital' as a way of linking health and health inequalities with Bourdieu's framework of social determinants (Kelly et al. 2019; Kriznik and Kelly 2016; Kriznik et al. 2018; Vineis and Kelly-Irving 2019). The term 'biological capital' has been applied to several different settings; farming professionals and environmentalists use it to represent biodiversity, for instance. However, in relation to sociological practices, there are two definitions. Natasha Kriznik and Michael Kelly (2016) contend that 'Biological capital [is] a way of theorising our own biological resources and their transmission.' Meanwhile, Paolo Vineis and Michelle Kelly-Irving (2019: 979) propose that 'biological capital represents the accumulated history of biological experiences.' Nonetheless, both pairs of researchers agree that when it comes to public health and health inequalities, biological capital intrinsically intersects with the foundational forms of capital: cultural, economic, social and symbolic.

There is a well-established correlation between deprived socio-economic status (SES) and ill health (Kelly and Green 2019; Vineis et al. 2017). The ancient Chinese, Roman and Greek civilizations noted the relationship between disease and the social environment. Similarly, in the nineteenth century, public health pioneers demonstrated the relationship between epidemics and social conditions. As a result, the discipline of epidemiology developed to study the determinants, patterns and processes of disease and health in the population (Kelly, Kelly and Russo 2014). Natasha Kriznik et al. (2018: 766) have identified contemporary research showing the relationship between social environment (class, poverty pollution), biological mechanisms (epigenetics: the moderation of gene expression) and the cross- and trans-generational transmission of health and social disadvantage. Vineis and Kelly-Irving (2019) contend that epidemiologists need to evidence the relationship between the biological and biographical. They argue that deoxyribonucleic acid (DNA) methylation modifications are a credible mechanism through which harmful environments determine people's biology and are indicators of disease (biomarkers). Consequently, physiological systems and cellular pathways are impacted, leading to disease vulnerability (ibid.: 980). For example, Natasha Kriznik (2016) has outlined the relationship between the maternal periconceptual and perinatal environment, epigenetics, development and subsequent impact on health and well-being across the life course. Reproductive health can be damaged during those periods, as well in the neonatal, adolescent and adult life stages (Tomova and Carroll 2019).

As outlined in Chapter 1, the influence of the environment on sperm has been well established (Bray, Gunnell and Smith 2006; Povey et al. 2012; Sartorius and Nieschlag 2010). The efficacy of sperm has been shown to decline from the age of 35, with research linking older fathers to genetic issues in babies (Goldberg 2014; Yatsenko and Turek 2018). In addition, age and socio-economic and cultural factors have been shown to have a significant influence on people's reproductive outcomes. The findings from my study highlight the interplay between the biological, cultural, social and symbolic in the participants' lived experience of involuntary childlessness. Therefore, I believe that there is justification for 'biological' and 'reproduction' to be considered as forms of 'capital'.

The addition of biological and reproductive capital to Bourdieu's theory of cultural, economic, social and symbolic capital strengthens the concept by acknowledging how an individual's 'life depends on inherited biological health/skills, epigenetic imprinting and the accumulation of embodied biological changes' (Vineis and Kelly-Irving 2019: 980). When I first encountered Bourdieu's theory I was baffled by the absence of biological reproduction, since his theory is based on reproduction: 'The convertibility of the different types of capital is the basis of the strategies aimed at ensuring the reproduction of capital (and the position occupied in social space)' (Bourdieu 1986). Therefore, I argue that examining parenting potential and dividends (Letherby 2010: 31), ageing (Simpson 2013), health, lineage and legacy using this perspective would give new insight into the multifaceted dynamics that exist between cultural, economic, social and symbolic capitals and all aspects of biological reproduction. Furthermore, I reason that there is legitimacy in viewing Bourdieu's social determinants through the lens of reproduction: what are the implications for individuals if we do not reproduce biologically, culturally, economically, socially and symbolically?

Appraisal

The main aim of this research was to explore the effect that involuntary childlessness had on older men. I did not intend to focus only on the factors in their childlessness, but also to explore the wider influences on the men's attitudes, beliefs and behaviours. As such, the study highlights the relationship between the participants' agency and social institutions in their many and varied forms. My findings demonstrate the myriad elements that influenced the participants' negotiation of the continuum of childlessness, from their awareness of fatherhood to non-fatherhood. The literature review, methodology and methods, and findings chapters provided the material to support the attainment of the research aims. To investigate the influences on how older men became involuntarily childless, my study aimed to:

- explore the participants' attitudes and behaviours in relation to the experience of involuntary childlessness;
- examine the influences on the participants' quality of life;
- suggest policy recommendations relating to the needs of involuntarily childless men as they age.

My research design, use of semi-structured interviews and employing of a latent thematic analysis resulted in all the aims being achieved. My experience as a counsellor helped me to collect rich, deep data. The participants' narratives were sometimes very emotional. Nonetheless, much of the material they spoke about reflected the findings of other life course, gerontological and infertility research. Forming the main themes from the data analysis facilitated an understanding of the interaction between formal and informal events in the social context of the participants' lives – for example, recognizing the influence the dominant pronatalist heteronormative had on all the men's reproductive decision-making. From the themes that emerged from the data analysis, it became evident that childlessness for older men was a complex intersection between many factors over time: age, class, economics, gender, familial aspects, health, identity, relationships, and sociocultural and psychological issues.

The evaluation of findings is critical in any research project and for any researcher, and both the quantitative and qualitative approaches have established criteria to ensure plausibility. The former draws on generalizability, reliability and validity to evidence means of repeatability and verification (Creswell 2003; Punch 2005). The subjective perspective of qualitative studies has been criticized for not matching the rigour and repeatability of quantitative research, and as offering 'mere idiosyncratic impressions of one or two cases that cannot provide solid foundations for rigorous scientific analysis' (Hammersley and Atkinson 2007: 7). In addition, Lincoln and Guba (1985) claim that it is not possible for those practising qualitative research to show more than 'credibility' for their research findings. The literature on thematic analysis does not offer specific guidelines (Boyatzis 1998; Braun, Clarke and Terry 2013; Braun and Clarke 2006; Guest, MacQueen and Namey 2012); therefore, I drew on the texts that had guided previous research (Creswell 2003; Denscombe 2007; Denzin and Lincoln 2005b; Silverman 2005; Strauss and Corbin 1998).

In order to show plausibility and 'truth value' (trustworthiness) in qualitative research, alternative means are used (Patton 2002: 93). The latter can be supported by a range of techniques, including audit trails, triangulation, thick description (Geertz 1973), trustworthiness and reflexivity (Lincoln and Guba 1985; Miles and Huberman 1994; Patton 2002). Letherby (2004: 175) stresses the importance of demonstrating the 'process and the product, between doing and knowing.' Furthermore, the feminist approach views all classes of data as biased and as reinforcing patriarchy via 'malestream' methods and values. Reflexivity is strongly associated with fulfilling validity in feminist research, as is the recognition of power. Examples of power in this study include the judgement of the reader (Morgan 1981). In addition, I, as the analyst, have control in who is represented and how (Cotterill 1992; Oakley 1981). As a method for mitigating the inherent power dynamics, I tried to locate myself in a number of ways that support the trustworthiness (Lincoln and Guba 1985; Webb 1970) of the research. Corbin and Strauss (1998) introduced the concept of reproducibility as a replacement for replication when evaluating qualitative research. The transparency and detail with which I have reported the stages of the research process adds weight to my belief that this study fulfils the criterion of reproducibility. Moreover, following Inhorn (2012: 18), I have reported the details of the research design and the procedures undertaken, and have given a thorough account of the data analysis. Chapter 3 examined the choice, design, testing and delivery of the research methodology. That chapter also highlighted the issues and challenges of conducting ethically appropriate research into a sensitive subject with a hard-to-access population. The absorption of ethics into the design of the study adds to its trustworthiness and credibility (Davies and Dodd 2002). I have addressed these issues in my study through the inclusion of an audit trail, expressed by the accounts of data collection and analysis, and the use of a research diary. Moreover, interview extracts illustrate not only technique, but also the quality of the interactions between me and the participants. Consequently, the 'trustworthiness' criterion is reflected in the breadth and depth of my engagement in the research and my immersion in the process. Similarly, by acknowledging my presence in the research process I have attempted to fulfil the reflexivity criterion.

All participants were supplied with verbatim transcripts of the first interview to ensure they agreed that they had been accurately represented (they all did). Uwe Flick (2009: 389) suggests that this is a form of 'communicative validation'. However, he notes that it does not go much beyond the participant's agreement. The interviewees were not involved in the analysis, interpretation or presentation of the data. I sought out the participants, and although they had their own motivations for being involved in the study, none were asked, or asked themselves, to approve my interpretations of their material. The participants did not agree to judge an analysis of themselves, and it has been considered unethical for researchers to take such a position (Fox 2009; Kvale 1999). The use of a two-interview strategy gave a form of member checking, as the participant was able to check that they were accurately represented. The one participant who did not want a second interview was satisfied that he had been accurately represented and agreed for his material to be included in the study. Chapter 3 highlighted the phases of a latent thematic analysis, demonstrating the techniques of familiarization with the data, memos, generation of initial codes, searching and reviewing themes and then defining and naming themes (Braun and Clarke 2006). NVivo 9 was used to store and aid organization of the data, and enabled the production of a graphic model that highlighted the relationships and links between codes, themes and memos.

I have produced this book based on my doctoral research and thesis, which examined male involuntary childlessness in the context of the life course and demonstrated the complexity and diversity in the lives of older men. Nevertheless, as with any study, there are limits to the research, and these are acknowledged in the following section.

Limitations of the Study

I believe the design and execution of the study to be detailed, thorough and coherent with its aims. However, the study is based on a small 'fortuitous sample' (Davidson 1998: 235), and therefore the findings are not generalizable to the population as a whole. The men I interviewed cannot be considered a representative sample of the involuntarily childless male population of the UK. I only interviewed one person from a non-White British background, and no one in residential or nursing-home accommodation. In addition, none of the men identified themselves as disabled, although most reported some form of health-related issue. This was not a problem, as the intention was to gain understanding of the experience of older involuntarily childless men. A significant part of the participants' narratives contained in this study are based on their retrospective accounts of their relationships over their life course. As in other social constructionist concepts, the men's subjective accounts are considered valid representations of how the participants constructed their social world (Allen and Wiles 2013; Kvale and Brinkman 2009; Lieblich, Tuval-Mashiach and Zilber 1998; McAdams, Josselson and Lieblich 2006).

The findings have been constructed from the biographical narratives of fourteen men. These accounts are set in the context of the meeting of two individuals, at a particular moment in time, at a particular place, according to a particular agenda. Furthermore, the participants were born and grew up in a time of great change in the United Kingdom and, as noted earlier in this chapter, later cohorts will be situated in and experience different historical and social contexts. With regard to the thematic analysis, West (2001) has pointed out that there must be some loss of essence and meaning in the deconstruction and reforming of data. Thomas and James (2006) believe that this type of analysis is not as valid as quantitative methods, and others suggest that it contains underlying post-positivist components (Charmaz 2006). I acknowledge and appreciate that these are my interpretations and constructions, and that others would have produced different elucidations. I acknowledge that my study cannot be said to be representative, but I do believe that the findings and discussion that I have presented are useful for understanding the experiences of both male involuntary childlessness and ageing.

Qualitative inquiry, and particularly biographical interviews, are known for the volume of material generated (Patton 2002), and as

Chambers (2002: 384) noted, 'the storyteller cannot possibly "tell all" the story'. Therefore, this narrative of the participants' stories is limited. I acknowledge that selection was carried out at each stage of the research process, in how I presented myself, in recruitment material, in every interaction with the participants, in the analysis, in the submitted thesis and in this book (Lieblich, Tuval-Mashiach and Zilber 1998; Nunkoosing 2005; Riessman 1993). Moreover, the attachment that I formed with the participants through meeting them and re-meeting them, and through analysing their stories, led to much angst in the choice of material utilized. I acknowledge that my background as a White British, heterosexual, born working-class but now possibly middle-class, hard-of-hearing male is one of privilege, and that my interpretations are therefore both limited and partial (Pease 2013). My background and life experience inform my subjectivity, and as I am integral to the research, the study is influenced by these. As it is impossible for me to be fully aware of its influence, I cannot be fully objective about my subjectivity. However, by acknowledging the patriarchal dividend, I have attempted to be transparent about its influence through incorporating reflexivity into my study.

In Chapter 3, I outlined the foundations, structures and processes I used to examine the lives of involuntarily childless men. In that chapter, I described how Chambers's (2002, 2005) 'feminist life course perspective' demonstrated that no single perspective would allow an in-depth understanding of later-life experience. I also acknowledged the great influence of feminisms on qualitative research generally and, in Chapters 1 and 2, on reproductive and gerontological perspectives in particular. Consequently, I drew on aspects of the 'profeminist' approach to research (Letherby 2003; Pease 2013; Pini and Pease 2013). Hearn (2000: 352) emphasizes that while men cannot be feminists, they can be profeminist. Pease (2000, 2013) suggests that profeminist researchers recognize patriarchy, undertake research using feminist theoretical insights and methodology, and acknowledge their male privilege and experience (Pease 2000: 6). It is with this in mind that I now look at 'me in the research'.

Concluding the Study

The aim of the study on which this book is based was to gain an in-depth understanding of older men's experiences of involuntary childlessness. Support from my wife, supervisors, counsellor, family, friends and fellow students all helped me in the endeavour of this research. The research community is very sympathetic to those going 'through the mill' and I was often moved by the empathy of strangers, for example at conferences. The other inspiration in this work has been my desire to make men's experiences of involuntary childlessness visible. The question that initiated my research journey (Hadley 2008a) reflected the lack of a narrative regarding male procreative consciousness (Marsiglio, Lohan and Culley 2013; Marsiglio 1991). I now recognize the complexity of the social constructs that promote the pronatalist ideal for women and mothering, and against men for nurturing. My own involuntary childlessness has been the inspiration for this study. Undertaking the research has taken a great deal of emotional effort, and the call of my working-class roots and feelings of unworthiness have surfaced (Ballinger 2012). Qualitative researchers sometimes describe themselves as 'bricoleurs', or makeshift artisans (Crotty 1998: 51), in order to convey the eclectic nature of their research (Denzin and Lincoln 2005a; Moulet 2005; West 2001). I adapt that description and view myself as a 'bateleur': a tightrope walker, juggler, acrobat, tumbler and buffoon. In my native Mancunian, however, this is pronounced 'battler', which I think is appropriate. I feel this reflects the personal as well as the practical processes that completing a study of this type involves. When I started my doctoral research, I did not fundamentally appreciate, as a man, how feminist research was not just another approach. Now, I believe I have an increased appreciation of feminists, and feminisms, with the understanding that I have privilege and power that I was not fully conscious of before this study.

In Chapter 3, I described a methodological framework that drew on the life course, biographical and critical gerontology approaches, and argued that this would be best suited for this study of the experiences of involuntarily childless older men. I outlined my method of fieldwork and depicted the use of an interview technique that would reach out and help the participants to voice their experiences. Feminist research literature stresses the collaborative nature of biographical research. In addition, it draws attention to the power issues that influence the interaction and the reflections that both interviewer and interviewee may experience. Feminist research highlights the issues surrounding power in the research process, and the interview is one of the most potent sites of power. Since Oakley's (1981) important treatise, feminist researchers have evolved an extremely nuanced appreciation of the dynamics within the interview process. Feminist research promotes the explicit use of reflexivity in the research process, to reflect the researcher's awareness (Cotterill 1992; Letherby 2003). Reflexivity means an attempt 'to make explicit the power relations and the exercise of power in the research process' (Ramazanoglu and Holland 2002: 118), by turning 'the mirror on the researcher's gaze' (Lohan 2000: 173). Moreover, Cotterill (1992) suggests that power probably shifts between the participant and the researcher, but that once the interaction has ended, the latter is in control (Letherby 2003: 85).

In this research I was an 'insider', and my status has received careful attention throughout the study. Concerns mainly centred on the consequences of self-disclosure to potential respondents and actual participants. The former may be discouraged from applying and the latter's responses influenced by my disclosure (see Reinharz 1992: 33 for an example). I chose not to self-disclose on any of the recruitment material. I was not averse to self-disclosure, but there is a need for sensitivity and care in doing so, as it can lead to 'competitive, or comparative, dynamics' within the interview, rather than mutuality and facilitation (Smith, Flowers and Larkin 2009: 66). However, in our initial exchanges all the interviewees enquired if I was 'childless'. At the time, I sensed that it was important for them to know my status, and I feel it helped build rapport in the research interview. For example, I noted on the respondent sheet that 'Russell seemed concerned to find out if I was involuntarily childless and I think his agreement to participate hinged on that.' The need of the participants to know of my reproductive status links to the 'insider–outsider' issues alluded to in Chapter 3. Being aware that the participants may present themselves as being powerful and autonomous (Schwalbe and Wolkomir 2001: 91), I adopted a number of strategies within the research design that were discussed in Chapter 3. I was aware of the power of being a PhD researcher from a university and tried to minimize the power differentials within the interviews (Oliffe and Mróz 2005: 258). For example, I was careful not to use jargon, to defer to the participants' wishes and for them to choose the time and location of our meeting.

The subject of this book is a sensitive one, and the men in my study may have been considering its implications for different durations at various points in their lives. I am a trained counsellor and brought with me skills related to the core conditions: congruence, empathy, genuineness and respect (Rogers 1951, 1957, 1961). Nevertheless, I had not been in practice for at least four years, and it was important that any interview did not become a counselling session (McLeod 1999, 2001, 2006). Kim Etherington (1996, 2004) has described her disquiet in negotiating the pull-push effect of her counselling background in her research interviews. One particular incident directly related to my counselling background. I was interviewing Russell and he referred to suicide. Immediately my counsellor training kicked in and I started to engage in his narrative. I then realized that I could not fully recall the standard procedure for managing clients who referred to suicide. At that point I realized I had moved away from being a researcher, and decided to be genuine in admitting I was out of my depth. However, Russell went on to give his views on life after death, and the interview continued for another one and a half hours. I reflected on this in a memo and my research diary. That the interview continued and Russell agreed to the second interview reflected the interview rapport Russell and I had built up.

Reflections on the Study

In this chapter, I have examined the key findings of this study, and discussed the implications in the context of issues raised in the material discussed in Chapters 1, 2 and 3. Subsequent to the discussion, I offered the contribution that my findings have made to the current evidence and knowledge base. I concluded the chapter by suggesting possible areas of further research and suggestions for policy and practice. This study has highlighted how the participants' relationships with the ideal of fatherhood were negotiated over time, through a diverse range of strategies that were unique to each individual and their circumstances. The scant attention paid to men's procreative scripts leads me to believe that future studies of men must appreciate their reproductive ideation, intention and history. Not to do so would help maintain the inequalities of patriarchy. By raising the importance of both the social and personal implications of reproduction for men, I have contributed to the larger enterprises of critical and social gerontology, social science and sociology.

The doctoral part of my research journey lasted for nearly five years, but my research journey as a whole stretches back ten years to the start of my Master's in Counselling. Over that period, I have not only been on an academic journey but also one of personal development. I knew that this research would be difficult and so it proved to be. The words of one of my counselling tutors have supported me through this piece: 'It's OK to struggle'. How I have struggled! My engagement with the men in this study has given me the chance to reflect in a different way about my life and my future. My understanding of men, and my attitude towards them, has grown, and I am now more aware of my social network and other social and biographical assets. I have developed more confidence in my abilities to engage people in my field of interest – the fascinating world of men, and in particular, how the reproductive domain is negotiated. In this book, I have been concerned to give voice to the lived experiences of men who wanted to fulfil a biological and sociological imperative. I hope I have done them justice.

The next chapter returns to the auto/biographical, and to what has happened between the ending of the study and the completion of the book. I will also consider how professionals may acknowledge the impact of involuntary male childlessness and people ageing without children in their working practices.

Note

1. Butera (2006) suggests five explanations for her struggle to recruit men to her study of friendship. First, men are not used to participating in research and feel no obligation to do so. Second, taking part in research is not typically part of performing a masculine identity. Third, a central element to the performance of masculinity is the partitioning of roles and the need for privacy, conditions that are challenged by an interview. Fourth, potential participants may have viewed the study as threatening or as a topic more associated with women. Finally, Butera acknowledges that the language used in her recruitment material might have put male respondents off by not providing an opportunity to perform a masculine identity. All these factors have probably to some degree contributed to my struggle to recruit participants. However, I wonder if more men would have participated had I declared my own involuntary childlessness in publicity material. Patricia and Peter Adler (2001: 527) propose that shared membership or expertise legitimizes 'entry into the setting'. In order not to bias any respondent, I had not referred to my own involuntary childlessness in any material. Without exception, and usually at first contact, all the interviewees enquired if I had children. My feeling was that their request was important, and I willingly self-disclosed my insider status as my intuition led me to believe it would help build rapport in the research relationship. Moreover, Adler and Adler (1987) argue that

there is a continuum of insider membership in research fieldwork that ranges between:

- Peripheral-member-researcher (PMR): The researcher interacts 'closely, significantly, and frequently' with a group but does not become involved in any central or functional role (ibid.: 36).
- Active-member-researcher (AMR): The researcher 'assumes a more central position' and moves from social activities to contribute to core roles (ibid.: 50).
- Complete-membership-researcher (CMR): The researcher 'immerse[s] themselves fully in the group.' They are equal with the group and share 'a common set of experiences, feelings, and goals'. (ibid.: 67)

The ability to occupy any of the above roles is limited by the researcher, the topic and the setting. In this study, I would have found it difficult to achieve CMR status, as there is no organization solely representing the involuntarily childless. Moreover, there would be issues regarding duration in, and disengagement from, the field.

Epilogue

Experience is by far the best Demonstration.

—Francis Bacon, *The Novum Organon*

In this Epilogue, I am going to discuss a range of subjects: myths around men, brief advice for practitioners of various disciplines and my experience of being that rare thing – a man researching men. In addition, the chapter is going to be in a more informal style. I will offer up thoughts, ideas and things that spark my interest, and I may well not justify them at all. In a way, this chapter is improvised in much the same way that back in 2007 (see Introduction), I improvised my response to Dr Liz Ballinger's question: 'What are you researching for your dissertation?' Using examples from business, jazz and theatre, Frank Barrett et al. (2018) highlighted the significance of improvisation in personal and organizational transformation. Barrett et al. argue that challenging conformity and learning to unlearn expected routines and disobey rules leads individuals to become more alive, alert and open to a horizon of new possibilities. When musicians and actors improvise, they trust in messiness, unexpected results and errors. Understanding discomfort and disharmony is an opportunity for learning. Barrett et al. (ibid.: 680) explain: 'Improvisation grows out of a receptivity to what the situation offers and thus the first move, this "yes to the mess," is a state of radical receptivity'. In this book – as a whole or in parts – and in this chapter in particular, please go with 'yes to mess.' I am afraid there are poems too.

Original Introduction

Before the coronavirus of 2019 struck, the following were the opening two paragraphs of this book.

'I am ending at the very beginning. It is an early autumn day in my home city of Manchester (UK) in 2019 and I am just starting to write this book. The leaves on the trees are beginning to change and the low, grey clouds softly weep as they move east across my home county of Lancashire to neighbouring Yorkshire. The political situation in the country is chaotic, as the government tries to negotiate a deal to exit the European Union. There is every possibility that the country will exit the EU (Brexit) with no deal in place at the end of this month. Should that happen, medical and food shortages and civil unrest are thought to be inevitable. The political directly influences my personal situation. In the five years since I was awarded my doctorate, I have had ten short-term contracts, and I have had little paid work since April 2019. Consequently, I have drawn down my small employee pension five years early so that at least we have some security of income.

I am in the small upstairs back room of our modest house. If we had had children this would have been a nursery at first. Instead of a crib and all the baby/child paraphernalia, there is office equipment, a desk, a computer, a printer/scanner, a filing cabinet and a big black IKEA bookcase. On the floor, instead of an activity centre, changing mat and other baby ephemera are scattered books, academic journals, boxes of the same and an overflowing bin. As the child or children grew, the flotsam and jetsam of various ages, stages and interests would coalesce to inform the room's usage. I am reading Marcia Inhorn's book *The New Arab Man* (2012) and am feeling overwhelmed, challenged and engaged. Following up on a reference, a quote from a Lebanese man in Marcia Inhorn and Emily Wentzell's paper (2011: 807) catches my eye: 'they equate having children with being a man.' Likewise, Silke Dyer et al.'s (2004: 960) paper emphasizes the importance of fatherhood to social status for South African men, using this quote in the title: 'You are a man because you have children.' Both quotes come from non-Western cultures, and yet my belief is that Western cultures also promote the same family ideal (pronatalism), just differently. Underpinning pronatalism is the concept of virility validated through fertility. In the majority of societies, women are still judged by the 'Motherhood Mandate' (Russo 1976). Therefore, women's validity is overtly and covertly linked to their internal reproductive and biological capital. Likewise, men are also judged on their reproductive capital(s). However, the difference is that men's reproductive capital is hidden in plain sight – hidden in the expectation for them to fill the traditional external 'provider role'. Although cultural differences need to be acknowledged, the provider role is often reduced to economic virility. I often wonder if the roles connected with men and women follow their biology. Sperm is effective outside of the body and men's roles mainly exist outside of their body.'

Some people do not want to be parents, for many and varied reasons. However, to label all men as not interested does harm to both individuals and society. As highlighted in Chapters 1 and 2, the majority of academic material has framed men as ambiguously ambivalent regarding reproduction, and they are often reduced to being defined by their functionality: typically their socio-economic status. As both Marcia Inhorn and Cynthia Daniels have indicated, this framing of men reduces and distorts them as individuals and as a group. Shockingly, this attitude is prevalent in contemporary academic literature. For example, Natalie Sappleton (2018a: 381) concludes that 'childless and childfree women (but not men) experience social stigmas as a consequence of being cast deviant.' Such attitudes reinforce William Collins's (2019) concept of an 'empathy gap' surrounding men's experience that is embedded in the micro, meso and macro levels of society. The perception that men are unaffected by and not interested in reproduction is 'false and reflect[s] out-dated and unhelpful gender stereotypes' (Fisher and Hammarberg 2017: 1307). Moreover, studies have found that fathers feel more happiness (Nelson-Coffey et al. 2019) and less isolation (Hadley 2009) than men who are childless not by choice. In the next section, I will further explore the perceptions of, and the myths around, men.

Myths around Men

I am a man who now finds men fascinating. My fascination concerns how men try to navigate through life, especially around reproduction, on such a limited social script. In this section, I am going to present a cross section of men talking about their experiences of childlessness and fatherhood. I then explore some of the myths surrounding men.

Let's 'grab a cab' and share some of the conversations I have had with taxi drivers. I have often taken a cab to or from the nearest main train station when I have attended a conference or meeting. I am going to briefly describe three 'cab-ride-chats'. I have only given broad descriptions of the men involved, and the dialogue is from memory, not from notes. I recall one cab ride from the very start of the study. Cabbie A was a White British man in his late sixties. He laughed when I described my research, and told me that he had been married for over forty years but was not a father. Because of his different careers – in the army, mining and the oil industry – he and his wife had decided not to have children. 'It wouldn't have been fair to leave her with the kids all the time. Especially with me being away with the mining and the oil jobs – they were for contractors but you didn't know how long they would last. You know?' I was just a pup-shark then, and my study was still waiting for ethical approval; I also did not have the confidence to ask if he would like to participate when the study was up and running. Nonetheless, I find it so very interesting that he was so open about his fertility history and the impact of economics on his decision-making.

On the return journey home from the train station, I often get an Uber cab. I like these because I can sit next to the driver, which makes it easier for me to hear (see Introduction). I am usually asked where I have travelled from and what I was doing. The following two conversations happened in the past three years. Cabbie B was Asian British, Muslim, aged in his mid-thirties, eleven years married and childless. On hearing about my research, he became very animated:

> My wife and I have no children. We both feel the pressure from her family, my family, friends and the community. She gets it directly with people asking when is she going to become a mother. I get the pressure but it is said in a different way. She is very upset when someone becomes pregnant or has a baby. I do all I can to reassure her. I say, 'Our time will come', but is been over ten years and I worry for her.

The passion and intensity with which Cabbie B spoke was very moving. He gave a telling insight to the stresses and strains of sociocultural expectations. Cabbie C was Black African, aged in his mid-forties and married with children. Following the usual exchange of pleasantries, I described how I had wanted to be a dad but did not become one. He told me he was a father of four and how important it was to him. 'My second eldest, she has done well at school and I had said she could have a new iPhone if she did. Haha! I now am working to get that for her. She has worked hard – she deserves it.' I mentioned the research that found that dads had increased enjoyment as their children developed and interaction grew. He cheerfully disagreed: 'I miss when they are babies, when they nuzzle and suck on your face' (at this point, he used his fingers to pull on his cheek) – 'I miss that. I would have another just [to] have that again.' I was swept along in his enthusiasm for his children and the joy he got from fatherhood – and moreover, the enthusiasm and energy he had to provide a good home and be a good father. Men talk. The cabbies' stories also show something else: how I have changed as a person. As Gay Becker (1994: 400) proposed, 'embodied knowledge of self is presented to others through biography.' I wrote this poem after striking up a conversation with an Irish man on a London tube train.

I am one of those

'It's crowded', he said and I agreed with the man

who looked like Richard Dreyfuss from Jaws

His Irish accent crested the noise of human shingle

that washes out and in and out

His voice dips and swells as he skims

the lifescapes of the Irish greats of the English

'I am one of those' when he heard about my research.

The few times he had had the chance

and if he could go back, he would do different

We are swimming in the sea of the unspoken

and the rip tides of experience unite and separate us.

The shark exits at Finchley Central.

(Hadley 2018e: 104)[1]

As stated in Chapter 1, Inhorn et al. (2009b) and Daniels (2006) have argued that men are minimized when it comes to reproduction and reproductive health. Daniels identified that traditional ideals of masculinity do not tolerate men's vulnerability – especially in reproductive health. Furthermore, she carefully highlighted how those ideals shape policy and practice. One way this is maintained is through the sociocultural narratives that people use in everyday interactions. I have been asked about men and childlessness many times. Here are answers to some common questions.

'Why Don't Men Talk?'

1. Men do talk. They are not used to being listened to in a non-judgemental or positive manner. However, when it comes to personal and sensitive subjects, many men struggle to

verbalize their feelings. A number of sociocultural factors influence why men default into traditional masculine behaviour. A key reason is that men fear embarrassment, humiliation, shame and stigma. Consequently, men are reluctant to reveal their emotions.

Why do men tend to default to stereotypical male behaviours of aggressiveness, inexpressiveness, emotional detachment, objectivity, control, risk-taking and action-orientated response (Lee 2003)? Glen Poole (2016) has argued that men respond through action: flight or fight, an impulse to 'fix things' rather than talk about things. The work of Stephen Wester et al. (2002), Joel Wong and Aaron Rochlen (2005), David Vogel et al. (2003) and Ann Fischer and Glenn Good (1997) identifies the elements, processes and outcomes that influence men's difficulties in describing, expressing and identifying feelings (alexithymia). Wester et al.'s (2002) literature review of sex differences in emotion found only small and variable differences between women and men's emotional experience. Similarly, Wong and Rochlen (2005) argued that although men and women have the same emotional experience, men are socialized to perceive the expression of feelings as weakness. Consequently, a fear of intimacy and emotional vulnerability is developed and emotional inexpressiveness becomes a norm. Fischer and Good (1997) highlight that restrictive emotionality and emotional inexpressiveness correlate with a fear of intimacy, leading to isolation and loneliness. They argue that men's emotional literacy represents the internalization of sociocultural expectations, not their ability to feel emotions. Men's inexpressiveness may thus reflect an internal conflict between feeling emotions and feeling unsafe to express them, or an external conflict between the men's emotional values and those of significant others (or both conflicts at once). Vogel et al. (2003) proposed that men who are emotionally vulnerable default to normative gender-role behaviour because it is easier, less risky and requires the least cognitive effort, and because they believe that it is what is expected of them (see also Fischer and Good 1997). Contemporary research by Simon Rice et al. (2020) found that shame was a significant factor in men's difficulties in describing and identifying their feelings. Ncil Humphreys et al. (2007) identified that social and emotional awareness (emotional intelligence) are skills that are necessary in navigating adult life and reduce the risk of dysfunctional mental health and risky behaviour.

Everyday examples of the age at which boys are socialized to be inexpressive can be readily found by examining social media. Look for the earliest age parents refer to their son as 'my/our little man'. Now look to see if daughters are called 'my/our little woman'. Older boys, teenagers and adult men are often told to 'man up'. Again, is there an equivalent 'woman up'? An acquaintance observed a mother's statement that 'he has to learn to man up' in response to her toddler's upset that another child had taken the toy he had been playing with. In my experience of counselling, I soon learned not to ask men how they felt. Often this led to the client looking puzzled and trying desperately to convey his feelings, before stating, 'I think I feel ...' That short statement is so revealing, and it supports the assertions made in the previous paragraph. Instead, I found asking 'What's happening inside?' to be more successful.

The lack of literature, research, practice and policy surrounding involuntarily childless men has implications for all types of professionals, including academics, counsellors, health and care workers, social workers and policymakers. The challenge for practitioners and professionals alike is to recognize that the effects of childlessness are unique to individual men, and shape their interactions on many levels. One possible approach is to acknowledge that the ongoing complex losses are very difficult to express due to the lack of a social script. Wong and Rochlen (2005) advise counsellors and psychotherapists that alternatives to face-to-face therapy talking, such as art and writing, may be more appropriate for male clients. Richard Nelson-Jones (2006: 438) outlined that practitioners should aim to help men recognize their self-worth and re-negotiate sociocultural stereotypes. Gay Becker (1994) identified how men and women receiving ART treatment used metaphor to make sense of the disruption of both their own expectations and sociocultural ones. She argued that metaphor 'enables individuals to recreate a sense of continuity and to reconnect themselves to the social and cultural order' (ibid.: 404). Jonathon Lloyd (2018), drawing on research, theory and practice, argued that the use of metaphor in therapy can be transformative, particularly for men.

Recently, *The Palgrave Handbook of Male Psychology and Mental Health* (Barry et al. 2019) has examined men's and boy's behaviour and mental health from a wide range of theoretical and clinical perspectives. In their review of literature on men and psychological treatment, Louise Liddon et al. (2019) proposed that therapy be more 'male-friendly'. The authors contend that men's needs are overlooked through implicit 'male gender blindness', because services are blind to 'the needs and preferences of men' (ibid.: 673). Liddon et al. make a range of suggestions for making most forms of intervention male-friendly. They identify that a key factor for practitioners to consider is a strengths-based approach of 'positive psychology/positive masculinity', and suggest moving away from a deficit model that focuses on the negatives of masculinity (ibid.: 680). Similarly, Joanna Smith, Sunil Lad and Syd Hiskey (2019) argue that compassion-focused therapy is particularly successful with men because it de-shames, engages and reframes men's view of themselves by reconceptualizing help-seeking as a practical and sensible course of action. Although they are based on psychological and counselling theory and practice, the approaches outlined above apply to any setting where professionals are interacting with men. We all make sense of our way of being in the world in the context of 'biological, physical, environmental, biographical and cultural givens' (Fischer 2006a: 430). It is necessary for academics, individuals, professionals, practitioners and all institutional stakeholders to understand and appreciate the 'givens' in why men do not feel it is safe to talk and why others do not listen.

'Men Can Have Children at Any Time in Their Lives.'
1. Sperm declines in efficacy after the age of 35.
2. All societies have sociocultural rules (the 'social clock') regarding the acceptable age to become parents.
3. The vast majority of men do not become parents after 50.

'Men aren't bothered about being a dad.'
1. Research has shown that a diagnosis of infertility for men and women causes the same distress as a diagnosis of cancer or a similar disease.
2. Childless men who wanted to be fathers reported being more angry, jealous and depressed than equivalent women.
3. Parenthood is mainly associated with women. Men who express the desire to perform nurturing roles are often stigmatized.
4. Any species that required a male and female to reproduce would not survive long if the majority of either sex 'was not interested' in reproduction. Similarly, would *Homo sapiens* have gone through its various technological and social advances if survival of the species was not a priority?

Research supporting the brief replies above can be found in Chapters 1 and 2. Moreover, my participants' lived experience of the impact of unwanted male childlessness is thoroughly examined in Chapters 4 to 7. However, let me give you another example from two men who are fathers. Following the publication of an academic paper of mine (Hadley 2018d), two former colleagues contacted me independently of each other. Both had become first-time dads in their early forties and both expressed similar sentiments. I combine their views here: 'Looking back, I was not really content in my thirties, I mean work was going well and I had a partner and all that. Yet, I was moody a lot of the time. Now I'm a dad I realize that's what was missing – I didn't realize it at the time. I love being a dad and I'm sorry for you that you didn't become one.' In this context, the word 'missing' is very significant because it emphasizes how disassociated men can be from their reproductive selves. The men I interviewed in my research – and many childless men I have informally talked with – all used the phrase 'something's missing'. This phrase is important because it highlights the absence of a social narrative that the men could draw on. The sense of 'something missing' prompted me to write this poem during my MA:

Something Missing
A conversation ended before it began
scatterling thoughts of cuda, shuda, wuda, dada
the latent maelstrom of the none man
There's something missing,
holding a life-wide gap,
breathing wallpaper,
I am whole and incomplete
There's something missing,
first to be left behind,
first to be sent in,
this line is not complete
(Hadley 2008a; 2018e: 103)[2]

Horace Sheffield (1979) wrote in the *Michigan Chronicle*'s 'As I See It' column that 'If you are not counted you do not count.' Sheffield was making the point to African Americans that electoral and census data directly influenced community funding. Sheffield's phrase is a very popular saying and has widespread usage across an extensive range of issues. As I stated in Chapter 1, the data on the level of male childlessness is difficult to extract, because in most of the world the reproductive history of men is not recorded at the registration of a birth. Consequently, for the majority of countries, the level of childlessness is underestimated, and this will have significant impact on individuals and institutions alike. In addition to 'missing out' on a fundamental sociocultural identity, childless men are a group that are deemed insignificant by many important institutions and social structures, such as academic scholarship, demographic statistics, government policy (nationally and worldwide), health and social care policy and practice, and wider social narratives. For example, in the USA, Tim Wong and Sean Cahil (2020) illustrate the importance of lesbian, gay, bisexual, transgender, queer, intersex and asexual (LGBTQIA) people completing the census by pointing out that 'It is impossible to overstate the importance of being counted.' They link analysis of the 2010 census to the federal funding of $16 billion in 2015 to support health, education, families, food, and housing programs in Massachusetts alone. Wong and Cahil explain: 'These programs are especially important for LGBTQ people, given the disproportionately high rates of poverty and homelessness and housing instability within our communities.' Ageing and childlessness will be significant factors in accommodation insecurity, homelessness and poverty too (Hadley 2018a). Contemporary sociological research highlights the issue of precarity in ageing. However, the recently published edited volume *Ageing and Precarity: Understanding Insecurity and Risk in Later Life* (Grenier, Phillipson and Setterson 2020) did not include any work on people ageing without children or family. When it comes to people ageing without children and male childlessness, may I offer this adaptation of Horace Sheffield's (1979) phrase: 'If you are not counted, you don't count, and if the people who do the counting won't count you, then you are doubly discounted.'

Childlessness in Later Life and Covid-19

As I explained in Chapters 1 and 2, health and care policies in a lot of countries are reliant on adult children acting in their parents' interests. In the UK, many people do not realize how difficult the system is concerning formal care in later life until they have to access it. Only in the last few years has social care in the UK started to come under the remit of the NHS. However, social care provision for older people is complex, with multiple agencies, including the NHS, local authorities, private companies and charities, all involved in providing in-the-home or residential care. Moreover, the social care system in the UK has been steadily underfunded for the last decade (Age UK 2019).

In my chapter (Hadley 2018b) in Josie Tetley et al.'s book for people starting their nursing and care careers, I highlighted how people ageing without children (AWOC) have similar issues to any other older person. However, they have additional concerns regarding being 'outsiders' in the social world and invisible to policymakers and service stakeholders. In addition to structural invisibility, a survey of childless older people (Beth Johnson Foundation/Ageing Without Children 2016) reported a number of issues. First, the widely held assumption that all older people have adult children or grandchildren added to their sense of invisibility. Frequently, reports on older people focus on adult children as the main source of care and support – the childless are omitted. Many childless older people in marginalized groups have not conformed to traditional family structures: this includes minority communities and LGBT+ people. Second, the language used in official documents and in everyday conversation can be hurtful and insensitive. Older people are habitually referred to as 'granny' or 'granddad', and for older childless people, this is isolating and inappropriate. Older childless people are a diverse group and such unthoughtful comments reflect embedded discrimination and exclusion. Third, many childless people reported being seen as available to care for ageing parents. For many, this raised concerns regarding who would care and advocate for them in later life. In particular, two strong fears were expressed: developing dementia and losing their personal and family history, including disposal of treasured items. Fourth, older childless people were apprehensive about how they were going to access services or help for even small practical issues. Finally, although older childless people wished to maintain or build such relationships with younger people, they felt that they were cut off from those relationships.

Covid-19 has severely tested the health and social care system in the UK, with deaths of residents in residential care being reported as 50 per cent higher than normal (Woodard 2020a, 2020b). The UK's Office for National Statistics (2020) reported that by 27 June 2020, care homes accounted for 30.2 per cent of deaths involving Covid-19 in England and Wales. This high mortality rate has been linked to the policy of the NHS to discharge people back to care homes untested in preparation for a surge of Covid-19 admissions

(Panjwani 2020). Although childless older people are overrepresented in residential care facilities (Dykstra 2009; Koropeckyj-Cox and Call 2007; Wenger 2009) it is difficult to ascertain what the population percentage is because that data is not collected. Moreover, those that are functionally childless (have no contact with their children) would be a confounding factor. Despite the media reporting on the high mortality rates, the focus was on the separation between older parents, adult children and grandchildren. Additionally, much of this coverage highlighted the use of technology to maintain social connections. Unfortunately, this hides the issue of the 'digital divide': less than 50 per cent of UK adults aged 75 or older have access to the internet (Marston, Musselwhite and Hadley 2020; Office for National Statistics 2018). However, the experiences of people who are ageing without the support of adult children or family were not reported (Woodard 2020a, 2020b).

No candle

No candle to light, no cake to cut, no nappies smelly, no teeth to keep, no hand to squeeze,

no stories read, no surprise to feign, no plays to see, no shoes to clean, no sports-day drama, no parties to piece/police, no presents to buy, no amends to make, no scrapes to clean,

no kiss-it-betters, no tears to dry, no hearts to mend, no embarrassment to give,

no graduation photos snapped, no 'Can you help with this?' No now-empty nest,

no grandchild to hold, no legacy to give, no one to call, no one to catch the fall,

no wishes heard, no life-lived described, few tears shed, no candle lit.

(Archetti 2020: 240; Hadley 2018f)[3]

Time Between

No dear, you would have to feel with me, else you would never know.

—George Eliot, *Middlemarch*

In Chapter 3, I described how qualitative research is 'messy', 'chaotic' and 'discombobulating', and parallels 'improvisation' as described earlier in this chapter. When I completed this research study, I was advised not to write a book but to publish academic papers. I anticipated the normal academic career path: short-term research or teaching contract followed by a permanent position. Since graduating and as of now (June 2020), I have had ten short-term contracts, written academic papers and chapters, and been interviewed for TV, radio, newspapers, podcasts and blogs. However, I have been lucky and have travelled to places that I had only dreamed of visiting to present my research. One of the privileges of researching male childlessness is how willing women and men are to share their fertility experiences. Particularly moving have been women's and men's experiences of miscarriage(s) – often following IVF treatment (see Bueno 2019). I believe the fact that people were willing to share their deeply private and intimate stories demonstrates how involved and interested people are in reproduction. Many women have told me that they were not interested in becoming parents but that their partner was. Typically, they would say, 'I wasn't bothered but he really wanted them.' When I have presented my research to non-academic, mixed and academic audiences, the overwhelming response has been a positive one. Often the audience are very emotionally moved; on occasion I have been asked if I can be hugged. However, there has also been some hostility (see Hadley 2020).

Very few studies report on the experiences of men working in areas that are heavily populated by women. Steve Robertson (2006) has argued that the sexuality of men researching gender is often regarded with suspicion (Frosh, Phoenix and Pattman 2002). Research illustrates similarly that patients who do not conform to traditional masculine gender norms have been viewed as lesser by staff in health and care settings (Dolan 2014; Gough and Robertson 2010; Hugill 2012; Watson 2000). In 2013, I attended a conference, 'Genetic Identities, Personal Lives and Assisted Donor Conception', based on a study funded by the Economic and Social Research Council (ESRC) of donor conception families. One incident in one of the presentations struck me at the time and has lived with me since. The co-investigator described an interview with a heterosexual couple in which the man was obviously struggling to deal with the situation. Consequently, he made various efforts to excuse himself from the interview. The speaker held the man's behaviour as an example of the difficulty typically encountered in collecting data from men. The audience responded with a laugh of understanding and a collective unspoken sentiment of 'typical man' (see my blog at the time, Hadley 2014a). Had a woman behaved in a similar fashion, would her behaviour be presented in the same manner? Looking back, I now believe that the man, rather than being held up as an example of the researcher's toil, deserved empathy, as he was obviously in a dilemma. Moreover, researchers have an ethical duty to do no harm, and that includes how they present and represent their participants. A similar occurrence happened at a more recent academic conference, where I was the only man at a presentation of research examining the interactions between midwives and fathers at the birth of the men's children. Much to the presenter's dismay, the audience laughed at a quote where a father had said something incongruous. The presenter and chair handled the situation beautifully. The presenter immediately voiced her alarm at the audience's reaction and highlighted her concern that her participant's narrative was being mocked. Similarly, the chair voiced her concern and drew attention to the fact that I was in the room. These examples highlight that there is an embedded view of men as lesser in reproduction scholarship.

An environment in which I did not expect to face hostility from academics was at a British Sociological Association (BSA) conferences (see Hadley 2020). I have experienced quite childish responses after I have described my research. Reactions have typically followed some or all of this script: 'Boo hoo! Why should I care? Oh, that's right, I don't', with exaggerated wiping away pretend tears and overstated eye rolling. I am sad to write that this reaction has always been from women – men have never behaved in such a manner. The most serious example of open hostility occurred when I presented at the British Sociological Association Human Reproduction Study Group Annual Conference. I was the only man at the conference, out of a minimum of thirty delegates. As is the norm at such events, at registration I introduced myself to other delegates, including Dr X. As I introduced myself, my offer of a handshake was disregarded. My question on whether she was presenting was summarily dismissed and Dr X turned her back and addressed another delegate. At the end of my presentation, Dr X called into question the validity of my research, saying of my participants, 'I bet they have had children.' I then attended Dr X's talk. I have made it my practice that when I am the sole male attendee, I sit in the front row and furthest away from the speaker and session chair. It is my aim not to be near the powerful figures in the room, and to enable all the other attendees to see me. I was horrified, shaken and shocked when in her talk, Dr X referred to the 'paedophile in the corner', stared at me and made a hand gesture

towards me. I glanced around and the chair of the session was looking directly at me in shock – her jaw had literally dropped. I am
still affected by Dr X's actions – someone I was completely unaware
of and had never met before. Although I complained to the BSA,
no action was taken against Dr X. Moreover, the BSA complaints
procedure at that time was not transparent, and I do not feel I was
believed; nor was I properly supported. What does this say about
academia's attitude towards men? Do the above examples reflect a
wider ambiguously ambivalent attitude towards men – 'manbiva-
lence' if you will – in society?

Feminist scholars have highlighted the exclusion of the male
experience in the disciplines of reproduction (Crawshaw 2013; Culley, Hudson and Lohan 2013; Earle and Hadley 2018; Inhorn et al.
2009b; Letherby 2010; Lohan 2015). Moreover, not only are men
excluded from participating as research subjects, they are also in
the minority in research groups in relevant research institutions.
The question is, what actual actions are being taken to address the
issue of the invisibility of men and the exclusion of their experiences in all levels of reproductive research?

Generalizing to the Mean Men

The popular media often presents polls where the average of the results is applied as representative of a population: generalizing to the
mean. For example, in national elections in the UK, mainstream
media often select a 'typical' town or city and produce a 'typical'
voter, drawn from averages of age, race, income, accommodation,
shopping preferences and the like. These are often called 'any-
whereville man/woman'. This generalizing from the mean may sell
papers, but it does not stand up to scrutiny, as it may very broadly
represent most people but only be true of very few. Moreover, it is
common to hear in television and radio debates people 'generalizing from the me' – for example, arguing that a national policy does
not make sense based solely on their experience. When it comes
to how men are represented in the media, the bad behaviour of a
few is often extrapolated and applied to all: generalizing from the
'mean men' to all men. There is an increasing trend in the media
and academia in which showing empathy for men often brings ac-
cusations of being a 'Men's Right Activist' (MRA). MRAs are seen
as being opposed to women's rights and feminisms. Psychologists
Martin Seager and John Barry (2019b) hypothesize that attitudes

to gender are subject to cognitive 'gender distortions', resulting in a 'gamma bias' in everyday experience, research, policy and practice. They contend that reports of poor behavior are magnified for men and minimized for women. Conversely, positive behavior is magnified in women and minimized in men. For example, they argue that the widely used phrase 'toxic masculinity' is a labelling form of cognitive distortion that builds self-fulfilling prophecies of men's negative behaviour. Likewise, they reason that the application of the term 'toxic' to any other characteristic – age, disability, ethnicity, faith – would not be acceptable. Consequently, societal and wider cultural narratives reinforce the idea that men are less valued, less vulnerable and disposable. Subsequently, Seager and Barry (2019a: 119) contend that it is attitudes towards men that have become 'toxic'. A pilot study of 203 men and fifty-two women reported that 92 per cent of male and 87 per cent of female participants agreed that the concept of 'toxic masculinity' negatively changed how all men were viewed (Barry et al. 2020: 16). The generalization of the poor behaviour of a few to all men – 'meneralization' – reinforces gender stereotypes and denies men's vulnerabilities.

Similarly to Daniels (2006) and Letherby (2012), Seager and Barry (2019a) identify that recognizing men's vulnerabilities benefits women and men equally. Furthermore, Seager and Barry (2019a) argue that sociological theory has dominated the debate on gender but failed to acknowledge the influence that biological and evolutionary processes have on behaviour. Additionally, they contend that much social theory on masculinities is based on little empirical research, splits the mind from the body and is close to social determinism. Seager (2019: 277) critiques the social constructionist view of gender as 'a collection of disposable social stereotypes, separated from and unrelated to biological sex.' Consequently, he outlines the case that current all-encompassing gender stereotypes (social behaviour) need revisiting to recognize instinctive behaviour (archetypes). Similarly, John MacInnes (1998: 12) has argued that there is no such thing as 'masculines', 'feminines' or 'gender'. He contends that seventeenth-century social contract theorists rationalized that social order was organized through 'relations between people [that] were governed by contract' (1998: 26–28). The concept of gender thus has its origins as a method of accounting for the sexual division of labour – which is both natural and social. Thus, the essential difference between men and women was socially constructed through the expression of sexual genesis as a process of socialization. Consequently, and over time, sex difference via gender, feminisms and masculinities became the default sociological construction. For example, in Georgian Britain (1714–1830) a man was considered brave and astute if he showed emotional vulnerability and reflected on his physical and psychological being. However, that all changed in the following Victorian period (1837–1901), in which the division of labour by sex led to the ideal of the of the tough, stoic male (Haggett 2014). MacInnes (1998: 2) argues that gender, feminisms and masculinity have become ideologies that do not 'exist as the property, character trait or aspect of identity of individuals'. Taking this perspective allows an understanding how men's experiences have been excluded from reproduction.

MacInnes (1998) criticizes the social sciences for reducing the influence of the natural sciences in people's behaviour purely to social construction. He argues that sociology overlooks one critical issue: 'we cannot socially construct babies' (ibid.: 9). Pulitzer Prize winner, prominent biologist and creator of three unifying concepts for the humanities and natural science Edward O. Wilson (2014: 187) argues that although the humanities and science are fundamentality different, they have a common origin: the evolution of the brain through the creative processes of sociobiology. He contends that to understand the human condition, it is necessary to accept both the cultural and the biological (instinct). Wilson (ibid.: 28–34) reasons that key to *Homo sapiens'* dominance is 'multilevel selection', where 'hereditary social behaviour improves the competitive ability' of both individuals in groups and the group as an entity. Consequently, in-group and between-group competition developed. The former depended on self-interest (selfishness), while the latter needed in-group altruism and cooperation with concomitant social understanding. Wilson (ibid.: 33) reasons that selfish individuals dominated altruistic individuals, but altruistic groups beat selfish groups. Thus, he argues that the human condition is permanently conflicted between the instinctive forces of self and group needs. Research by Laurie Rudman and Stephanie Goodwin (2004: 507) on implicit gender attitudes found that women had an automatic in-group bias through 'a dramatically greater liking for women than men show for men'. Similar findings have been reported from a wide range of different fields. For example, Nathan Hook (2019) found that females identified more strongly with computerized fictional characters of their own gender, whereas males identified equally with either gender. Seager and Barry (2019a: 107) argue that men's behaviour points more to 'an archetypal instinct to protect the social group' rather than 'power, dominance and aggression towards women.' Similarly, Belinda Brown (2019: 191) reports that males engage in 'costly altruism' when the beneficiary is female. She contends that it makes evolutionary sense to protect the source of reproduction. This may link to Daniels and Chadwick's (2018: 825) contention that fathers who participated in homebirth engaged in 'selfless masculinity' linked to the 'involved father' ideal. Moreover, some men merged 'selfless masculinity', 'best father' and traditional 'provider' ideals to form a 'selfless breadwinner' epitome.

Wilson (2014) draws on psychological studies (although he references few) to support his claims regarding individual and group behaviour. Acknowledging the complex relationship between the biological, psychological and sociological would lead to a greater understanding of men and of the human condition overall.

Conclusion

In this book, I have shown that many of the stereotypes surrounding men are dubious – especially those concerning reproduction and ageing. Moreover, common myths reinforce gender stereotypes that are harmful to men, women, children, families and wider society. Cynthia Daniels (2006: 6) captures this beautifully when she asserts, 'But only through the recognition of the vulnerabilities of men can gender injustices be transformed. We must see, and believe, evidence of male weaknesses and vulnerability. We must see, and recognize, men's intimate connection to human reproduction.' I advocate a change in attitude towards men and boys, facilitated through the acknowledgement that the biopsychosocial complexity of life that is applied to others is also shown to men. Men are people too.

The global pandemic has changed so much for so many. As I type, my wife and I are in our twelfth week of self-isolation. We are lucky. We have the internet and can get essentials delivered. We have a garden we can sit in and take in nature. We do not have to risk going out to work or to shop. Our dog helps keep us distracted; her need for exercise and food puts structure into our lives. Writing this book has given me daily focus and structure. We have friends and relatives to virtually connect with. I am lucky.

A life lived is encapsulated in the '–' between two numbers on memorials. During that 'dash' we are 'doing being': negotiating between our personal needs and navigating the messiness and chaos of the surrounding environment. I am legion (Grant, Judd and Naylor 1993): the sum of biological, cultural, economic, historical, physiological, psychological and sociological contexts. I am legion – like you, like everyone else. I am a mediated childless-by-circumstance man; I am a man who wanted to be a dad and did not become one. I hope you have enjoyed reading this book – even if it has annoyed, changed, challenged, disappointed, engaged, frustrated or moved you. It has me.

Notes

1. Originally published in Hadley, Robin A. 2018. 'The Lived Experience of Older Involuntary Childless Men', *The Auto/Biography Yearbook* 2017: 93–108.
   https://www.britsoc.co.uk/groups/study-groups/
   autobiography-study-group/yearbook/.
2. Originally published in Hadley, Robin A. 2018. 'The Lived Experience of Older Involuntary Childless Men', *The Auto/Biography Yearbook* 2017: 93–108.
   https://www.britsoc.co.uk/groups/study-groups/
   autobiography-study-group/yearbook/.
3. From: *Childlessness in the Age of Communication: Deconstructing Silence.* Archetti, C. Copyright (© 2020 Cristina Archetti). Routledge: London. Reproduced by permission of Taylor & Francis Group.

PEN PORTRAITS, IN INTERVIEW ORDER, AND INTERVIEWER REFLECTIONS

George

Contacted me by email after reading a leaflet. George is 60 years old, slim, tanned, fit-looking, slightly taller than my 5'6", silver-grey-haired, very articulate and well spoken. Since his teenage years, he had loved the outdoors, including activities such as walking and sailing. He has held, and been active in, the Christian faith for a similar period. He was born in a peninsula town in north-west England, where his father worked in the family business and his mother gave up work to look after George and his younger sister by three years. He had a very happy childhood and went to boarding school at age 13, at his father's insistence, and left at age 18 to attend teacher training college. He taught mainly in schools in the south-east for twenty-six years, before making a small number of moves northwards back to the north-west. He left the teaching profession in his late forties, successfully pursued a research doctorate and now has a career as a researcher. He was forced to take his teacher's pension on his sixtieth birthday, but does not view himself as retired. He and his wife have lived in their present location in a small city for the past four years, due to her career – she has a high-status, full-time position in higher education. They live in a modernized house in the middle of a small row of stone-fronted Victorian terraced houses. He, following his parents, married late – in his early forties. His wife is ten years younger and he loves her very much. Although there were times when he thought he was going to become a father in his mid- to late forties, he and his wife decided after a long discussion not to pursue full medical intervention, but to let nature take its course. Although this decision meant that they could have a more 'artistic' and flexible lifestyle, he has become increasingly aware of the relationship he has missed as a father and grandfather. Similarly, he became aware during his career of not being part of his 'childed' colleagues' peer group and not fitting in with younger 'childless' colleagues. He is aware of a gradual decline in his hearing and sight, and this leads to frustration regarding his performance and another 'gap' between himself and others. However, his and his wife's interest in environmental issues has led them to rationalize the 'green' advantage of not having children. He is conscious of his health and accesses the doctor when necessary. Both his parents had dementia. His wish is to age gracefully. His closest blood relatives apart from his sister are his cousins, with whom he keeps in contact via email and Skype. His wife and his sister are his closest relationships, followed by his wife's family and his cousins.

It was George's fate to be the first interviewee, and my nerves and unsureness permeate my notes. I am in awe of his use of and ease with language and I sense he feels my unease: I noted that I feel I had disappointed him and that he had been annoyed by some of my 'on-the-fly' enquiries. Moreover, he does become emotional, but quickly regains control, and my intervention suggesting we could stop recording sounds scratchy and tentative.

John

Apart from our interview meetings, all other contact with John, 59, was by telephone. John was recruited through the first advertisement in *The Oldie*. Later, it became apparent that he did not want his partner to know of his participation, and to this end he would shred the transcript and all written communication. John is in a long-term relationship, and is a tall, obese man, dressed in a loose-fitting jumper and leggings, who is temporarily using a walking frame. The house is large and detached, on an estate that was built in the 1970s, and was bought to accommodate the children they were planning to have. He was born in a working-class area of a large city in the south-east of England, and has lived in central-east England since his mid-twenties, when he moved for both his and his partner's employment opportunities. His childhood was one of 'aversive' treatment by both parents. He boarded at a specialist school from age 9, where he was bullied, and returned home at 13. His father was a skilled workshop engineer, and both his parents were local councillors, which meant he was denied the attention he felt a child needed when young. He is the oldest of three boys and has two nephews to the middle brother, but has little contact with them. He has chronic health conditions, including type 2 diabetes, cellulitis, erectile dysfunction, venous hypertension, atrial fibrillation, dilated cardiomyopathy and neurophia (damaged nerves) in his hands and feet. These he links directly to heavy drinking following his partner's decision not have children with him in their mid-thirties (they are the same age). They had delayed trying for children because the interest rate rise meant they both had to work to cover their mortgage. They met through friends in their early twenties and initially agreed on a common desire to become parents; however, he now believes that his partner's fear of pain and the pain of childbirth was the reason for his not being a father. Fear of not being wanted or being unable to find another partner stopped him leaving the relationship, although once, in his mid-forties, he did leave for another woman and her children. However, she decided against living with him and he returned, the same day, to his home. His partner is a leading professional in her field and works for high-profile national companies, and her focus on her work frustrates him. He qualified as an electronics technician and worked for a local company that closed down when the company switched operations overseas about five years ago, and where his size was a subject of discrimination. He had been a political activist, but reorganization and change of political direction led him to leave. As a result, he has little social contact with former colleagues or activists. His well-being is merged with his health, and he acknowledged that a substantial loss of weight would reduce all other conditions. However, he refuses to have a gastric band, because food and drink are the only two things he has in common with his partner. Moreover, the one thing he would change to improve the quality of his life is 'himself' by having some self-confidence and self-esteem. John notes that as a young man, he was invincible, but now he is vulnerable. He has contemplated suicide in the past and would prefer to control his own demise rather than lose further functionality – in particular loss of sight. He sets great store by his CD music collection (two thousand discs) and six guitars, and cites space as a reason against sheltered accommodation in later life.

I felt I performed better in these interviews, and although there was a lot of anger, I did not feel it was directed at me. However, I did have an escape strategy planned as a precaution. The ambiguity and ambivalence that surrounded John also settled in my view of him: I wasn't quite sure how or what to make of him.

David

David was recruited through my personal network and outside of our interview meetings, all contact was through email. David is 60 years old, has been married for five and half years, and is thin, lightly tanned and dressed in slacks and a shirt; he has quick brown eyes and is well spoken. He is a Christian Scientist, as was his mother, and has taken an active role in church and lives by its principles. He was born in central-east England, the eldest of three children (a brother and sister followed), but the family moved to south-east England when he was aged around 10. His career path has led him to move around the south-east before settling in a large detached house in a commuter town. The industry he worked in had many female employees, but he had a strong sense of not risking his position to form a relationship with an employee. Since leaving full-time employment, and with his wife working from home, he feels they are 'rootless' due to the difficulty in building social connections in a transitory population. He attained a high position in the telecommunications industry before regime change led him to retire at 58. His father was a schoolmaster, his mother was a full-time homemaker, and he had a very good childhood. He noted how his sister had from an early age a large circle of friends and a vibrant social life compared to him and his brother. In his teenage years, he was aware of being sensitive about the subject of girlfriends, and did 'not see the point in having one until after university and starting a career'. His brother and sister both had two boys each, although since his sister's death, the link with those nephews has withered. David has had a number of intense relationships, but has suffered from what he terms 'girlfriend phobia'. Here, a pattern was painted according to which having become involved in a relationship to the extent of thinking of marriage, he had what may be described as an intense anxiety attack that led him to end the relationship. This happened with his wife, but he rectified the situation by talking to a friend. He met his wife through work; she is now 37, has many relatives and now runs her own company from their home. Although they both agreed that they would have children, she has focused on her business and David acknowledged that time is running out. He described his present occupation as split between part-time business consultancy, volunteer work, church and hobbies such as sailing and motorcycling.

I enjoyed talking with David, but had the feeling I was missing something and that I had not gone deep enough. Moreover, I had the impression that he did not see the point in the second interview. Interestingly, he gave me the transcript back at the start of the second interview to correct some items.

Harry

Harry, 64, was recruited through my personal network, and was contacted through email and telephone messages. Harry lives in the suburbs of a city in the south-east of England; he was born in the poorer area of the city and moved to his present address about thirty years ago. He lives in one of a row of artisan cottages in a picture-postcard location with three old dogs. The room we sit in is full of brass and wooden antiques, and there are many clocks that 'ticktock' and randomly strike. Harry half sits and half lies in the centre of a settee, while I perch on the edge an armchair that is about a metre and half from, and diagonally facing, him. He is a widower of two years, a large, tall man with a strong local accent and a slightly dazed demeanour. He was the only child to working-class parents and describes himself as firmly working class; he left school at 15 with no qualifications and worked in various jobs before getting married at 24. As a married man, he felt he had to have a 'proper' job, and so became a bus driver and worked his way to a management role before taking voluntary redundancy at 44 to pay off the mortgage. He divorced when he was 30 and started dating H (now deceased), who worked for the same company and in the same location. He then worked in the prison service until recently, when he retired due to issues surrounding his ongoing bereavement. H and he had tried for children, but it seems that she had a gynaecological problem, although he did not enquire what it was. They went through the adoption procedure but withdrew because of the focus on their different religious practices. He always believed that he would die first, and set up financial devices for that eventuality. H's death, and battle with cancer, has left Harry bereft in many ways, not least because having children would have been a connection with her.

Moreover, he fears being viewed as a paedophile, and will not let the local children visit his dogs as they used to when H was alive. He has a lot of support from his neighbours, but feels a gap when any of H's large family calls. He has two old male friends that he would call if he had any problems, and knows many people from walking the dogs and his interest in antiques. Life is 'passable' but not what he would have chosen. Financially, he has three pensions, including a widow's allowance from L's pension, which he was granted after contacting the chief executive of the company.

I saw Harry the evening of the day I held the second interview with John. My overriding feeling after the interview was of a man lost in grief. When I contacted him to arrange the second interview, I was not surprised when he said he had said all he wanted to. Moreover, I was relieved at not having to witness his pain, bereavement and bewilderment.

Martin

Martin, 70, responded by email to the first advert in *The Oldie* magazine. He is tall and slim, with a slight south-eastern accent; he has grey hair and lively eyes. He and his second wife, 'A', have lived in an 1820s farmhouse in rural Wales for the past three years. He and 'A' run a vintage marque motorcycle club, and he restores and maintains motorcycles of that make. They both take an active volunteer role locally, and both are learning Welsh. The house is whitewashed and set back from the road; inside, the ceilings are low with dark beams and the walls white, with the wooden furniture a warm biscuit colour. He is the only son to working-class parents, both of whom worked; his father was an engineer and his mother a telephone operator. He does feel that being an only child, he is self-sufficient and not in need of anybody else; he has been shy most of his life and has to work not to fade into the background. He was born and raised in a large city in the south-east, and he speaks fondly of a childhood in a supportive community with strong family connections. In his early teens, the family moved to one of the post-war new towns, and he left school at 16 with three GCEs. He completed an engineering apprenticeship and worked his way from the shop floor via the design office to management. That company closed in the mid-1990s, and he took early retirement both to pay off the mortgage and have some income. He then started his own consultancy business, despite some reservations surrounding becoming self-employed and having to push himself forward. He retired three years ago and now describes himself as retired and volunteering. He married for the first time at age 26 and divorced in the mid-1980s; although his first wife was scared of childbirth, he does not believe that not having children was a reason for the divorce. In his twenties and thirties he felt a duty to carry on the family name, but eventually accepted that it wasn't possible. In their later years, Martin supported his parents as a matter of repayment for what they had done for him. He married his wife, A, in 1990, and it was while trying for a baby in the following few years that he found out he was infertile and had been from his mid-teens. In order not to deny A the experience of motherhood, and after some period of reflection on his part regarding donor sperm, they tried donor insemination. However, they ended the treatment after two cycles because of the physical and emotional affect to A. Due to their age, treatment was not available on the NHS. A has a large family and it is through her niece that Martin has become a 'Sgrampy': a surrogate grandfather. This is a role he was determined to fill: as soon as he had knowledge of the pregnancy, he talked with A and then contacted the niece 'before anyone else got there'. He would like to see the granddaughter's eighteenth birthday (she is presently aged 3). His health is 'very good', although he has had a pacemaker for the past twenty years and has age-related deterioration in sight and hearing. His felt age is physically 55 and mentally 35.

I enjoyed interviewing Martin; there was a lot of laughter, and he came across as very calm and grounded. He also returned the transcript with corrections to be made; interestingly, A had read it, and said that she only went through the infertility treatment so that he could experience fatherhood.

Raymond

Raymond, 69, was recruited through an LGBT over-50s group in the north-west. He is the same height as me, slightly plumper, and he is wearing dark trousers and a plain shirt. He sees himself as a widower since his partner P died some eight years ago. He has a soft Lancashire accent and the dialect permeates his speech. He shuffles as he walks due to an ongoing foot problem that is being treated at a local outpatients' clinic. He lives in the ground-floor flat of a housing association property in a leafy suburb of a north-western town. The room we sit in is neat and tidy, and has a small display case of ornaments to one side. He was born in a village, not far from his present address, in a working-class family in which his dad was a gas engineer and his mother cleaned for 'the big houses in the village'. He has a sister seven years younger, and his sexuality has been an issue for some of her partners: it is only relatively recently that he has seen her children. His partner P had a large family, and he has maintained contact with some of them. From his mid-twenties he travelled the country with P in their role as waiters in hotels and restaurants. They passed themselves off as stepbrothers and this was never questioned in any situation. This strategy allowed him and his long-term partner to 'pass' as staff, and they often shared quarters: the unsocial working hours suited their relationship. In the late 1980s Raymond and P opened their own business in a city in the north-west, but following a series of robberies they lost both the business and a house they had bought together. As a result, the local council housed them before they moved to the present accommodation. They returned to 'waiting on' before working for the catering section of a local NHS facility. They worked there for about eight years before the facilities were closed and they were offered early retirement. Raymond knew he was gay at 15, and with the societal norms of the time insisting on marriage before children, at that time put all thoughts of fatherhood aside. However, he has always enjoyed meeting and interacting with children and would enjoy a grandparental relationship where he could pass on knowledge and experience. As a result, he feels his missing of the father-type role is not due to recent events, but has always been there, although not consciously acknowledged. However, he is wary of being seen as a paedophile and is reluctant to voice his wish to be in a grandparental role. Raymond's income comprises the state pension and a small NHS pension. He works in the pub as a way of 'making ends meet' since P's death. This also serves as a point of social contact. Due to his foot problem, his social life has been reduced: he sometimes travels on public transport to hear people's voices and suffers a low mood if he has to stay in for more than few days. In this respect, the LGBT group has been of great support. His felt age is the same physically and mentally.

The two strands that dominated my thoughts and feelings following my meetings with Raymond were a sense of loneliness and of the change in society, which has shifted from one in which marriage is the only route to parenthood to one where gay men can have surrogate babies.

Colin

Colin, 61, diagnosed with motor neurone disease at 51, was recruited through my personal network. The interview was conducted via email because of Colin's concern that his MND affects him in various ways when he is emotional. MND is a huge factor in his life: he cannot walk without a frame and has breathing difficulties. As a result, we agreed that we would use one document with individual questions, replies, follow-up questions and replies following sequentially. Colin has lived within twenty miles of his hometown in central-southern England all his life. He has been married twice and has lived with his female partner, who has grown-up children, for the past seven years. Colin is a retired mechanical design engineer who was very good at sport. He holds a Christian faith and believes that marriage is for the purpose of having children. He had a very happy childhood in a working-class area and was the youngest of three brothers. From a young age he was conscious of the desire to get married, have children and continue the family name, but not to have the structure of job, house and so on. He married his 'childhood sweetheart' at 26; he had wanted to have children, but she had wanted to concentrate on her career. They divorced when he was 33 and he waited twelve years before having another relationship and meeting his next wife, who had three children already and whom he married when he was 48. Only when married did she tell him that she had had surgery to prevent having any more children. It was at this point he accepted he would not be becoming a father. As the children of his partner were adults, Colin did not feel that he was in a father role with them, but had noted that there seemed to be a deeper bond between sibling and parent. He rated his health as terrible and his felt age as 80. If he could change one thing, it would be his MND, and he has planned for hospice care when his condition worsens. Colin's core social ties are his partner, brothers and half a dozen or so close friends, and he has an outer circle of forty or so.

I was aware of the effect my questions might have not only on Colin but also on those who support him, and this made me wary of pushing for too much detail. Interviewing by email was difficult, as there were no non-verbal cues, and even 'open' questions were subject to yes/no answers. Therefore, in the follow-up questions I highlighted the experiences of others: for instance by asking, 'Some men say ... what is your experience?' However, these questions also often drew a single reply.

Frank

Outside of our interview meetings, all contact with Frank, 56, was through email, and he found out about the study through reading a friend's copy of the first advert in *The Oldie*. He has lived in his present location of a large village in Wales for approximately thirty years. Originally from central England, he is articulate, with a strong Midlands accent, and is tall and slightly stooped, with light brown hair and a thin face; he lives in a two-bedroomed, single-story miner's cottage. The cottage had a high ceiling and small windows, and consequently was dark. The second interview took place in his friend's house overlooking a picturesque bay: he could not see why anyone would live in that location. Frank is the youngest of three children; his eldest brother has no children and his sister has two adult sons, the younger of which Frank gets on with very well. However, he does not feel close to anyone in particular, and his social life is restricted by his financial and health situation. Raised in a lower-middle-class family, he reports his childhood as nothing special and recalls having to entertain himself. His father died suddenly when Frank was 17, and despite being shy and quiet, he assumed the role of man of the house. His mother, now 87, moved to a coastal town fifteen miles from Frank about twelve years ago, and they see each other regularly. He is not in a caring role, but is her first point of contact. This situation has caused some conflict regarding money and inheritance, and he no longer speaks with his sister. Frank left the Midlands in his late twenties after completing an arts degree. He undertook various jobs, including as a care assistant and driver, and manual work such as building and gardening. However, in his forties he suffered a back injury and, in addition, for the past ten years has lived with ME, which he struggled to have diagnosed due to his rural location. He supplements his benefits allowance by doing odd jobs for people. However, the nature of his ailments means that he cannot find regular work, and he is in dispute with the benefits agency. Frank had his first serious and intimate relationship when he was 34, which lasted ten years. His ex-partner was ten years his junior, and due to trust issues, he took control of contraception. He has not had a relationship since they split up and there is an ongoing dispute regarding the property. Frank has strong environmental concerns and supports local efforts and groups; however, he believes that his education and intelligence separates him from local men. He is actively seeking a partner but believes that his health, economics and location do not aid his quest. Moreover, he uses free online dating agencies and is not interested in the older women who contact him: he would prefer someone younger with whom he could father a child or be in a father role to an existing child. He does realize that his age may count against him but does not account for how old he would be when the child is older.

I found Frank both fascinating and frustrating: the former because of his question, 'how is a man supposed to be a man?', and the latter because of his constant ambivalence. This last point was particularly frustrating during the coding. I have struggled to pinpoint what it is that Frank says that exasperated me, unless it is at some subliminal level of recognition of self. Moreover, Frank's attempts to 'move' in any direction regarding work, relationships and health all seem to be frustrated.

Alan

Alan, 82, was recruited through an LGBT over-50s group in northwest England. Initially, he telephoned to see if he was suitable for the study: he made it very clear that he never wanted to be a father but had been 'adopted' as a grandfather. Alan lives in the suburbs of a large conurbation on a road that has a wide range of housing, from Victorian terraces to new builds with residential homes. This is not far from where he was born and baptized. Both interviews took place in his ground-floor flat in a two-story building probably built in the 1970s. He has lived in the flat for approximately eight years; it was rented from a private landlord. He is a small, trim man, with a close-cropped grey and white beard to match his hair. He wears spectacles, and his hearing had deteriorated, meaning that he needed to lip read. He is a wit and raconteur, and enjoys speaking: he has a broad local accent. He is very active in an LGBT group, in church and in voluntary work for various charities, including those for young and older LGBT people. Furthermore, he suffers from a low mood if he cannot get out. He uses a cane – temporarily, he says, after falling a few months previously. He had an industrial injury to his thumbs in his late 1950s that forced him to take retirement through ill health: he now struggles to grip things in either hand. He had taken part in research previously and had another researcher visiting soon. He handed me a sheet containing his early life story that had been used in a local paper on residents' histories. Alan related the story of his being born out of wedlock and his subsequent adoption to a widow with three children, the nearest in age to him being some 15 years older. As a gay man, he had no sexual interest in women: to become a father, marriage was a prerequisite, and therefore it was dismissed absolutely. His working life had consisted of a number of roles; a twenty-five-year stint in the Royal Navy, and work as an industrial librarian, a licensee and in stores personnel for a heating manufacturer. Apart from the RN, he had lived in a port in eastern-central England, and moved back to his hometown with his then partner in the 2000s. He had taken an active role in various G.A.Y. organizations from the 1950s until the present day. He split from his long-time partner some ten years ago, and he is not in a romantic relationship. However, he has a very strong bond with B, a man in his mid-forties who he has known for some fifteen years. He and B call each other 'dad' and 'son', with B having power of attorney. Alan does not fear losing physical functionality, but does fear losing his mental capacity. He had a keen interest is sports; he had run marathons and only stopped a few years ago. He was also a season ticket holder for his local football club. It was at a match that another supporter approached him to ask if he would be an 'adopted' grandfather to the man's twin sons, aged 12, for a school project. The role lasted about three years and ended around five years ago, and it gave Alan a sense of belonging. This was reinforced recently when one of his 'boys' shouted 'Hello granddad!' to him at a match.

My impression was of being in the presence of a professional performer. My interventions were tolerated and then used to link back to his script. For all that, I had the feeling that Alan wanted to tell his story, and I was left with a sense of Alan and his loneliness. I noted that I would like to have a beer and a chat with him, but would be wary of always being the audience. Afterwards, as I wrote my notes in the car, two men and a little van were sweeping the pavements: they were collecting the fallen leaves and so was I.

Michael

Michael, 63, was recruited from my online response to an article in *The Telegraph* Online, and with the exception of our Skype interviews, all contact was via email. Technical issues meant that there are no clear images of Michael. He is erudite and well-spoken, with a deprecating sense of humour, and referred to himself as 'eccentric' and 'an artsy-fartsy drama teacher'. He likes beautiful things, fashion ('I like Paul Smith'), theatre and art, and expensive treats. He calls himself a cultural Christian, but does not believe in god or a spiritual being: he is known in the Asia Pacific region as a 'free thinker'. He is employed as a drama teacher where he has worked for approximately two years. He lives in a rented villa with its own grounds and a swimming pool. He previously worked in Japan, and had a ten-year relationship with a Japanese woman and mother of a teenage daughter. Michael always expected that he would be a father, with a desire that had 'bubbled along' with no particular peak. As he aged, he had noted the change of his self-reflection, from the 'when will I get married and have children' of earlier years to 'when will I die'. He was born in a small, 'idyllic' town in south-west England, where he has a sister who is six years older, and had a 'very happy' childhood. His upbringing was very middle class. In his teens, he played in a rock band and was very extroverted in public, but very self-conscious and shy in his personal life. After meeting his godparents' children, he found children fascinating. He trained in education and drama and taught in this country for a few years, before flying off at thirty to teach overseas in various countries. However, he feels that this is his last post before retiring. He became emotional when describing teaching Year 7: how 'lovely' they are and how jealous of the parents he is at times. The one thing in his life he would change would be to be a parent. Similarly, he related how he sobbed 'with envy' on a flight when watching the film *Kokowääh*, the story of a man faced with suddenly having to look after his unknown daughter. Michael feels he has little in common with male colleagues, and sometimes feels isolated not only in the staff room but also in the evenings and weekends. However, he feels that single 'childless' men have to work harder to form and maintain social contacts. He noted feeling now that he had to say not only that he wasn't married, but also that he wasn't gay, in social situations. His inner social circle consists of five friends, but his outer circle is quite large and he has kept in touch with friends in his hometown and the various countries he has worked in. He described himself as healthy, but not fit; he takes tablets for high blood pressure and eye drops for ocular hypertension, and initiates regular check-ups with the doctors and dentist. He has no firm plans about retiring, as he gets so much from his job; however, he thinks he might return to his hometown when he does retire.

I found Michael very easy to talk to and very open about his thoughts and feelings; he reminded me of David. The technical issues meant that the video feed often failed, and I felt that having a poor image distracted from the interview. I was moved when he described becoming emotional about the Year 7 children and the film *Kokowääh*.

Edward

Edward, 60, contacted me after reading my piece in the MoreToLife (MTL) newsletter. He is about 5'10" and well built, but not fat. He has short, dark, curly hair that is receding away from his forehead. He is well spoken, with the hint of a south-west accent and an easy-going manner. He and his partner have lived for over thirty years in their 1920s semi-detached house in a large commuter town in the south-east. He fairly recently became self-employed after spending most of his working life as a salaried architect. For the past few years, he has been a volunteer guide at a local historical building. He had a very good childhood, being the youngest of four children, and the family remain close. He enjoys his role of uncle and is particularly close to the son of the brother he is closest to. All his siblings are now grandparents and he is aware of not enjoying the grandchild–grandparent relationship. He was very aware of his father's strict Edwardian values, and grew up appreciating the role of a father in a family: he feels he is becoming more like his father as he grows older. He was shy at school and still has difficulty in broaching conversation with strangers. He said he is not ambitious and is happy to be a 'backroom boy'. He went to grammar school before going to university in the East Midlands to qualify as an architect. The duration (seven years) and choice of course meant that he did not have much contact with women: he was in his late twenties when he had his first intimate relationship with his current partner, M. They delayed trying for children until she had retrained, at which point she was in her mid-thirties and he in his early forties. He had not been worried about their age, as his parents were in their forties when he was born. A few years later, they tried IVF, but stopped, as the process was stressful, particularly for M. Although they discussed adoption and fostering, they were not happy to pursue it. The details of the IVF treatment had not been widely shared with friends and family. Edward believed that people should know that they did want a family. It was because of the IVF treatment that he and M joined MTL, and he believed that this had been of great benefit in supporting them. He noted that as friends and peers had children, their relationship would fade away.

However, he had found himself being particularly jealous of one friend who had children, so much so that Edward had avoided him for a number of years. Twenty-five years ago, Edward set up a pension plan, but the economic situation has meant that he has to keep working. Furthermore, over the past decade, he has been made redundant twice before becoming self-employed. Although he likes the freedom of choice available in being self-employed, he would prefer to have the freedom of being retired. He rates his quality of life as good and formed by 'simple pleasures', citing his deep love for M, having a close circle of friends and family nearby and owning his own home. Edward is in good health but takes tablets for high cholesterol and gastric reflux, and also sees himself as a 'bit of a hypochondriac'. Edward hopes to retire to his birth town and live near his brother. However, he has not really considered issues surrounding late life or the end of life.

I found talking to Edward very easy, and he was very open about IVF, I think because of his connection with MTL. However, he did say that I had teased the information about his retirement out of him, and I had the feeling that he did not see the point of the second interview.

James

James, 65, was recruited via a flyer handed to a fellow PhD student from another university. Both interviews were held at his partner's home. The house is on a narrow, twisty road between a town and a village; there is no front garden, and the house is one of a row of Victorian terraces that have been extended and modernized. The front door opens directly into a wooden-floored, square living room, with a door directly facing the one just entered. To the right is a long, low pine table, faced at either end by a light-coloured settee; I sat on a low sofa that backs onto the front-room window. James has a soft north-east accent; moreover, he sat with his head back and his chin pointing to the ceiling. I was concerned that the microphone would not pick his speech up clearly. He has white hair and a lightly tanned face with sparkling blue eyes; he is slim and about 5'8". He was raised in a small working-class town in the north-east and is seven years younger than his brother. He regards himself now as bridging the gap between working and middle class. His father, a signalman, died when he was young, and he helped care for his mother and lived near her before she died. He attended mixed primary and grammar school but left at 15, before any exams, because he 'knocked around' with the lads from the local pit village and they had started work. However, he never wanted to be a pitman. He trained as a printer and was one until retiring five years ago. He refers to his early adulthood as quite boozy and 'quite an incestuous crowd', many of whom he is still friends with. However, the drinking culture of the environment helped with his shyness and he had his first intimate relationship at 18. From his mid-thirties he had planned to retire when he was 60. He now draws his final salary pension and the state pension. James has a strong relationship with his brother, and that extended to his brother's two daughters when they were younger. He is as at home with children as he is with adults. James says that there were three relationships of significant length in his life, of three, ten and (with his current partner) twelve years respectively. The first was in his late twenties and the second in his late thirties. It was in this relationship that his thoughts turned to fatherhood. However, his then partner made it very clear that she did not want children because of her fear of childbirth. When they split up, he felt that he was too old to become a father because of the parent–child age gap. James met his current partner through the singles column in a newspaper, and they have 'lived apart together' for over a decade. However, he believes that he will soon move to live with his partner. He is confident in his ability to socialize and not worried about change. Quality of life for James is related to health, the best thing being not working and being financially secure. His health is good and he has become fitter after retiring through taking up cycling. He stopped smoking when he was 40 and has been a vegetarian for a long time. His partner has a daughter, A, who lives overseas, and a son, and both have one young child each. It was while visiting A that James spent a lot time caring for her baby. As a result, he has a role as a grandfather, and is called 'Pappous' – the Greek for grandfather.

James had a laid-back air and it was easy to see why he had no difficulty in fitting in with different social environments. My feeling was that he was a man who could hold a conversation with someone with completely different views and not lose his temper.

Russell

Russell, 55, was recruited via a flyer in a location close to Keele University. He lodges with two older spinster sisters with whom he has a very close friendship. He has lived in the area for approximately eight years and in the UK for around twenty-five. He is very protective of the sisters and values the relationship very much, becoming emotional when he talks about them. Initial conversations were by telephone and involved me phoning a telephone box. The following communications were mainly by email. From very early on it was apparent from Russell's use of language and the authority in his voice that he had been in the role of an academic supervisor. Our first conversations were centred on the study and the rationale behind it, and this was very clearly due to his interest in the subject. The interviews took place on campus. Russell is wiry and about my height, lightly tanned and with short, light, receding hair. He speaks quickly and succinctly and with a slight Australian accent. Occasionally he uses Australian colloquialisms. He was very aware of the tape and often stated his actions and emotions for its benefit and mine. For example, he often explained why he was avoiding eye contact. He is quick witted, intelligent, knowledgeable, self-effacing and open. He was dressed casually for both interviews. His was a turbulent upbringing: he left Australia when very young and, in England, was placed in foster care followed by an orphanage. From age 9 to 11 he lived with his birth father, who was both violent and very loving, and Russell stated several times a wariness of possibly being genetically or socially influenced by that behaviour. However, he does consider his strong sense of duty to be a provider as an attribute from his birth father. He was then reunited with his birth mother and they returned to Australia. When he was in his mid-teens, Russell suffered a breakdown and was admitted to various psychiatric establishments. Here, he had many traumas and was treated with different psychotropic drugs. Following his discharge at around 20, Russell worked in the voluntary sector before coming to England to reconnect with his father. It was here that he met his wife and got a job in the finance business sector. He was very successful in that sector; however, in his forties he left it and completed an MBA. He then took a teaching qualification and changed career, moving into the higher education sector. He has held a handful of academic posts. Presently he has been between posts for about nine months. His marriage lasted about ten years, and although both wanted to have children (they regularly bought baby items), they both agreed that everything, such as finance and accommodation, would have to be in place. A number of factors meant that they divorced before trying for a baby. Although he assumed he would be a father, Russell was very aware of contraception, and during the marriage used the Billings method. He was also conscientious in the use of contraception in the two serious relationships subsequent to his divorce. A younger junior colleague had initiated one relationship. This partner offered to have his child, but the relationship broke up soon after he had fully committed to it. He has not had an intimate relationship for the past ten years. He said that he was coming to terms with not becoming a father. In the second interview, he acknowledged the loss of not becoming a grandfather. In forming relationships, Russell states that he is often seduced and not the seducer. Moreover, although he is able to socialize well at parties and similar events, his shyness has been a factor in forming intimate relationships. He is conscious of not being the typical 'rugger-bugger' Australian, and liked art, drama, ballet and musicals. He sees himself as being in 'disgustingly good health', although he has had a hernia. He is aware of deterioration in his eyesight, but compares himself favourably against peers and family, stating that he has a felt age of being in his thirties. He measures his quality of life by the contentment of being able to choose what he wants to do. He misses the intimate closeness of a relationship, and that is one thing that parenthood would bring him. Both his birth mother and father divorced and had subsequent relationships. Russell has thirteen assorted half- and stepsiblings. However, he is only in contact with his birth mother and birth sister, who live in Australia.

Although our interviews lasted a long time, I found that in fact, the time flew by when listening to Russell. He is an intense man who is very self-aware. For example, he mentioned how the second interview was a time of grief because we would not meet again. I was very touched by his story and more than a little in awe of his knowledge. He mentioned suicide and suicidal ideation at one point, and my initial reaction was to try and remember what the protocol was when counselling. However, I quickly recovered my position.

Stephen

Stephen, 49, was recruited through my personal network. Both interviews took place over the telephone; emails would have taken too long to type, and it was difficult to find a suitable and convenient location for face-to-face meetings. Stephen presently lives in a one-bedroom flat that he and his elderly mother (with whom he shares it) bought from the council. They have lived there for nearly thirty years. One of the reasons for using email and telephone for our conversations was to avoid his mother finding out about the interviews. Stephen was born and raised in a working-class council estate in a small village in east-central England; he is a single child and has never known his father. His early childhood, he believed, was not very positive, due in some part to his mother's alcohol and mental health issues and the lack of a positive role model. His mother left him with his grandmother in his late childhood and moved to a large city in the south-east, where he joined her in his late teens. Although not one of the most popular boys in school, he does not believe he was especially shy. The most significant factor in his life has been his severe acne, which started 'nice and early' and has been central to his view of himself. Only in the past five years has he found a treatment that clears it completely, and this is a source of some frustration, as the treatment has been available for decades. Moving to the anonymity of the city also meant that being working class did not have the same impact as it did in his birth village. At 19, during his degree, he spent six months in America and had his first serious and intimate relationship. Although the relationship ended badly, his confidence grew with regard to meeting people and forming relationships. However, after just passing his degree, work was hard to find and he became a gardener in a park in a select area for a few years, before moving into the social sector. At the park, a hedonistic culture included a heter-onormative, predatory male sexual lifestyle, which he adopted. As a result, he spent the time between his mid-twenties and his early forties drinking and having short-term sexual relationships with women who were only visiting the country for a week. His attitude to fatherhood and any norm of traditional family life was very dismissive at that time. He worked to live and paid no attention to future financial or career issues. However, in his early forties he realized that because a lot of his behaviour was centred on the consumption of alcohol, his body could not sustain this 'reckless' lifestyle. Because of the AIDS scare he was very careful to use condoms, and so is positive that there are no offspring as a result of his relationships. During that period he purposefully avoided relationships with women resident in the UK; however, having decided that he had to change, he noted two relationships that he would have liked to develop. In both cases, the women rejected his offer, claiming that they didn't want a long-term relationship with him.

Although one of the women wanted children, at 42 he was too old, as she wanted a partner her own age (35) or younger. In the period since, Stephen has reflected that his lifestyle had consequences not only with regards to his relationships. For example, he has little pension provision, having opted out of several schemes. He feels that he will therefore have to work until he is 70 or older. Moreover, by focusing on his social life, his career has not developed, and he is now trying to retrain to further his career opportunities. He is also aware that his job is seen as being on 'the frontline of social care', and that this is usually the preserve of younger people. As such he feels he is treated differently and that his sector of the profession is quite ageist. Furthermore, because of his living arrangements, colleagues have believed that he is gay or to be avoided. His present job he describes as a low-grade middle-management position. He has two good friends and is happy with his own company, describing himself as interested in art and sport, but a solitary individual. He does not get lonely or understand why people say they do, but he does believe that as an older single man he is vulnerable to discrimination. He says that he now travels to venues that commuters use because of incidents in the past where, as a solo man, he has been subject to unwanted or unwarranted attention from groups of people. Stephen contacts his only uncle, who is also childless, regularly and is concerned that he may be singled out because of that status. Stephen acknowledged that the opportunity for a meaningful relationship that would produce children was receding, and that he had spent the last few years regretting his previous lifestyle. Moreover, he felt that the rejection of his offer of a deeper committed relationship was a form of 'payback' for his earlier lifestyle, adding to the deep regrets he feels about the latter. Looking to the future, he would prefer to have a relationship and then children, but the priority would be to be in a relationship. He rates his quality of life as low, believing that quality of life consists of work–life balance, a good relationship and a family. The best things about his life at present are swimming and reading, and the worst are his work–life balance and the stress of work. Although he doesn't get lonely, he wishes he had someone to share 'the ups and downs' with and go on holiday with. The disadvantage to ageing for Stephen is the limitations it is putting on his chance of forming a relationship and becoming a father. He spoke of an emerging spirituality and, relatedly, preferred not to think of the future.

I found interviewing Stephen quite puzzling, not least because he insisted on walking as we spoke. Thus, there was a soundscape wherever he went, including when he went into a shop to enquire about some shoes. There was an air of recovery about Stephen: he described himself as having been addicted, at one point, to that hedonistic lifestyle.

Appendix 2

INTERVIEW SCHEDULE – FIRST INTERVIEW GUIDE

Introduction

'My name is Robin Hadley and I am a researcher from Keele University, Staffordshire. I am conducting interviews as part of my PhD study exploring the experiences of involuntarily childless men aged over 50. This involves listening to your experiences, in relation to involuntary childlessness, and the impact that may have on your life, for example on your relationships with friends and relations, how you see yourself, and your health.

You are being invited to help in this research because there are very few studies on the actual experiences of involuntarily childless men. By recounting your experiences, you will be helping increase the knowledge of the issues facing older involuntarily childless men. The findings from the study will be used to raise awareness of the issues faced by older involuntarily childless men to relevant organizations and other interested parties. On completion of the study I would be delighted to send you a summary of the findings should you want them.'

Researcher: Ethics

Talk through the information sheet and ensure that participant understands what the research involves, including steps for anonymizing data, confidential storage, etc.; talk through and invite participant to sign consent forms. Choose pseudonym.

Researcher, Section 1: Involuntary Childlessness

'I will describe the main steps involved in the interview. After starting the audio recorder, I will confirm the name you have chosen and use throughout the transcript. I will then ask you about your experiences as an involuntarily childless man. Following that, I would be grateful if you could give me some information about quality of life, and your health. This will help demonstrate how this study fits in with other research. At the end of the interview I will then ask how you found the meeting and confirm that you still want to participate in the study. We will then discuss the details of contacting you and the arrangements regarding the next interview. Finally, I will go through a checklist to ensure that I have covered everything. Is that acceptable – have you any questions or anything you want raise? As I said before, if there is anything you find difficult then please let me know and we'll move on. Have I been clear? I am about to start audio recording – is that alright? We are now recording and I'm just confirming that you are happy to be known as XXXXX.'

1. Can I just check you would have liked children, but you have never had any?
2. Tell me a little about yourself?

(Prompt: For example, if you were describing yourself to someone for the first time over the phone or to a pen pal.)

Researcher, Section 1a: Involuntary Childlessness

'Are you happy to continue? In telling me about how involuntary childlessness has affected your life it may be helpful to think of when you very first became aware of the idea of fatherhood and what affect that had on what you thought and did? As time went by perhaps certain events occurred that impacted on your opportunity to become a father? As you recall different occasions it would be good to know how you saw yourself in relation to your colleagues, friends and family? As we talk, and move from the past to the present, it would be good to know how you see yourself now, and in the future. So, does that feel all right? Are you happy to talk along these lines?'

3. I would be grateful if you could just tell me about when you
   first became aware of fatherhood – of being a father?

(Prompts: what would being a father have meant to you? So having
a child would mean … ?)

How important do you think being a father is? So you saw yourself
as … ? How do you think others saw you … ? What do you feel has
been the biggest challenge to you in not being a father? And as you
age? What do you feel are the greatest challenges facing older people without children? How do you think older people overcome, if
they do, these challenges? What would you see as the particular issues for men who wanted to be a father but aren't? Do these issues
change as with age? Are there advantages to not being a father?
Are there disadvantages to not being a father? And in the future?
Follow the participants' events as he describes them. It is important
to allow the participant to express his views and allow time to develop his response).

4. Finally: is there anything else you would like to add or make
   clear?

Section 2: Quality of Life (QoL), Social Networks, Ageing and Demographic Material

'Now I would like to ask some questions about your quality of life
and your health.'

Researcher, Section 2a: QoL and Health

5. Generally speaking, what would you say defines a good
   quality of life?
6. How would you describe your own quality of life?
7. What parts of your life right now give your life quality?
8. What parts of your life right now reduce your life quality
   (what things limit it)?
9. Which of those is the most important to you?
10. What has changed or stayed the same since the age of 50?
11. If you could change one thing what would it be?
12. In general, how would you describe your health?
13. What is important to you about your health?
14. What aspects of your health right now give your life quality?

15. What aspects of your health right now reduce your life quality?
16. Which of those is the most important to you?
17. What has changed or stayed the same since the age of 50?
18. If you could change one thing what would it be?
19. How often do you see your GP?

(Prompts: do you organize that? Have you always done that?)

Researcher, Section 2b: Social Networks

'The people we have relationships with are important, so I just want to ask you a few questions about your family and friends, if that would be all right?'

20. How do you relax?
21. What would you say is your main way of socializing?

(Prompts: do you attend meetings, social groups and hobbies? How many roughly (large: > 8, medium: 4–7, small: 0–3)).

22. Do you feel you are treated differently because of not being a father?
23. Whom do you socialize with?

(Prompts: equal numbers of friends and family or more one than the other?)

24. Who you are in touch with regularly?

(Prompts: more friends than family? Weekly? By phone?)

25. And you know them from … ?

(Prompts: family, friends, work?)

26. How long have you known them? Do they live far away?
27. Who of these are important to you?

(Prompts: if you had something to share/had a problem who would you contact?)

28. Who are you closest too?
29. Do you feel that your relationships are equal?

(Prompts: that you give equally or one or other gives more? Has it always been like that?)

30. Has your involuntary childlessness ever affected relationships?
31. Are there ever occasions when you feel isolated?

(Prompts: tell me more; has it always been like that?)

32. Do you feel you are understood?
33. Or perhaps you may feel not considered?
34. Do you believe that childlessness has affected relationships?
35. If there were one thing you could change in your relationships with others, what would it be?

Researcher, Section 2c: Ageing

'I just want to ask you a few questions about the future if that would be all right?'

36. What would you say the advantages to ageing were?
37. What are the disadvantages?
38. Do you feel you see changes in how you think about yourself since 50?
39. Do you feel you are treated differently because of your age?
40. What do you look forward to in the future?
41. What are your doubts about the future?
42. Have you made a will or a living will?
43. My friend used to say he would like to die at 90 being shot by the jealous boyfriend of a younger lover … and you?

Alternative to 43:

There are two certainties in life. One is tax … ? Now I'd like to ask you about your working life.

44. How would you describe yourself: employed, not working, volunteer, retired, carer, other?
45. How many hours a week do you do that?
46. How would you describe your main occupation at this present time?

I would just like to remind you that everything you say is confidential and you do not have to answer if you do not want to. I am saying that because I am about to ask a question about your income:

47. How would you describe your main source of income?

(Prompts: salary, state pension, work pension, benefits, private means.)

Researcher, Section 2d: Demographic Material

'We are nearly finished now. I would like to confirm a few details about you.'

48. You were born in ... ?
49. That makes you ... years old?
50. Where were you born?
51. How long have you lived in this area?
52. What form of transport do you use?
53. How would you describe your ethnicity?

(Prompts: I am White British ...).

54. How would you describe your present relationship status?

(Prompts: married, in a relationship, single, widower, living alone, divorced or separated).

55. What is your highest qualification?
56. Do you hold a faith?
57. If there is a message you would like to put out to the world in general about being an involuntarily childless man, what will that be?
58. Finally, is there anything else you would like to add or make clear?

Researcher, Section 3: Debriefing/Ending

59. How did you find taking part in this research?

Check participant is OK and is satisfied with the meeting. Give list of support organizations and explain why you are doing so. Remind the participant that the contact details are on the information sheet and that they should not hesitate to get in touch if they have any queries or concerns. Outline next stage of research and check that the participant is happy to receive the transcript. Agree the most suitable way of doing this, and how they would like to be addressed in letters, email or on the phone. If phoning, what would be a convenient time (between what hours; in the morning/afternoon/evening). Mention possible reactions to typed transcript and reassure. Confirm informed consent, permission to use quotes etc. Collect equipment. Thank participant for taking part in the study. Post-interview write field notes and contact supervisors confirming safety.

Appendix 3

INTERVIEW SCHEDULE – SECOND
INTERVIEW GUIDE

Researcher: Ethics and Introduction

Ensure that participant understands what the research involves. Clarify any issues that are outstanding from the previous interview. Invite participant to reconfirm their consent to participate.

'Thank you for participating so far. To begin with, I will confirm the name you chose last time, and once again, we use this name throughout the transcript. Following that, we will discuss the transcript of the previous interview. For example, you may have something to discuss, clarify, add, change or remove. Finally, we will discuss the next stages of the research – what happens next, contact arrangements, permissions and so on. I will go through a checklist to ensure that I have covered everything. Is that acceptable – have you any questions or anything you want to raise? As I said before, if there is anything you find difficult then please let me know and we will move on. I am about to start audio recording – is that all right? We are now recording and I'm just confirming that you are still happy to be known as XXXXX.'

Researcher: Transcript Discussion

1. How did you find reading the transcript of our last interview?
2. Was there anything in particular that struck you about it?

(Prompts: is there anything in there that you would like to say more on? Anything you wish to remove? So being a father would have made what sort of difference ... ? Having a child at that time would have ... ? That particular moment stood out because ... ? Tell me a little more about ... ?)

3. Anything further to add?

Researcher: Data Analysis Outcomes

Bring in any issues that are being realized in the data analysis.

4. What is your reaction to ... ?
5. Others have mentioned ... ?
6. Have you experienced ... ?
7. Is there anything else you would like to add or make clear?
8. We are nearly finished now, so if there was one message that you would like me to pass on about men in your situation what would that be?

Researcher: Debriefing/Ending

Check participant is OK and is satisfied with the meeting.

9. How did you find taking part in this research?

Remind the participant that the contact details are on the information sheet and that they should not hesitate to get in touch if they have any queries or concerns at all. Clarify that the participant agrees to the next stage in the research, confirm informed consent and permission to use quotes. Check the participant wants a summary of findings and what format would be most suitable. As the study draws to a close, he will be contacted regarding the key points/summary sheet. At that time confirmation of informed consent and permission for the use of direct quotations will be checked. Thank participant for taking part. Collect equipment. Post-interview write field notes and contact supervisor(s) confirming safety.

GLOSSARY

Assisted reproductive technology (ART): fertility treatments that typically involve retrieving eggs, combining them with sperm in the laboratory, and then returning them to the woman's body or to another woman's body. IVF is probably the most well-known ART technique.

Auto/biography: an approach to research that views the relationship between the researcher and the participants' biographies as an important factor in research. The auto/biographical approach is closely linked to feminist research through its emphasis on reflexivity and focus on identity, subjectivity, power and privilege in the research process.

Critical gerontology: the study of ageing from a political-economic perspective (Phillips, Ajrouch and Hillcoat-Nalletamby 2010).

Demography: the scientific study of populations – typically using statistical measures and analysis of records, and research and surveys of births, disease, education, employment, health, geopolitical location and mortality.

Epigenetics: the study of changes in gene function that do not entail a change in DNA sequence.

Gamete: a mature sexual reproductive cell – either a female egg or a male sperm – that has unpaired chromosomes.

Gerontology: the study of ageing. Although it covers all ages, it is mostly associated with studies of older people. It is multi-disciplinary and includes biological, critical, chronological age, environmental, life course, medical, psychological, sociological and technological perspectives (Phillips, Ajrouch and Hillcoat-Nalletamby 2010).

Heteronormative: a view of the world that promotes heterosexuality as the normal sexual orientation.

Intracytoplasmic sperm injection (ICSI): IVF procedure where a single sperm is injected into the centre of the egg. The technique of surgical sperm retrieval is widely associated with ICSI.

Intrauterine insemination: a fertility treatment where sperm is directly inserted into a woman's uterus.

In vitro fertilization: a fertility treatment that involves the retrieval of eggs, which are then combined with sperm in the laboratory. The fertilized eggs develop into embryos, which are then cultured for five to six days before being transferred into the woman's uterus.

Life course perspective: an emphasis on the context of ageing that examines biographical and cultural aspects, roles and statuses, social characteristics (e.g. class, gender, race) and social and economic institutions and policies across a historical time period (Phillips, Ajrouch and Hillcoat-Nalletamby 2010).

Lifespan: a view of human development as lifelong, occurring in stages and unidirectional. In psychology, lifespan is primarily concerned with individual behaviour over social factors (Phillips, Ajrouch and Hillcoat-Nalletamby 2010).

Male factor infertility: any reason for which sperm may be less effective or incapable of fertilization.

Metaphor: describing something in terms of something else.

Periconceptual: the period from before conception to early pregnancy.

Perinatal: the period from during pregnancy until up to a year after birth.

Pronatalism: the political, religious or cultural attitudes that promote parenthood as an ideal.

Positive psychology: the scientific study of human functioning in order to understand and promote the factors that allow individuals and communities to flourish and thrive.

Social gerontology: an approach to the study of ageing concerned with the demographic, economic, life course and social characteristics of ageing populations and older people (Phillips, Ajrouch and Hillcoat-Nalletamby 2010).

Surgical sperm retrieval: a surgical procedure in which sperm cells are extracted directly from the testis – either from the epididymis or the testicles. This procedure is carried out in men who have no sperm in their ejaculate.

Unexplained (idiopathic) infertility: cases where no obvious medical cause for a couple's infertility is found.

REFERENCES

Aarseth, H., L. Layton and H. Bjerrum Nielsen. 2016. 'Conflicts in the Habitus: The Emotional Work of Becoming Modern', *The Sociological Review* 64(1): 148–65.

Adams, R.G. 1987. 'Patterns of Network Change: A Longitudinal Study of Friendships of Elderly Women', *The Gerontologist* 27(2): 222–27.

Adler, N.E. 1991. 'Forward', in A.L. Stanton and C. Dunkel-Schetter (eds), *Infertility: Perspectives from Stress and Coping Research*. New York: Plenum Press, pp. vii–ix.

Adler, P., and P. Adler. 1987. *Membership Roles in Field Research*. Thousand Oaks, CA: SAGE Publications.

_____. 2001. 'The Reluctant Respondent', in J.F. Gubrium and J.A. Holstein (eds), *Handbook of Interview Research: Context and Method*. Thousand Oaks, CA: SAGE Publications, pp. 515–35.

Age UK. 2019. 'Briefing: Health and Care of Older People in England 2019'. London.

Albertini, M., and M. Kohli. 2009. 'What Childless Older People Give: Is the Generational Link Broken?', *Ageing & Society* 29(8): 1261–74.

_____. 2017. 'Childlessness and Intergenerational Transfers in Later Life', in M. Kreyenfeld and D. Konietzka (eds), *Childlessness in Europe: Contexts, Causes, and Consequences*. New York: Springer, pp. 351–67.

Albertini, M., and L. Mencarini. 2011. 'Childlessness and Support Networks in Later Life: A New Public Welfare Demand? Evidence from Italy'. Turin: Collegio Carlo Alberto.

Allan, G. 2008. 'Flexibility, Friendship, and Family', *Personal Relationships* 15(1): 1–16.

Allan, G., and G. Crow. 2001. *Families, Households and Society*. Basingstoke: Palgrave Macmillan.

Allan, G., and G. Jones. 2003. 'Introduction', in G. Allan and G. Jones (eds), *Social Relations and the Life Course*. Basingstoke: Palgrave Macmillan, pp. 1–12.

Allen, K.R., R. Blieszner and K.A. Roberto. 2011. 'Perspectives on Extended Family and Fictive Kin in the Later Years: Strategies and Meanings of Kin Reinterpretation', *Journal of Family Issues* 32(9): 1156–77.

Allen, R.E.S., and J.L. Wiles. 2013. 'How Older People Position Their Late-Life Childlessness: A Qualitative Study', *Journal of Marriage and Family* 75(1): 206–20.

Alley, D., and E.M. Crimmins. 2010. 'Epidemiology of Ageing', in D. Dannefer and C. Phillipson (eds), *The SAGE Handbook of Social Gerontology*. London: SAGE Publications, pp. 75–95.

Amieva, H., R. Stoykova, F. Matharan, C. Helmer, T.C. Antonucci and J-F. Dartigues. 2010. 'What Aspects of Social Network Are Protective for Dementia? Not the Quantity but the Quality of Social Interactions is Protective up to 15 Years Later', *Psychosomatic Medicine* 72(9): 905–11.

An, J.S., and T.M. Cooney. 2006. 'Psychological Well-Being in Mid to Late Life: The Role of Generativity Development and Parent–Child Relationships across the Lifespan', *International Journal of Behavioral Development* 30(5): 410–21.

Anderson, K. 2014. 'Book Review: Conceiving Masculinity: Male Infertility, Medicine, and Identity by Liberty Walther Barnes', *Gender & Society* 29(4): 605–7.

Ando, K. 2005. 'Grandparenthood: Crossroads between Gender and Aging', *International Journal of Japanese Sociology* 14(1): 32–51.

Antonucci, T.C., and H. Akiyama. 1987. 'Social Networks in Adult Life and a Preliminary Examination of the Convoy Model', *The Journal of Gerontology* 42(5): 519–27.

Antonucci, T.C. 1986. 'Social Support Networks: Hierarchical Mapping Technique', *Generations* 10(4): 10–12.

Arber, S., and J. Ginn. 1991. *Gender and Later Life: A Sociological Analysis of Resources and Constraints*. London: SAGE Publications.

Arber, S., and V. Timonen (eds). 2012. *Contemporary Grandparenting: Changing Family Relationships in Global Contexts*. Bristol: Policy Press.

Arber, S., L. Andersson and A. Hoff. 2007. 'Changing Approaches to Gender and Ageing: Introduction', *Current Sociology* 55(2): 147–53.

Arber, S., K. Davidson and J. Ginn. 2003. 'Changing Approaches to Gender and Later Life', in S. Arber, K. Davidson and J. Ginn (eds), *Gender and Ageing: Changing Roles and Relationships*. Maidenhead: Open University Press, pp. 1–14.

Arber, S., J. Ginn and K. Davidson. 2005. 'Older Men: Their Social World and Healthy Lifestyles'. Swindon, UK: Economic and Social Research Council.

Arber, S., D. Price, K. Davidson and K. Perren. 2003. 'Re-Examining Gender and Marital Status: Material Well-Being and Social Involvement', in S. Arber, K. Davidson and J. Ginn (eds), *Gender and Ageing: Changing Roles and Relationships*. Maidenhead: Open University Press, pp. 148–67.

Archbishops' Council. 2013. 'Statistics for Mission 2011'. London: The Archbishops' Council of the Church of England.

Archetti, C. 2019. 'No Life without Family: Film Representations of Involuntary Childlessness, Silence and Exclusion', *International Journal of Media & Cultural Politics* 15(2): 175–96.

———. 2020. *Childlessness in the Age of Communication: Deconstructing Silence*. London: Routledge.

Aries, P. 1980. 'Two Successive Motivations for the Declining Birth Rate in the West', *Population and Development Review* 6(4): 645–50.

Armitage, C.J., and M. Conner. 2001. 'Efficacy of the Theory of Planned Behaviour: A Meta-analytic Review', *British Journal of Social Psychology* 40(4): 471–99.

Atchley, R.C. 1989. 'A Continuity Theory of Normal Aging', *The Gerontologist* 29(2): 183–90.

———. 1999. *Continuity and Adaption in Aging*. Baltimore, MD: The Johns Hopkins University Press.

Atkinson, M. 2011. *Deconstructing Men & Masculinities*. Ontario: Oxford University Press.

Ayers, G. 2010. '"I Could Be a Father, but I Could Never Be a Mother": Values and Meanings of Women's Voluntary Childlessnessin Southern Alberta', Master's thesis. Alberta: University of Lethbridge.

Baars, J., J. Dohmen, A. Grenier and C. Phillipson (eds). 2013. *Ageing, Meaning and Social Structure: Connecting Critical and Humanistic Gerontology*. Bristol: Policy Press.

Baars, J., and C. Phillipson. 2013. 'Connecting Meaning with Social Structure: Theoretical Foundations', in J. Baars, J. Dohmen, A. Grenier and C. Phillipson (eds), *Ageing, Meaning and Social Structure: Connecting Critical and Humanistic Gerontology*. Bristol: Policy Press, pp. 11–30.

Bacon, F. 1855. *The Novum Organon, Or a True Guide to the Interpretation of Nature*. Boston, MA: Adamant Media Corporation.

Bagozzi, R.P., and M.F. Van Loo. 1978. 'Toward a General Theory of Fertility: A Causal Modeling Approach', *Demography* 15(3): 301–20.

Bailey, J. 2008. 'First Steps in Qualitative Data Analysis: Transcribing', *Family Practice* 25(2): 127–31.

Ballinger, L. 2012. 'The Role of the Counsellor Trainer: The Trainer Perspective', PhD thesis. Manchester: The University of Manchester.

Bampton, R., and C.J. Cowton. 2002. 'The E-Interview', *Forum Qualitative Sozialforschung* 3(2). Retrieved 11 March 2009 from http://www.qualitative-research.net/index.php/fqs/article/view/848.

Bancroft, A. 2001. 'The Chosen Lives of Childfree Men' [book review], *Journal of Biosocial Science* 33(3): 477–80.

Barden, G. 2014. *My Little Soldiers*. New York: Piranha Press.

Barnes, L. 2014. *Conceiving Masculinity: Male Infertility, Medicine, and Identity*. Philadelphia, PA: Temple University Press.

Barresi, J. 2006. 'The Identities of Malcolm X', in D.P. McAdams, R. Josselson and A. Lieblich (eds), *Identity and Story: Creating Self in Narrative*. Washington, DC: American Psychological Association, pp. 201–21.

Barrett, F., J. Huffaker, C. Fisher and D. Burgaud. 2018. 'Improvisation and Transformation: Yes to the Mess', in Judi Neal (ed.), *Handbook of Personal and Organizational Transformation*. Cham: Springer International Publishing, pp. 671–94.

Barry, J.A., R. Kingerlee, M. Seager and L. Sullivan (eds). 2019. *The Palgrave Handbook of Male Psychology and Mental Health*. Cham: Palgrave Macmillan.

Barry, J.A., R. Walker, L. Liddon and M. Seager. 2020. 'Reactions to Contemporary Narratives about Masculinity: A Pilot Study', *Psychreg Journal of Psychology* 4(2): 8–21.

Basten, S. 2009. 'Voluntary Childlessness and Being Childfree', The Future of Human Reproduction Working Paper 5. Oxford: University of Oxford.

Beck, U. 1992. *Risk Society: Towards a New Modernity*. London: SAGE Publications.

Beck, U., and E. Beck-Gernsheim. 1995. *The Normal Chaos of Love*. Cambridge: Polity Press.

_____. 2002. *Individualization: Institutionalized Individualism and Its Social and Political Consequences*. London: SAGE Publications.

Becker, G. 1999. *Disrupted Lives: How People Create Meaning in a Chaotic World*. Berkeley, CA: University of California Press.

_____. 1994. 'Metaphors in Disrupted Lives: Infertility and Cultural Constructions of Continuity', *Medical Anthropology Quarterly* 8(4): 383–410.

Becker, H.S. 1963. *Outsiders*. New York: Free Press.

Beeson, D., P. Jennings and W. Kramer. 2013. 'A New Path to Grandparenthood: Parents of Sperm and Egg Donors', *Journal of Family Issues* 34(10): 1205–316.

Bengtson, V. 2001. 'Beyond the Nuclear Family: The Increasing Importance of Multigenerational Bonds', *Journal of Marriage and Family* 63(1): 1–16.

Bengtson, V.L., G.H. Elder and N.M. Putney. 2005. 'The Lifecourse Perspective on Ageing: Linked Lives, Timing and History', in V.L. Bengtson, M.L. Johnson, P.G. Coleman and T.B. Kirkwood (eds), *The Cambridge Handbook of Age and Ageing*. Cambridge: Cambridge University Press, pp. 493–501.

Bengtson, V.L., and A. Lowenstein (eds). 2003. *Global Aging and Challenges to Families*. New York: Aldine de Gruyter.

Bengtson, V.L., C. Rosenthal and L. Burton. 1990. 'Families and Aging: Diversity and Heterogeneity', in R.H. Binstock and L. George (eds), *Handbook of Aging and Social Sciences*. New York: Academic Press, pp. 263–87.

Bennett, K.M., L. Arnott and L. Soulsby. 2013. '"You're Not Getting Married for the Moon and the Stars": The Uncertainties of Older British

Widowers about the Idea of New Romantic Relationships', *Journal of Aging Studies* 27(4): 499–506.

Bennett, K.M., G. Hughes and P. Smith. 2003. '"I Think a Woman Can Take It": Widowed Men's Views and Experiences of Gender Differences in Bereavement', *Ageing International* 28(4): 408–24.

Bennett, K.M., and K. Morgan. 1993. 'Ageing, Gender and the Organisation of Physical Activities', in S. Arber and M. Evandrou (eds), *Ageing, Independence and the Life-Course*. London: Jessica Kingsley Publishers, pp. 78–90.

Bennett, K.M., and L. Soulsby. 2012. 'Wellbeing in Bereavement and Widowhood', *Illness, Crisis and Loss* 20(4): 321–37.

Bennett, K.M. 2005. '"Was Life Worth Living?" Older Widowers and Their Explicit Discourses of the Decision to Live', *Mortality* 10(2): 144–54.

———. 2007. '"No Sissy Stuff": Towards a Theory of Masculinity and Emotional Expression in Older Widowed Men', *Journal of Aging Studies* 21(4): 347–56.

Benton, T., and I. Craib. 2001. *Philosophy of Social Science: The Philosophical Foundations of Social Thought*. Basingstoke: Palgrave Macmillan.

Bernard, M., B. Bartlam, S. Biggs and J. Sim. 2004. *New Lifestyles in Old Age: Health, Identity and Well-Being in Berryhill Retirement Village*. Bristol: Policy Press.

Bernard, M., and T. Scharf. 2007. 'Critical Perspectives on Ageing Societies', in M. Bernard and T. Scharf (eds), *Critical Perspectives on Ageing Societies*. Bristol: Policy Press, pp. 3–12.

Berrington, A. 2004. 'Perpetual Postponers? Women's, Men's and Couple's Fertility Intentions and Subsequent Fertility Behaviour', *Population Trends* 117: 9–19.

Beth Johnson Foundation/Ageing Without Children. 2016. 'Our Voices', *Beth Johnson Foundation & Ageing Without Children Report*. London: Beth Johnson Foundation.

Biggs, S. 1993. *Understanding Ageing: Images, Attitudes and Professional Practice*. Buckingham: Open University Press.

———. 1999. *The Mature Imagination: Dynamics of Identity in Midlife and Beyond*. Buckingham: Open University Press.

———. 2004. 'Age, Gender, Narratives, and Masquerades', *Journal of Aging Studies* 18(1): 45–58.

Billari, F.C., A. Goisis, A. Liefbroer, R. Settersten, A. Aassve, G. Hagestad and Z. Spéder. 2011. 'Social Age Deadlines for the Childbearing of Women and Men', *Human Reproduction* 26(3): 616–22.

Bingham, J. 2013. 'Men "Just as Broody as Women", Study Suggests', *The Telegraph*, 3 April 2013. Retrieved 9 April 2013 from http://www.telegraph.co.uk/women/mother-tongue/9966713/Men-just-as-broody-as-women-study-suggests.html.

Birch, M. 1998. 'Re/constructing Research Narratives: Self and Sociological Identity in Alternative Settings', in J. Ribbens and R. Edwards (eds),

Feminist Dilemmas in Qulitative Research: Public Knowledge and Private Lives. London: SAGE Publications pp. 171–83.

Blackstone, A., and M. Stewart. 2012. 'Choosing to be Childfree: Research on the Decision Not to Parent', *Sociology Compass* 6(9): 718–27.

Blaikie, N. 2010. *Designing Social Research: The Logic of Anticipation.* Cambridge: Polity Press.

Blyth, E., and R. Moore. 2001. 'Involuntary Childlessness and Stigma', in T. Mason, C. Carlisie, C. Watkins and E. Whitehead (eds), *Stigma and Social Exclusion in Healthcare.* London: Routledge, pp. 217–25.

Boddington, B., and R. Didham. 2008. 'Busy Making Other Plans: Increases in Childlessness in New Zealand', *Demographic Trends.* Wellington: Statistics New Zealand, pp. 2–11.

_____. 2009. 'Increases in Childlessness in New Zealand', *Journal of Population Research* 26(2): 131–51.

Bodin, M., L. Plantin and E. Elmerstig. 2019. 'A Wonderful Experience or a Frightening Commitment? An Exploration of Men's Reasons to (Not) Have Children', *Reproductive Biomedicine & Society Online* 9: 19–27.

Boivin, J. 2003. 'A Review of Psychosocial Interventions in Infertility', *Social Science and Medicine* 57(12): 2325–41.

Boivin, J., L. Bunting, J. Collins and K. Nygren. 2007. 'International Estimates of Infertility Prevalence and Treatment-Seeking: Potential Need and Demand for Infertility Medical Care', *Human Reproduction* 22(6): 1506.

Boivin, J., L. Bunting, N. Kalebic and C. Harrison. 2018. 'What Makes People Ready to Conceive? Findings from the International Fertility Decision-Making Study', *Reproductive Biomedicine & Society Online* 6: 90–100.

Boivin, J., K. Sanders and L. Schmidt. 2006. 'Age and Social Position Moderate the Effect of Stress on Fertility', *Evolution and Human Behavior* 27(5): 345–56.

Bond, T. 2004. 'Ethical Guidelines for Researching Counselling and Psychotherapy'. BACP. Retrieved 8 February 2008 from http//:www.bacp.co.uk/research.

Borell, K., and S. Ghazanfareeon Karlsson. 2003. 'Reconceptualising Intimacy and Ageing: Living Apart Together', in S. Arber, K. Davidson and J. Ginn (eds), *Gender and Ageing: Changing Roles and Relationships.* Maidenhead: Open University Press, pp. 47–62.

Borgatti, S.P., and D.S. Halgin. 2011. 'On Network Theory', *Organization Science* 22(5): 1168–81.

Bos, H., F. van Balen and D.C. van den Boom. 2003. 'Planned Lesbian Families: Their Desire and Motivation to Have Children', *Human Reproduction* 18(10): 2216–24.

Bottero, W. 2011. 'Personal Life in the Past', in V. May (ed.), *Sociology of Personal Life.* Basingstoke: Palgrave Macmillan, pp. 22–34.

Bourdieu, P. 1986. 'The Forms of Capital'. Marxist Internet Archive. Retrieved 7 May 2020 from https://www.marxists.org/reference/subject/philosophy/works/fr/bourdieu-forms-capital.htm.

_____. 1989. 'Reproduction interdite. La dimension symbolique de la domination économique', Études rurales 113/114: 15–36.

_____. 2008. *The Batchelors Ball: The Crisis of Peasant Society in Béarn*. Oxford: Polity Press.

Bourdieu, P., and L.Wacquant 1992. *An Invitation to Reflexive Sociology*. Cambridge: Polity Press.

Bowlby, J. 1979. *The Making and Breaking of Affectional Bonds*. London: Tavistock.

Bowling, A. 2009. 'The Psychometric Properties of the Older People's Quality of Life Questionnaire, Compared with the CASP-19 and the WHOQOL-OLD', *Current Gerontology and Geriatrics Research*, Article ID 298950: 1–12.

Bowling, A., and P. Dieppe. 2005. 'What is Successful Ageing and Who Should Define It?', *British Medical Journal* 331: 1548–51.

Bowling, A., Z. Gabriel, J. Dykes, L.M. Dowding, O. Evans, A. Fleissig, D. Banister and S. Sutton. 2003. 'Let's Ask Them: A National Survey of Definitions of Quality of Life and Its Enhancement among People Aged 65 and Over', *International Journal of Aging & Human Development* 56(4): 269–306.

Boyatzis, R.E. 1998. *Transforming Qualitative Data: Thematic Ananlysis and Code Development*. Thousand Oaks, CA: SAGE Publications.

Brannen, J., P. Moss and A. Mooney. 2004. *Working and Caring over the Twentieth Century*. Basingstoke: Palgrave Macmillan.

Brannen, J., and A. Nilsen. 2006. 'From Fatherhood to Fathering: Transmission and Change among British Fathers in Four-Generation Families', *Sociology* 40(2): 335–52.

Brannon, R. 1976. 'The Male Sex Role – and What It's Done for Us Lately', in R. Brannon and D. Davids (eds), *The Forty-Nine Percent Majority: The Male Sex Role*. Reading, MA: Addison-Wesley Publishing Company, pp. 1–40.

Braun, V., and V. Clarke. 2006. 'Using Thematic Analysis in Psychology', *Qualitative Research in Psychology* 3(2): 77–101.

_____. 2013. *Successful Qualitative Research: A Practical Guide for Beginners*. London: SAGE Publications.

Braun, V., V. Clarke and G. Terry. 2013. 'Thematic Analysis', in P. Rohleder and A. Lyons (eds), *Qualitative Research in Clinical and Health Psychology*. Basingstoke: Palgrave MacMillan, pp. 95–113.

Bray, I., D. Gunnell and G.D. Smith. 2006. 'Advanced Paternal Age: How Old is Too Old?', *Journal of Epidemiol Community Health* 60(10): 850–53.

Brennan, M., and G. Letherby. 2017. 'Auto/Biographical Approaches to Researching Death and Bereavement: Connections, Continuums, Contrasts', *Mortality* 22(2): 155–69.

Brescoll, V.L., and E.L. Uhlman. 2005. 'Attitudes Toward Traditional and Non-Traditional Parents', *Psychology of Women Quarterly* 29(4): 436–45.

Bretherton, I. 1992. 'The Origins of Attachment Theory: John Bowlby and Mary Ainsworth', *Developmental Psychology* 28(5): 759–75.

Brian, K. 2009. *The Complete Guide to IVF: An Inside View of Fertility Clinics and Treatment*. London: Piatkus Books.

British Broadcasting Corporation. 2000. 'Paediatrician Attacks: "Ignorant" Vandals"'. Retrieved 12 March 2015 from http://news.bbc.co.uk/1/hi/wales/901723.stm.

_____. 2012. 'April Jones Abduction: Child Got into Van Willingly Say Police'. Retrieved 12 March 2015 from http://www.bbc.co.uk/news/uk-wales-19800140.

_____. 2014. 'Jimmy Saville Scandal'. Retrieved 12 March 2015 from http://www.bbc.co.uk/news/uk-20026910.

British Society of Gerontology. 2008. 'BSG Guidelines on Ethical Research with Human Participants'. Retrieved 7 March 2021 from https://www.britishgerontology.org/about-bsg/bsg-ethical-guidelines.

British Sociological Association. 2004. 'Statement of Ethical Practice for the British Sociological Association'. Durham.

Broom, A., K. Hand and P. Tovey. 2009. 'The Role of Gender, Environment and Individual Biography in Shaping Qualitative Interview Data', *International Journal of Social Research Methodology* 12(1): 51–65.

Brown, B. 2019. 'From Hegemonic to Responsive Masculinity: The Transformative Power of the Provider Role', in John A. Barry, Roger Kingerlee, Martin Seager and Luke Sullivan (eds), *The Palgrave Handbook of Male Psychology and Mental Health*. Cham: Palgrave Macmillan, pp. 183–204.

Brown, C., and M.J. Lowis. 2003. 'Psychosocial Development in the Elderly: An Investigation into Erikson's Ninth Stage', *Journal of Aging Studies* 17(4): 415–26.

Brown, J.A., and M.M. Ferree. 2005. 'Close Your Eyes and Think of England: Pronatalism in the British Print Media', *Gender and Society* 19(5): 5–24.

Bryman, A. 2001. *Social Research Methods*. Oxford: Oxford University Press.

Bueno, J. 2019. *The Brink of Being: Talking About Miscarriage*. London: Virago Press.

Bugajska, B.E. 2016. 'The Ninth Stage in the Cycle of Life – Reflections on E.H. Erikson's Theory', *Ageing and Society* 37(6): 1095–110.

Bulcroft, R., and J. Teachman. 2004. 'Ambiguous Constructions: Development of a Childless or Child-Free Life Course', in M. Coleman and L. Ganong (eds), *Handbook of Contemporary Families*. Thousand Oaks, CA: SAGE Publications, pp. 116–35.

Bures, R.M., T. Koropeckyj-Cox and M. Loree. 2009. 'Childlessness, Parenthood, and Depressive Symptoms Among Middle-Aged and Older Adults', *Journal of Family Issues* 30(5): 670–87.

Burholt, V., and C. Wenger. 1998. 'Differences over Time in Older People's Relationships with Children and Siblings', *Ageing & Society* 18(5): 537–62.

Burr, V. 1995. *Social Constructionism*. Gove: Routledge.

Bury, V. 1995. 'Ageing, Gender and Society', in S. Arber and J. Ginn (eds), *Connecting Gender and Ageing: A Sociological Approach*. Buckingham: Open University Press, pp. 15–29.

Butera, K. 2006. 'Manhunt', *Qualitative Inquiry* 12(6): 1262–82.

Butler, J. 2004a. 'Bodily Inscriptions, Performative Subversions (1990)', in S. Salih and J. Butler (eds), *The Judith Butler Reader*. Malden, MA: Blackwell Publishing, pp. 90–118.

_____. 2004b. 'Changing the Subject: Judith Butler's Politics of Radical Resignification', in S. Salih and J. Butler (eds), *The Judith Butler Reader*. Malden, MA: Blackwell Publishing, pp. 325–56.

_____. 2004c. 'Variations on Sex and Gender: Beauvoir, Wittig, Foucault (1987)', in S. Salih and J. Butler (eds), *The Judith Butler Reader*. Malden, MA: Blackwell Publishing, pp. 21–38.

Butt, J., and J. Moriarty. 2004. 'Social Support and Ethnicity in Old Age', in A. Walker and C. Hagan Hennessey (eds), *Quality of Life in Old Age*. Maidenhead: Open University Press, pp. 167–87.

Bytheway, B. 1995. *Ageism*. Buckingham: Open University Press.

_____. 1997. 'Talking about Age: The Theoretical Basis of Social Gerontology', in A. Jamieson, S. Harper and C. Victor (eds), *Critical Approaches to Ageing and Later Life*. Buckingham: Open University Press, pp. 7–15.

_____. 2005. 'Age-Identities and the Celebration of Birthdays', *Ageing & Society* 25(4): 463–77.

_____. 2011. *Unmasking Age: The Significance of Age for Social Research*. Bristol: Policy Press.

Calasanti, T. 2004. 'Feminist Gerontology and Old Men', *The Journals of Gerontology Series B: Psychological Sciences and Social Sciences* 59(6): S305–S14.

Calasanti, T., and N. King. 2005. 'Firming the Floppy Penis', *Men and Masculinities* 8(1): 3–23.

Calasanti, T., and K. Slevin. 2001. 'Introduction', in Toni Calasanti and Kathleen Slevin (eds), *Gender, Social Inequalities and Aging*. Walnut Creek, CA: AltaMira Press, pp. 3–12.

Cameron, D. 1985. *Feminism & Linguistic Theory*. Basingstoke: Palgrave Macmillan.

Campbell, L.D., I.A. Connidis and L. Davies. 1999. 'Sibling Ties in Later Life', *Journal of Family Issues* 20(1): 114–48.

Cannold, L. 2000. 'Who's Crying Now? Chosen Childlessness, Circumstantial Childlessness and the Irrationality of Motherhood. A Study of the Fertility Decisions of Australian and North American Women', PhD thesis. Melbourne: The University of Melbourne.

_____. 2004. 'Declining Marriage Rates and Gender Inequity in Social Institutions: Towards an Adequately Complex Explanation for Childlessness', *People and Place* 12(4): 1–11.

_____. 2005. *What, No Baby? Why Women Are Losing the Freedom to Mother, and How They Can Get It Back*. Fremantle: Curtin University Books.

Carers UK. 2015. 'Facts about Carers: Policy Briefing, October 2015'. London.

Carroll, K. 2013. 'Infertile? The Emotional Labour of Sensitive and Feminist Research Methodologies', *Qualitative Research* 13(5): 546–61.

Carroll, M. 2019. 'Preface', in Michael Carroll (ed.), *Clinical Reproductive Science*. Hoboken, NJ: Wiley-Blackstone, p. xvii.

Carstensen, L.L. 1992. 'Social and Emotional Patterns in Adulthood: Support for Socioemotional Selectivity Theory', *Psychol Aging* 7(3): 331–38.

Caspi, A., G.H. Elder and D.J. Bem. 1988. 'Moving Away from the World: Life-Course Patterns of Shy Children', *Developmental Psychology* 24(6): 824–31.

Cavanagh, A. 2007. 'Taxonomies of Anxiety: Risks, Panics, Paedophilia and the Internet', *Electronic Journal of Sociology*. Retrieved 12 March 2014 from http://www.sociology.org/content/2007/__cavanagh_taxonomies. pdf.

Chambers, P. 2002. 'Hidden Lives: Multiple Narratives of Later Life Widowhood', PhD thesis. Keele: Keele University.

_____. 2005. *Older Widows and the Life Course: Multiple Narratives of Hidden Lives*. Aldershot: Ashgate Publishing.

Chambers, P., G. Allan, C. Phillipson and M. Ray. 2009. *Family Practices in Later Life.* Bristol: Policy Press.

Chamie, J., and B. Mirkin. 2012. 'Childless by Choice'. Yale Center for the Study of Globalization, Yale University. Retrieved 13 February 2018 from https://yaleglobal.yale.edu/content/childless-choice.

Chancey, L, and S.A. Dumais. 2009. 'Voluntary Childlessness in Marriage and Family Textbooks, 1950–2000', *Journal of Family History* 34(2): 206–23.

Chandra, A., and E. Stephen. 1998. 'Impaired Fecundity in the United States: 1982–1995', *Family Planning Perspectives* 30(1): 34–42.

Chang, E., K. Wilber and M. Silverstein. 2010. 'The Effects of Childlessness on the Care and Psychological Well-Being of Older Adults with Disabilities', *Aging & Mental Health* 14(6): 712–19.

Charmaz, K. 2006. *Constructing Grounded Theory*. London: SAGE Publications.

_____. 2008. 'Grounded Theory', in Jonathan A. Smith (ed.), *Qualitative Psychology: A Practical Guide to Research Methods*. London: SAGE Publications, pp. 81-110

Cheng, A., and M. Evans. 2009. 'An in-Depth Look Inside the Twitter World'. Sysmos. Retrieved 7 March 2021 from https://sysomos.com/inside-twitter

Chodzko-Zajko, W., A. Schwingel and C.H. Park. 2009. 'Successful Aging: The Role of Physical Activity', *American Journal of Lifestyle Medicine* 3(1): 20–28.

Christians, C.G. 2005. 'Ethics and Politics in Qualitative Research', in N.K. Denzin and Y.S. Lincoln (eds), *The SAGE Handbook of Qualitative Research*. Thousand Oaks, CA: SAGE Publications, pp. 139–64.

Cohen-Bacrie, P., Belloc, S., Ménézo, Y.J.R, Clement, P., Hamidi, J. and Benkhalifa, M. 2008. 'Correlation between DNA Damage and Sperm

Parameters: A Prospective Study of 1,633 Patients', *Fertility and Sterility* 91(5): 1801–5.

Coleman, J.S. 1988. 'Social Capital in the Creation of Human Capital', *American Journal of Sociology* 94: S95–S120. Retrieved 21 December 2020 from http://www.jstor.org/stable/2780243.

Coles, T. 2008. 'Finding Space in the Field of Masculinity: Lived Experiences of Men's Masculinities', *Journal of Sociology* 44(3): 233–48.

———. 2009. 'Negotiating the Field of Masculinity: The Production and Reproduction of Multiple Dominant Masculinities', *Men and Masculinities* 12(1): 30–44.

Collins, P. 1998. 'Negotiated Selves: Reflections on "Unstructured" Interviewing', *Sociological Research Online* 3(3): 70–83.

Collins, T.L. 2011. 'Managing Transition: A Longitudinal Study of Personal Communities in Later Life Widowhood', PhD thesis. Keele: Keele University.

Collins, Wi. 2019. *The Empathy Gap: Male Disadvantage and the Mecahnisms of Their Neglect*. LPS Publishing.

Connell, R.W. 1995. *Masculinities*. Cambridge: Polity Press.

———. 2000. *The Men and the Boys*. Cambridge: Polity Press.

———. 2009. *Gender: In World Perspective*. Cambridge: Polity Press.

Connell, R.W., and J.W. Messerschmidt. 2005. 'Hegemonic Masculinity', *Gender & Society* 19(6): 829–59.

Connidis, I.A. 2001. *Family Ties and Aging*. Thousand Oaks, CA: SAGE Publications.

Connidis, I.A., and J.A. McMullin. 2002. 'Sociological Ambivalence and Family Ties: A Critical Perspective', *Journal of Marriage and Family* 64(3): 558–67.

Connidis, I.A., and J.A. McMullin. 1993. 'To Have or Have Not: Parent Status and the Subjective Well-Being of Older Men and Women', *The Gerontologist* 33(5): 630–36.

———. 1999. 'Permanent Childlessness: Perceived Advantages and Disadvantages among Older Persons', *Canadian Journal on Aging & Mental Health* 18(4): 447–65.

Cornwell, B. 2011. 'Independence through Social Networks: Bridging Potential among Older Women and Men', *The Journals of Gerontology, Series B: Psychological Sciences and Social Sciences* 66(6): 782–94.

Corr, C.A. 2004. 'Revisiting the Concept of Disenfranchised Grief', in K.J. Doka (ed.), *Disenfranchised Grief: New Directions, Challenges, and Strategies for Practice*. Champaign, IL: Research Press, pp. 39–60.

Corsetti, S. 2017. 'Childless Couples "on Track to Be Australia's Most Common Family Type"'. ABC News. Retrieved 12 February 2021. https://www.abc.net.au/news/2017-05-15/childless-households-on-the-rise/8528546.

Cotterill, P. 1992. 'Interviewing Women: Issues of Friendship, Vulnerability, and Power', *Women's Studies International Forum* 15(5–6): 593–606.

Cotterill, P., and G. Letherby. 1993. 'Weaving Stories: Personal Auto/Biographies in Feminist Research', *Sociology* 27(1): 67–79.

Crawshaw, M. 2013. 'Male Coping with Cancer-Fertility Issues: Putting the "Social" into Biopsychosocial Approaches', *Reproductive Biomedicine Online* 27(3): 261–70.

Crawshaw, M., and R. Balen. 2010. 'Introduction', in M. Crawshaw and R. Balen (eds), *Adopting after Infertility: Messages from Practice, Research, and Personal Experience*. Jessica Kingsley Publishers: London, pp. 9–18.

Creswell, J.W. 2003. *Research Design: Qualitative, Quantitative and Mixed Methods Approaches*. Thousand Oaks, CA: SAGE Publications.

Creswell, J.W., and A.L. Garrett. 2008. 'The "Movement" of Mixed Methods Research and the Role of Educators', *South African Journal of Education* 28(3): 321–33.

Critcher, C. 2009. 'Widening The Focus: Moral Panics as Moral Regulation', *British Journal of Criminology* 49(1): 17–34.

Crotty, M. 1998. *The Foundations of Social Research: Meaning and Perspective in the Research Process*. London: SAGE Publications.

Cruz, J.M. 2003. *Sociological Analysis of Aging: The Gay Male Perspective*. New York: Harrington Press.

Crystal, S., A. Akincigil, U. Sambamoorthi, N. Wenger, J.A. Fleishman, D.S. Zingmond, R.D. Hays, S.A. Bozzette and M.F. Shapiro. 2003. 'The Diverse Older HIV-Positive Population: A National Profile of Economic Circumstances, Social Support, and Quality of Life', *Journal of Acquired Immune Deficiency Syndromes* 33: S76–S83.

Culley, L., and N. Hudson. 2009. 'Commonalities, Differences and Possibilities: Culture and Infertility in British South Asian Communities', in L. Culley, N. Hudson and F. van Rooij (eds), *Marginalized Reproduction: Ethnicity, Infertility and Reproductive Technologies*. London: Earthscan, pp. 97–116.

Culley, L., N. Hudson and M. Lohan. 2013. 'Where Are All the Men? The Marginalization of Men in Social Scientific Research on Infertility', *Reproductive Biomedicine Online* 27(3): 225–35.

D'Augelli, A R., H.J. Rendina, K.O. Sinclair and A.H. Grossman. 2007. 'Lesbian and Gay Youth's Aspirations for Marriage and Raising Children', *Journal of LGBT Issues in Counseling* 1(4): 77–98.

Daly, I., and S. Bewley. 2013. 'Reproductive Ageing and Conflicting Clocks: King Midas' Touch', *Reproductive Biomedicine Online* 27(6): 722–32.

Daly, K.J. 1999. 'Crisis of Genealogy: Facing the Challenges of Infertility', in H. McCubbin, E. Thompson, A. Thompson and J. Futrell (eds), *The Dynamics of Resilient Families*. Thousand Oaks, CA: SAGE Publications.

Dalzell, A. 2005. '"I Can Just Imagine Someone Calling Me Daddy": Narratives of Men without Children', MSc Dissertation. Bristol: University of Bristol.

Dalzell, A. 2007. '"The Expectation Has Always Been That I'll Not Have Kids" – The Narratives of Childless Gay Men', Master's dissertation. Bristol: University of Bristol.

Daniels, C. 2002. 'Between Fathers and Fetuses: The Social Construction of Male Reproduction and the Politics of Fetal Harm', in D.L. Dickenson (ed.), *Ethical Issues in Maternal-Fetal Medicine*. Cambridge: Cambridge University Press, pp. 113–30.

———. 2006. *Exposing Men: The Science and Politics of Male Reproduction*. New York: Oxford University Press.

Daniels, N.M., and R.J. Chadwick. 2018. 'Doing Homebirth Like a Man? Constructions of Masculinity in South African Men's Narratives of Homebirth', *Journal of Gender Studies* 27(6): 725–39.

Daniluk, J.C. 1988. 'Infertility: Intrapersonal and Interpersonal Impact', *Fertility and Sterility* 49(6): 982–90.

———. 2001. 'Reconstructing Their Lives: A Longitudinal, Qualitative Analysis of the Transition to Biological Childlessness for Infertile Couples', *Journal of Counseling and Development* 79(4): 439–49.

Daniluk, J.C., and E. Koert. 2012. 'Childless Canadian Men's and Women's Childbearing Intentions, Attitudes towards and Willingness to Use Assisted Human Reproduction', *Human Reproduction* 27(8): 2405–12.

———. 2013. 'The Other Side of the Fertility Coin: A Comparison of Childless Men's and Women's Knowledge of Fertility and Assisted Reproductive Technology', *Fertility and Sterility* 99(3): 839–46.

Dannefer, D., and R. Settersten. 2010. 'The Study of the Life Course: Implications for Social Gerontology', in D. Dannefer and C. Phillipson (eds), *The SAGE Handbook of Social Gerontology*. London: SAGE Publications, pp. 3–19.

Data Protection Act. 1998. 'Data Protection Act 1998 (c.29)'. Information Commissioner's Office. Retrieved 31 March 2020 from http://www.legislation.gov.uk/ukpga/1998/29/contents.

Davidson, C.R. 2009. 'Transcription: Imperatives for Qualitative Research', *International Journal of Qualitative Methods* 8(2): 35–52.

Davidson, K. 1998. 'Gender, Age and Widowhood: How Older Widows and Widowers Differently Realign Their Lives', PhD thesis. Guildford: University of Surrey.

———. 2001. 'Late-Life Widowhood, Selfishness, and New Partnership Choices: A Gendered Perspective', *Ageing and Society* 21(3): 297–317.

———. 2002. 'Gender Differences in New Partnership Choices and Constraints for Older Widows and Widowers', *Ageing International* 27(4): 43–60.

———. 2004. '"Why Can't a Man Be More Like a Woman?": Marital Status and Social Networking of Older Men', *Journal of Men's Studies* 13(1): 25–43.

———. 2006. 'Flying Solo in Old Age: Widowed and Divorced Men and Women in Later Life', in J. Vincent, C. Phillipson and M. Downs (eds), *The Futures of Old Age*. London: SAGE Publications, pp. 172–79.

Davidson, K., and S. Arber. 2004. 'Older Men – Their Health Behaviours and Partnership Status', in A. Walker and C. Hagan Hennessey (eds), *Quality of Life in Old Age*. Maidenhead: Open University Press, pp. 127–48.

Davidson, K., T. Daly and S. Arber. 2003a. 'Exploring the Social Worlds of Older Men', in S. Arber, K. Davidson and .J Ginn (eds), *Gender and Ageing: Changing Roles and Relationships*. Maidenhead: Open University Press, pp. 168–85.

Davidson, K., T. Daly and S. Arber. 2003b. 'Older Men, Social Integration and Organisational Activities', *Social Policy and Society* 2(2): 81–89.

Davidson, K., L. Warren and M. Maynard. 2005. 'Social Involvement: Aspects of Gender and Ethnicity', in A. Walker (ed.), *Understanding Quality of Life in Old Age*. Maidenhead: Open University Press, pp. 84–99.

Davidson, K., and G. Fennell. 2002. 'New Intimate Relationships in Later Life', *Ageing International* 27(4): 3–10.

Davidson, K., and R. Meadows. 2009. 'Older Men's Health: The Role of Marital Status and Masculinities', in B. Gough and S. Robertson (eds), *Men, Masculinities and Health: Critical Perspectives*. Basingstoke: Palgrave Macmillan, pp. 109–23.

Davies, D., and J. Dodd. 2002. 'Qualitative Research and the Question of Rigor', *Qualitative Health Research* 12(2): 279–89.

Day, J. 2013. *Rocking the Life Unexpected: 12 Weeks to Your Plan B for a Meaningful and Fulfilling Life Without Children*. London: Gateway Women.

_____. 2016. *Living the Life Unexpected: 12 Weeks to Your Plan B for a Meaningful and Fulfilling Future Without Children*, 2nd edn. London: Bluebird/Pan Macmillan.

De Jong Gierveld, J. 2003. 'Social Networks and Social Well-Being of Older Men and Women Living Alone', in S. Arber, K. Davidson and J. Ginn (eds), *Gender and Ageing: Changing Roles and Relationships*. Maidenhead: Open University Press, pp. 95–110.

_____. 2004. 'Remarriage, Unmarried Cohabitation, Living Apart Together: Partner Relationships Following Bereavement or Divorce', *Journal of Marriage and the Family* 66(1): 236–43.

De Medeiros, K., and R. Rubinstein. 2018. 'Age-Identity in Progress Narratives of Never-Married Childless Older Women', in N. Sappleton (ed.), *Voluntary and Involuntary Childlessness: The Joys of Otherhood?* Bingley: Emerald Publishing, pp. 193–213.

Deindl, C., and M. Brandt. 2013. 'Support Networks of Childless Elders: Informal and Formal Support in Europe'. International Union for the Scientific Study of Population. Retrieved 19 January 2018 from http://www.iussp.org/sites/default/files/event_call_for_papers/brandt_deindl_busan_0.pdf.

Denscombe, M. 2007. *The Good Research Guide for Small-Scale Social Research Projects*. Maidenhead: Open University Press.

Denzin, N.K., and Y.S. Lincoln. 1994. 'Introduction: Entering the Field of Qualitative Research', in N.K. Denzin and Y.S. Lincoln (eds), *Handbook of Qualitative Research*. Thousand Oaks, CA: SAGE Publications, pp. 1–22.

_____. 2005a. 'Introduction: The Discipline and Practice of Qualitative Research', in N.K. Denzin and Y.S. Lincoln (eds), *The SAGE Handbook of Qualitative Research*. Thousand Oaks, CA: SAGE Publications, pp. 1–32.

_____. 2005b. 'Paradigms aand Perspectives in Contention', in N.K. Denzin and Y.S. Lincoln (eds), *The SAGE Handbook of Qualitative Research*. Thousand Oaks, CA: SAGE Publications, pp. 183–90.

_____ (eds). 2005c. *The SAGE Handbook of Qualitative Research*. Thousand Oaks, CA: SAGE Publications.

_____. 2008. 'Introduction: The Discipline and Practice of Qualitative Research', in N.K. Denzin and Y.S. Lincoln (eds), *Strategies of Qualitative Inquiry*. Los Angeles: SAGE Publications, pp. 1–43.

Department of Work and Pensions. 2014. 'Retirement Age'. Department of Work and Pensions. London: Her Majesty's Stationery Office.

Dermott, E. 2003. 'The "Intimate Father": Defining Paternal Involvement', *Sociological Research Online* 8(4): 28–38.

_____. 2008. *Initimate Fatherhood: A Sociological Analysis*. Abingdon: Routledge.

Dickson-Swift, V., E. L James and P. Liamputtong. 2008. *Undertaking Sensitive Research in the Health and Social Sciences: Managing Boundaries, Emotions and Risk*. Cambridge: Cambridge Univesity Press.

Dickson-Swift, V., E.L. James, S. Kippen and P. Liamputtong. 2008. 'Risk to Researchers in Qualitative Research on Sensitive Topics: Issues and Strategies', *Qualitative Health Research* 18(1): 133–44.

_____. 2009. 'Researching Sensitive Topics: Qualitative Research as Emotion Work', *Qualitative Research* 9(1): 61–79.

Didham, R. 2016. 'Childlessness in New Zealand 1976 to 2013', *New Zealand Sociology* 31(1): 155–72.

Doka, K.J. (ed.). 2002. *Disenfranchised Grief: New Directions, Challenges, and Strategies for Practice*. Champaign, IL: Research Press.

Dolan, A. 2013. '"I Never Expected It to Be Me": Men's Experiences of Infertility', *Men, Infertility and Infertility Treatment Seminar, 29th November 2013*. Warwick: Economic and Social Research Council.

_____. 2014. '"I've Learnt What a Dad Should Do": The Interaction of Masculine and Fathering Identities among Men Who Attended a "Dads Only" Parenting Programme', *Sociology (Online)* 48(4): 812–28.

Domar, A., A. Broome, P.C. Zuttermeister, M. Seibel and R. Friedman. 1992. 'The Prevalence and Predictability of Depression in Infertile Women', *Fertility and Sterility* 58(6): 1158–63.

Domar, A.D., P.C. Zuttermeister and R. Friedman. 1993. 'The Psychological Impact of Infertility: A Comparison with Patients with Other Medical Conditions', *Journal of Psychosomatic Obstetrics and Gynaecology* 14 (special issue): 45–52.

Doucet, A. 2006. *Do Men Mother? Fatherhood, Care, and Domestic Responsibility*. Toronto: University of Toronto Press.

Doucet, A., and R. Lee. 2014. 'Fathering, Feminism(s), Gender, and Sexualities: Possibilities, Tensions, and New Pathways', *Journal of Family Theory & Review* 6(4): 355–73.

Dudgeon, M., and M. Inhorn. 2003. 'Gender, Masculinity and Reproduction: Anthropological Perspectives', *International Journal of Men's Health* 2(1): 31–56.

_____. 2004. 'Men's Influences on Women's Reproductive Health: Medical Anthropological Perspective', *Social Science & Medicine* 59(7): 1379–95.

Duncombe, J., and J. Jessop. 2002. '"Doing Rapport" and the Ethics of "Faking Friendship"', in M. Mauthner, M. Birch, J. Jessop and J. Miller (eds), *Ethics in Qualitative Research*. London: SAGE Publications, pp. 107–22.

Dunne, G.A. 1997. *Lesbian Lifestyles: Women's Work and the Politics of Sexuality*. London: Macmillan.

Dyer, S.J., N. Abrahams, N.E. Mokoena and Z.M. van der Spuy. 2004. '"You Are a Man Because You Have Children": Experiences, Reproductive Health Knowledge and Treatment-Seeking Behaviour among Men Suffering from Couple Infertility in South Africa', *Hum Reprod* 19(4): 960–67.

Dykstra, P.A. 1995. 'Network Composition', in K. Knipscheer, J. de Jong Gierveld, T. van Tilburg and P.A. Dykstra (eds), *Living Arrangements and Social Networks of Older Adults*. Amsterdam: VU University Press, pp. 97–114.

_____. 2004. 'Diversity in Partnerships Histories: Implications for Older Adults' Social Integration', in C. Phillipson, G. Allan and D. Morgan (eds), *Social Networks and Social Exclusion: Sociologocal and Policy Perspectives*. Aldershot: Ashgate Publishing, pp. 117–41.

_____. 2006. 'Off the Beaten Track: Childlessness and Social Integration in Late Life', *Research on Aging* 28(6): 749–67.

_____. 2009. 'Childless Old Age', in P. Uhlenberg (ed.), *International Handbook of Population Ageing*. Houten: Springer, pp. 671–90.

_____. 2010. *Intergenerational Family Relationships in Ageing Societies*. New York and Geneva: United Nations.

Dykstra, P.A., and T. Fokkema. 2011. 'Relationships between Parents and Their Adult Children: A West European Typology of Late-Life Families', *Ageing and Society* 31(4): 545–69.

Dykstra, P.A., and G.O. Hagestad. 2007a. 'Childlessness and Parenthood in Two Centuries: Different Roads Different Maps?', *Journal of Family Issues* 28(11): 1518–32.

_____. 2007b. 'Roads Less Taken: Developing a Nuanced View of Older Adults Without Children', *Journal of Family Issues* 28(10): 1275–310.

Dykstra, P.A., and R. Keizer. 2009. 'The Wellbeing of Childless Men and Fathers in Mid-Life', *Ageing & Society* 29(8): 1227–42.

Earle, S., and R.A. Hadley. 2018. 'Men's Views and Experiences of Infant Feeding: A Qualitative Systematic Review', *Maternal & Child Nutrition* 14(13): e12586.

Earle, S., and G. Letherby. 2003. 'Introducing Gender, Identity and Reproduction', in S. Earle and G. Letherby (eds), *Gender, Identity and Reproduction: Social Perspectives*. Basingstoke: Palgrave Macmillan pp. 1–11.

Eggebeen, D.J., and C. Knoester. 2001. 'Does Fatherhood Matter for Men?', *Journal of Marriage and Family* 63(2): 381–93.

Elder, G.H. 1999. 'The Life Course and Aging: Some Reflections', *Distinguished Scholar Lecture: Section on Aging. American Sociological Association*. Chapel Hill, NC: University of North Carolina, pp. 1–25.

Elder, G.H., M. Kirkpatrick Johnson and R. Crosnoe. 2003. 'The Emergence and Development of Life Course Theory', in J. Mortimer and M. Shanahan (eds), *Handbook of the Life Course*. New York: Springer, pp. 3–19.

Eliot, George. 1871–72. *Middlemarch*. Harmondsworth: Penguin Books.

Elliot, Stacy. 1998. 'The Relationship between Fertility Issues and Sexual Problems in Men', *The Canadian Journal of Human Sexuality* 7(3): 1–8.

Ellis, C. 2007. 'Telling Secrets, Revealing Lives: Relational Ethics in Research with Intimate Others', *Qualitative Inquiry* 13(1): 3–29.

Equality Act. 2010. 'Equality Act (c.15)'. London: The Stationery Office. Retrieved 15 August 2017 from http://www.legislation.gov.uk/ukpga/2010/15/introduction

Erikson, E. 1959. *Identity and the Life Cycle: Selected Papers*. New York: International Universities Press.

_____. 1964. *Childhood and Society*. New York: W.W. Norton & Company.

_____. 1980. *Identity and the Life Cycle*. New York: W.W. Norton & Company.

Erikson, E., and J. Erikson. 1997. *The Life Cycle Completed: Extended Version with New Chapter on the Ninth Stage of Development by Joan M. Erikson*. New York: W.W. Norton & Company.

Estes, C. 2005. 'Women, Ageing and Inequality: A Feminist Perspective', in M.L. Johnson (ed.), *Cambridge Handbook Of Age and Ageing*. Cambridge: Cambridge University Press, pp. 552–59.

Estes, C., S. Biggs and C. Phillipson. 2003. *Social Theory, Social Policy and Ageing: A Critical Introduction*. Maidenhead: Open University Press.

Etherington, K. 1996. 'The Counsellor as Researcher: Boundary Issues and Critical Dilemmas', *British Journal of Guidance & Counselling* 24(3): 339–47.

_____. 2004. *Becoming a Reflexive Researcher*. London: Jessica Kingsley Publishers.

_____. 2007. 'Ethical Research in Reflexive Relationships', *Qualitative Inquiry* 13(5): 599–616.

European Commission. 2009. 'Intergenerational Solidarity: Analytical Report, Flash Eurobarometer (Online)'. European Commission. Retrieved 12 March 2014 from http://ec.europa.eu/public_opinion/flash/fl_269_en.pdf.

Evans, T, and P. Wallace. 2008. 'A Prison within a Prison?: The Masculinity Narratives of Male Prisoners', *Men and Masculinities* 10(4): 484–507.

Exley, C., and G. Letherby. 2001. 'Managing a Disrupted Lifecourse: Issues of Identity and Emotion Work', *Health* 5(1): 112–32.

Fairhurst, E. 2003a. '"If You Had a Whole Year of Weekends It Would Be a Very Long Day": Situating and Assessing Time in the Context of Paid and Unpaid Work', in G. Allan and G. Jones (eds), *Social Relations and the Life Course*. Basingstoke: Palgrave Macmillan, pp. 187–98.

———. 2003b. 'New Identities in Ageing: Perspectives on Age, Gender and Life after Work', in S. Arber, K. Davidson and J. Ginn (eds), *Gender and Ageing: Changing Roles and Relationships*. Maidenhead: Open University Press, pp. 31–46.

Featherstone, B. 2009. *Contemporary Fathering: Theory, Policy, and Practice*. Bristol: Policy Press.

Featherstone, M., and A. Wernick. 1995. 'Introduction', in M. Featherstone and A. Wernick (eds), *Images of Aging*. London: Routledge, pp. 1–15.

Feng, Z. 2017. 'Childlessness and Vulnerability of Older People in China', *Age and Ageing* 47(2): 275–81.

Fennell, G., and K. Davidson. 2003. '"The Invisible Man?" Older Men in Modern Society', *Ageing International* 28(4): 315–25.

Fertility Fairness. 2018. 'IVF Provision in England'. Retrieved 23 February 2020 from http://www.fertilityfairness.co.uk/nhs-fertility-services/ivf-provision-in-england/.

Finch, J. 2004. 'Feminism and Qualitative Research', *International Journal of Social Research Methodology* 7(1): 61–64.

———. 2007. 'Displaying Families', *Sociology* 41(1): 65–81.

Finch, J., and J. Mason. 1993. *Negotiating Family Responsibilities*. London: Routledge.

Fischer, A.R., and G.E. Good. 1997. 'Men and Psychotherapy: An Investigation of Alexithymia, Intimacy and Masculine Gender Roles', *Psychotherapy* 43(2): 160–70.

Fischer, C.T. 2006a. 'Glossary', in C.T. Fischer (ed.), *Qualitative Research Methods for Psychologists: Introduction through Empirical Studies*. Burlington, MA: Academic Press, pp. 429–21.

———. 2006b. 'Introduction', in Constance T. Fischer (ed.), *Qualitative Research Methods for Psychologists: Introduction through Empirical Studies*. Burlington, MA: Academic Press, pp. xv–xlii.

Fisher, J., G. Baker and K. Hammarberg. 2010. 'Long-Term Health, Well-Being, Life Satisfaction, and Attitudes toward Parenthood in Men Diagnosed as Infertile: Challenges to Gender Stereotypes and Implications for Practice', *Fertility and Sterility* 94(2): 574–80.

Fisher, J., and K. Hammarberg. 2017. 'Psychological Aspects of Infertility among Men', in M. Simoni and I. Huhtaniemi (eds), *Endocrinology of the*

Testis and Male Reproduction. Cham: Springer International Publishing, pp. 1287–317.

Flick, U. 2009. *An Introduction to Qualitative Research*. London: SAGE Publications.

Forste, R. 2002. 'Where are All the Men?', *Journal of Family Issues* 23(5): 579–600.

Fox, C. 2009. 'Tales of the Unexpected: Analysing Disabled Women's Accounts of Abusive Relationships', PhD thesis. Keele: Keele University.

Franklin, S. 1990. 'Deconstructing "Desperateness": The Social Construction of Infertility in Popular Representations of New Reproductive Technologies', in M. McNeil, I. Varcoe and S. Yearley (eds), *The New Reproductive Technologies*. Basingstoke: Macmillan Press, pp. 200–29.

———. 1997. *Embodied Progress: A Cultural Account of Assisted Conception*. London: Routledge.

Friend, R.A. 1989. 'Older Lesbian and Gay People: Responding to Homophobia', *Marriage & Family Review* 14(3–4): 241–63.

Frosh, S., A. Phoenix, and R. Pattman. 2002. *Young Masculinities*. London: Palgrave.

Gabb, J., M. Klett-Davies, J. Fink and M. Thomae. 2013. 'Enduring Love? Couple Relationships in the 21st Century. Survey Findings: An Interim Report', *Economic and Social Research Council (ESRC RES-062-23-3056) Research Project*. Milton Keynes: The Open University.

Gabb, J., and E.B. Silva. 2011. 'Introduction to Critical Concepts: Families, Intimacies and Personal Relationships', *Sociological Research Online* 16(4): 23.

Gabriel, Z., and A. Bowling. 2004. 'Quality of Life in Old Age from the Perspectives of Older People', in A. Walker and C. Hagan Hennessey (eds), *Quality of Life in Old Age*. Maidenhead: Open University Press, pp. 14–34.

Gatrell, C. 2006. 'Interviewing Fathers: Feminist Dilemmas in Fieldwork', *Journal of Gender Studies* 15(3): 237–51.

Gatrell, C., S. Burnett, C. Cooper and P. Sparrow. 2015. 'The Price of Love: The Prioritisation of Childcare and Income Earning among UK Fathers', *Families, Relationships and Societies* 4(2): 225–38.

Geertz, C. 1973. *The Interpretation of Cultures*. New York: Basic Books.

Gergen, M.M. 1992. 'Life Stories: Pieces of a Dream', in G. Rosenwald and R. Ochberg (eds), *Telling Lives*. New Haven: Yale University Press.

Gerson, K. 1985. *Hard Choices: How Women Decide about Work, Career and Motherhood*. Berkeley, CA: University of California Press.

Ghauri, L. 2014. 'Review of Marcia Claire Inhorn, The New Arab Man: Emergent Masculinities, Technologies, and Islam in the Middle East', *Religion and Gender* 4(2): 234–36).

Gibson, D. 1996. 'Broken down by Age and Gender: "The Problem of Old Women" Redefined', *Gender & Society* 10(4): 433–48.

Giddens, A. 1977. *Studies in Social and Political Theory*. London: Hutchinson.

_____. 1991. *Modernity and Self-Identity: Self and Society in the Late Modern Age*. Cambridge: Polity Press.

Gilleard, C., and P. Higgs. 2000. *Cultures of Ageing: Self, Citizen and the Body*. Harlow: Pearson Educational.

_____. 2005. *Contexts of Ageing: Class, Cohort and Community*. Cambridge: Polity Press.

_____. 2010. 'Aging without Agency: Theorizing the Fourth Age', *Aging and Mental Health* 14(2): 121–28.

Gillespie, R. 2000. 'When No Means No: Disbelief, Disregard and Deviance as Discourses of Voluntary Childlessness', *Women's Studies International Forum* 23(2): 223–34.

_____. 2003. 'Childfree And Feminine: Understanding the Gender Identity of Voluntarily Childless Women', *Gender Society* 17(1): 122–36.

Gilligan, C. 1993. *In a Different Voice: Psychological Theory and Women's Development*. Cambridge, MA: Harvard University Press.

Ginn, J., and S. Arber. 1995. '"Only Connect": Gender Relations and Ageing', in S. Arber and J. Ginn (eds), *Connecting Gender and Ageing: A Sociological Approach*. Buckingham: Open University Press, pp. 1–14.

Global Action on Aging. 2002. 'Final Declaration and Recommendations of the World NGO Forum on Ageing'. Retrieved 27 May 2014 from http://www.cruzroja.es/pls/portal30/docs/PAGE/SITE_CRE/ARBOL_CARPETAS/BB_QUE_HACEMOS/B10_INTERVENCION_SOCIAL/PERSONASMAYORES/FORO_ENVEJECIMIENTO/TR02%20138_%20DOCUMENTO%20FINAL_ENG.PDF.

Goffman, E. 1963. *Stigma: Notes on the Management of Spoiled Identity*. Englewood Cliffs, NJ: Prentice-Hall.

Goldacre, B. 2008. *Bad Science*. London: Fourth Estate.

_____. 2012. *Bad Pharma*. London: Fourth Estate.

Goldberg, W.A. 2014. *Father Time: The Social Clock and the Timing of Fatherhood*. Basingstoke: Palgrave Macmillan.

Goldstein, J.R. 2009. 'How Populations Age', in P. Uhlenberg (ed.), *International Handbook of Population Aging*. Houten: Springer, pp. 7–18.

Gorman, G. 2016. 'The Untold Grief of Childless Men', News.com.au, 14 February 2016. Retrieved 19 February 20201 from https://www.news.com.au/lifestyle/parenting/kids/the-untold-grief-of-childless-men/news-story/afd12390a8e450d5b9c04e7db6e9d88b.

Gott, M., and S. Hinchcliff. 2003. 'Sex and Ageing: A Gendered Issue', in S. Arber, K. Davidson and J. Ginn (eds), *Gender and Ageing: Changing Roles and Relationships*. Maidenhead: Open University Press, pp. 168–85.

Gough, B. 2010. 'Promoting "Masculinity" over Health: A Critical Analysis of Men's Health Promotion with Particular Reference to an Obesity Reduction "Manual"', in B. Gough and S. Robertson (eds), *Men, Masculinities and Health: Critical Perspectives*. Basingstoke: Palgrave Macmillan, pp. 125–42.

Gough, B., and S. Robertson. 2010. *Men, Masculinities and Health: Critical Perspectives*. Basingstoke: Palgrave Macmillan.

Granovetter, M.S. 1973. 'The Strength of Weak Ties', *American Journal of Sociology* 78(6): 1360–80.

———. 1983. 'The Strength of Weak Ties: A Network Theory Revisited', *Sociological Theory* 1: 201–33.

Grant, R., J. Judd and D. Naylor. 1993. 'Legion', season 6, episode 2, *Red Dwarf*. Broadcast 14 October 1993. London.

Gray, A. 2009. 'The Social Capital of Older People', *Ageing & Society* 29(1): 5–31.

Gray, B. 2009. 'The Emotional Labour of Nursing 1: Exploring the Concept', *Nursing Times* 105(8): 26–29.

Green, D.O., J.W. Creswell, R.J. Shope and V.L. Plano Clarke. 2007. 'Grounded Theory and Racial/Ethnic Diversity', in A. Bryant and K. Charmaz (eds), *The SAGE Handbook of Grounded Theory*. London: SAGE Publications, pp. 472–92.

Greene, M., and A. Biddlecom. 2000. 'Absent and Problematic Men: Demographic Accounts of Male Reproductive Roles', *Population and Development Review* 26(1): 81–115.

Greil, A., K. Slauson-Blevins and J. McQuillan. 2010. 'The Experience of Infertility: A Review of Recent Literature', *Sociology of Health & Illness* 32(1): 140–62.

Grenier, A. 2012. *Transitions and the Lifecourse: Challenging the Constructions of 'Growing Old'*. Bristol: Policy Press.

Grenier, A., C. Phillipson and R. Setterson (eds). 2020. *Precarity and Ageing: Understanding Insecurity and Risk in Later Life*. Bristol: Policy Press.

Grenier, E. 2017. 'More Canadians Living Alone and without Children, Census Figures Show', CBC, 2 August 2017. Retrieved 11 May 2020 from https://www.cbc.ca/news/politics/census-2016-marriage-children-families-1.4231163.

Grinion, P. 2005. 'The BioPsycosocial Stress of Infertility: Grappling with the Ethical and Moral Concerns vis-à-vis Assisted Reproductive Technologies', *NACSW Convention 2005*. Grand Rapids, MI: North American Association of Christians in Social Work.

Grundy, E., and S. Read. 2012. 'Social Contacts and Receipt of Help among Older People in England: Are There Benefits of Having More Children?', *The Journals of Gerontology Series B: Pyschological Sciences and Social Sciences* 67(6): 742–54.

Grundy, E., and O. Kravdal. 2008. 'Reproductive History and Mortality in Late Middle Age among Norwegian Men and Women', *American Journal of Epidemiology* 167(3): 271–79.

———. 2010. 'Fertility History and Cause-Specific Mortality: A Register-Based Analysis of Complete Cohorts of Norwegian Women and Men', *Social Science & Medicine* 70(11): 1847–57.

Guasp, A. 2011. 'Lesbian, Gay and Bisexual People in Later Life'. London: Stonewall.

Guba, E.G., and Y.S. Lincoln. 2005. 'Pradigmatic Controversies, Contradictions, and Emerging Influences', in N.K. Denzin and Y.S. Lincoln (eds), *The SAGE Handbook of Qualitative Research*. Thousand Oaks, CA: SAGE Publications, pp. 191–213.

Guest, G., K, M. MacQueen and E.E. Namey. 2012. *Applied Thematic Analysis*. Los Angeles, CA: SAGE Publications.

Gullette, M.M. 1997. *Declining to Decline: Cultural Combat and the Politics of Midlife*. Charlottesville, VA: University Press of Virginia.

Guralnik, J.M., S. Butterworth, K. Patel, G. Mishra and D. Kuh. 2009. 'Reduced Midlife Physical Functioning among Never Married and Childless Men: Evidence from the 1946 British Birth Cohort Study', *Aging Clinical and Experimental Research* 21(2): 174–81.

Gutmann, D.L. 1987. *Reclaimed Powers: Towards a New Psychology of Men and Women in Later Life*. New York: Basic Books.

Gutmann, M. 2009. 'The Missing Gamete? Ten Common Mistakes or Lies about Men's Sexual Destiny', in M. Inhorn., T. Tjørnhøj-Thomsen, H. Goldberg and M. la Cour Mosegard (eds), *Reconceiving the Second Sex: Men, Masculinity, and Reproduction*. New York: Berghahn Books, pp. 21–44.

Hackett, E. 2008. 'Gender as Mere Difference', *Men and Masculinities* 11(2): 211–18.

Hadley, R.A., and T.S. Hanley. 2011. 'Involuntarily Childless Men and the Desire for Fatherhood', *Journal of Reproductive and Infant Psychology* 29(1): 56–68.

Hadley, R.A. 2008a. 'Involuntarily Childless Men: Issues Surrounding the Desire for Fatherhood', Master's dissertation. Manchester: The University of Manchester.

_____. 2008b. 'This Man's Story', *MoreToLife Newsletter*. Infertility Network UK.

_____. 2009. 'Navigating in an Uncharted World: How Does the Desire for Fatherhood Affect Men?', Master's dissertation. Manchester: The University of Manchester.

_____. 2012a. 'The Heather Stott Show', BBC Radio Manchester, 2 February 2012.

_____. 2012b. 'Not Even Tomorrow's Chip Paper', *MoreToLife Newsletter*. Infertility Network UK.

_____. 2013. 'Robin Hadley: I Know All about Broody Men Who Long to Be Dads: I Am One', *The Daily Telegraph*, 4 April 2013, 27.

_____. 2014a. 'Condemned as a "Typical" Man?'. The ReValuing Care Research Network blog. Retrieved 19 February 2021 from https://revaluingcare.net/condemned-as-a-typical-man/.

_____. 2014b. 'The Impotence of Earnestness and the Importance of Being Earnest: Recruiting Older Men for Interview', in A. Tarrant and J. Watts (eds), *Studies of Ageing Masculinities: Still in Their Infancy?* London: The Centre for Policy on Ageing, pp. 68–83.

_____. 2015. 'Life without Fatherhood: A Qualitative Study of Older Involuntarily Childless Men', PhD thesis. Keele: Keele University.

_____. 2016a. 'Men and Infertility', *The Times: Weekend Section*, 16 July 2016, 7.

_____. 2016b. 'Review: Reconceiving the Second Sex: Men, Masculinity, and Reproduction', *Journal of Reproductive and Infant Psychology* 34(5): 535–36.

_____. 2018a. 'Ageing without Children, Gender and Social Justice', in S. Westwood (ed.), *Ageing, Diversity and Equality: Social Justice Perspectives.* Abingdon: Routledge, pp. 66–81.

_____. 2018b. 'Ageing without Children', in J. Tetley, N. Cox, K. Jack and G. Witham (eds), *Nursing Older People at a Glance.* Chichester: John Wiley & Sons, pp. 76–77.

_____. 2018c. 'How Involved Are Men in "Involved Fathering"?' Male Psychology Network blog. Retrieved 19 February 2021 from https://malepsychology.org.uk/2018/05/11/how-involved-are-men-in-involved-fathering/.

_____. 2018d. '"I'm Missing out and I Think I Have Something to Give": Experiences of Older Involuntarily Childless Men', *Working with Older People* 22(2): 83–92.

_____. 2018e. 'The Lived Experience of Older Involuntary Childless Men', *The Annual Journal of the British Sociological Association Study Group on Auto/Biography* 2017: 93–108.

_____. 2018f. '"There's Something Missing in My Life": Non-Fatherhood on "Fathers Day"'. Centre for Reproduction Research Blog. Retrieved 19 February 2021 from https://centreforreproductionresearch962893217.wordpress.com/2018/06/15/168/.

_____. 2019a. 'Deconstructing Dad', in J.A. Barry, R. Kingerlee, M. Seager and L. Sullivan (eds), *The Palgrave Handbook of Male Psychology and Mental Health.* Cham: Palgrave Macmillan, pp. 47–66.

_____. 2019b. '"It's Most of My Life – Going to the Pub or the Group": The Social Networks of Involuntarily Childless Older Men', *Ageing and Society* 41(1): 51–76.

_____. 2020. 'Men and me(n)', *Methodological Innovations* 13(2): 1–11.

Hadley, R.A., C. Newby and J.A. Barry. 2019. 'Anxious Childhood Attachment Predicts Childlessness in Later Life', *Psychreg Journal of Psychology* 3(3): 7–27.

Hagestad, G., and V. Call. 2007. 'Pathways to Childlessness: A Life Course Perspective', *Journal of Family Issues* 28(10): 1338–61.

Haggett, A. 2014. 'Looking Back: Masculinity and Mental Health – The Long View', *Psychologist* 27: 426–29.

Hall, J.C. 2008. 'The Impact of Kin and Fictive Kin Relationships on the Mental Health of Black Adult Children of Alcoholics', *Health and Social Work* 33(4): 259–66.

Hammarberg, K., V. Collins, C. Holden, K. Young and R. McLachlan. 2017. 'Men's Knowledge, Attitudes and Behaviours Relating to Fertility', *Human Reproduction Update* 23(4): 458–80.

Hammersley, M., and P. Atkinson. 1983. *Ethnography: Principles in Practice*. London: Routledge.

———. 2007. *Ethography. Principles in Practice*, 3rd edn. London: Routledge.

Hank, K., and M. Wagner. 2013. 'Parenthood, Marital Status, and Well-Being in Later Life: Evidence from SHARE', *Social Indicators Research* 114(2): 639–53.

Haralambos, Michael, and Martin Holborn. 2008. *Sociology: Themes and Perspectives*. London: HarperCollins Publishers, pp. 458–519.

Haraway, D. 1988. 'Situated Knowledges: The Science Question in Feminism and the Privilege of Partial Perspective', *Feminist Studies* 14(3): 575–99.

———. 1991. *Simians, Cyborgs, and Women: The Reinvention of Nature*. London: Free Association Books.

Heaphy, B. 2007. 'Sexualities, Gender and Ageing', *Current Sociology* 55(2): 193–210.

———. 2009. 'Choice and Its Limits in Older Lesbian and Gay Narratives of Relational Life', *Journal of GLBT Family Studies* 5(1–2): 119–38.

Hearn, J. 1995. 'Imaging the Aging of Men', in M. Featherstone and A. Wernick (eds), *Images of Aging: Cultural Representations of Later Life*. London: Routledge, pp. 97–118.

———. 2000. '"Men, (Pro-)Feminism, Organizing and Organizations"', *Finnish Journal of Business Economics* 3(00): 350–72.

———. 2004. 'From Hegemonic Masculinity to the Hegemony of Men', *Feminist Theory* 5(1): 49–72.

———. 2013. 'Methods and Methodologies in Critical Studies on Men and Masculinities', in B. and B. Pease (eds), *Men, Masculinities and Methodology*. Basingstoke: Palgrave Macmillan, pp. 26–38.

Heaton, T.B., C.K. Jacobson and K. Holland. 1999. 'Persistence and Change in Decisions to Remain Childless', *Journal of Marriage and the Family* 61(2): 531–39.

Helosfan, K., and G. Hagestad. 2012. 'Transformations in the Role of Grandparents across Welfare States', in S. Arber and V. Timonen (eds), *Contemporary Grandparenting: Changing Family Relationships in Global Contexts*. Bristol: Policy Press, pp. 27–49.

Hendricks, J. 2010. 'Age, Self, and Identity in the Global Century', in D. Dannefer and C. Phillipson (eds), *The SAGE Handbook of Social Gerontology*. London: SAGE Publications, pp. 251–79.

Heslin, K.C., A.B. Hamilton, T.K. Singzon, J.L. Smith and N.L.R. Anderson. 2011. 'Alternative Families in Recovery: Fictive Kin Relationships among Residents of Sober Living Homes', *Qualitative Health Research* 21(4): 477–88.

Hicks, S. 2005. 'Lesbian and Gay Foster Care and Adoption: A Brief UK History', *Adoption & Fostering* 29(3): 42–56.

Hill, A. 2020. 'Favouring Young over Old in Covid-19 Treatment Justifiable, Says Ethicist', *The Guardian*, 22 April 2020. Retrieved 19 February 2021 from https://www.theguardian.com/world/2020/apr/22/favouring-young-over-old-in-covid-19-treatment-justifiable-says-ethicist.

Himmel, W., E. Ittner, M.M. Kochen, H.W. Michelmann, B. Hinney, M. Reuter, M. Kallefhoff and R-H. Ringert. 1997. 'Management of Involuntary Childlessness', *British Journal of General Practice*, 47(415): 111–18.

Hinton, Lisa, and Tina Miller. 2013. 'Mapping Men's Anticipations and Experiences in the Reproductive Realm: (In)Fertility Journeys', *Reproductive Biomedicine Online* 27(3): 244–52.

Hirschman, A.O. 1970. *Exit, Voice and Loyalty: Responses to Decline in Firms, Organizations and States*. Cambridge, MA: Harvard University Press.

Hobson, B., and D. Morgan. 2002. 'Introduction: Making Men into Fathers', in B. Hobson (ed.), *Making Men into Fathers: Men, Masculinities and the Social Politics of Fatherhood*. Cambridge: Cambridge University Press, pp. 1–24.

Hochschild, A. 1983. *The Managed Heart: Commercialization of Human Feeling*. Berkeley, CA: University of California Press.

Hodgekiss, A. 2013. 'Men without Children Are "More Depressed and Sad" Than Childless Women', *Daily Mail*, 2 April 2014.

Hofberg, K., and I.F. Brockington. 2000. 'Tokophobia: An Unreasoning Dread of Childbirth: A Series of 26 Cases', *The British Journal of Psychiatry* 176(1): 83–85.

Hoff, A. 2015. 'Current and Future Challenges of Family Care in the UK : Future of an Ageing Population. Evidence Review: March 2015'. London: Government Office for Science.

Hoffman, L.W. 1975. 'The Value of Children to Parents and the Decrease in Family Size', *Proceedings, American Philosophical Society* 119(6): 430–38.

Hoffman, L.W., and J.D. Manis. 1979. 'The Value of Children in the United States: A New Approach to the Study of Fertility', *Journal of Marriage and Family* 41(3): 583–96.

Holden, K. 2007. *The Shadow of Marriage: Singleness in England, 1914–1960*. Manchester: Manchester University Press.

Hollway, W., and T. Jefferson. 2000. *Doing Qualitative Research Differently: Free Association, Narrative and the Interview Method*. London: SAGE Publications.

Holstein, J.A., and J.F. Gubrium. 2005. 'Interpretive Practice and Social Interaction', in N.K. Denzin and Y.S. Lincoln (eds), *The SAGE Handbook of Qualitative Research*. Thousand Oaks, CA: SAGE Publications, pp. 483–505.

Holstein, M., and M. Minkler. 2007. 'Critical Gerontology: Reflections for the 21st Century', in M. Bernard and T. Scharf (eds), *Critical Perspectives on Ageing Societies*. Bristol: Policy Press, pp. 13–23.

Hook, N. 2019. 'May the Force of Gender Be with You: Identity, Identification and "Own-Gender Bias"', in J.A. Barry, R. Kingerlee, M. Seager and L. Sullivan (eds), *The Palgrave Handbook of Male Psychology and Mental Health*. Cham: Palgrave Macmillan, pp. 165–82.

Houghton, D., and P. Houghton. 1984. *Coping with Childlessness*. London: Unwin Hyman.

Houseknecht, S.K. 1977. 'Reference Group Support for Voluntary Childlessness: Evidence for Conformity', *Journal of Marriage and Family* 39(2): 285–92.

_____. 1980. 'Timing of the Decision To Remain Voluntarily Childless: Evidence for Continuous Socialization', *Psychology of Women Quarterly* 4(1): 81–96.

_____. 1987. 'Voluntary Childlessness', in M.B. Sussman and S.K. Steinmetz (eds), *Handbook of Marriage and the Family*. New York: Plenum Press, pp. 369–95.

HPV Action. 2020. 'Jabs for Boys'. Retrieved 27 June 2020 from http://jabsfortheboys.uk/.

Hudson, N.A. 2008. 'Infertility in British South Asian Communities: Negotiating the Community and the Clinic', PhD thesis. Leicester: De Montfort University.

Hugill, K. 2012. 'The "Auto/Biographical" Method and Its Potential to Contribute to Nursing Research', *Nurse Researcher* 20(2): 28–32.

Human Fertilisation and Embryology Authority. 2007/8. 'The HFEA Guide to Infertility'. London: Human Fertilisation and Embryology Authority.

_____. 2009a. 'IVF – Chance of success'. Retrieved 16 June 2014 from http://www.hfea.gov.uk/ivf-success-rate.html.

_____. 2009b. 'Surrogacy'. Retrieved 9 June 2014 from http://www.hfea.gov.uk/fertility-treatment-options-surrogacy.html.

_____. 2019. 'Fertility Treatment 2017: Trends and Figures'. Retrieved 10 June 2019 from https://www.hfea.gov.uk/media/3189/fertility-treatment-2017-trends-and-figures.pdf.

Humphreys, N., A. Curran, E. Morris, P. Farrell and K. Woods. 2007. 'Emotional Intelligence and Education: A Critical Review', *Educational Psychology* 7(2): 235–54.

Hussain, R., R. Marino, and I. Coulson. 2005. 'The Role of Health Promotion in Healthy Ageing', in V. Minichiello and I. Coulson (eds), *Contemporary Issues in Gerontology: Promoting Positive Ageing*. London: Routledge, pp. 34–52.

Hutchison, E.D. 2011. 'A Life Course Perspective', in E.D. Hutchison (ed.), *Dimensions of Human Behaviour: The Changing Life Course*. Thousand Oaks, CA: SAGE Publications, pp. 1–38.

Huyck, M.H., and D.L. Gutmann. 2006. 'Men and Their Wives: Why are Some Married Men Vunerable at Midlife?', in V. Hilkevitch Bedford and B. Formaniak Turner (eds), *Men in Relationships*. New York: Springer Publishing, pp. 27–50.

Infertility Network UK. 2014. 'More-To-Life'. Retrieved 27 May 2014 from https://healthunlocked.com/moretolifeuk.

Inhorn, M. (ed.). 2007. *Reproductive Disruptions: Gender, Technology, and Biopolitics in the New Millennium*. New York: Berghahn Books.

Inhorn, M., and E. Wentzell. 2011. 'Embodying Emergent Masculinities: Men Engaging with Reproductive and Sexual Health Technologies in the Middle East and Mexico', *American Ethnologist* 38(4): 801–15.

Inhorn, M. 2012. *The New Arab Man: Emergent Masculinities, Technologies, and Islam in the Middle East*. Princeton, NJ: Princeton University Press.

Inhorn, M., T. Tjørnhøj-Thomsen, H. Goldberg and M. la Cour Mosegard (eds). 2009a. *Reconceiving the Second Sex: Men, Masculinity, and Reproduction*. New York: Berghahn Books.

———. 2009b. 'The Second Sex in Reproduction? Men, Sexuality, and Masculinity', in Inhorn, M., T. Tjørnhøj-Thomsen, H. Goldberg and M. la Cour Mosegard (eds), *Reconceiving the Second Sex: Men, Masculinity, and Reproduction*. New York: Berghahn Books, pp. 1–17.

Ivanova, K., and P.A. Dykstra. 2015. 'Aging Without Children', *Public Policy & Aging Report* 25(3): 98–101.

Ives, J., H. Draper, H. Pattison and C. Williams. 2008. 'Becoming a Father/ Refusing Fatherhood: An Empirical Bioethics Approach to Paternal Responsibilities and Rights', *Clin Ethics* 3(2): 75–84.

Jager, E. 2015. *The Pater: My Father, My Judasim, My Childlessness*. New York: The Toby Press.

James, N. 1989. 'Emotional Labour: Skill and Work in the Social Regulation of Feelings', *The Sociological Review* 37(1): 15–42.

Jamieson, L. 1998. *Intimacy: Personal Relationships in Modern Societies*. Cambridge: Polity Press.

Jamieson, L., K. Backett-Milburn, R. Simpson and F. Wasoff. 2010. 'Fertility and Social Change: The Neglected Contribution of Men's Approaches to Becoming Partners and Parents', *The Sociological Review* 58(3): 463–91.

Jamieson, L., F. Wasoff and R. Simpson. 2009. 'Solo-Living, Demographic and Family Change: The Need to Know More about Men', *Sociological Research Online* 14(2).

Järvinen, M. 2001. 'Accounting for Trouble: Identity Negotiations in Qualitative Interviews with Alcoholics', *Symbolic Interaction* 24(3): 263–84.

Jeffries, S., and C. Konnert. 2002. 'Regret and Psychological Well-Being among Voluntarily and Involuntarily Childless Women and Mothers', *The International Journal of Aging and Human Development* 54(2): 89–106.

Jensen, A.-M. 2010. 'A Gender Boomerang on Fertility? How Increasing Expectations of Fatherhood May Avert Men from Having Children', *Quetelet Seminar: Stalls, Resistances and Reversals in Demographic Transitions,*

24–26 November 2010. Louvain-la-Neuve, Belgium: Norwegian University of Science and Technology.

_____. 2016. 'Ideas about Childbearing among Childless Men', *Families, Relationships and Societies* 5(2): 193–207.

Jewkes, Y., and G. Letherby. 2001. 'Insiders and Outsiders: Complex Issues of Identification, Difference and Distance in Social Research', *Auto/Biography Studies* 16(2): 41–50.

Joffe, H., and L. Yardley. 2004. 'Content and Thematic Analysis', in D.F. Marks and L. Yardley (eds), *Research Methods for Clinical and Health Psychology*. London: SAGE Publications, pp. 56–68.

Jones, K., M. Robb, S. Murphy and A. Davies. 2019. 'New Understandings of Fathers Experiences of Grief and Loss Following Stillbirth and Neonatal Death: A Scoping Review', *Midwifery* 79: 102531.

Jordan, C., and T.A. Revenson. 1999. 'Gender Differences in Coping with Infertility: A Meta-Analysis', *Journal of Behavioral Medicine* 22(4): 341–58.

Jutla, K.K. 2011. 'Caring for a Person with Dementia: A Qualitative Study of the Experiences of the Sikh Community in Wolverhampton', PhD thesis. Keele: Keele University.

Kafcaloudes, P. 2013. 'How Childlessness Affects Men and Why Some Are Choosing Singlehood'. ABC Radio: 7 April 2013.

Kamo, Y., T.L. Henderson and K.A. Roberto. 2011. 'Displaced Older Adults' Reactions to and Coping with the Aftermath of Hurricane Katrina', *Journal of Family Issues* 32(10): 1346–70.

Kampf, A. 2015. 'Liberty Walther Barnes Conceiving Masculinity: Male Infertility, Medicine, and Identity', *Social History of Medicine* 28(2): 402–4.

Kanuha, V.K. 2000. '"Being" Native versus "Going Native": Conducting Social Work Research as an Insider', *Social Work* 45(5): 439–47.

Karp, D.A. 2000. 'A Decade of Reminders: Changing Age Consciousness between Fifty and Sixty Years Old', in J.F. Gubrium and J.A. Holstein (eds), *Aging and Everyday Life*. Malden, MA: Blackwell Publishers, pp. 65–86.

Kaufman, M. 1994. 'Men, Feminisim, and Men's Contradictory Experiences of Power', in H. Brod and M. Kaufman (eds), *Theorizing Masculinities*. Thousand Oaks, CA: SAGE Publications, pp. 142–63.

Keizer, R. 2010. 'Remaining Childless. Causes and Consequences from a Life Course Perspective', PhD thesis. Utrecht: Utrecht University.

Keizer, R., P.A. Dykstra and M. Jansen. 2007. 'Pathways into Childlessness: Evidence of Gendered Life Course Dynamics', *Journal of Biosocial Science* 40(6): 1–16.

Keizer, R., P.A. Dykstra and A.-R. Poortman. 2009. 'Life Outcomes of Childless Men and Fathers', *European Sociological Review* 26(1): 1–15.

Kellehear, A. 2007. *A Social History of Dying*. Cambridge: Cambridge University Press.

_____. 2008. 'Dying as a Social Relationship: A Sociological Review of De-
bates on the Determination of Death', *Social Science & Medicine* 66(7):
1533–44.

Kelly, M. 2009. 'Women's Voluntary Childlessness: A Radical Rejection of
Motherhood?', *Women's Studies Quarterly* 37(3 & 4): 157–72.

Kelly, M., and J. Green. 2019. 'What Can Sociology Offer Urban Public
Health?', *Critical Public Health* 29(5): 517–21.

Kelly, M., R. Kelly and F. Russo. 2014. 'The Integration of Social, Behavioral, and Biological Mechanisms in Models of Pathogenesis', *Perspectives
in Biology and Medicine* 57(3): 308–28.

Kelly, M., N. Kriznik, A.L. Kinmonth and P. Fletcher. 2019. 'The Brain,
Self and Society: A Social-Neuroscience Model of Predictive Processing',
Social Neuroscience 14(3): 266–76.

Kemkes-Grottenhaler, A. 2003. 'Postponing or Rejecting Parenthood?
Results of a Survey among Female Academic Professionals', *Journal of
Biosocial Science* 35(2): 213–26.

Kendig, H., P.A. Dykstra, R.I. van Gaalen and T. Melkas. 2007. 'Health of
Aging Parents and Childless Individuals', *Journal of Family Issues* 28(11):
1457–86.

Kidd, S.A., B. Eskenazi and A. Wyrobek. 2001. 'Effects of Male Age on
Semen Quality and Fertility: A Review of the Literature', *Fertility and
Sterility* 75(2): 237–48.

Kimmel, M., J. Hearn and R. Connell (eds). 2005. *Handbook of Studies on
Men and Masculinities*. Thousand Oaks, CA: SAGE Publications.

Kimmel, M. 1994. 'Masculinity as Homophobia: Fear, Shame, and Silence
in the Construction of Gender Identity', in H. Brod and M. Kaufman
(eds), *Theorizing Masculinities*. Thousand Oaks, CA: SAGE Publications,
pp. 119–41.

King, A., and A. Cronin. 2016. 'Bonds, Bridges and Ties: Applying Social
Capital Theory to LGBT People's Housing Concerns Later in Life', *Quality
in Ageing and Older Adults* 17(1): 16–25.

King, R.B. 2003. 'Subfecundity and Anxiety in a Nationally Representative
Sample', *Social Science & Medicine* 56(4): 739–51.

Kluwer, E., and G. Mikula. 2013. 'Gender-Related Inequalities in the Division of Family Work in Close Relationships: A Social Psychological
Perspective', *European Review of Social Psychology* 13(1): 185–216.

Kneale, D., E. Coast and J. Stillwell. 2009. 'Fertility, Living Arrangements,
Care and Mobility', in J. Stillwell, E. Coast and D. Kneale (eds), *Fertility,
Living Arrangements, Care and Mobility*. Dordrecht: Springer, pp. 1–22.

Knijn, T., I. Ostner and C. Schmitt. 2006. 'Men and (Their) Families: Comparative Perspectives on Men's Roles and Attitudes Towards Family
Formation', in J. Bradshaw and A. Hatland (eds), *Social Policy, Employment and Family Change in Comparative Perspective*. Cheltenham: Edward
Elgar Publishing, pp. 179–97.

Knipscheer, K., J. de Jong Gierveld, T. van Tilburg and P.A. Dykstra (eds). 1995. *Living Arrangements and Social Networks of Older Adults*. Amsterdam: VU University Press.

Knodel, J. 2001. 'Book Review: The Chosen Lives of Childfree Men By Patricia Lunneborg', *Gender Issues* 19(1): 96–98.

Knodel, J., and M.B. Ofstedal. 2003. 'Gender and Aging in the Developing World: Where Are the Men?', *Population and Development Review* 29(4): 677–98.

Kohli, M. 1988. 'Ageing as a Challenge for Sociological Theory', *Ageing & Society* 8(4): 367–94.

———. 1999. 'Private and Public Transfers between Generations: Linking the Family and the State', *European Societies* 1(1): 81–104.

Kohli, M., H. Künemund and J. Lüdicke. 2005. 'Family Structure, Proximity and Contact'. Retrieved 8 March 2021 from https://www.researchgate.net/publication/255559579_Family_structure_proximity_and_contact.

Kohli, M., and M. Albertini. 2009. 'Childlessness and Intergenerational Transfers: What is at Stake?', *Ageing & Society* 29 (Special Issue 8): 1171–83.

Koo, M. 2002. 'The Missing Critical Friends' Voices: An Angel's Heart or a Beautiful Mind?', *Australian Association for Research in Education Annual Conference 2002*. Brisbane: Australian Association for Research in Education.

Koropeckyj-Cox, T. 2003. 'Three Childless Men's Pathways into Old Age', in J.F. Gubrium and J.A. Holstein (eds), *Ways of Aging*. Malden, USA: Blackwell Publishing, pp. 75–95.

Koropeckyj-Cox, T., and G. Pendell. 2007a. 'Attitudes about Childlessness in the United States: Correlates of Positive, Neutral, and Negative Responses', *Journal of Family Issues* 28(8): 1054–82.

———. 2007b. 'The Gender Gap in Attitudes about Childlessness in the United States', *Journal of Marriage and Family* 69(4): 899–915.

Koropeckyj-Cox, T, and V.R.A. Call. 2007. 'Characteristics of Older Childless Persons and Parents – Cross-National Comparisons', *Journal of Family Issues* 28(10): 1362–414.

Kranz, D., H. Busch and C. Niepel. 2018. 'Desires and Intentions for Fatherhood: A Comparison of Childless Gay and Heterosexual Men in Germany', *Journal of Family Psychology* 32(8): 995–1004.

Krekula, C. 2007. 'The Intersection of Age and Gender: Reworking Gender Theory and Social Gerontology', *Current Sociology* 55(2): 155–71.

Kreyenfeld, M., and D. Konietzka (eds). 2017. *Childlessness in Europe: Contexts, Causes, and Consequences*. Cham: Springer.

Kriznik, N. 2016. 'Integrated Mechanisms Describing the Relationship between the Social and the Biological', *The Rank Prize Fund Mini-Symposium on Developmental Programming of Human Disease: Preconception Nutrition and Lifelong Health*. Cambridge: The Rank Prize Fund.

Kriznik, N., and M. Kelly. 2016. 'Social Capital, Biological Capital and Health Inequalities: Bourdieu Meets Developmental Programming', *British Sociological Association Annual Conference 2016*. Aston University: St John's College Reading Group on Health Inequalities.

Kriznik, N., A.L. Kinmonth, T. Ling and M. Kelly. 2018. 'Moving beyond Individual Choice in Policies to Reduce Health Inequalities: The Integration of Dynamic with Individual Explanations', *Journal of Public Health* 40(4): 764–75.

Kruse, A. 2012. 'Active Ageing: Solidarity and Responsibility in an Ageing Society'. Centre for European Studies. Retrieved 8 March 2021 from https://www.martenscentre.eu/publication/active-ageing-solidarity-and-responsibility-in-an-ageing-society/.

Kûbler-Ross, E. 1970. *On Death and Dying*. London: Routledge.

Kvale, S. 1996. *InterViews: An Introduction to Qualitative Research Interviewing*. Thousand Oaks, CA: SAGE Publications.

_____. 1999. 'The Psychoanalytic Interview as Qualitative Research', *Qualitative Inquiry* 5(1): 87–113.

Kvale, S., and S. Brinkman. 2009. *Interviews: Learning the Craft of Qualitative Research Interviewing*. Thousand Oaks, CA: SAGE Publications.

Laceulle, H. 2013. 'Self-Realisation and Ageing: A Spiritual Perspective', in J. Baars, J. Dohmen, A. Grenier and C. Phillipson (eds), *Ageing, Meaning and Social Structure: Connecting Critical and Humanistic Gerontology*. Bristol: Policy Press, pp. 97–118.

Lalos, A., L. Jacobsson and B. von Schoultz. 1985. 'The Wish to Have a Child: A Pilot Study of Infertile Couples', *Acta Pyschiatrica Scandinavica* 72(5): 476–81.

Langdridge, D. 2007. *Phenomenological Pyschology: Theory, Research and Method*. Harlow: Pearson Education.

Langdridge, D., K. Connolly and P. Sheeran. 2000. 'Reasons for Wanting a Child: A Network Analytic Study', *Journal of Reproductive and Infant Psychology* 18(4): 321–88.

Langdridge, D., P. Sheeran and K. Connolly. 2005. 'Understanding the Reasons for Parenthood', *Journal of Reproductive and Infant Psychology* 23(2): 121–33.

Laslett, P. 1989. *A Fresh Map of Life*. London: Weidenfield and Nicholson.

Layard, R., A.E. Clark, F. Cornaglia, N. Powdthavee and J. Vernoit. 2014. 'What Predicts a Successful Life? A Life-Course Model of Well-Being', *The Economic Journal* 124(580): F720–F38.

Lechner, L., C. Bolman and A. van Dalen. 2007. 'Definite Involuntary Childlessness: Associations between Coping, Social Support and Psychological Distress', *Human Reproduction* 22(1): 288–94.

Legacy Foresight. 2007. 'Executive Summary: Baby Boomers and Posterity'. East Chiltington.

_____. 2010. 'Executive Summary: Baby Boomers Revisited, 2010'. East Chiltington.

Lee, D. 1997. 'Interviewing Men: Vulnerabilities and Dilemmas', *Women's Studies International Forum* 20(4): 553–64.

Lee, R.M. 1993. *Doing Research on Sensitive Topics*. London: SAGE Publications.

Lee, S. 1996. *Counselling in Male Infertility*. Oxford: Blackwell Science.

_____. 2003. 'Myths and Reality in Male Infertility', in Jane Haynes and Juliet Miller (eds), *Inconceivable Conceptions: Psychological Aspects of Infertility and Reproductive Technology*. Hove: Brunner-Routledge, pp. 73–85.

Leontowitsch, M. 2012. 'Interviewing Older Men', in M. Leontowitsch (ed.), *Researching Later Life and Ageing – Expanding Qualitative Research Horizons*. London: Palgrave Macmillan, pp. 104–23.

_____. 2013. 'Interviewing Older Men Online', in B. Pini and B. Pease (eds), *Men, Masculinities and Methodology*. Basingstoke: Palgrave Macmillan, pp. 223–35.

Letherby, G. 1994. 'Mother or Not, Mother or What? Problems of Definition and Identity', *Women's Studies International Forum* 17(5): 525–32.

_____. 1997. '"Infertility" and "Involuntary Childlessness" Definition and Self-Identity', PhD thesis. Stoke-on-Trent: Staffordshire University.

_____. 1999. 'Other Than Mother and Mothers as Others: The Experience of Motherhood and Non-Motherhood in Relation to "Infertility" and "Involuntary Childlessness"', *Women's Studies International Forum* 22(3): 359–72.

_____. 2002a. 'Challenging Dominant Discourses: Identity and Change and the Experience of "Infertility" and "Involuntary Childlessness"', *Journal of Gender Studies* 11(3): 277–88.

_____. 2002b. 'Childless and Bereft?: Stereotypes and Realities in Relation to "Voluntary" and "Involuntary" Childlessness and Womanhood', *Sociological Inquiry* 72(1): 7–20.

_____. 2002c. 'Claims and Disclaimers: Knowledge, Reflexivity and Representation in Feminist Research', *Sociological Research Online* 6(4).

_____. 2003. *Feminist Research in Theory and Practice*. Maidenhead: Open University Press.

_____. 2004. 'Quoting and Counting: An Autobiographical Response to Oakley', *Sociology* 38(1): 175–89.

_____. 2010. 'When Treatment Ends: The Experience of Women and Couples', in M. Crawshaw and R. Balen (eds), *Adopting after Infertility: Messages from Practice, Research, and Personal Experience*. London: Jessica Kingsley Publishers, pp. 29–42.

_____. 2012. '"Infertility" and "Involuntary Childlessness": Losses, Ambivalences and Resolutions', in S. Earle, C. Komaromy and L. Layne (eds), *Understanding Reproductive Loss: Perspectives on Life, Death and Fertility*. Farnham: Ashgate Publications, pp. 9–21.

_____. 2016. '"Infertility" and "Involuntary Childlessness": Losses, Ambivalences and Resolutions', in S. Earle, C. Komaromy and L. Layne (eds), *Understanding Reproductive Loss: Perspectives on Life, Death and Fertility*. Abingdon: Routledge, pp. 9–22.

Letherby, G., and C. Williams. 1999. 'Non-Motherhood: Ambivalent Auto-biographies', *Feminist Studies* 25(3): 719–28.

Levinson, D., C. Darrow, E. Klein, M. Levinson and B. McKee. 1978. *The Seasons of a Man's Life*. New York: Ballantine Books.

Liamputtong, P. 2007. *Researching the Vulnerable: A Guide to Sensitive Research Methods*. Thousand Oaks, CA: SAGE Publications.

Liddon, L., R. Kingerlee, M. Seager and J.A. Barry. 2019. 'What Are the Factors That Make a Male-Friendly Therapy?', in J.A. Barry, R. Kingerlee, M. Seager and L. Sullivan (eds), *The Palgrave Handbook of Male Psychology and Mental Health*. Cham: Palgrave Macmillan.

Lieblich, A., R. Tuval-Mashiach and T. Zilber. 1998. *Narrative Research: Reading, Analysis, and Interpretation*. Thousand Oaks, CA: SAGE Publications.

Lincoln, Y.S., and E.G. Guba. 1985. *Naturalistic Inquiry*. Newbury Park, CA: SAGE Publications.

Lisle, L. 1996. *Without Child: Challenging the Stigma of Childlessness*. New York: Ballantine Books.

Littleton, F., and S. Bewley. 2019. 'Honouring "Patient 38" – A Mother of All IVF Mothers?', *Reproductive Biomedicine & Society Online* 8(7–9).

Litwin, H., and R. Landau. 2000. 'Social Network Type and Social Support among the Old-Old', *Journal of Aging Studies* 14(2): 213–28.

Litwin, H., and K.J. Stoeckel. 2013. 'Social Networks and Subjective Well-being among Older Europeans: Does Age Make a Difference?', *Ageing & Society* 33(7): 1263–81.

Livingston, G., and D'V. Cohn. 2010. 'Childlessness up among All Women; Down among Women with Advanced Degrees'. Pew Research Center. Retrieved 10 May 2018 from https://www.pewsocialtrends.org/2010/06/25/childlessness-up-among-all-women-down-among-women-with-advanced-degrees/.

Lloyd, J. 2018. *Whales in The Desert: The Use of Metaphors in Therapy*. London: PublishNation.

Lloyd, M. 1996. 'Condemned to Be Meaningful: Non-Response in Studies of Men and Infertility', *Sociology of Health & Illness* 18(4): 433–54.

Lockwood, G. 2008. 'Biopsies/Sperm Retrieval'. National Infertility Day, 18 July 2008. London: Infertility Newtwork UK.

Lohan, M. 2000. 'Extending Feminist Methodologies: Researching Masculinities and Technologies', in A. Byrne and R. Lentin (eds), *(Re)searching Women: Feminist Methodologies in the Social Sciences in Ireland*. Dublin: Institute of Public Administration, pp. 167–87.

———. 2015. 'Advancing Research on Men and Reproduction', *International Journal of Men's Health* 14(3): 214–24, 26–32.

Lopata, H.Z. 1981. 'Widowhood and Husband Sanctification', *Journal of Marriage and the Family* 43(2): 439–50.

———. 1996. *Current Widowhood: Myths and Realities*. London: SAGE Publications.

Lou, V.W.Q. 2011. 'Depressive Symptoms of Older Adults in Hong Kong: The Role of Grandparent Reward', *International Journal of Social Welfare* 20(s1): S135–S47.

Lowenstein, A., and R. Katz. 2010. 'Family and Age in a Global Perspective', in D. Dannefer and C. Phillipson (eds), *The SAGE Handbook of Social Gerontology*. London: SAGE Publications, pp. 190–201.

Luborsky, M.R. 1994. 'The Identification and Analysis of Themes and Patterns', in A. Sankar and J.F. Gubrium (eds), *Qualitative Methods in Ageing Research*. Thousand Oaks, CA: SAGE Publications, pp. 189–210.

Lunneborg, P.W. 1999. *The Chosen Lives of Childfree Men*. Westport, CT: Bergin & Garvey.

Lupton, D., and L. Barclay. 1997. *Constructing Fatherhood: Discourses and Experience*. London: SAGE Publications.

_____. 1999. 'The Experiences of New Fatherhood: A Socio-Cultural Analysis', *Journal of Advanced Nursing* 29(4): 1013–20.

Lynch, M. 2000. 'Against Reflexivity as an Accidental Virtue and Privileged Source of Knowledge', *Theory, Culture and Society* 17(3): 26–54.

Mac an Ghaill, M., and C. Haywood. 2007. *Gender, Culture and Society: Contemporary Feminities and Masculinities*. Basingstoke: Palgrave Macmillan.

Machielse, A., and R. Hortulanus. 2013. 'Social Ability or Social Frailty? The Balance between Autonomy and Connectedness in the Lives of Older People', in J. Baars, J. Dohmen, A. Grenier and C. Phillipson (eds), *Ageing, Meaning and Social Structure: Connecting Critical and Humanistic Gerontology*. Bristol: Policy Press, pp. 119–38.

Machin, A.J. 2015. 'Mind the Gap: The Expectation and Reality of Involved Fatherhood', *Fathering: A Journal of Theory and Research about Men as Parents* 13(1): 36–59.

MacInnes, J. 1998. *The End of Masculinity*. Buckingham: Open University Press.

MacRae, H. 1992. 'Fictive Kin as a Component of the Social Networks of Older People', *Research on Aging* 14(2): 226–47.

Mahlstedt, P.P. 1985. 'The Psychological Component of Infertility', *Fertility and Sterility* 43(3): 335–46.

Malacrida, C. 2007. 'Reflexive Journaling on Emotional Research Topics: Ethical Issues for Team Researchers', *Qualitative Health Research* 17(10): 1329–39.

Malik, S., and N. Coulson. 2008. 'The Male Experience of Infertility: A Thematic Analysis of an Online Infertility Support Group Bulletin Board', *Journal of Reproductive and Infant Psychology* 26(1): 18–30.

Mann, R. 2007. 'Out of the Shadows?: Grandfatherhood, Age and Masculinities', *Journal of Aging Studies* 21(4): 281–91.

Marcé, L.V. 1858. *Traite de la Folie des Femmes Enceintes, des Nouvelles Accouchees et des Nourrices*. Paris: Baillière.

Marchbank, J., and G. Letherby. 2007. *Introduction to Gender: Social Science Perspectives*. Harlow: Pearson Education.

Marsh, I., and G. Melville. 2011. 'Moral Panics and the British Media – A Look at Some Contemporary "Folk Devils"', *Internet Journal of Criminology* (Online) ISSN 2045-6743.

Marsh, S. 2017a. 'The Agony of Being a Childless Man: Women Have Talked for Years about the Longing for a Baby. Now Would-Be Dads Are Sharing Their Pain', *Daily Mail*, 29 October 2017.

———. 2017b. '"The Desire to Have a Child Never Goes Away": How the Involuntarily Childless Are Forming an New Movement', *The Guardian*, 3 October 2017.

Marshall, V.W., and P.J. Clarke. 2010. 'Agency and Social Structure in Ageing and Life-Course Research', in D. Dannefer and C. Phillipson (eds), *The SAGE Handbook of Social Gerontology*. London: SAGE Publications, pp. 294–305.

Marsiglio, W., M. Lohan and L. Culley. 2013. 'Framing Men's Experience in the Procreative Realm', *Journal of Family Issues* 34(8): 1011–36.

Marsiglio, W. 1991. 'Male Procreative Consciousness and Responsibility', *Journal of Family Issues* 12(3): 268–90.

Marston, H.R., C.B.A. Musselwhite and R.A. Hadley. 2020. 'COVID-19 vs Social Isolation: The Impact Technology Can Have on Communities, Social Connections and Citizens'. Ageing Issues blog. Retrieved 22 August 2020 from https://ageingissues.wordpress.com/2020/03/18/covid-19-vs-social-isolation-the-impact-technology-can-have-on-communities-social-connections-and-citizens/.

Marston, H.R. 2019. 'Millennials and ICT – Findings from the Technology 4 Young Adults (T4YA) Project: An Exploratory Study', *Societies* 9(4): 80.

Marston, H.R., R. Genoe, S. Freeman, C. Kulczycki and C.B.A. Musselwhite. 2019. 'Older Adults' Perceptions of ICT: Main Findings from the Technology in Later Life (TILL) Study', *Healthcare* 7(3): 86.

Marston, H.R., S. Freeman, K.A. Bishop and C.L. Beech. 2016. 'A Scoping Review of Digital Gaming Research Involving Older Adults Aged 85 and Older', *Games Health J* 5(3): 157–74.

Martinengo, G., J.I. Jacob and J.E. Hill. 2010. 'Gender and the Work-Family Interface: Exploring Differences across the Family Life Course', *Journal of Family Issues* 31(10): 1363–90.

Masebe, L., and M. Ramosebudi. 2016. 'Trends and Levels of Childlessness among Educated Women in South Africa', *African Population Studies* 30(2): 2897–909.

Mason, J. 2002. *Qualitative Researching*. London: SAGE Publications.

———. 2006. 'Mixing Methods in a Qualitatively Driven Way', *Qualitative Research* 6(1): 9–25.

———. 2011. 'What It Means to Be Related', in V. May (ed.), *Sociology of Personal Life*. Basingstoke: Palgrave Macmillan, pp. 59–71.

Mason, M-C. 1993. *Male Infertility – Men Talking*. London: Routledge.

Matthews, A,. and R. Matthews. 1986. 'Infertility and Involuntary Child-lessness: The Tranistion to Nonparenthood', *Journal of Marriage and Family* 48(3): 641–49.

Mauthner, N., and A. Doucet. 1998. 'Reflections on a Voice-Centred Relational Method: Analysing Maternal and Domestic Voices', in J. Ribbens and R. Edwards (eds), *Feminist Dilemmas in Qualitative Research: Public Knowledge and Private Lives*. London: SAGE Publications, pp. 119–46.

May, V. 2011a. 'Introducing a Sociology of Personal Life', in V. May (ed.), *Sociology of Personal Life*. Basingstoke: Palgrave Macmillan, pp. 1–10.

——— (ed.). 2011b. *Sociology of Personal Life*. Basingstoke: Palgrave Macmillan.

——. 2013. *Connecting Self to Society: Belonging in a Changing World*. Basingstoke: Palgrave Macmillan.

Mayhew, E. 2006. 'The Parental Employment Context', in J. Bradshaw and A. Hatland (eds), *Social Policy, Employment and Family Change in Comparative Perspective*. Cheltenham: Edward Elgar Publishing, pp. 37–59.

McAdams, D., R. Josselson and A. Lieblich (eds). 2006. *Identity and Story: Creating Self in Narrative*. Washington, DC: American Psychological Association.

McAdams, D, and E. de St Aubin. 1992. 'A Theory of Generativity and Its Assessment through Self-Report, Behavioral Acts, and Narrative Themes in Autobiography', *Journal of Personality and Social Psychology* 62(6): 1003–15.

McAdams, D., and A. Diamond. 1997. 'Stories of Commitment : The Psychosocial Construction of Generative Lives', *Journal of Personality and Social Psychology* 72(3): 678–94.

McCarthy, B., J. Hagan and M. Martin. 2002. 'In and out of Harm's Way: Violent Victimisation and the Social Capital of Fictive Street Families', *Criminology* 40(4): 831–66.

McKee, L., and M. O'Brien. 1983. 'Interviewing Men: Taking Gender Seriously', in E. Gamarnikow, D. Morgan, J. Purvis and D. Taylorson (eds), *The Public and the Private*. London: Heinemann, pp. 147–61.

McKeering, H., and K.I. Pakenham. 2000. 'Gender and Generativity Issues in Parenting: Do Fathers Benefit More Than Mothers from Involvement in Child Care Activities?', *Sex Roles* 43(7): 459–80.

McLeod, J. 1994. *Doing Counselling Research*. London: SAGE Publications.

——. 1999. *Practitioner Research in Counselling*. London: SAGE Publications.

——. 2001. *Qualitative Research in Counselling and Psychotherapy*. London: SAGE Publications.

——. 2006. *Qualitative Research in Counselling and Psychotherapy*. London: SAGE Publications.

McMullin, J. 1995. 'Theorizing Age and Gender Relations', in S. Arber and J. Ginn (eds), *Connecting Gender and Ageing: A Sociological Approach*. Buckingham: Open University Press, pp. 30–41.

McNeil, C., and J. Hunter. 2014. *The Generation Strain: The Collective Solutions to Care in an Ageing Society*. London: Institute for Public Policy Research.

McQuillan, J., A.L. Greil, L. White and M.C. Jacob. 2003. 'Frustrated Fertility: Infertility and Psychological Distress Among Women', *Journal of Marriage and Family* 65(4): 1007–18.

Mead, G.H. 1934. *Mind, Self and Society: From the Standpoint of a Social Behaviorist*. Chicago: University of Chicago Press.

Meadows, R., and K. Davidson. 2006. 'Maintaining Manliness in Later Life: Hegemonic Masculinities and Emphasized Feminities', in Toni Calasanti and Kathleen Slevin (eds), *Ageing Matters: Realigning Feminist Thinking*. New York: Taylor & Francis Group, pp. 295–312.

Meil, G. 2006. 'The Consequences of the Development of a Beanpole Kin Structure on Exchanges Between Generations: The Case of Spain', *Journal of Family Issues* 27(8): 1085–99.

Melville, J. 2013. 'Promoting Communication and Fostering Interaction between the Generations: A Study of the UK's First Purpose-Built Intergenerational Centre', PhD thesis. Keele: Keele University.

Menning, B.E. 1980. 'The Emotional Needs of Infertile Couples', *Fertility and Sterility* 32(4): 313–19.

Mensfe. 2008. 'Men's Fertility Forum – MENSFE Matters'. Retrieved 15 December 2008 from www.mensfe.net/.

Merrill, B., and L. West. 2009. *Using Biographical Methods in Social Research*. London: SAGE Publications.

Miall, C.E. 1986. 'The Stigma of Involuntary Childlessness', *Social Problems* 33(4): 268–82.

Miles, M.B., and A.M. Huberman. 1994. *Qualitative Data Analysis*. Thousand Oaks, CA: SAGE Publications.

Miller, R.L. 2000. *Researching Life Stories and Family Histories*. London: SAGE Publications.

Miller, T. 2011. *Making Sense of Fatherhood: Gender, Caring and Work*. Cambridge: Cambridge University Press.

Miller, T., and E. Dermott. 2015. 'Contemporary Fatherhood: Continuity, Change and Future', *Families, Relationships and Societies* 4(2): 179–81.

Moller, M. 2007. 'Exploiting Patterns: A Critique of Hegemonic Masculinity', *Journal of Gender Studies* 16(3): 263–76.

Monach, J.H. 1993. *Childless, No Choice: The Experience of Involuntary Childlessness*. Abingdon: Routledge.

Moore, R., M. Allbright and K. Strick. 2016. 'Childlessness in Midlife: Increasing Generativity Using a Narrative Approach', *The Family Journal* 25(1): 40–47.

Morgan, D.H.J. 1981. 'Men, Masculinity and Sociological Enquiry', in H. Roberts (ed.), *Doing Feminist Research*. London: Routledge, pp. 83–113.

_____. 1992. *Discovering Men*. London: Routledge.

_____. 1996. *Family Connections: An Introduction to Family Studies*. Cambridge: Polity Press.

_____. 1999. 'Risk and Family Practices: Accounting for Change and Fluidity in Family Life', in E.B. Silva and C. Smart (eds), *The New Family?* London: SAGE Publications, pp. 13–30.

_____. 2011a. 'Locating "Family Practices"', *Sociological Research Online* 16(4): 14.

_____. 2011b. *Rethinking Family Practices*. London: Palgrave Macmillan.

Morgan, S.P. 1991. 'Late Nineteenth and Early Twentieth Century Childlessness', *American Journal of Sociology* 97(3): 779–807.

_____. 2003. 'Is Low Fertility a Twenty-First Cemtury Demographic Crisis?', *Demography* 40(4): 589–603.

Morison, T. 2013. 'Heterosexual Men and Parenthood Decision Making in South Africa: Attending to the Invisible Norm', *Journal of Family Issues* 34(8): 1125–44.

Morrow, S.L. 2006. 'Honor and Respect: Feminist Collaborative Research with Sexually Abused Women', in Constance T. Fischer (ed.), *Qualitative Research Methods for Psychologists: Introduction through Empirical Studies*. Burlington, MA: Academic Press.

Motor Neurone Disease Association. 2012. 'What is MND?' Retrieved 20 November 2019 from http://www.mndassociation.org/.

Moulet, C. 2005. 'Neither "Less" nor "Free": A Long-Term View of Couples' Experience and Construction of Involuntary Childlessness', PhD thesis. Melbourne: Australian Catholic University.

Mullins, A. 2018. 'Capital in Pronatalist Fields: Exploring the Influence of Economic, Social, Cultural and Symbolic Capital on Childbearing Habitus', in N. Sappleton (ed.), *Voluntary and Involuntary Childlessness: The Joys of Otherhood?* Bingley: Emerald Publishing, pp. 97–124.

Murphy, M. 2009. 'Where Have All the Children Gone? Women's Reports of More Childlessness at Older Ages Than When They Were Younger in a Large-Scale Continuous Household Survey in Britain', *Population Studies: A Journal of Demography* 63(2): 115–33.

National Health Service. 2017. 'Infertility'. Retrieved 17 August 2018 from https://www.nhs.uk/conditions/infertility/.

National Institute for Clinical Excellence. 2004. 'Fertility: Assessment and Treatment for People with Fertility Problems'. London.

Nelson-Coffey, S.K., M. Killingsworth, K. Layous, S.W. Cole and S. Lyubomirsky. 2019. 'Parenthood is Associated with Greater Well-Being for Fathers Than Mothers', *Personality and Social Psychology Bulletin* 45(9), 1378–1390.

Nelson-Jones, R. 2006. *The Theory and Practice of Counselling and Therapy*. London: SAGE Publications.

Neuberger, J. 2009. 'What Does It Mean to Be Old?', in P. Cann and M. Dean (eds), *Unequal Ageing: The Untold Story of Exclusion in Old Age*. Bristol: Policy Press, pp. 101–22.

Neugarten, B., and N. Datan. 1973. 'Sociological Perspectives on the Life Cycle', in P.B. Baltes and K.W. Schaie (eds), *Life-Span Developmental Psychology*. New York: Academic Press, pp. 53–69.

Neugarten, B., and G. Hagestad. 1976. 'Age and the Life Course', in R.H. Binstock and E. Shanas (eds), *Handbook of Aging and the Social Sciences*. New York: Van Nostrand Rheinhold.

Neugarten, B., J. Moore and J. Lowe. 1965. 'Age Norms, Age Constraints and Adult Socialisation', *American Journal of Sociology* 70(6): 701–17.

Neugarten, B. 1969. 'Continuities and Discontinuities of Psychological Issues into Adult Life', *Human Development* 12(2): 81–130.

_____. 1970. 'The Old and the Young in Modern Societies', *American Behavioral Scientist* 14(1): 13–24.

_____. 1974. 'Age Groups in American Society and the Rise of the Young-Old', *The ANNALS of the American Academy of Political and Social Science* 415(1): 187–98.

_____. 1976. 'Adaptation and the Life Cycle', *The Counseling Psychologist* 6(1): 16–20.

_____. 1979. 'Time, Age, and the Life Cycle', *Am J Psychiatry* 136(7): 887–94.

Newton, N., and I. Baltys. 2014. 'Parent Status and Generativity within the Context of Race', *International Journal of Aging & Human Development* 78(2): 171–95.

Nicholson, V. 2007. *Singled Out: How Two Million Women Survived without Men after the First World War*. London: Viking.

_____. 2012. *Millions Like Us: Women's Lives in the Second World War*. London: Penguin.

Nightingale, A. 2003. 'A Feminist in the Forest: Situated Knowledges and Mixing Methods in Natural Resource Management', in *ACME: An International E-Journal for Critical Geographies* 2(1): 77–90.

Nilsson, M., J-E. Hagberg and E.J. Grassman. 2013. 'To Age as a Man: Ageing and Masculinity in a Small Rural Community in Sweden', *Nordic Journal for Masculinity Studies* 8(1): 58–76.

Nunkoosing, K. 2005. 'The Problems With Interviews', *Qualitative Health Research* 15(5): 698–706.

Nye, R. 2013. 'The Transmission of Masculinities', in P.S. Gorski (ed.), *Bourdieu and Historical Analysis*. Durham, NC: Duke University Press, pp. 286–302.

O'Driscoll, R., and J. Mercer. 2018. 'Are Loneliness and Regret the Inevitable Outcomes of Ageing and Childlessness?', in Natalie Sappleton (ed.), *Voluntary and Involuntary Childlessness*. Bingley: Emerald Publishing, pp. 173–91.

Oakley, A. 1981. 'Interviewing Women: A Contradiction in Terms', in H. Roberts (ed.), *Doing Feminist Research*. London: Routledge, pp. 30–61.

Oakley, A. 2005. 'The Invisible Woman: Sexism in Sociology', in A. Oakley (ed.), *The Ann Oakley Reader: Gender, Women and Social Science*. Bristol: Policy Press, pp. 189–205.

Office for National Statistics. 2009. 'National Population Projections, 2008-Based'. Retrieved 10 February 2015 from http://www.statistics. gov.uk/pdfdir/pproj1009.pdf.

_____. 2012a. 'Religion in England and Wales 2011'. Retrieved 11 December 2019 from http://www.ons.gov.uk/ons/dcp171776_290510.pdf.

_____. 2012b. 'Young Adults Living with Parents in the UK, 2013'. Retrieved 21 January 2020 from http://www.ons.gov.uk/ons/rel/family-demography/young-adults-living-with-parents/2013/sty-young-adults.html.

_____. 2018. 'Internet Access – Households and Individuals, Great Britain'. Retrieved 22 January 2020 from https://www.ons.gov.uk/peoplepopulationandcommunity/householdcharacteristics/homeinternetandsocialmediausage/bulletins/internetaccesshouseholdsandindividuals/2018#:~:text=In%202018%2C%20of%20all%20households,had%20access%20to%20the%20internet.&text=However%2C%20these%20households%20had%20the,percentage%20points%20in%20all%20households.

_____. 2020. 'Deaths Registered Weekly in England and Wales, Provisional: Week Ending 19 June 2020'. London.

Oliffe, J. 2009. 'Bugging the Cone of Silence with Men's Health Interviews', in B. Gough and S. Robertson (eds), *Men, Masculinities and Health: Critical Perspectives*. Basingstoke: Palgrave Macmillan, pp. 67–90.

Oliffe, J., and L. Mróz. 2005. 'Men Interviewing Men about Health and Illness: Ten Lessons Learned', *The Journal of Men's Health & Gender* 2(2): 257–60.

Organisation for Economic Co-operation and Development. 2015. 'OECD Family Database: SF2.5. Childlessness', OECD Family Database. Paris.

Osborne, R. 1992. *Philosophy for Beginners*. London: Zidane Press.

Owens, D. 1982. 'The Desire to Father: Reproductive Ideologies and Involuntarily Childless Men', in L. Mckee and M. O'Brien (eds), *The Father Figure*. London: Tavistock, pp. 72–86.

Pahl, R., and L. Spencer. 2004. 'Personal Communities: Not Simply Families of "Fate" or "Choice"', *Current Sociology* 52(2): 199–221.

Panjwani, A. 2020. 'Yes, Patients Were Discharged to Care Homes without Covid-19 Tests'. Full Fact. Retrieved 2 July 2020 from https://fullfact.org/health/coronavirus-care-homes-discharge/.

Park, K. 2002. 'Stigma Management among the Voluntarily Childless', *Sociological Perspectives* 45(1): 21–45.

_____. 2005. 'Choosing Childlessness: Weber's Typology of Action and Motives of the Voluntarily Childless', *Sociological Inquiry* 75(3): 372–402.

Parr, N. 2007. 'Which Men Remain Childless: The Effects of Early Lifecourse, Family Formation, Working Life and Attitudinal Variables'. Melbourne Institute. Retrieved 26 October 2015 from http://melbourneinstitute.com/downloads/hilda/conf-papers/Parr_Childless_Men.pdf.

_____. 2009. 'Childlessness Among Men in Australia', *Population Research and Policy Review* 29(3): 319–38.

_____. 2010. 'Satisfaction with Life as an Antecedent of Fertility: Partner + Happiness = Children?', *Demographic Research* 22(21): 635–62.

Parsons, T. 1942. 'Age and Sex in the Social Structure of the United States', *American Sociological Review* 7(5): 604–16.

_____. 1943. 'The Kinship System of the Contemporary United States', *American Anthropologist* 45(1): 22–38.

_____. 1949. 'The Social Structure of the Family', in R.N. Ashen (ed.), *The Family*. New York: Haynor, pp. 241–74.

_____. 1956. 'The American Family: Its Relations to Personality and to the Social Structure', in T. Parsons and R. Bales (eds), *Family, Socialization and Interaction Process*. Abingdon: Routledge, pp. 3–33.

Patton, M.Q. 2002. *Qualitative Research & Evaluation Methods*. Thousand Oaks, CA: SAGE Publications.

Pease, B. 2000. *Recreating Men: Postmodern Masculinity Politics*. London: SAGE Publications.

_____. 2013. 'Epistemology, Methodology and Accountability in Researching Men's Subjectivities and Practices', in B. Pini and B. Pease (eds), *Men, Masculinities and Methodology*. Basingstoke: Palgrave Macmillan, pp. 39–52.

Perren, K., S. Arber and K. Davidson. 2003. 'Men's Organisational Affiliations in Later Life: The Influence of Social Class and Marital Status on Informal Group Membership', *Ageing & Society* 23(1): 69–82.

_____. 2004. 'Neighbouring in Later Life: The Influence of Socio-Economic Resources, Gender and Household Composition on Neighbourly Relationships', *Sociology* 38(5): 965–84.

Pesando, L.M. 2018. 'Childlessness and Upward Intergenerational Support: Cross-National Evidence from 11 European Countries', *Ageing and Society* 39(6): 1219–54.

Petchesky, R.P. 1980. 'Reproductive Freedom: Beyond "A Woman's Right to Choose"', *Signs: Journal of Women in Culture and Society* 5(4): 661–85.

Petrou, S. 2018. *I Only Wanted to be a Dad: A Man's Journey on the Road to Fatherhood*. Newall: VASPX Publishing.

Pfeffer, N., and A. Wollett. 1983. *The Experience of Infertility*. London: Virago Press.

Phillips, J. 2007. *Care*. Cambridge: Polity Press.

Phillips, J., K. Ajrouch and S. Hillcoat-Nalletamby. 2010. *Key Concepts in Social Gerontology*. London: SAGE Publications.

Phillips, N., L. Taylor and G. Bachmann. 2019. 'Maternal, Infant and Childhood Risks Associated with Advanced Paternal Age: The Need for Comprehensive Counseling for Men', *Maturitas* 125: 81–84.

Phillipson, C. 1982. *Capitalism and the Construction of Old Age*. London: Palgrave Macmillan.

_____. 1999. 'The Social Construction of Retirement: Perspectives from Critical Theory and Political Economy', in Meredith Minkler and Carroll Estes (eds), *Critical Gerontology: Perspectives from Political and Moral Economy*. New York: Baywood Publishing Company, pp. 315–27.

_____. 2003. 'From Family Groups to Personal Communities: Social Capital and Social Change in the Family Life of Older Adults', in V.L. Bengtson and A. Lowenstein (eds), *Global Aging and Challenges to Families*. New York: Aldine de Gruyter, pp. 54–74.

_____. 2004. 'Social Networks and Social Support in Later Life', in C. Phillipson, G. Allan and D. Morgan (eds), *Social Networks and Social Exclusion: Sociological and Policy Perspectives*. Aldershot: Ashgate Publishing, pp. 35–49.

_____. 2013. *Ageing*. Cambridge: Polity Press.

Phillipson, C., G. Allan and D. Morgan. 2004a. 'Introduction', in C. Phillipson, G. Allan and D. Morgan (eds), *Social Networks and Social Exclusion: Sociological and Policy Perspectives*. Aldershot: Ashgate Publishing, pp. 1–6.

_____. (eds). 2004b. *Social Networks and Social Exclusion: Sociological and Policy Perspectives*. Aldershot: Ashgate Publishing.

Phillipson, C., M. Bernard, J. Phillips and J. Ogg. 2001. *The Family and Community Life of Older People: Social Networks and Social Support in Three Urban Areas*. London: Routledge.

Phillipson, C., and A. Walker. 1987. 'The Case for Critical Gerontology', in S. Di Gregorio (ed.), *Social Gerontology: New Directions*. New York: Croom Helm, pp. 1–18.

Pickard, L. 2015. 'A Growing Care Gap? The Supply of Unpaid Care for Older People by Their Adult Children in England to 2032', *Ageing and Society* 35(1): 96–123.

Pickard, L., R.W. Wittenberg, A. Comas-Herrera, D. King and J. Malley. 2012. 'Mapping the Future of Family Care: Receipt of Informal Care by Older People with Disabilities in England to 2032', *Social Policy and Society* 11(4): 533–45.

Pickard, L., R. Wittenberg, D. King, J. Malley and A. Comas-Herrera. 2009. 'Informal Care for Older People by Their Adult Children: Projections of Supply and Demand to 2041 in England'. London: Personal Social Services Research Unit, London School of Economics and Political Science. Retrieved 15 May 2018 from https://www.lse.ac.uk/LSEHealthAndSocialCare/MAP2030/docs/InfCare_Pickardetal_2009.pdf.

Pidd, H. 2010. 'Elton John and David Furnish Have Christmas Baby', *The Guardian*, 28 December 2010. Retrieved 20 January 2018 from https://www.theguardian.com/music/2010/dec/28/elton-john.

Pike, E.C.J. 2011. 'The Active Aging Agenda, Old Folk Devils and a New Moral Panic', *Sociology of Sport Journal* 28(2): 209–25.

Pini, B., and B. Pease. 2013. 'Gendering Methodologies in the Study of Men and Masculinities', in B. Pini and B. Pease (eds), *Men, Masculinities and Methodology*. Basingstoke: Palgrave Macmillan.

Pleck, J.H. 1987. 'The Contemporary Man', in M. Scher, M. Stevens, G.E. Good and G.A. Eichenfield (eds), *Handbook of Counselling and Psychotherapy with Men*. Newbury Park, CA: SAGE Publications, pp. 16–27.

Plummer, K. 1995. *Telling Sexual Stories: Power, Change and Social Worlds*. London: Routledge.

Poole, G. 2016. *How You Can Stop Male Suicide in 7 Simple Steps*. Blackpool: Lightworks Publications.

Porche, M.V., and D.M. Purvin. 2008. '"Never in Our Lifetime": Legal Marriage for Same-Sex Couples in Long-Term Relationships', *Family Relations* 57(2): 144–59.

Portacolone, E. 2011. 'Precariousness among Older Adults Living Alone in San Francisco: An Ethnography', PhD thesis. San Francisco, CA: University of California.

Poston, D .L. 1976. 'Characteristics of Voluntarily and Involuntarily Childless Wives', *Social Biology* 23(3): 198–209.

Poston, Dudley L., K.B. Kramer, K. Trent and M.-Y. Yu. 1983. 'Estimating Voluntary and Involuntary Childlessness in the Developing Countries', *Journal of Biosocial Science* 15(4): 441–52.

Povey, A.C., J.-A. Clyma, R. McNamee, H. Moore, H. Baillie, A. Pacey and N. Cherry. 2012. 'Modifiable and Non-Modifiable Risk Factors for Poor Semen Quality: A Case-Referent Study', *Human Reproduction* 27(9): 2799–806.

Powdthavee, N. 2011. 'Life Satisfaction and Grandparenthood: Evidence from a Nationwide Survey'. Bonn: Institute of Labor Economics (IZA).

Präg, P., T. Sobotka, A. Lappalainen, A. Mettinen, A. Rotkirch, J. Takács, A. Donno, M. Tanturri and M. Mills. 2017. 'Childlessness and Assisted Reproduction in Europe: Summary Report of Key Findings for WP4, Families and Societies Working Paper 69'. Brussels: European Commission.

Punch, K.F. 2005. *Introduction to Social Research: Quantitative and Qualitative Approaches*. London: SAGE Publications.

Purewal, S., and O. van Den Akker. 2007. 'The Socio-Cultural and Biological Meaning of Parenthood', *Journal of Psychosomatic Obstetrics & Gynaecology* 28(2): 79–86.

Qu, L., and R. Weston. 2004. 'Family Size: Men's and Women's Expectations over the Years', *Family Matters* 69: 18–23.

Quesnel-Vallée, A., and S.P. Morgan. 2003. 'Missing the Target? Correspondence of Fertility Intentions and Behavior in the U.S.', *Population Research and Policy Review* 22(5–6): 497–525.

Ramazanoglu, C., and J. Holland. 2002. *Feminist Methodology: Challenges and Choices*. London: SAGE Publicatons

Ranson, G. 2012. 'Review: Reconceiving the Second Sex: Men, Masculinity and Reproduction', *Canadian Studies in Population* 39(3–4): 135–36.

Rawlings, D., and K. Looi. 2007. 'Yes, Men Want Kids Too', *Journal of Fertility Counselling* 14(1): 23–28.

Ray, M.R. 2000. 'Continuity and Change: Sustaining Long-Term Marriage Relationships in the Context of Emerging Chronic Illness', PhD thesis. Keele: Keele University.

_____. 2013. 'Critical Perspectives on Social Work with Older People', in J. Baars, J. Dohmen, A. Grenier and C. Phillipson (eds), *Ageing, Meaning and Social Structure: Connecting Critical and Humanistic Gerontology*. Bristol: Policy Press, pp. 139–56.

Read, S., and E. Grundy. 2010. 'Mental Health among Older Married Couples: The Role of Gender and Family Life', *Social Psychiatry and Psychiatric Epidemiology* 46(4): 331–41.

Reinharz, S. 1992. *Feminist Methods in Social Research*. New York: Oxford University Press.

Reay, D. 2015. 'Habitus and the Psychosocial: Bourdieu with Feelings', *Cambridge Journal of Education* 45(1): 9–23.

Reid, M., and C. Reczek. 2011. 'Stress and Support in Family Relationships after Hurricane Katrina', *Journal of Family Issues* 32(10): 1397–418.

Rendall, M., L. Clarke, H.E. Peters, N. Ranjit and G. Verropoulou. 1999. 'Incomplete Reporting of Men's Fertility in the United States and Britain: A Research Note', *Demography* 36(1): 135–44.

Research Directorate. 2008. 'Thailand: Situation and Treatment of Homosexuals, Transsexuals and Transgender Persons; Whether the Government Updated the Constitution to Provide Rights to Homosexuals, Transsexuals and Transgender Persons (2005–2007)'. Ottawa: Immigration and Refugee Board of Canada. Retrieved 26 April 2015 from http://www.refworld.org/docid/47d6547d28.html.

Rice, S., D. Kealy, J. Oliffe, M. Treeby and J. Ogrodniczuk. 2020. 'Shame and Guilt Mediate the Effects of Alexithymia on Distress and Suicide-Related Behaviours among Men', *Psychology, Health & Medicine* 25(1): 17–24.

Riessman, C.K. 1993. *Narrative Analysis*. Newbury Park, CA: SAGE Publications.

Robb, M., and S. Ruxton. 2018. 'Young Men and Gender Identity', in H. Montgomery and M. Robb (eds), *Children and Young People's Worlds*. Bristol: Policy Press.

Roberts, B. 2002. *Biographical Research*. Maidenhead: Open University Press.

Roberts, E., A. Metcalfe, M. Jack and S.C. Tough. 2011. 'Factors That Influence the Childbearing Intentions of Canadian Men', *Human Reproduction* 6(5): 1202–8.

Roberston, S. 2006. 'Masculinity and Reflexivity in Health Research with Men', *Auto/Biography Studies* 4(14): 302–19.

_____. 2007. *Understanding Men and Health: Masculinities, Identity and Well-being*. Maidenhead: Open University Press.

Robinson, K., T. Schmidt and D.M. Teti. 2005. 'Issues in the Use of Longitudinal and Cross-Sectional Designs', in D.M. Teti (ed.), *Handbook of*

Research Methods in Developmental Science. Malden, MA: Blackwell Publishing, pp. 1–20.

Roelfs, D., E. Shor, K. Davidson and J. Schwartz. 2011. 'Losing Life and Livelihood: A Systematic Review and Meta-Analysis of Unemployment and All-Cause Mortality', *Social Science & Medicine (1982)* 72(6): 840–54.

Rogers, C.R. 1951. *Client-Centred Therapy*. London: Constable & Robinsons.

———. 1957. 'The Necessary and Sufficient Conditions of Therapeutic Personality Change', *Journal of Consulting and Clinical Psychology* 21(2): 95–103.

———. 1961. *On Becoming a Person: A Therapist's View of Psychotherapy*. London: Constable.

Roodin, P.A. 2004. 'Global Intergenerational Research, Programs and Policy', *Journal of Intergenerational Relationships* 2(3–4): 215–19.

Rooij, F. van, F. van Balen and J. Hermanns. 2006. 'Migrants and the Meaning of Parenthood: Involuntary Childless Turkish Migrants in The Netherlands', *Human Reproduction* 21(7): 1832–38.

Rosenfeld, D. 2003a. *The Changing of the Guard: Lesbian and Gay Elders, Identity, and Social Change*. Philadelphia, PA: Temple University Press.

———. 2003b. 'Identity Careers of Older Gay Men and Lesbians', in J.F. Gubrium and J.A. Holstein (eds), *Ways of Aging*. Malden, MA: Blackwell Publishing, pp. 160–81.

Rothrauff, T., and T. Cooney. 2008. 'The Role of Generativity in Psychological Well-Being: Does it Differ for Childless Adults and Parents?', *Journal of Adult Development* 15(3): 148–59.

Rowe, J.W., and R.L. Khan. 1997. 'Successful Aging', *The Gerontologist* 37(4): 433–40.

Rozer, J., G. Mollenhorst and A-R. Poortman. 2017. 'Fertility Rate'. Our World in Data. Retrieved 10 February 2020 from https://ourworldindata.org/fertility-rate.

Rubinstein, R.L. 1986. *Singular Paths: Old Men Living Alone*. New York: Columbia University Press.

Rudman, L., and S. Goodwin. 2004. 'Gender Differences in Automatic In-Group Bias: Why Do Women Like Women More Than Men Like Men?', *Journal of Personality and Social Psychology* 87(4): 494–509.

Russell, C. 2007. 'What Do Older Women and Men Want?', *Current Sociology* 55(2): 173–92.

Russo, N.F. 1976. 'The Motherhood Mandate', *Journal of Social Issues* 32(3): 143–53.

Sabo, D. 2005. 'The Study of Masculinities and Men's Health', in M. Kimmel, J. Hearn and R.W. Connell (eds), *Handbook of Studies on Men and Masculinities*. Thousand Oaks, CA: SAGE Publications, pp. 326–52.

Saleh, R., G. Ranga, R. Raina, D. Nelson and A. Agarwal. 2003. 'Sexual Dysfunction in Men Undergoing Infertility Evaluation: A Cohort Observational Study', *Fertility and Sterility* 79(4): 909–12.

Sampson, H., M. Bloor and B. Fincham. 2008. 'A Price Worth Paying? Considering the "Cost" of Reflexive Research Methods and the Influence of Feminist Ways of "Doing"', *Sociology* 42(5): 919–33.

Sandberg, L. 2009. 'Getting Intimate: Old Age, Masculinity and New (?) Heterosexual Morphologies', in Jeff Hearn (ed.), *GEXcel Work in Progress Report, Volume V: Proceedings from GEXcel Theme 2: Deconstructing the Hegemony of Men and Masculinities*. Linköping: Institute of Thematic Gender Studies, pp. 61–78.

Sappleton, N. 2018a. 'Postscript', in N. Sappleton (ed.), *Voluntary and Involuntary Childlessness: The Joys of Otherhood?* Bingley: Emerald Publishing, pp. 379–85.

———. (ed.). 2018b. *Voluntary and Involuntary Childlessness: The Joys of Otherhood?* Bingley: Emerald Publishing.

Sargent, P. 2000. 'Real Men or Real Teachers? Contradictions in the Lives of Men Elementary School Teachers', *Men and Masculinities* 2(4): 410–33.

———. 2001. *Real Men or Real Teachers? Contradictions in the Lives of Men Elementary School Teachers*. Harriman, TN: Men's Studies Press.

Sartorius, G.A., and E. Nieschlag. 2010. 'Paternal Age and Reproduction', *Human Reproduction Update* 16(1): 65–79.

Scambler, G. 2009. 'Health-Related Stigma', *Sociology of Health & Illness* 31(3): 441–55.

Scharf, T., and B. Bartlam. 2008. 'Ageing and Social Exclusion in Rural Communities', in N. Keating (ed.), *Rural Ageing: A Good Place to Grow Old?* Bristol: Policy Press, pp. 97–108.

Schoen, R., N. Astone, Y. Kim, C. Nathanson and J. Fields. 1999. 'Do Fertility Intentions Affect Fertility Behavior?', *Journal of Marriage and Family* 61(3): 790–99.

Schoen, R., Y. Kim, C. Nathanson, J. Fields and N. Astone. 1997. 'Why Do Americans Want Children?', *Population and Development Review* 23(2): 333–58.

Schwalbe, M., and M. Wolkomir. 2001. 'The Masculine Self as Problem and Resource in Interview Studies of Men', *Men and Masculinities* 4(1): 90–103.

Scollato, A., and R. Lampasona. 2013. 'Tokophobia: When Fear of Childbirth Prevails', *Mediterranean Journal of Clinical Psychology* 1(1): 1–18.

Scott, A., and C. Wenger. 1995. 'Gender and Social Support Networks in Later Life', in S. Arber and J. Ginn (eds), *Connecting Gender and Ageing: A Sociological Approach*. Buckingham: Open University Press, pp. 158–72.

Scrutton, S. 1996. 'Ageism: The Foundation of Age Discrimination', in J. Quadagno and D. Street (eds), *Aging for the Twenty-First Century*. New York: St. Martin's Press, pp. 141–54.

Seager, M. 2019. 'From Stereotypes to Archetypes: An Evolutionary Perspective on Male Help-Seeking and Suicide', in J.A. Barry, R. Kingerlee, M. Seager and L. Sullivan (eds), *The Palgrave Handbook of Male Psychology and Mental Health*. Cham: Palgrave Macmillan, pp. 227–48.

Seager, M., and J.A. Barry. 2019a. 'Positive Masculinity: Including Masculinity as a Valued Aspect of Humanity', in J.A. Barry, R. Kingerlee, M. Seager and L. Sullivan (eds), *The Palgrave Handbook of Male Psychology and Mental Health*. Cham: Palgrave Macmillan, pp. 105–22.

Seager, M., and J.A. Barry. 2019b. 'Cognitive Distortion in Thinking about Gender Issues: Gamma Bias and the Gender Distortion Matrix', in J.A. Barry, R. Kingerlee, M. Seager and L. Sullivan (eds), *The Palgrave Handbook of Male Psychology and Mental Health*. Cham: Palgrave Macmillan, pp. 87–104.

Seltzer, J.A. 2004. 'Cohabitation in the United States and Britain: Demography, Kinship, and the Future', *Journal of Marriage and Family* 66(4): 921–28.

Seymour-Smith, S., M. Wetherell and A. Phoenix. 2002. '"My Wife Ordered Me to Come!": A Discursive Analysis of Doctors' and Nurses' Accounts of Men's Use of General Practitioners', *Journal of Health Psychology* 7(3): 253–67.

Sharkey, W. 1997. 'Erik Erikson'. Muskingum University. Retrieved 22 February 2020 from http://mu-internal.net/~psych/psycweb/history/erikson.htm.

Sheffield, H. 1979. 'As I See It: If You Don't Get Counted, You Don't Really Count', *Michigan Chronicle*, 24 February 1979.

Shirani, F. 2013. 'The Spectre of the Wheezy Dad: Masculinity, Fatherhood and Ageing', *Sociology (Online)* 0(0): 1–16.

Shirani, F., K. Henwood and C. Coltart. 2012. '"Why Aren't You at Work?": Negotiating Economic Models of Fathering Identity', *Fathering* 10(3): 274–90.

Silva, E.B., and C. Smart. (eds). 1999. *The New Family?* London: SAGE Publications.

Silverman, P. 2005. *Doing Qualitative Research*. London: SAGE Publications.

Silvers, R., and R. Burnside. 2011. 'England Expects', in *A Rod Silvers' Film*. London: ElstreeDV Media Production.

Simpson, P. 2011. 'Differentiating the Self: How Midlife Gay Men in Manchester Respond to Ageing and Ageism', PhD thesis. Manchester: The University of Manchester.

———. 2013. 'Alienation, Ambivalence, Agency: Middle-Aged Gay Men and Ageism in Manchester's Gay Village', *Sexualities* 16(3–4): 283–99.

Simpson, R. 2006. 'Delayed Childbearing and Childlessness in Britain: Research Briefing 29'. Edinburgh: Centre for Research on Families and Relationships, The University of Edinburgh. Retrieved 8 March 2021 from https://era.ed.ac.uk/handle/1842/2782.

———. 2009. 'Delayed Childbearing and Childlessness', in J. Stillwell, E. Coast and D. Kneale (eds), *Fertility, Living Arrangements, Care and Mobility*. Dordrecht: Springer, pp. 23–40.

Siristatidis, C., and S. Bhattacharya. 2007. 'Unexplained Infertility: Does It Really Exist? Does It Matter?', *Human Reproduction* 22(8): 2084–87.

Sixsmith, J., M. Boneham and J.E. Goldring. 2003. 'Accessing the Community: Gaining Insider Perspectives From the Outside', *Qualitative Health Research* 13(4): 578–89.

Smart, C. 2007. *Personal Life: New Directions in Sociological Thinking*. Cambridge: Polity Press.

Smith, A., F. Wasoff and L. Jamieson. 2005. 'Solo Living across the Life Course'. Edinburgh: Centre for Research on Families and Relationships, The University of Edinburgh. Retrieved 23 April 2015 from https://era.ed.ac.uk/handle/1842/2822.

Smith, C.D. 1998. '"Men Don't Do this Sort of Thing": A Case Study of the Social Isolation of House Husbands', *Men and Masculinities* 1(2): 138–72.

Smith, I., T. Knight, R. Fletcher and J. Macdonald. 2019. 'When Men Choose to Be Childless: An Interpretative Phenomenological Analysis', *Journal of Social and Personal Relationships* 37(1), 325–44.

Smith, J., A. Braunack-Mayer, G. Wittert and M. Warin. 2007. '"I've Been Independent for So Damn Long!": Independence, Masculinity and Aging in a Help Seeking Context', *Journal of Aging Studies* 21(4): 325–35.

Smith, J., S. Lad and S. Hiskey. 2019. 'Of Compassion and Men: Using Compassion Focused Therapy in Working with Men', in J.A. Barry, R. Kingerlee, M. Seager and L. Sullivan (eds), *The Palgrave Handbook of Male Psychology and Mental Health*. Cham: Palgrave Macmillan, pp. 483–507.

Smith, J., P. Flowers and M. Larkin. 2009. *Interpretative Phenomenological Analysis: Theory, Method and Research*. London: SAGE Publications.

Smith, J., and M. Osborn. 2008. 'Interpretative Phenomenological Analysis', in J. Smith (ed.), *Qualitative Psychology: A Practical Guide to Research Methods*. London: SAGE Publications, pp. 53–80.

Smith, K. 2015. 'Paternal Age Bioethics', *Journal of Medical Ethics* 41(9): 775–79.

Sobotka, T. 2004. *Postponement of Childbearing and Low Fertility in Europe*. Amsterdam: Dutch University Press.

Spector-Mersel, G. 2006. 'Never-Aging Stories: Western Hegemonic Masculinity Scripts', *Journal of Gender Studies* 15(1): 67–82.

Spencer, L., and R. Pahl. 2006. *Rethinking Friendship: Hidden Solidarities Today*. Princeton, NJ: Princeton University Press.

Stanley, L. 1992. *The Auto/Biographical I: The Theory and Practice of Feminist Auto/Biography*. Manchester: Manchester University Press.

———. 1993. 'On Auto/Biography in Sociology', *Sociology* 27(1): 41–52.

Steck, N., M. Egger and M. Zwahlen. 2018. 'Assisted and Unassisted Suicide in Men and Women: Longitudinal Study of the Swiss Population', *British Journal of Psychiatry* 208(5): 484–90.

Stelle, C., C.A. Fruhauf, N. Orel and L. Landry-Meyer. 2010. 'Grandparenting in the 21st Century: Issues of Diversity in Grandparent–Grandchild Relationships', *Journal of Gerontological Social Work* 53(8): 682–701.

Stöbel-Richter, Y., M. Beutel, C. Finck and E. Brähler. 2005. 'The "Wish to Have a Child", Childlessness and Infertility in Germany', *Human Reproduction* 20(10): 2850–57.

Stoetzler, M., and N. Yuval-Davis. 2002. 'Standpoint Theory, Situated Knowledge and the Situated Imagination', *Feminist Theory* 3(3): 315–33.

Strauss, A., and J. Corbin. 1998. *Basics of Qualitative Research*. Thousand Oaks, CA: SAGE Publications.

Strawbridge, W., M. Wallhagen and R. Cohen. 2002. 'Successful Aging and Well-Being: Self-Rated Compared with Rowe and Kahn', *The Gerontologist* 42(6): 727–33.

Suen, Y.T. 2010. 'Reflecting on Studying Older Men's Lives: Thinking across Boundaries', in M.E. Harrison and P.W. Schnaars (eds), *The 17th Annual American Men's Studies Association Conference Proceedings*. Atlanta, GA: Men's Studies Press, pp. 198–204.

_____. 2011. 'Do Older Women or Older Men Report Worse Health? Questioning the "Sicker" Older Women Assumption through a Period and Cohort Analysis', *Social Theory & Health* 9(1): 71–86.

Swan, V. 1998. 'Narrative Therapy, Feminism and Race', in B.I. Seu and C.M. Heenan (eds), *Feminism & Psychotherapy: Reflections on Comtemporary Theories and Practices*. London: SAGE Publications, pp. 30–42.

Tarrant, A. 2010. '"Maturing" a Sub-Discipline: The Intersectional Geographies of Masculinities and Old Age', *Geography Compass* 4(10): 1580–91.

_____. 2012a. 'Grandfathering as Spatio-Temporal Practice: Conceptualizing Performances of Ageing Masculinities in Contemporary Familial Carescapes', *Social & Cultural Geography* 14(2) [online-first version]: 1–19.

_____. 2012b. 'Grandfathering: The Construction of New Identities and Masculinities', in S. Arber and V. Timonen (eds), *Contemporary Grandparenting: Changing Family Relationships in Global Contexts*. Bristol: Policy Press, pp. 181–201.

Taylor, M.F., J. Brice, N. Buck and E. Prentice-Lane. 2010. 'British Household Panel Survey User Manual Volume A: Introduction, Technical Report and Appendices'. Colchester: University of Essex.

Teddlie, T., and A. Tashakkori. 2003. 'Major Issues and Controversies in the Use of Mixed Methods in the Social and Behavioral Sciences', in A. Tashakkori and T. Teddlie (eds), *Handbook of Mixed Methods in Social & Behavioral Research*. Thousand Oaks, CA: SAGE Publications, pp. 3–50.

Tetley, J., N. Cox, K. Jack and G. Witham (eds). 2018. *Nursing Older People at a Glance*. Chichester: John Wiley & Sons.

Thane, P. (ed.). 2005. *The Long History of Old Age*. London: Thames and Hudson.

Thomas, G., and D. James. 2006. 'Reinventing Grounded Theory: Some Questions about Theory, Ground and Discovery', *British Educational Research Journal* 32(6): 797–95.

Thompson, E., and P. Whearty. 2004. 'Older Men's Social Participation: The Importance of Masculinity Ideology', *The Journal of Men's Studies* 13(1): 5–24.

Thompson, E.H. 1994. 'Older Men as Invisible Men in Contemporary Society', in E.H. Thompson (ed.), *Older Men's Lives*. Thousand Oaks, CA: SAGE Publications, pp. 1–21.

_____. 2006. 'Images of Old Men's Masculinity: Still a Man?', *Sex Roles* 55(9–10): 633–48.

Thompson, R., and C. Lee. 2011a. 'Fertile Imaginations: Young Men's Reproductive Attitudes and Preference', *Journal of Reproductive and Infant Psychology* 29(1): 43–55.

_____. 2011b. 'Sooner or Later? Young Australian Men's Perspectives on Timing of Parenthood', *Journal of Health Psychology* 16(5): 807–18.

Throsby, K., and R. Gill. 2004. '"It's Different for Men": Masculinity and IVF', *Men and Masculinities* 6(4): 330–48.

Timonen, V., and S. Arber. 2012. 'A New Look at Grandparenting', in S. Arber and V. Timonen (eds), *Contemporary Grandparenting: Changing Family Relationships in Global Contexts*. Bristol: Policy Press, pp. 1–24.

Tomova, A.-M., and M. Carroll. 2019. 'Lifestyle and Environmental Impacts on Fertility', in M. Carroll (ed.), *Clinical Reproductive Science*. Hoboken, NJ: Wiley-Blackwell, pp. 205–14.

Tong, R.P. 2009. *Feminist Thought: A More Comprehensive Introduction*. Boulder, CO: Westview Press.

Tonkin, L. 2010. 'Making Sense of Loss: The Disenfranchised Grief of Women Who Are "Contingently Childless"', *Journal of Motherhood Initiative for Research and Community Involvement* 1(2): 177–87.

Tornstam, L. 1989. 'Gero-Transcendence: A Reformulation of the Disengagement Theory', *Aging Clinical and Experimental Research* 1(1): 55–63.

_____. 1992. 'The Quo Vadis of Gerontology: On the Scientific Paradigm of Gerontology', *The Gerontologist* 32(3): 318–26.

Townsend, N.W. 2002. *The Package Deal: Marriage, Work and Fatherhood in Men's Lives*. Philadelphia, PA: Temple University Press.

Townsend, P. 1957. *The Family Life of Older People: An Inquiry in East London*. Harmondsworth: Penguin.

_____. 1962. *The Last Refuge: A Survey of Residential Institutions and Homes for the Aged in England and Wales*. London: Routledge & Kegan Paul.

_____. 2010. 'Section VI – The Structured Dependency of the Elderly', in C. Phillipson (ed.), *The Peter Townsend Reader*. Bristol: Policy Press, pp. 449–64.

Tracey, J. 2015. 'I Can Fill up with the Thought of My Imaginary Child', iPM, BBC Radio 4, 5 December 2015.

Turner, J. 2016. 'Book Review: Conceiving Masculinity: Male Infertility, Medicine, and Identity', *Men and Masculinities* 20(1): 126–28.

Umberson, D., T. Pudrovska and C. Reczek. 2010. 'Parenthood, Childlessness, and Well-Being: A Life Course Perspective', *Journal of Marriage and Family* 72(3): 612–29.

Urry, J. 2007. *Mobilities*. Cambridge: Polity Press.

Valuing Older People. 2013. 'Manchester City Council'. Manchester City Council. Retrieved 8 March 2018 from https://www.manchester.gov.uk/info/200091/older_people/7116/our_age-friendly_work.

van Balen, F., and T.C. Trimbos-Kemper. 1995. 'Involuntarily Childless Couples: Their Desire to Have Children and Their Motives', *Journal of Psychosomatic Obstetrics & Gynecology* 16(3): 137–44.

van Balen, F., and M. Inhorn. 2002. 'Introduction. Interpreting Infertility: A View from the Social Sciences', in M. Inhorn and F. van Balen (eds), *Infertility around the Globe: New Thinking on Childlessness, Gender, and Reproductive Technologies*. Berkeley, CA: University of California Press, pp. 3–32.

van Bavel, J., P.A. Dykstra, B. Wijckmans and A.C. Liefbroer. 2010. 'Demographic Change and Family Obligations'. Geneva: United Nations Economic Commission for Europe.

van de Kaa, D.K. 2002. 'The Idea of a Second Demographic Transition in Industrialized Countries', *Sixth Welfare Policy Seminar of the National Institute of Population and Social Security*. Tokyo: The National Institute of Population and Social Security.

van den Hoonaard, D.K. 2007. 'Aging and Masculinity: A Topic Whose Time Has Come', *Journal of Aging Studies* 21(4): 277–80.

_____. 2010a. *By Himself: The Older Man's Experiences of Widowhood*. Toronto: University of Toronto Press.

van den Hoonaard, D.K., K.M. Bennett and E. Evans. 2012. '"I Was There When She Passed": Older Widowers' Narratives of the Death of Their Wife', *Ageing & Society (Online)* 0(0): 1–18.

van Tilburg, T.G. 1995. 'Delineation of the Social Network and Differences in Network Size', in K. Knipscheer, J. de Jong Gierveld, T. van Tilburg and P.A. Dykstra (eds), *Living Arrangements and Social Networks of Older Adults*. Amsterdam: VU University Press, pp. 83–96.

van Wormer, K. 2019. '"I Always Expected to Have Grandchildren Some Day": The Long Road from Sense of Loss to Gradual Acceptance', *Journal of Human Behavior in the Social Environment* 29(2): 245–55.

Veevers, J.E. 1972. 'The Violation of Fertility Mores: Voluntary Childlessness as Deviant Behaviour', in C.L. Boydell, C.F. Grindstaff and P.C. Whitehead (eds), *Deviant Behaviour and Societal Reaction*. Toronto: Holt, Rinehart and Winston, pp. 571–92.

_____. 1973. 'Voluntary Childlessness: A Neglected Area of Family Study', *The Family Coordinator* 22(2): 199–205.

_____. 1975. 'The Moral Careers of Voluntarily Childless Wives: Notes on the Defense of a Variant World View', *The Family Coordinator* 24(4): 473–87.

_____. 1979. 'Voluntary Childlessness', *Marriage & Family Review* 2(2): 1–26.

_____. 1980. *Childless by Choice*. Toronto: Butterworth & Co.

Victor , C., S. Scrambler and J. Bond. 2009. *The Social World of Older People: Understanding Loneliness and Social Isolation in Later Life*. Maidenhead: Open University Press.

Victor, C., S. Scrambler, A. Bowling and J. Bond. 2005. 'The Prevalence of, and Risk Factors for, Loneliness in Later Life: A Survey of Older People in Great Britain', *Ageing & Society* 25(6): 357–75.

Victor, C., and T. Scharf. 2005. 'Social Isolation and Loneliness', in A. Walker (ed.), *Understanding Quality of Life in Old Age*. Maidenhead: Open University Press, pp. 100–16.

Vincent, J. 1995. *Inequality and Old Age*. London: University College London Press.

Vineis, P., et al. 2017. 'The Biology of Inequalities in Health: The LIFEPATH Project', *Longitudinal and Life Course Studies* 8(4), 417–49.

Vineis, P., and M. Kelly-Irving. 2019. 'Biography and Biological Capital', *European Journal of Epidemiology* 34(10): 979–82.

Vogel, D., S. Wester, M. Heesacker and S. Madon. 2003. 'Confirming Gender Stereotypes: A Social Role Perspective', *Sex Roles* 48(11): 519–28.

Vrtička, P., D. Sander and P. Vuilleumier. 2012. 'Influence of Adult Attachment Style on the Perception of Social and Non-Social Emotional Scenes', *Journal of Social and Personal Relationships* 29(4): 530–44.

Wadensten, B. 2007. 'The Theory of Gerotranscendence as Applied to Gerontological Nursing – Part I', *International Journal of Older People Nursing* 2(4): 289–94.

Wagner, B., and K. McLaughlin. 2015. 'Politicising the Psychology of Social Class: The Relevance of Pierre Bourdieu's Habitus for Psychological Research', *Theory & Psychology* 25(2): 202–21.

Wall, G., and S. Arnold. 2007. 'How Involved is Involved Fathering? An Exploration of the Contemporary Culture of Fatherhood', *Gender & Society* 21(4): 508–27.

Wallroth, V. 2016. 'Men Do Care! A Gender-Aware and Masculinity-Informed Contribution to Caregiving Scholarship', PhD Dissertation. Linköping: Linköping University.

Walz, T. 2002. 'Crones, Dirty Old Men, Sexy Seniors: Representations of the Sexuality of Older Persons', *Journal of Aging and Identity* 7(2): 99–112.

Waren, W. 2008. 'Characteristics of Voluntary Childless Men', *Annual Meeting of the Population Association of America, New Orleans, 29 March 2008*. New Orleans, LA: Population Association of America

Waren, W., and H. Pals. 2013. 'Comparing Characteristics of Voluntarily Childless Men and Women', *Journal of Population Research* 30(1): 151–70.

Watson, J. 2000. *Male Bodies: Health, Culture, and Identity*. Buckingham: Open University Press.

Webb, E.J. 1970. 'Unconventionality, Triangulation and Inference', in N.K. Denzin (ed.), *Sociological Methods*. Chicago: Aldine Publications, pp. 449–57.

Webb, R.E., and J.C. Daniluk. 1999. 'The End of the Line: Infertile Men's Experiences of Being Unable to Produce a Child', *Men and Masculinities* 2(1): 6–25.

Weeks, J., B. Heaphy, and C. Donovan. 2001. *Same Sex Intimacies: Familes of Choice and Other Life Experiments*. New York: Routledge.

Weitoft, G., B. Burström and M. Rosén. 2004. 'Premature Mortality among Lone Fathers and Childless Men', *Social Science & Medicine* 59(7): 1449–59.

Wellman, B., and S. Wortley. 1990. 'Different Strokes from Different Folks: Community Ties and Social Support', *The American Journal of Sociology* 96(3): 558–88.

Wenger, G.C. 1984. *The Supportive Network: Coping with Old Age*. London: George Allen & Unwin.

_____. 1990. 'Change and Adaptation in Informal Support Networks of Elderly People in Wales 1979–1987', *Journal of Aging Studies* 4(4): 375–89.

_____. 1992. *Help in Old Age – Facing up to Change: A Longitundinal Network Study*. Liverpool: Liverpool University Press.

_____. 2009. 'Childlessness at the End of Life: Evidence from Rural Wales', *Ageing & Society* 29(8): 1243–59.

Wenger, G.C., A. Scott and N. Patterson. 2000. 'How Important is Parenthood? Childlessness and Support in Old Age in England', *Ageing & Society* 20(2): 161–82.

Wenger, G.C., P.A. Dykstra, T. Melkas and K.C.P.M. Knipscheer. 2007. 'Social Embeddedness and Late-Life Parenthood Community Activity, Close Ties, and Support Networks', *Journal of Family Issues* 28(11): 1419–56.

Wengraf, T. 2001. *Qualitative Research Interviewing: Biographic Narratives and Semi-Structured Methods*. London: SAGE Publications.

Wengraf, T., and P. Chamberlayne. 2006. 'Interviewing for Life-Histories, Lived Situations and Personal Experience: The Biographic-Narrative Interpretive Method (BNIM). (Longer) Short Guide to BNIM Interviewing and Interpretation'. London: University of East London. Retrieved 8 March 2021 from https://www.researchgate.net/publication/333389503_1_SHORT_GUIDE_May_2019_update.

Wentzell, E., and M. Inhorn. 2011. 'Masculinities: The Male Reproductive Body', in F.E. Mascia-Lees (ed.), *A Companion to the Anthropology of the Body and Embodiment*. Chichester: Wiley-Blackwell, pp. 307–19.

West, C., and D. Zimmerman. 1987. 'Doing Gender', *Gender and Society* 1(2): 125–51.

West, W. 2001. 'Beyond Grounded Theory: The Use of a Heuristics Approach to Qualitative Research', *Counselling and Psychotherapy Research* 1(2): 126–31.

Wester, S., D. Vogel, P. Pressly and M. Heesacker. 2002. 'Sex Differences in Emotion: A Critical Review of the Literature and Implications for Counseling Psychology', *The Counseling Psychologist* 30(40): 630–52.

Weston, K. 1991. *Families We Choose: Lesbians, Gays, Kinship*. New York: Cambridge University Press.

Westwood, S. 2016a. *Ageing, Gender and Sexuality: Equality in Later Life*. London: Routledge.

_____. 2016b. '"We See It as Being Heterosexualised, Being Put into a Care Home": Gender, Sexuality and Housing/Care Preferences among Older LGB Individuals in the UK', *Health and Social Care in the Community* 24(6): e155–e63.

White, M., and J. McQuillan. 2006. 'No Longer Intending: The Relationship between Relinquished Fertility Intentions and Distress', *Journal of Marriage and Family* 68(2): 478–90.

Whiteford, L.M., and L. Gonzalez. 1995. 'Stigma: The Hidden Burden of Infertility', *Social Science & Medicine* 40(1): 27–36.

Williams, C.L., and J.E. Heighe. 1993. 'The Importance of Researcher's Gender in the In-Depth Interview: Evidence from Two Case Studies of Male Nurses', *Gender and Society* 7(2): 280–91.

Williams, R. 2010. 'The Health Experiences of African-Caribbean and White Working-Class Fathers', in B. Gough and S. Robertson (eds), *Men, Masculinities and Health: Critical Perspectives*. Basingstoke: Palgrave Macmillan, pp. 143–58.

Williams, R. 1978. *Marxism and Literature*. Oxford: Oxford University Press.

Willig, C. 2001. *Introducing Qualitative Research in Psychology: Adventures in Theory and Method*. Maidenhead: Open University Press.

Wilson, E.O. 2014. *The Meaning of Human Existence*. New York: W W Norton & Co.

Wirtberg, I. 1999. 'Trying to Become a Family; or Parents Without Children', in B. Settles, S. Steinmetz, G. Peterson and M. Sussman (eds), *Concepts and Definitions of Family for the 21st Century*. New York: Haworth Press, pp. 121–33.

Wittenberg, R., L. Pickard, J. Malley, D. King, A. Comas-Herrera and R. Darton. 2008. 'Future Demand for Social Care, 2005 to 2041: Projections of Demand for Social Care for Older People in England'. London: Personal Social Services Research Unit, London School of Economics and Political Science.

Wolff, K. 1950. *The Sociology of Georg Simmel*. New York: Free Press.

Wong, J.Y., and A.B. Rochlen. 2005. 'Demystifying Men's Emotional Behaviour: New Research Directions and Implications for Counseling and Research', *Psychology of Men and Masculinity* 6(1): 62–72.

Wong, T., and S. Cahil. 2020. 'The 2020 Census: If You Aren't Counted, We Don't Count'. Fenway Health. Retrieved 1 June 2020 from https://fenwayhealth.org/the-2020-census-if-you-arent-counted-we-dont-count/.

Wong, Y.J.K., A. Pituch and A.B. Rochlen. 2006. 'Men's Restrictive Emotionality: An Investigation of Associations with Other Emotion-Related Constructs, Anxiety, and Underlying Dimensions', *Psychology of Men & Masculinity* 7(2): 113–26.

Woodard, K. 2020a. 'The Invisible Million'. The Silver Line blog. Retrieved 21 February 2021 from https://www.thesilverline.org.uk/coronavirus-news-and-views/the-invisible-million/.

_____. 2020b. 'When You're Not Counted, You Don't Count'. Ageing without Children Consultancy blog. Retrieved 5 March 2021 fromttps://ageingwithoutchildrenconsultancy.   com   /2020/06/19/when-youre-not-counted-you-dont-count/.

Woodward, K., and S. Woodward. 2009. *Why Feminism Matters: Feminism Lost and Found*. Basingstoke: Palgrave Macmillan.

Woollett, A. 1985. 'Childlessness: Strategies for Coping with Infertility', *International Journal of Behavioral Development* 8(4): 473–82.

Wright Mills, C. 1959. *The Sociological Imagination*. New York: Oxford University Press.

Yatsenko, A., and P. Turek. 2018. 'Reproductive Genetics and the Aging Male', *Journal of Assisted Reproduction and Genetics* 35(6): 933–41.

Young, M., and T. Schuller. 1991. *Life After Work: The Arrival of the Ageless Society*. London: HarperCollins Publishers.

Yow, V.R. 2005. *Recording Oral History. A Guide for the Humanities and Social Science*. Walnut Creek, CA: AltaMira Press.

Zar, M., K. Wijma and B. Wijma. 2001. 'Pre- and Postpartum Fear of Childbirth in Nulliparous and Parous Women', *Scandinavian Journal of Behaviour Therapy* 30(2): 75–84.

Zevallos, Z. 2014. 'Bringing Sociology to the Media: Robin Hadley' [video]. YouTube (uploaded 5 March 2014). Retrieved 21 February 2021 from https://www.youtube.com/watch?v=PsxJO_Kl58k.

Zhang, Z., and M.D. Hayward. 2001. 'Childlessness and the Psychological Well-Being of Older Persons', *The Journals of Gerontology Series B: Psychological Sciences and Social Sciences* 56(5): S311–S20.

Ziegler, F., and T. Scharf. 2013. 'Community-Based Participatory Action Research: Opportunities and Challenges for Critical Gerontology', in J. Baars, J. Dohmen, A. Grenier and C. Phillipson (eds), *Ageing, Meaning and Social Structure: Connecting Critical and Humanistic Gerontology*. Bristol: Policy Press, pp. 157–79.

INDEX

www.ingramcontent.com/pod-product-compliance
Lightning Source LLC
Chambersburg PA
CBHW070608030426
42337CB00020B/3717